LANGUAGES AND LITERATURE

PATRON

TUN DR MAHATHIR MOHAMAD

EDITORIAL ADVISORY BOARD

CHAIRMAN

Tan Sri Dato' Seri (Dr) Ahmad Sarji bin Abdul Hamid

MEMBERS OF THE BOARD

Tan Sri Dato' Dr Ahmad Mustaffa Babjee

Prof. Dato' Dr Asmah Haji Omar

Puan Azah Aziz

Dr Peter M. Kedit

Dato' Dr T. Marimuthu

Ms Patricia Regis

Tan Sri Datuk Dr Wan Zahid Noordin

Dato' Mohd Yusof bin Hitam

Mr P. C. Shivadas

The *Encyclopedia of Malaysia* was first conceived by Editions Didier Millet and Datin Paduka Marina Mahathir. The Editorial Advisory Board, made up of distinguished figures drawn from academic and public life, was constituted in March 1994. The project was publicly announced in October that year, and eight months later the first sponsors were in place. In 1996, the structure of the content was agreed; later that year the appointment of Volume Editors and the commissioning of authors were substantially complete, and materials for the work were beginning to flow in. By early 2004, nine volumes were completed for publication. Upon completion, the series will consist of 15 volumes.

The Publishers wish to thank the following people for their contribution to the first seven volumes:
Dato' Seri Anwar Ibrahim,
who acted as Chairman of the Editorial Advisory Board;
and
Tan Sri Dato' Dr Noordin Sopiee
Tan Sri Datuk Augustine S. H. Ong
the late Tan Sri Zain Azraai
Datuk Datin Paduka Zakiah Hanum bt Abdul Hamid
Datin Noor Azlina Yunus

EDITORIAL TEAM

Series Editorial Team

PUBLISHER
Didier Millet

GENERAL MANAGER
Charles Orwin

PROJECT COORDINATOR
Marina Mahathir

EDITORIAL DIRECTOR
Timothy Auger

PROJECT MANAGER
Martin Cross

PUBLISHING MANAGER
Dianne Buerger

PRODUCTION MANAGER
Sin Kam Cheong

DESIGN DIRECTOR
Tan Seok Lui

EDITORS
Ameena Siddiqi
Stephen Chin
Shoba Devan
E. Ravinderen a/l Kandiappan
Fong Peng Khuan
Tanja Jonid
Yvonne Lee
Ridzwan Othman

DESIGNERS
Kevin SJ Francis
Lawrence Kok
Yusri bin Din

Volume Editorial Team

VOLUME COORDINATOR
Martin Cross

EDITORS
Fong Peng Khuan
Wendy (Khadijah) Moore
Jacinth Lee-Chan

DESIGNER
Kevin SJ Francis

ILLUSTRATORS
Chai Kah Yune
Chua Kheng Leng
Eva bte Mohd Ali
Flex Art and Illustration
Jerry ak David
Khoo Kim Chuan
Lim Joo
Tan Hong Yew
Yeap Kok Chien
Yeong Sook Bee

SPONSORS

The *Encyclopedia of Malaysia* was made possible thanks to the generous and enlightened support of the following organizations:

- DRB-HICOM BERHAD
- MAHKOTA TECHNOLOGIES SDN BHD
- MALAYAN UNITED INDUSTRIES BERHAD
- MALAYSIA NATIONAL INSURANCE BERHAD
- MINISTRY OF EDUCATION MALAYSIA
- NEW STRAITS TIMES PRESS (MALAYSIA) BERHAD
- TRADEWINDS CORPORATION BERHAD
- PETRONAS BERHAD
- UEM WORLD BERHAD
- STAR PUBLICATIONS (MALAYSIA) BERHAD
- SUNWAY GROUP
- TENAGA NASIONAL BERHAD

- UNITED OVERSEAS BANK GROUP
- YAYASAN ALBUKHARY
- YTL CORPORATION BERHAD

PNB GROUP OF COMPANIES
- PERMODALAN NASIONAL BERHAD
- NCB HOLDINGS BERHAD
- GOLDEN HOPE PLANTATIONS BERHAD
- SIME DARBY BERHAD
- MALAYAN BANKING BERHAD
- MNI HOLDINGS BERHAD
- PERNEC CORPORATION BERHAD

CONTRIBUTORS

Assoc. Prof. Dr Asiah Sarji
Universiti Kebangsaan Malaysia

Prof. Dr Asmah Haji Omar
Universiti Pendidikan Sultan Idris

Balan Moses
New Straits Times

the late Assoc. Prof. Dr P. Balasubramaniam
Universiti Malaya

Assoc. Prof. Dr Geoffrey Benjamin
Nanyang Technological University

Dr Michael E. Boutin
Summer Institute of Linguistics

Richard Brewis
Summer Institute of Linguistics

Chong Siew Ling
Universiti Malaya

Prof. Dr James Collins
Universiti Kebangsaan Malaysia

Assoc. Prof. Dr Faridah Ibrahim
Universiti Kebangsaan Malaysia

Prof. Dr Ismail Hamid
Universiti Kebangsaan Malaysia (retired)

Jim Johansson
Summer Institute of Linguistics

Assoc. Prof. Dr Juli Edo
Universiti Malaya

Khalid M. Hussain
Dewan Bahasa dan Pustaka (retired)

Julie K. King
Summer Institute of Linguistics

Krishnan a/l Ramasamy
Universiti Malaya

Prof. Lim Chee Seng
Universiti Malaya

Prof. Emeritus Dr Mohd Taib Osman
Universiti Malaya

Prof. Dr Mohd Yusoff Hashim
Kolej Islam Melaka

Prof. Dr Elaine Morais
Universiti Malaya

Prof. Dr Muhammad Haji Salleh
Universiti Sains Malaysia

Dr Ng Pek Hoon
Universiti Malaya (retired)

Dr Noriah Taslim
Universiti Sains Malaya

Pang Khee Teik
Writer-photographer

Rajakumahran
Editor

P. Rajendran
President, Malaysian Tamil Writers' Association

Prof. Dr Siti Hawa Salleh
Universiti Putra Malaysia

Assoc. Prof. Dr Solehah Ishak
Universiti Kebangsaan Malaysia

Assoc. Prof. Dr K. Thilagawathi
Universiti Malaya (retired)

Prof. Dr Ungku Maimunah Mohd Tahir
Universiti Kebangsaan Malaysia

Assoc. Prof. Dr Wong Soak Koon
Universiti Sains Malaysia (retired)

Assoc. Prof. Margaret Yong
Universiti Malaya (retired)

Prof. Dr Zawiah Yahya
Universiti Kebangsaan Malaysia (retired)

THE ENCYCLOPEDIA OF
MALAYSIA

Volume 9

LANGUAGES AND LITERATURE

Volume Editor

Prof. Dato' Dr Asmah Haji Omar

Universiti Pendidikan Sultan Idris

ARCHIPELAGO PRESS

Contents

ABOVE: Malay language learning materials on display in a large Kuala Lumpur bookstore.

FAR RIGHT: Elephant Brand sarongs for men advertised on a large chick-blind in two languages and three scripts: Jawi and Romanized Malay, and Chinese.

TITLE PAGE: Rare double-sided Royal Malay seal used by the Tengku Besar Indra Raja in the court of the Sultan of Kelantan. The side shown is dated AH 1311, which corresponds with 1893 CE.

HALF TITLE PAGE: Young soldiers reading a Malay newspaper in the Jawi script in 1947.

Introduction

Traditional Jawi writing equipment.

With some 80 languages spoken in the country, Malaysia represents one of the world's densest language communities. This volume seeks to provide an insight into both the linguistic and the literary complexity of the country. In doing so, account is taken of competing academic viewpoints, while maintaining an objective stance. With so many languages and accompanying literatures, a degree of selectivity has been necessary. While the less widely spoken languages are examined, including those of the Orang Asli and the numerous Sarawak and Sabah ethnic groups, the dominant languages—Malay, Chinese, Tamil and English—and their respective literatures are covered in greater depth.

GERAKAN CINTAILAH BAHASA KITA

BAHASA JIWA BANGSA

Poster from one of several campaigns organized by Dewan Bahasa dan Pustaka (Institute of Language and Literature) to promote the national language, Malay

CENTRE: Malaysian literature is published in several languages including Malay, Chinese, Tamil and English.

Road safety signboard in Sabah in the 1960s. Multilingual notices are essential in a country where citizens speak many different first languages.

Malaysia's many languages

In addition to hosting such a large total number of languages, Malaysia can boast of having thriving language communities in at least four languages, with locally produced media reaching relatively large communities of speakers of each. This linguistic landscape developed primarily as a result of waves of migration at different periods of history.

Academics agree that language migration commenced in Malaysia with the arrival of Austroasiatic and then Austronesian language speakers several thousand years ago. It is an Austronesian language, Malay, that has achieved the position of dominant language. Malay in its widest sense—which includes Indonesian—is a major world language and has been used as an international language of diplomacy for many hundreds of years. It is on the one hand a highly developed language with a great literary tradition, while on the other it is able to be used and understood by speakers with only a relatively low level of proficiency, often making it the language of choice for immigrant communities.

A large number of other Austronesian languages are spoken by the many ethnic groups residing in the states of Sarawak and Sabah, on the island of Borneo. The incredible density of languages within these two states illustrates the relative historical novelty of international borders. Indeed, many of the comparatively small language groups in these states are merely parts of larger groups found in Kalimantan (Indonesian Borneo) or the Philippines.

Several Austroasiatic languages, known as the Aslian languages, which have the longest association with the Malay Peninsula, continue to be spoken by relatively small groups of the aboriginal Orang Asli (Malay for 'original people'). The Aslian languages are related to the national languages of Cambodia and Vietnam.

The three languages that, together with Malay, dominate the country only began to achieve this position in the 19th and early 20th centuries, with the immigration of large numbers of Chinese and Indian workers, and the colonial British administration. Several Chinese dialects are spoken in Malaysia, with a complex distribution. Tamil is the first language of the majority of Malaysian Indians, although other Indian languages are also spoken. English retains an important place even after Independence.

KESELAMATAN JALAN RAYA MULA-NYA DARI KAMU!

PEMANDU 2
ORANG 2 JALAN KAKI
PENUNGGANG 2
PENUMPANG 2

乘客 行人
駕駛員
交通安全靠你!
1968 ROAD SAFETY CAMPAIGN COMMITTEE

ROAD SAFETY BEGINS WITH you!
DRIVERS
PEDESTRIANS
RIDERS
PASSENGERS

ESSO

Linguistic classification and selection

In a linguistic scenario such as Malaysia's, the difficulties of precisely and properly classifying the various languages and speech variants are immense. All languages are in a constant state of flux, often as a result of interaction between speakers of other languages. This is particularly true in Malaysia, where the meeting of many different language communities has generated a linguistic and literary synergy between them, and has led to the development of contact languages and their more established counterparts, creoles. Many Malaysians are multilingual and may speak, and mix, different languages in different situations throughout an average day.

Certain languages spoken in Malaysia are not covered in depth in this volume. Thai is one of these, as only a very small number of first language Thai speakers of Malaysian nationality reside in the country. Arabic and Sanskrit on the other hand are excluded as they are primarily used in Malaysia for religious purposes. As for the many other languages spoken in the country by travellers, tourists and migrant workers, these groups of speakers are not permanent enough to be classed as language communities.

An 1858 edition of the quarterly magazine *Cermin Mata* ('Eye Glass'). Featuring literature and instruction, the magazine was published in Malay by the Mission Press. It was one of the most beautiful early Malay printed works, finely lithographed with colours.

From traditional to contemporary literature

Malaysia has an ancient literary tradition, which initially developed in oral form among the indigenous peoples. The process of handing down stories from generation to generation continues, although with the adoption or development of writing systems (as recently as the 1980s, for some Aslian, Sabah and Sarawak languages), these began to be written down, allowing easier transmission.

The Malay written tradition predates those of the other indigenous groups, yet did not truly develop until the advent of Islam, probably between the 13th and 15th centuries. This precipitated the adoption of the Arabic-based Jawi script and enabled the rich Malay oral traditions to be recorded in works such as the Hikayat.

In the 20th century, Roman script (*Rumi*) superseded Jawi, and modern Malay literature began to be produced. The novel, short story and free verse forms have been adopted by the Malay speech community from English literature, which was taught in schools during colonial times. Each local form has subsequently developed and matured to take on a truly Malaysian style and perspective. This literary evolution has similarly occurred in Malaysian literature in the other major languages. Local Chinese and Tamil literature, reflecting the transient nature of the speakers of these languages, initially focused in both content and style on their homelands; shifting to domestic issues only upon Independence. Meanwhile English literature, previously the domain of expatriate writers, only started to appear after Independence. Locally written drama in Malay with more modern formats and plays in English by local playwrights also only appeared post-Independence.

Over 200,000 people attended the Kuala Lumpur Book Fair in 2003. Organized by the National Book Council, the fair was first held in 1991.

Language policy

The authorities recognize the right of every group to use and maintain its own language. However, the Federal Constitution states that Malay is the national language. Malay is thus the language for official purposes, and the first language of education. A national organization, Dewan Bahasa dan Pustaka (Institute of Language and Literature), has been established to develop the language and promote its use. In the media, the plurality of the linguistic scenario has been allowed to be expressed, with all of the dominant languages, and some of the less-widely spoken ones, represented.

Language Family Trees

Phylum (over 5,000 years time-depth)	e.g. Austric phylum
Stock (2,500–5,000 years time-depth)	e.g. Austronesian stock
Family	e.g. Indonesian family
Sub-family/sub-group	e.g. Malayic sub-family
Language, dialect or speech variant	e.g. Malay

History of scripts

The scripts used to write Malaysian languages all have their origins in other parts of the world.

1. *Utusan Melayu*, the last daily Jawi Malay newspaper, ceased publication in 2003.
2. Eighteenth-century manuscript written in Arabic. The Jawi script was adapted from Arabic.
3. Kuala Lumpur signposts in Romanized Malay (*Rumi*).
4. Latin inscription from a statue of the governor of Roman Britain.
5. A local Chinese magazine article on Taiwan's tallest building.
6. Chinese poem on a Song dynasty (960–1279 CE) ceramic pillow.
7. Prayer times displayed in Tamil at a Hindu temple.
8. Tamil temple inscription in India.

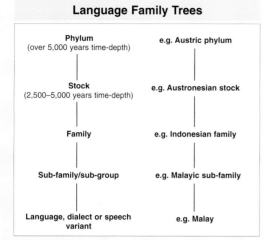

Key events in the development of the language families of Malaysia

The timeline below shows selected events from the histories of the six main language stocks and families represented in Malaysia. Events in Roman type are directly related to Malaysia. Those in italics relate to events overseas. The Afro-Asiatic family of languages, of which Arabic is a member, is not included as very few Malaysians speak these languages as first languages.

3000 BCE   **1 CE**   **1000 CE**   **1800 CE**

Austroasiatic
e.g. Aslian languages

c. 2000 BCE Latest date Austroasiatic speakers arrived in the Malay Peninsula.

The way of life of the Orang Asli changed little from the group's prehistoric arrival to the 20th century.

1901 CE First work on the languages of the Orang Asli, by German scholar Wilhelm Schmidt, published.

Austronesian
e.g. Malay
Iban
Kadazandusun

682 CE Date of oldest known Malay text, the Kedukan Bukit inscription.

c. 1000 CE The Malay and Iban languages began to evolve separately.

c. 1400 CE Melaka became Islamized. Arabic influence increased and Jawi script began to develop.

1600–1800 CE Major Bugis migration to the Malay Peninsula.

1889 CE First Austronesian homeland theory proposed.

c. 1800 CE Major Iban migrations into Sarawak from Kalimantan ended.

Sino-Tibetan
e.g. Chinese
Burmese

c. 1300 CE Overland routes across China were closed, leading to increased maritime trade involving Southeast Asia.

1405 CE Admiral Zheng He (Cheng Ho) visited Melaka.

1600–1900 CE Major Chinese migration to the Malay Peninsula, Sarawak and Sabah, peaking in the 19th century.

1922 CE Mandarin became the official language of China.

Dravidian
e.g. Tamil
Telegu
Malayalum

c. 700 BCE The present Tamil script first appeared in India.

c. 300 BCE The Tamil grammar book, the Tolkappiyam, was written.

Indian immigrants disembarking in Penang. Between 1900 and 1930, over half a million Indians landed on the island.

c. 1890 CE Huge numbers of south Indian labourers began to migrate to the Malay Peninsula to work on rubber estates and infrastructure construction.

1911–1921 CE Indian immigration to the Malay Peninsula peaked.

Indo-European
e.g. English
Portuguese
Dutch
Sanskrit
Punjabi

Archaeological finds in the Bujang Valley (above) include this Sanskrit inscription (right).

c. 400 CE Date of earliest known Sanskrit inscription in the Malay World.

1511 CE Portuguese conquest of Melaka.

1641 CE Dutch rule of Melaka began.

Dutch gravestone in Melaka dated 1660.

1786 CE British gained control of Penang.

1816 CE First English language school opened, in Penang.

The Penang Free School was founded by the British in 1816.

Tai-Kadai
e.g. Thai

c. 1400 CE Tai-Kadai speakers first appeared in the northern Malay Peninsula.

1700–1900 Period of major Thai migration to the northern Thai states.

2000 CE

c. 1970 CE
The term 'Aslian' was coined.

Iskandar Carey's study of the Temiar Language (1961).

1997 CE
Kadazandusun first taught in schools.

1957 CE
Malay became the official language of Malaya.

Chinese writing skills seminar organized by the Malaysian Chinese Writers Association in 1983.

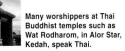

Many worshippers at Thai Buddhist temples such as Wat Rodharom, in Alor Star, Kedah, speak Thai.

CLASSIFYING LANGUAGES

Languages may be classified in a number of ways, one of the most general being by family. Languages within a family share systems and structures that form the rules of language. Linguists group languages based on these similarities, which are the result of linguistic evolution from a limited number of original language stocks. At least six of the world's language stocks and families are represented in Malaysia. The classification of Malaysian languages into stocks and families provides a useful basis for examining their antiquity. Although some academic disagreement remains, the weight of opinion is that at some point all of the language stocks and families represented in what is now Malaysia arrived from outside the archipelago. Even more debate surrounds the origins of the individual languages themselves. Nevertheless, certain languages from the Austronesian and Austroasiatic stocks may be classified as indigenous to Malaysia.

Languages may also be grouped by typology. Malay and the languages of Sabah and Sarawak use affixes to form words, and are termed agglutinative, whereas the Chinese languages are tonal: different tones generate different meanings to a given word. The languages of India, meanwhile, are largely inflectional. They make use of affixes, and undergo changes in the shape of their words to derive new words.

Several writing systems are employed in Malaysia. Malay utilizes two writing systems: the Arabic-based Jawi and the more recent Roman (*Rumi*). In line with mainland China, the Chinese script has evolved from the complex classical form to the modern simplified Pinyin form. The Indian languages have many different scripts. The languages of Sabah and Sarawak and the Aslian languages of the Peninsula never developed indigenous written traditions. Perhaps partly as a result of this, a number of these languages have yet to be thoroughly researched.

Part of a tourist guidebook on Malaysia published in Arabic, one of the rare occasions that the language is used for non-religious purposes in Malaysia.

Other less well-defined areas of classification are the many contact languages: a feature of a society comprising speakers of different first languages. Contact languages range from languages of wider communication to more established pidgins and creoles. Classificatory difficulties are compounded by the constantly shifting boundaries of these various speech forms. Indeed, the precise use of the term 'language' itself causes some difficulty; even linguists themselves sometimes interchange the use of the terms 'language' and 'dialect'. In this volume, where the distinction is indeterminate, the term 'speech variant' has been used.

Language usage in multilingual Malaysia is particularly complex. Basic academic classification techniques often cannot be applied. A key example of this is the tendency of Malaysians to 'code-switch', i.e. change language or dialect, sometimes frequently, in the course of a single communication, often within a single sentence.

Language stocks and families

Since the late 18th century, languages have been grouped into stocks and families according to uniquely shared linguistic changes and innovations. Languages from several of these are spoken in Malaysia. The languages with the longest association with the country belong to the Austroasiatic and Austronesian stocks. Other languages—from the Tai-Kadai, Sino-Tibetan, Dravidian, Indo-European, and Afro-Asiatic families—have a relatively more recent association with the country.

There is evidence, such as this inscription from the Bujang Valley, that Sanskrit, an Indo-European language, was used in the Malay Peninsula over 1300 years ago.

Evolution of modern linguistics

In 1786, British official William Jones delivered an academic paper in Calcutta demonstrating that India's ancient language, Sanskrit, was related— through descent from a single ancestral language—to Europe's ancient languages, Greek and Latin. This genetic relationship developed into the study of the Indo-European language family, heralded the beginning of modern linguistics in Asia, and laid the foundation for the rigorous, scientific study of language stocks and families throughout the world.

The languages of island Southeast Asia soon became part of that scholarly discourse and, through the efforts of 19th-century scholar Herman N. van der Tuuk, became subject to the same sophisticated methodology of comparative historical linguistics.

Despite advances in linguistic studies over the course of the 19th and 20th centuries, the basic principle that languages can be classified according to their stocks or family membership remains fundamental for organizing knowledge about genetic relationships between them. Thanks to van der Tuuk and other more recent scholars, Malay and the other languages of island Southeast Asia have been in the forefront of this scholarly evolution.

Pioneer linguist

Aside from pioneering the description of several Southeast Asian languages, including Malay, Herman N. van der Tuuk edited the first Malay dialect dictionary, a lexicon of Jakarta Malay published in 1868. Other writers from that period had noted a link between Malay, Madagascan and the Polynesian languages, but it was van der Tuuk who first applied comparative linguistics to explain these relationships within the framework of a language family. His observations about patterns of similarity (cognation) later came to be known as 'van der Tuuk's laws'.

Herman N. van der Tuuk was born to Dutch-Eurasian parents in Melaka in 1824.

Title page of the lexicon of Batavia (Jakarta) Malay edited by van der Tuuk.

Austronesian, Austroasiatic and Tai-Kadai

Austronesian, formerly known as Malayo-Polynesian, is one of the world's most far-flung language stocks. The term 'Austronesian', which comes from the Greek words meaning 'south' and 'island', is now widely used for the language stock spoken within the area stretching from Madagascar, off the coast of Africa in the southeast Indian Ocean, all the way to Easter Island (Rapanui), off the west coast of South America in the southeast Pacific Ocean. With more than 1,000 member languages being spoken by at least 270 million people, Austronesian is second only to the largest language stock, Niger-Congo.

In Malaysia, the Austronesian language having the most speakers is Malay, with about 11 million people using it as their first language. Besides Malay, there are at least 50 other indigenous Austronesian languages, mostly spoken in Sabah and Sarawak. Iban, with more than half a million speakers, mainly in Sarawak, is the most widely spoken of these. Other Austronesian languages are spoken in Malaysia by about two and a half million people. Amongst these, some long-standing immigrant groups retain their original Austronesian languages. The largest of these is the Javanese-speaking minority located in the Peninsula's south-east, although use of the language is declining. Other immigrant Austronesian groups who settled in the peninsula, including the Acehnese, Bugis, Kerinchi and Mandailing, have, by way of contrast, integrated culturally and linguistically into the Malay community. In Sabah, more recent immigrants belong to the Maranao and Sama groups of speakers.

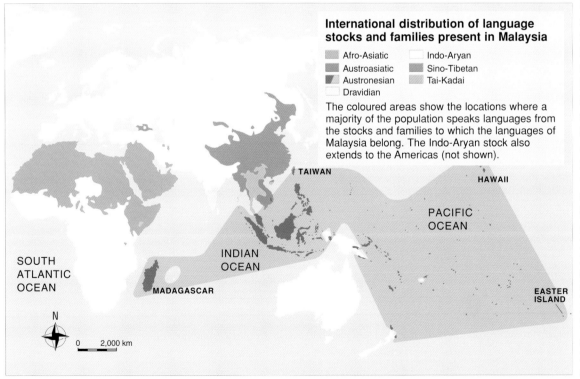

International distribution of language stocks and families present in Malaysia

- Afro-Asiatic
- Austroasiatic
- Austronesian
- Dravidian
- Indo-Aryan
- Sino-Tibetan
- Tai-Kadai

The coloured areas show the locations where a majority of the population speaks languages from the stocks and families to which the languages of Malaysia belong. The Indo-Aryan stock also extends to the Americas (not shown).

TAIWAN

HAWAII

PACIFIC OCEAN

SOUTH ATLANTIC OCEAN

INDIAN OCEAN

MADAGASCAR

EASTER ISLAND

N

0   2,000 km

The Austronesian language stock

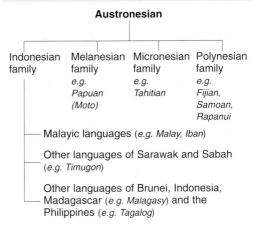

Austronesian
- Indonesian family *e.g. Papuan (Moto)*
- Melanesian family *e.g. Tahitian*
- Micronesian family
- Polynesian family *e.g. Fijian, Samoan, Rapanui*

— Malayic languages (*e.g. Malay, Iban*)

— Other languages of Sarawak and Sabah (*e.g. Timugon*)

— Other languages of Brunei, Indonesia, Madagascar (*e.g. Malagasy*) and the Philippines (*e.g. Tagalog*)

A simplified vocabulary comparison from west to east

Malagasy	Malay	Iban	Timugon	Tagalog	Tahitlan	Papuan (Moto)	Fijian	Samoan	Rapanui	English
Rua	**Dua**	Dua	Duo	Dalawa	Piti	Rua	Rua	Lua	Rua	**Two**
Efata	**Empat**	Pat	Apat	Apat	Maha	Hani	Va	Fa	Ha	**Four**
Enina	**Enam**	Nam	Onom	Anim	Ono	Tauratoi	Ono	Ono	Ono	**Six**
Vuruna	**Burung**	Burong	Susuit	Manok	Manu	Manu	Manumanu	Manu	Manu	**Bird**
Masu	**Mata**	Mata	Mato	Mata	Mata	Mata	Mata	Mata	Mata	**Eye**
Sufina	**Telinga**	Pending	Talingo	Tenga	Tiaria	Taia	Dalinga	Talinga	Talinga	**Ear**
Manga-hazu	**Ubi Kayu**	Ubi Kayu	Mundok	Kamote	Maniota	Maniota	Tavioca	Maniota	Manioka	**Tapioca**
Kisua	**Babi**	Jani	Bawi	Baboy	Pua'a	Boroma	Vuaka	Pua'a	Oru	**Pig**

The Austroasiatic stock is spread over India, China and Southeast Asia, and includes two national languages, Khmer (Cambodian) and Vietnamese. In Malaysia, several different Austroasiatic languages belong to the same branch of the stock, known by Western scholars as Aslian. These Aslian languages are spoken in Orang Asli communities spread throughout almost all the Peninsular states. Of these, the Semai language, with a wide range of dialects mostly spoken in Perak, is the largest, with about 20,000 speakers (see 'Aslian languages').

The Tai-Kadai family is spread throughout mainland Southeast Asia and southwestern China, and is represented in Malaysia. Along the northern border, especially in Perlis, Kedah and Kelantan, there are small communities who speak Pak Thai, a southern dialect of Thai, the national language of Thailand. These communities were probably established by immigrants from the north no earlier than the late 18th century.

Families from beyond Southeast Asia

The largest non-indigenous language family in Malaysia, Sino-Tibetan, has at least five million speakers using languages of the Chinese branch of the family. Significant inbound migration of Chinese speakers began in the 15th century, but most arrived in the late 19th and 20th centuries. These immigrants were mostly speakers of three Chinese dialect groups or languages, namely Min, Yue and Kejia, which remain the most widely spoken today (see

'Distribution of Chinese dialects'). Mandarin, China's national language, is also taught in Malaysia and used by many ethnic Chinese as a language of wider communication (see 'Contact languages'). The use of Mandarin as a first language is growing, particularly by families in which parents belong to different Chinese dialect groups.

The Dravidian family of languages indigenous to India has a long history of contact with Malaysia. Today, more than one million Malaysians speak Dravidian languages, mainly Tamil, while much smaller communities speak Telugu or Malayalam as their first language. Other Indian and Sri Lankan languages, for example, Bengali, Gujerati, Hindi, Punjabi, Sindhi, Urdu, and Sinhalese, are also spoken by small communities (see 'Indian languages'), and belong to the Indo-European family of languages.

Kristang, a creole of another Indo-European language, Portuguese, is spoken as a first language by perhaps no more than 1,500 Malaysians living in a small enclave in Melaka. These speakers are recognized as a remnant community that has survived since the end of Portuguese political control in 1641. By far the most widely spoken Indo-European language in Malaysia, however, is English. Yet, while more than 30 per cent of Malaysians speak it, the number of first language speakers is small—but on the rise with active government encouragement in schools.

The Semitic or Afro-Asiatic family is also represented in Malaysia, in the form of Arabic, which has a special status as it is the language of Islam, the official religion. Over half the population are Muslims and familiar with Arabic, at least at the formulaic level. It is widely taught in schools, especially religious ones. However, despite being an influential language in Malaysia for well over a millennium, the number of Malaysians who speak it as a first language is probably fewer than the corresponding figure for English or Mandarin.

The Dhammikarama Temple, built by the Burmese community who migrated to Penang in the mid-19th century.

LEFT: Eurasian dancers, descended from the first European colonizers of the Peninsula, performing a traditional dance in front of the ruins of the ancient Portuguese fort in Melaka. Kristang, a Portuguese creole, is still spoken by some of the Eurasian community.

BELOW: Often displayed in Muslim households, the Ayat Qursi, a Qur'anic verse written in Arabic, declares that there is no other god but Allah.

Language diffusion

Though the spread of languages can occur in many ways, the migration of speakers remains the most important. The majority of languages spoken in Malaysia arrived in this way, although often the precise manner in which this occurred is disputed. Other methods of diffusion include prestige, for example in the case of Arabic and Sanskrit, and government intervention, which largely drove the introduction of English to Malaysia. The story of language diffusion is a continuing one.

Orang Asli children of the Jahai ethnolinguistic group. Theirs is an Aslian language, part of the Austroasiatic stock.

Earliest arrival: Austroasiatic languages

Austroasiatic is the oldest surviving language family in the Malay Peninsula, dating back at least 4,000 years (evidenced by numerous archaic features of today's languages and archaeological findings), although details of the migration of Austroasiatic speakers remain unclear. The 14 or more Austroasiatic languages now spoken in Malaysia belong to the Aslian branch of the family, and are spoken only in the Malay Peninsula (see 'Aslian languages'). The number and distinctiveness of these Aslian languages strongly support other linguistic evidence of the antiquity of their migration from the centre of mainland Southeast Asia to the Peninsula.

The genesis of Malay

Other than recent immigrant languages, there is only one Austronesian language spoken in Peninsular Malaysia: Malay. Various hypotheses exist as to the origin and route of migration of Malay speakers, and these are closely tied to the prehistory of the Austronesian language stock, for which a number of theories have also been proposed.

One disputed theory, put forward by Bernd Nothofer in 1996, is that the Malayic family, which includes present-day Malay, Iban and Selakau, and has emerged as a major Austronesian branch, developed in the rivers and deltas of western Borneo. Thereafter, Malay speakers migrated to Sumatra, the Malay Peninsula and elsewhere more than 2,000 years ago.

Less controversial is the existence of a core Malay language area. This encompasses the locations of early Malay kingdoms. The earliest records of these are *batu yupa* (stone inscriptions) dated circa 4th century CE found in the Kutai area of southeast Kalimantan (Indonesian Borneo). Written in Sanskrit in the Pallava script, the first king's name is of indigenous origin. Other stone inscriptions from kingdoms in south Sumatra and Bangka Island are traceable to the 7th century CE. Population movement between these sub-regions of Malay speakers, with their various dialectal forms of the language, occurred throughout—and possibly prior to—this period, motivated by trade, family ties, and the need to start new livelihoods.

During the Melaka Sultanate (1401–1511) the number of Malay speakers was swelled by merchants and Islamic scholars from Sumatra. They were followed in the 17th and 18th centuries by influxes of Sumatran soldiers, mercenaries and miners. Also during the 17th and 18th centuries the Bugis, speakers of the Austronesian language of that name, arrived from Sulawesi (then known as Celebes).

Seven stone pillars (*batu yupa*) inscribed with Sanskrit verses have been discovered in southeast Kalimantan.

Austronesian origin theories

Malay is only a single language in the Malayic branch of the Austronesian language stock. In 1889, Dutch linguist Hendrik Kern proposed a theory about the homeland of Austronesian-speaking peoples based on archaeological research of William Solheim II and extensive linguistic studies. He believed the ancient language stock originated from coastal Vietnam and dispersed to the Malay Peninsula, Southeast Asia and Pacific islands. Subsequently, Kern's homeland theory was elaborated by other scholars, some of whom contended that Yunnan in the mountains of southeast China was the ultimate homeland of the Austronesian languages, with later dispersal along the coasts of mainland Southeast Asia.

An alternative theory is that the homeland of the Austronesian languages is the island of New Guinea or eastern Indonesia. However, this theory has not been well received by historical linguists.

More recently, in 1997, comparative linguists, including Peter Bellwood, have claimed that the indigenous languages of the remote mountain regions of Taiwan (known in early literature as Formosa), such as Rukai and Tsou, are related to the Austronesian languages of Polynesia and the Malay World. They claim that these early Taiwanese languages form a separate and archaic branch of Austronesian from which the other Austronesian languages later split. Their argument is supported by late 20th-century archaeological evidence of prehistoric Austronesian settlements in Taiwan. Linguistic and archaeological evidence therefore points to the possibility that southeast China and Taiwan may be the homeland of the Austronesian language family. The theory also addresses the question of why the Austronesians embarked on a course of such widespread expansion, and concludes that it was a result of their early adoption of agriculture in a region mainly populated by hunter gatherers.

Early Austronesians were expert sailors. It is likely that their vessels were a kind of early windsurfing craft.

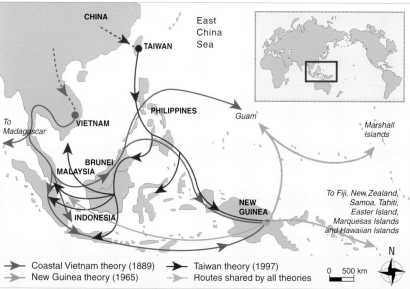

Coastal Vietnam theory (1889)
New Guinea theory (1965)
Taiwan theory (1997)
Routes shared by all theories

0   500 km

N

CHINA

TAIWAN

East China Sea

To Madagascar

VIETNAM

PHILIPPINES

Guam

Marshall Islands

BRUNEI
MALAYSIA

INDONESIA

NEW GUINEA

To Fiji, New Zealand, Samoa, Tahiti, Easter Island, Marquesas Islands and Hawaiian Islands

Core area of the Malay language

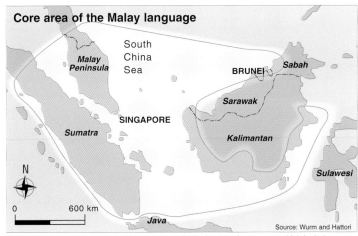

Malay has been spoken for several hundred years in the language's core area which includes parts of modern-day Malaysia, Singapore, Brunei and Indonesia.

Then in the 19th century, large numbers of people from other Muslim Austronesian groups migrated to the Peninsula. Among the most numerous of these were the Mandailing from Sumatra, the Javanese from Java, and the Boyanese and Madurese from islands north of Java. Smaller groups included families from Jambi in Sumatra who settled in Johor. With limited exceptions, these immigrant communities have become established speakers of Malay.

Migration of other languages

Speakers of Thai, a major Tai-Kadai language, first appeared in the northern Malay Peninsula in the 14th century. They moved southward and eventually imposed suzerainty over Malay-speaking areas such as Patani (now part of Thailand), Perlis, Kedah, Kelantan and Terengganu. However, most present-day Malaysian Thai-speaking communities can trace their origins only to the 18th and 19th centuries.

Another small language diffusion—this time of an Indo-European language—took place with the Portuguese conquest of Melaka in 1511. The descendants of the original Portuguese who settled there during the 16th and 17th centuries speak Kristang (pronounced Kristao), a Portuguese language diluted with many Malay loan words.

In the 19th century, the growing power of imperial Britain in Malaya introduced another Indo-European language, English, particularly for the purposes of commerce, administration and education. No massive movement of English speakers was involved—diffusion was merely accomplished by government programmes.

However, from 1600 to 1800, and especially in the 19th century, large numbers of speakers of Indo-European (Hindi, Punjabi and Bengali), Dravidian (Tamil, Telugu and Malayalam) and Sino-Tibetan (Chinese and Burmese) languages moved to the Malay Peninsula, and to a lesser extent to Sabah and Sarawak. Other languages have spread due to the prestige associated with their links to religion, for

An 1806 copy of the *Government Gazette* published by the British colonial authorities. This was one of several ways in which the English language was propagated.

example Sanskrit due to its association with Hinduism and Buddhism, and Arabic as the language of Islam.

Iban speakers today constitute the largest ethnic group in Sarawak. Prior to the 19th century, large numbers of Iban moved from their homeland around the lakes and rivers of western Borneo (now Kalimantan, Indonesia) northward to Sarawak and eventually northeastward into Brunei and Sabah. Other Sarawakian groups, such as the Kayan and Kenyah, also moved within the last few hundred years from homelands outside what is now Malaysia, in the Apo Kayan area of eastern Borneo (also now Kalimantan, Indonesia). In the western corner of Sarawak, the Selakau group originated in the west of Borneo near the Selakau River, where their closest language relatives are located today (see 'Languages of Sarawak').

Recent diffusions

Malaysia's late 20th-century economic boom, as well as warfare and civil unrest elsewhere in the region, has led to further immigration by speakers of other languages. Most follow long-established patterns of regional migration: Filipinos into Sabah; Bengalis (from Bangladesh) and southern coastal Muslim Myanmar-ese, particularly into the northern states of the Peninsula; and Javanese, Madurese, and Malay-speakers as well as other Muslim groups from Sumatra, mainly to the Peninsula's west coast. The arrival of speakers of other languages, even as temporary workers, has had a linguistic impact on modern Malaysian society, and illustrates that the process of diffusion still continues.

Inscribed in Arabic, the oldest indigenous coin discovered in the Peninsula dates from 1445–59 CE.

The Malaysian-Indonesian border at Tebedu in Sarawak. Intra-Borneo population movement continues to shape the languages of Sabah and Sarawak.

The arrival of new languages
Speakers of many different languages arrived in the Malay Peninsula from across the seas.

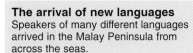

Many of the Chinese who migrated during the 19th century arrived on so-called 'fish-eye' ships.

A reconstruction in Melaka of the flagship *Flore de la Mare* which led the Portuguese fleet that conquered the Melakan empire in 1511.

Foreign language speakers continue to migrate to Malaysia, many of them illegally. Here a group of Myanmarese is turned away by the authorities.

Contact languages

The interaction of speakers of different languages in a wide range of social activities has led to the development of several contact languages in Malaysia, including pidgins. As more Malaysians have become proficient in Malay, colloquial Malay (bahasa basahan) has become the contact language most widely spoken; other contact languages are often limited to particular regions of the country. All of the contact languages exhibit some degree of linguistic simplification and hybridization; this is particularly so with pidginized versions.

Pidgin, or bazaar, Malay is often the preferred mode of communication in public places such as wet markets.

Colloquial Malay

The comedy group Senario makes use of colloquial Malay in their popular television series.

Malay, the most important language of wider communication, is spoken by members of all ethnic groups in Malaysia. For centuries, at least two kinds of Malay have been used throughout what is now known as Malaysia. One of these, colloquial Malay, is a largely unwritten form of Malay. It is used among Malay speakers in both single and multi-dialect situations, as well as in inter-ethnic social situations. Televised dramas and comedies also make use of this everyday language. Almost all Malaysians can speak this variant, with some regional differences (see 'Regional varieties of Malay'). The other variant, standard Malay (also known as formal Malay) is primarily a written variant associated with education and administration.

Colloquial Malay differs from formal Malay in that the former is only used in spoken form, while the latter is both written and spoken. Further differences are that formal Malay is characterized by a complex system of affixation (the addition of prefixes and suffixes to a root word), which is largely omitted in colloquial Malay as is the use of many conjunctions (see 'Social varieties of Malay'). Colloquial Malay is also marked by a reduced vocabulary in certain fields, although it is rich in social and cultural terms.

Other languages of wider communication

English has been taught in Malaysia's schools for about 200 years, and came to be associated with the dominant social class during the colonial period. Through these means it has become a language of wider communication in Malaysia. Many Malaysians speak a variant of English which differs considerably from the English taught in schools (see 'English'). While this makes some use of correct grammar, many features are adopted from local languages, especially Malay, including vocabulary and the way in which tenses are used. Other Malaysians speak a pidginized Malaysian variety of English.

There are other languages too that function as languages of wider communication in various parts of Malaysia, particularly Sarawak. For example, in the remote upper reaches of the Rajang, the Kayan language serves as an important vernacular language among the diverse ethno-linguistic groups located there, including the Kejaman, Kenyah and Penan, as well as Malays and Chinese in the town of Belaga. A Malay-Iban contact language is also spoken in the Lower Rajang area. However, these vernacular languages have only been cursorily studied. Indeed, more research needs to be conducted on hybrid languages throughout Malaysia. Mandarin too, may be classed as a language of wider communication, as it is often used to communicate with and between speakers of different Chinese dialects.

Pidgins

When two groups without a shared language meet for trade and other purposes, the result may be a pidgin: a mixed speech form usually heard in areas where members of different speech communities converge while carrying out their daily activities. It is not a first or home language and has no community of native speakers. Although established pidgins have governing conventions, generally their grammar is simpler than those of the source languages.

A Sarawakian hybrid language

Along the lower Rajang River in Sarawak, a Malay-based contact language, heavily influenced by Iban, often serves as an inter-ethnic language. A typical conversation involving this language might be as follows (Iban elements in italics):

- *Makai*, Datuk
  Eat, Datuk

- Au, aya, lapar bendar saya seharitu. Pikir saya *enda ngenyauh tu rumah aya ditu*.
  Yes, uncle, I'm very hungry. I thought your house was not that far.

- Dari mana *pengangkat nuan tu tadi*, Datuk?
  Where did you start your journey, Datuk?

- Dari Kuching.
  Kuching.

- *Ngirup kopi nya*, Datuk. Sudah sejuk.
  Drink your coffee, Datuk. It's already cold.

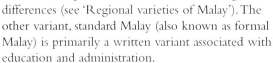
The town of Sibu, on the Rajang River, is a meeting point for Sarawakians from the state's diverse ethnolinguistic groups.

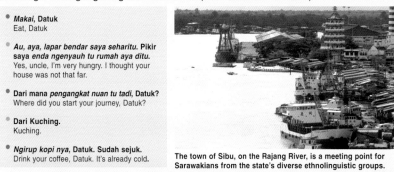

- Sibu
- Sarikei
- Rajang River
- Kapit
- Kalibas River
- Saratok

MALAY PENINSULA
South China Sea
Sabah
Sarawak
INDONESIA

Malay-Iban contact language
0   50 km

Code-switching

A characteristic feature of Malaysia's sociolinguistic profile which serves to maximize the effectiveness of communication is the extensive occurrence of code-switching. This is the ability of speakers to switch from one language or social register to another, depending on the place, topic and participants. Most Malaysians are able to change from one language to another with great facility.

A speaker may begin a formal speech in Malay and continue in English; bargaining near Ipoh may start in Mandarin and switch to Cantonese for greater solidarity; a doctor may use English to explain a medical problem to her patient but switch to Tamil for greater clarity. Choice of language is indeed both flexible and pragmatic.

Switching mid-sentence

As the example below shows, code-switching between Malay and English at the intra-sentential level—common practice among many of Malaysia's multilingual population—may involve the adoption of single words or phrases, or even whole clauses.

Peperiksaan yang diadakan adalah secara umum. Calon tak payah prepare.
The exam that was held was a public one. The candidates didn't prepare seriously.

Mungkin some of them overconfident. *Jadi dalam* exam *itu,* blindly *jawab.*
Perhaps some of them were overconfident. So in the exam they answered blindly.

We are not testing *apa yang diperolehi di universiti.* Knowledge-wise, the clerks know better, *kerana mungkin dia membaca.*
We are not testing what can be gained by the university. Knowledge-wise, the clerks know better, perhaps because they have read.

Mixing languages

Sabahan friends may meet in a Kota Kinabalu Chinese restaurant, greet each other in Kadazandusun, change to Sabah Malay to place their order, then resume their conversation in English.

'*Poingkuo ko no?*' (How are you?)
'*Avasi.*' (Fine.)

'*Ikan masam manis.*' (Sweet and sour fish.)

'As I was saying.....'

Several pidgins can be differentiated in Malaysia, including a Malay pidgin (*bahasa Melayu pasar,* or bazaar Malay), an English pidgin, a Cantonese pidgin and a Hokkien pidgin. In common with other pidgins, these are not always mutually intelligible with their source languages.

The Malay pidgin is spoken with regional variations throughout Malaysia, particularly in marketplaces, and is the most widespread pidgin. The mainly Malay vocabulary is reduced, and grammar, sometimes derived from Chinese or Tamil, is usually simplified. For example, in formal, written Malay, a conditional conjunction (usually *kalau* ('if')), appears at the beginning of a conditional clause, e.g. *kalau hujan* ('if it rains'), whereas in bazaar Malay *kalau* (or *kalu*) often

Immigrant workers, including Bangladeshis, often speak only a rudimentary, pidginized form of Malay.

appears at the end of a conditional clause, or at both the beginning and the end of the clause, e.g. [*kalu*] *ujan kalu* ('if it rains'). Recent immigrants, often temporary workers, often use a form of pidgin Malay with a particularly limited vocabulary (often mixed with English), and simplified grammatical structures. This makeshift Malay can be labelled a 'jargon', as it is a pidgin in a very early stage of development.

As speakers become more proficient in the Malay language, their vocabulary expands and their grammar becomes conventional. While some older Malaysians may still speak pidgin Malay, most

Malaysians are now fluent in the colloquial form. Nevertheless, the user-friendly nature of pidgin Malay has made it a relatively stable language of great utility that belongs in the continuum of Malay variants.

The English pidgin is often heard in shopping centres in cities and larger towns, with its mainly English vocabulary mixed with words from other languages, particularly Malay. Grammar is heavily influenced by Malay, with little regard for tenses, number or gender. Pronunciation and intonation may be Malay, Chinese or Indian, depending on the ethnolinguistic group of the speaker. As with pidgin Malay, the English pidgin is often adapted to reflect regional languages and dialects, particularly in Sabah and Sarawak. With such a wide range of standards of English spoken it is sometimes difficult to classify a variant as pidgin English as opposed to another more standard form; one method is to class as pidgins those forms that are unintelligible to non-Malaysian native English speakers (see 'English').

A form of pidgin Hokkien appears to be used when speakers of other Chinese dialects interact with first-language Hokkien speakers, particularly in Penang. Similarly, a Cantonese pidgin may be used in areas where Cantonese speakers form the majority, such as Ipoh and parts of Kuala Lumpur (see 'Distribution of Chinese dialects').

Trilingual bazaar Malay phrasebook

The English-bazaar Malay-Lun Dayeh (Murut) phrasebook published by the Borneo Literature Bureau in 1971 was written to assist members of the Lun Dayeh community who were still learning Malay and English, as well as English-speaking visitors. The choice of bazaar Malay rather than standard Malay highlights the widespread use of the former in everyday situations.

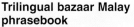

Creoles

The term 'creole' refers to a hybrid language that originated in contact situations and subsequently became the first language of a particular ethnic group. The evolution of a contact language into a first language involves an enormous and immediate expansion of vocabulary as well as regularization of grammar. A number of languages in Malaysia can be considered creoles, or at least creole-like, the best known being those of the Melaka Portuguese and the Straits Chinese.

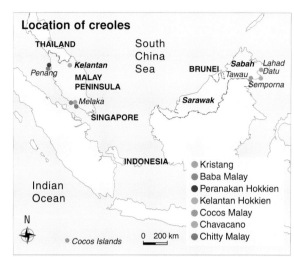

Location of creoles

- Kristang
- Baba Malay
- Peranakan Hokkien
- Kelantan Hokkien
- Cocos Malay
- Chavacano
- Chitty Malay

0 200 km

Small creole-speaking communities are found from Penang on the west coast of the Peninsula to Semporna in eastern Sabah. The Cocos Islands, where the Cocos Malay creole developed, are now part of Australia.

The city of Melaka has a particularly rich linguistic history, and is home to three creoles: Melaka Portuguese, Baba Malay and Chitty Malay.

The evolution of Malaysian creoles

A creole is a mixed speech form which has a community of native speakers. Alternatively, a creole may be described as a fully developed pidgin (see 'Contact languages'). This happens when a sizeable number of speakers adopt a pidgin as their home language and then hand this language down from generation to generation. This was how the three best-known Malaysian creoles—Melaka Portuguese, Baba Malay and Peranakan Hokkien—came into being, developing in the multicultural Straits Settlements of Penang, Melaka and Singapore. The Chitty Malay creole also developed in this way, in Melaka. Less well-known creoles that developed more recently include Cocos Malay and Chavacano, both in Sabah, and Kelantan Hokkien.

The number of speakers of most Malaysian creoles is declining steadily, largely due to intermarriage with speakers of other speech communities. The increasing numbers of Melaka Portuguese intermarrying with Malaysians of Chinese and Indian descent, for example, has led to their native creole being replaced by another language, usually English. Similarly, the offspring of Straits Chinese intermarriages with Chinese of other dialect groups tend not to adopt the Baba Malay creole. Meanwhile, members of the small Cocos Malay community in Sabah, being Muslim, often intermarry with local Malays and their offspring naturally adopt the local variety of Malay.

Melaka Portuguese

Melaka Portuguese is spoken by the descendants of Portuguese settlers who intermarried with the local Malay population following the capture of Melaka by the Portuguese in 1511. Also known as Melaka Eurasians, the Melaka Portuguese form a unique community in the ethnic mix of Malaysia. In Malay, the creole is known as *Bahasa Kristang*, which may be loosely translated as 'the language of the Christians'. The term '*Kristang*' is derived from the Portuguese *cristaõ*, meaning 'Christian', and served as a distinction from the mainly Muslim inhabitants of Melaka at the time of its fall. The creole was used in Roman Catholic church services in Melaka until World War II.

The creole uses many Portuguese words, a number of which date back to the 16th century, as well as a mixture of Malay and English loan words. Its grammar has undergone much simplification compared to the grammar of modern-day Portuguese as spoken in Portugal or Brazil. For example, the inflections of the original Portuguese verbs have been lost, and one form serves all moods, tenses, numbers and persons. For instance, *Eu vai* stands for 'I go', 'I went', or, 'I will go', with the tenses not being distinguished at all.

Today, the number of Melaka Portuguese speakers is estimated to be between 1,000 and 1,500, making it a much-endangered mode of communication. Similarly threatened are related speech systems spoken in parts of Singapore, and Pulau Tikus, Penang. Indeed the latter is now virtually extinct.

Assunta Peste Contrôle
Pessoas De Profissional
Peste Contrôle
Desde 1988

Kristang compared with bazaar Malay

Kristang sentence structure often parallels that of bazaar Malay, a remarkable case of language convergence towards intertranslatability.

Kristang:	Eli	ja	kotrá aké	kandri	ku	fake.
Bazaar Malay:	Dia	sudah	potong itu	daging	sama	pisau.
English:	He cut the meat with a knife.					

Kristang:	Eli	ja	kaza ku	femi	Malayu.
Bazaar Malay:	Dia	sudah	kawin sama	perempuan	Melayu.
English:	He married a Malay woman.				

Kristang:	Yo	ja	dá ku	Maria	sa pai.
Bazaar Malay:	Gua	sudah	tengok sama	Maria	punya bapa.
English:	I saw Maria's father.				

Top: Inhabitants of the Portuguese village in Melaka continue to communicate in Kristang, both in speech and writing. There is some evidence to suggest the small number of speakers may be increasing.

Left: The letterhead of a Melaka pest control company, written in Kristang.

Right: Popular singing group *Tres Amigos* performed in Kristang at the Independence celebrations in 1957.

Creoles of the Straits Chinese

Baba Malay

The Malaysian creole with the largest number of speakers is Baba Malay, although perhaps no more than 5,000 speakers remain, primarily in Melaka. They maintain their ethnic Chinese identity but speak a form of Malay as their first language.

Some of the members of this community are descended from the Chinese who settled in Melaka from the 15th century onwards. The assimilation and intermarriage of these early Chinese settlers with Malay-speaking women led to the creation of a Malay-based creole with Hokkien elements. Baba Malay is also spoken in Penang and Singapore by Babas who moved there from Melaka from the early 19th century onwards, although there is some opinion that Malaysian Baba Malay is more refined.

Baba Malay has a grammar often reminiscent of bazaar Malay, both having resulted from Chinese-Malay interaction, but is distinguishable from other regional Malay dialects (see 'Contact languages' and 'Regional varieties of Malay'). As a spoken language, it developed into a patois of Malay mixed with the Chinese Hokkien dialect. Gradually, the creole was influenced by the British colonial administration, with many popular English expressions and words being adopted by the end of the 19th century. Publications appeared in this creole in the 19th and 20th centuries.

Straits Chinese Mr and Mrs Wee Thiam Thye are pictured here at their wedding in 1940. Alternatively known as Peranakans (Malay for 'locally born'), male Straits Chinese are more specifically referred to as Babas and females as Nyonyas.

Baba Malay vocabulary

Baba Malay	Malay	English
From Chinese		
cangkir	cawan	cup
toh	meja	table
From Malay		
pane	panas	hot
sampei	sampai	to arrive
senduk	sudu	spoon
tiker	tikar	mat
From Portuguese via Malay		
menyelah	jendela	window
From Tamil		
taci	kakak	elder sister
From English		
tempeh	kuil	temple

Baba Malay has many loan words from a variety of languages, and differs both phonologically and semantically from other Malay dialects.

LEFT: Although most Babas were illiterate until the 20th century, a number of publications in Baba Malay appeared, including translations such as Bunyan's *Pilgrims' Progress*.

Peranakan Hokkien

This creole is spoken by the Straits Chinese in Penang, the earliest of whom arrived from Fujian province in China and thus spoke Hokkien. Peranakan Hokkien consists of Hokkien with a large number of words and phrases borrowed from Malay. These borrowed Malay words are spoken with the typical high-low pattern of Hokkien intonation. This alternative vocabulary has been incorporated to the exclusion of the original Hokkien terms to the extent that Peranakan Hokkien speakers may have difficulty understanding the equivalent Hokkien term. However, to the outsider perhaps the most pervasive element of the creole is the addition of the suffix 'lah' to the last word of a sentence.

Nyonyas at a *toh panjang* (long table) meal at the Cheong Fatt Tze mansion in Penang wear *kebaya*, a Peranakan blouse which displays a Malay influence—as does the Peranakan Hokkien creole.

Cocos Malay and other creoles

Two other creoles spoken by recent immigrant groups in Sabah did not originate and evolve in Malaysia. Cocos Malay, or Bahasa Cocos, is a creole spoken by the Cocos Malay community. They migrated to Sabah (mainly near Tawau and Lahad Datu) from the Cocos (Keeling) Islands in the south Indian Ocean after World War II. They now number around 3,000, far more than the 500 speakers still living on the Cocos Islands; speakers are also found in Western Australia. Some scholars identify this Malay variant as a creole, or more specifically, a pidgin-derived Malay variant, based on its reduced morphology and complex historical development. This particular form of speech has a mixture of Malay, Chinese, English, Javanese and Dutch elements; it has no literary tradition. Near Semporna, also on Sabah's east coast, a Spanish creole, Chavacano (also known as Zamboangueño), is spoken by a tiny community linked with the Philippines, where Chavacano functions as a major language with a written tradition in some areas. Chavacano has a largely Spanish lexicon, but with a grammatical system that is said to be similar to other languages in the Philippines.

Kelantan's Peranakan Chinese have integrated both linguistically and culturally with the Kelantan Malays and Thais.

A small group of fewer than 500 speakers, the Chitties of Kampung Tujung, Gajah Behrang, Melaka, are Straits-born Indians, the offspring of 15th-century Indian traders from the Coromandel Coast. Hindu by faith, they have Tamil names, eat Indian food and observe traditional rituals, but speak Malay as their first language. Chitty Malay has similarities with Baba Malay, but is distinguished by Tamil loan words related to cultural and religious practices such as their annual Mariamman festival.

Another Malaysian creole, only recently documented, is spoken as a first language by the Chinese inhabitants of more than 40 villages in Kelantan. The creole is a variety of Hokkien that has been heavily influenced by the vocabulary and syntax of both Malay and Thai. This Kelantan Hokkien can be considered a creole-like Hokkien variant, that arose historically through intermarriage between Hokkien-speaking men and Thai-speaking women, with the additional pressure of the predominant Kelantan Malay culture.

Cocos Malays in traditional costume waving Union Jacks to welcome HRH Queen Elizabeth II on her visit to the Cocos Islands in 1955.

A Chitty couple at home in the Chitty village of Kampung Tujung, Melaka.

Language usage

Although four major world languages—Malay, Chinese, Tamil and English—predominate in Malaysia, at least 80 different tongues are spoken as first languages. Many Malaysians speak second, third and even fourth languages too. Language choice varies according to the situation, as well as the age and ethnic membership of the speaker. Certain groups have even chosen to permanently change their first language. Malaysians are also often literate in more than one language, and literacy rates continue to rise.

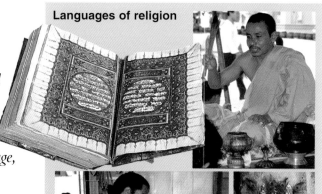

Language priority

It is a legal requirement in Peninsular Malaysia for shop and other business signs to have Malay as the most prominent language, as seen in these signs belonging to a coffee shop (top), a money-changer (middle), and the 'Gap Rest House' (bottom).

Malay: the dominant language

The 2000 census counted over 11.2 million Malays, amounting to 53.6 per cent of Malaysian citizens. It may be assumed that virtually all of these use Malay as their first language, making it the language with the largest number of speakers in Malaysia. These speakers are distributed throughout the country, in contrast to the one and a half million speakers of Hokkien Chinese, the next largest first language (or dialect), who mainly live in Peninsular Malaysia. Tamil and Khek (Hakka) Chinese are the only two other languages with more than a million speakers, with other languages having considerably fewer.

Malay is the country's national and official language, and this legal sovereignty is articulated in both the education and administrative systems where it dominates. Its long history as a regional language of wider communication, as well as government policies which strengthen its use, has resulted in 85–95 per cent of Malaysians speaking Malay as a first or additional (second or third) language. Although oral and literary competence in Malay, English and Mandarin has increased dramatically since Independence in 1957, Malay remains incontestably the dominant language. Not only the default language when all others have failed, it is also the language of choice in a wide range of social situations. A sign language, Malaysian Sign Language, has even been developed to enable the hearing impaired to communicate in Malay.

Situational choice in language

In certain fields and regions, however, Malay may not be the language of choice. For example, Malay is not chiefly used in religious practices. Among

Muslims, Arabic, the sacred language of Islam, is the predominant religious language, while Malay is an auxiliary language used in sermons and instruction. Ritual worship is conducted exclusively in Arabic, and religious specialists study in that language.

Malaysia's Hindu minority use Sanskrit as their major ritual language, with Tamil and other Dravidian languages playing an auxiliary role. Buddhists similarly preserve Sanskrit and Pali for a wide range of ritual activities. Among Chinese Buddhists and Taoists, Chinese languages play an important role, while Thai-speaking Buddhists maintain Thai as an auxiliary religious language.

Malay is probably the most widespread language of Christianity, especially in Sabah and Sarawak, although other languages are also used, including English, Tamil, Malayalam, Chinese, Iban, Bidayuh, Kenyah, Kayan, Kadazandusun and Lundayeh.

In the corporate world, both English and Mandarin are widely used by executives and professionals. Strong efforts have been made to expand the use of Malay, with some success including the development of Malay training manuals. Malay retains a strong position in daily interactions in the manufacturing and service industries, although in certain parts of the country other languages compete with it.

Acronyms

The Malaysian languages are replete with acronyms (words or phrases formed by the combination of letters or syllables from two or more other words, such as 'radar' in English (radio detecting and ranging). Acronyms differ from mere abbreviations, as they are pronounceable as words.

Many acronyms are purely Malay based, such as PERNAS (Perdagangan Nasional), PERKIM (Pertubuhan Kebajikan Islam Malaysia), JAIS (Jabatan Agama Islam Selangor) and UPSI (Universiti Pendidikan Sultan Idris). Other well-known examples have entered the vocabularies of Malay and other local languages from English, for example UMNO (United Malays National Organisation), FELDA (Federal Land Development Authority), and FRIM (Forestry Research Institute Malaysia).

The *Institut Kefahaman Islam Malaysia* (Malaysian Institute of Islamic Understanding) radio station uses the acronym 'IKIM'.

Malaysian students gathering to celebrate their graduation from the University of Liverpool in England. Thousands of Malaysian students study in English-speaking countries every year.

Changing affiliations

Due to the large number of languages used in daily life, their different status, and the large number of Malaysians who speak more than one language, speakers can and do permanently change their language affiliation. They may decide to use a first language different from that of their parents. For example, some Malay parents who have been educated in English-speaking countries may choose English as their first language, assuming that the children will learn Malay in school.

The Chinese in particular have made numerous choices with regard to language use. Whilst most have chosen to retain their ancestral dialects, Mandarin is studied, and some have chosen to speak English as their first language. In Kelantan, for example, at the intersection of the Malay- and Thai-speaking regions, many Chinese communities have maintained Hokkien, but modified it to parallel the languages spoken around them, namely Thai and Kelantan Malay (see 'Creoles').

Language shift occurs when entire communities change their language allegiance, as when the Melakan Straits Chinese switched from their native Chinese to Malay for daily communication (see 'Creoles'). Throughout history, many communities have changed their language allegiance and, in some cases, their cultural identities as well. For instance, the first language of the Muslim Utsat ethnic group—who migrated to Pangkor Island, Perak, in the early 20th century from the Chinese island of Hainan—was originally a Chamic language related to those of Vietnam, although they also spoke Chinese languages. After settling, building a mosque, and engaging in trade, they chose Malay as their first language. Today, the Utsat community has totally integrated into the Malay community of Pangkor with no trace of their own ancestral language.

Language choice is also determined by ethnic membership and age. For example, Javanese is spoken as a home language in Pontian (Johor), Meru

Malaysian Sign Language

Malaysian Sign Language (MSL), also known as Bahasa Malaysia Kod Tangan (BMKT) or Manually Coded Bahasa Malaysia, was officially implemented for the teaching of Malay in schools for the hearing impaired in 1985. It was formulated based on the concept of 'total communication' (*komunikasi seluruh*), that is, it makes use of signing with both hand and finger movements, finger-spelling, and lip-reading.

Linguistically, MSL closely reflects spoken Malay. Both the meaning of the basic word, and the grammatical elements that constitute it, are signed. Malay is an agglutinative language (i.e. it uses affixes) and makes use of reduplication; both of these characteristic elements are reflected in MSL. For instance, the word *tulis* (write) can be simply signed by simulating the action of the hand writing, but MSL requires that the prefix *me-* in *menulis* (to write) be also indicated. This is done by using finger-spelling. For the letters of the alphabet and numbers, MSL uses the internationally accepted signs.

TOP RIGHT: The Malay word '*emak*' (mother) is signed using the international sign for mother (left). The sign for the alternative Malay word, '*ibu*' (mother), is similar but only the little finger is raised, representing the letter 'i' (right).

LEFT: Two alternatives for the word 'I' in Malay are '*saya*' and '*aku*'. The sign for the former is the standard international sign for 'I' (left). For '*aku*' the fist is closed to represent the letter 'a'.

and Sabak Bernam (both in Selangor). Although children in these communities speak Malay outside the home due to their schooling, Javanese is the language of communication with their own family members. Many are bilingual in Javanese and Malay, but only the older generation prefers to speak Javanese. Middle-aged villagers use either Javanese or Malay, depending on the social context and the participants, but those under 20 only know a few formulaic phrases in Javanese and are unable to use the original language of their ancestors. In any case, the influence of Malay has caused a divergence from the Javanese spoken in Java.

As with young people in other countries around the world, Malaysian youths—for a variety of reasons including group identity—continue to develop their own language, particularly in urban areas. As they are mostly multilingual, they have even wider scope for creating new slang terminology. This is particularly the case among those whose dominant language is Malaysian English.

Youth magazines such as *Apo*? ('What?') use slang to communicate with their audience. For example at the top of the cover is the code-mixed word '*Terbest*' in the Malay phrase '*Lawak Terbest Masakini*' ('The Best Jokes Now').

Reading and literacy

Until the 20th century, the literacy rate was very low. At Independence in 1957, the literacy rate in the Malay Peninsula in any language was only 51 per cent, and in Malay only 25 per cent (46 per cent of the Malay population, 3 per cent of the Chinese population, and 5 per cent of Indians). These rates have since increased.

As the literacy rate has risen, the number of public libraries has increased, and the size of the tertiary student population grown. Malaysians are spending more time reading for both education and pleasure. Many, particularly the younger generation, are able to read and write at least two languages. Daily newspapers, magazines and books are published in all the major languages, offering a wide choice of reading material (see 'Languages and the print media').

Literacy rate in any language for population aged 10 years and above by ethnic group	
Ethnic group	Rate (%)
Total Malaysian Citizens	**91.0**
Total Bumiputera	90.3
Malays	93.0
Other Bumiputera	77.4
Chinese	92.3
Indians	92.9
Others	84.4
Non-Malaysian Citizens	**74.7**
ALL MALAYSIANS	**90.0**

Source: Population and Housing Census, 2000

Libraries

Malaysia has a National Library (Perpustakaan Negara Malaysia) located in Kuala Lumpur with a large collection of reading materials in both Malay and English, as well as a substantial collection of historical manuscripts. Each state also has a central public library, a number of branch libraries and, in some cases, mobile libraries. Both the national and state libraries coordinate activities aimed particularly at children to promote literacy and raise interest in reading.

There is also a large number of common-user specialist libraries attached to various government departments and statutory bodies, including universities, which hold titles in a wide range of local and foreign languages. However, access to these is subject to some restrictions. Finally, there is a small number of private non-common user specialist libraries, again with restrictions as to access.

ABOVE: Watercolour of a 1980s mobile library sponsored by multinational oil company, Esso.

LEFT: Located in Kuala Lumpur, the National Library holds over 1.5 million books.

1. *Lumba Kuda*, the Malay term for 'racehorse', dominates a billboard advertising the Racehorse brand of tea in Melaka.

2. Multilingual sign dating from the communist Emergency period (1948–1960) marking the edge of a 'white' or communist-free area. It is written in English, Malay (Jawi), Chinese and Tamil.

3. Iban bards singing during the Gawai Kenyalang festival at Rumah Kaong Ili, Ulu Batang Ai, in the Lubok Antu district of Sarawak's Sri Aman division in August 1975.

4. Cinema in Kuantan displaying English and Chinese writing. A smaller Malay (Jawi) notice is between the centre and right-hand entrances.

5. Motorists at Snake Road, Tanjung Malim, Perak, in 1932, posing by a road sign written in English, Malay (Jawi), Tamil, and Chinese.

6. Kadazandusun and Malay banner promoting Sabah's harvest festival.

7. Numerous magazines are published and sold in Malaysia in the Malay, Chinese and Tamil languages. English publications are also popular.

LANGUAGE DIVERSITY

At least 80 languages are spoken in Malaysia, making it one of the most complex linguistic communities in the world. Of these, some—drawn from the Austronesian and Austroasiatic language stocks—may be deemed indigenous to the Malay Archipelago. The Austronesian languages include Malay, the majority of the languages of Sarawak and Sabah, and more recent immigrant languages such as Acehnese, Javanese, Mandailing and Madurese. These latter languages are however not covered in this section, being spoken primarily by sojourners, and thus lacking stable speech communities.

The versatile Malay language has been used in a wide range of contexts for many centuries, and remains the most widely spoken language in the country, with several geographical and social variants. Most of the numerous Sarawakian and Sabahan languages are from the same Austronesian stock as Malay, and have close links to the languages of the rest of Borneo. In Sarawak it is Iban, a language that is closely related to Malay, that has the largest number of first language speakers. In Sabah the Dusunic languages spoken by the Kadazandusun ethnic group dominate. Unsurprisingly, these dominant languages are the best researched.

The survival of some minority languages of Sarawak and Sabah, and of several Aslian languages, spoken on the Peninsula by the aboriginal Orang Asli, is under threat. Some have already disappeared.

The numerous other languages used in Malaysia originate from outside the Malay World. Although Chinese speakers began to settle in Melaka in the 15th century, these early arrivals assimilated with the Malay population and adopted the Baba Malay creole (see 'Creoles'). It was only in the second half of the 19th century that large numbers of Chinese settled in the country and formed distinct speech communities of the South-eastern Chinese languages. Indian language speakers, primarily of Tamil, arrived at about the same time. English too became firmly established with the extension of British colonial administration to Malaya. Even after Independence, and despite there being only a small and transient first-language speaking population, English has evolved to become the de facto second language in Malaysia.

All of the non-indigenous Malaysian languages have undergone some degree of localization from their original form.

TOP LEFT: *Bés Hyang Dnèy and other Jah Hut Stories* presents four Orang Asli folk tales in Jah Hut and English.

TOP: Technology has enabled members of isolated communities, such as this elderly Iban man in Sarawak, to communicate with the outside world.

ABOVE: Traditional calligraphy is still preferred to printing in certain areas of Chinese culture.

History of Malay

Spoken by over 200 million people in Southeast Asia, Malay is now the fifth most widely spoken world language. Written Malay dates back at least 1,500 years, making it as old as English. The history of the language may conveniently be divided into four periods, in the course of which it has undergone many changes and, more recently, standardization. While local dialectal differences remain, these have become less pervasive since Malay was made the national language in 1957.

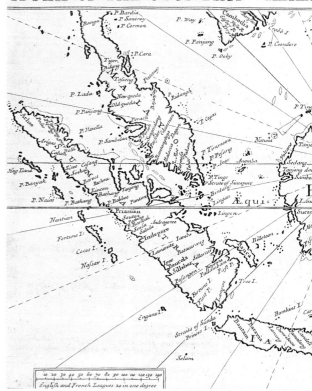

ABOVE: A map from Bowrey's A Dictionary of English and Malayo, Malayo and English published in London in 1701 showing the wide distribution of Malay-speaking communities. This distribution has changed little since.

RIGHT: The dictionary's title page and entries for 'Br'.

Classical Malay

From its introduction in the 14th century, the Jawi script enabled the Malays to record their experiences, religious laws, and what had hitherto been oral literature. This development led to the emergence in the 17th century of the great romances known as Hikayat. In his study of Malay literature, Sir Richard Winstedt categorized the Hikayat as classical Malay literature. The language of the Hikayat has itself come to be known as classical Malay or *Bahasa Melayu klasik*.

Winstedt's *A History of Classical Malay Literature* (1958) had a major impact on the teaching of Malay literature in schools and universities.

Old Malay

The oldest known Malay text, dated 682 CE, is the Kedukan Bukit inscription found near Palembang, Sumatra. Several other inscriptions, dating from the 7th to 9th centuries, have been found in Sumatra and western Java. These ancient texts are considered examples of 'Old Malay' or 'Early Malay', paralleling the nomenclature in historical studies of English and other European languages.

All these inscriptions were in an Indian script, Pallava, and characterized by extensive incorporation of Sanskrit loan words. This reflects the elevated status of these ritual and royal texts, and also indicates the importance of the commercial and cultural links of Malay polities to the Indian subcontinent. Other Malay-language inscriptions written in Indic-based scripts, though few in number, have been found as far afield as Luzon Island in the Philippines, including an inscription found near Manila dated to 900 CE.

The discovery of Malay texts from one end of the Malay Archipelago (Sumatra) to the other (Luzon) shows the early widespread use of Malay as a language of ritual and government. The tradition of writing Malay in Indic-based scripts persisted until the early 17th century. In Malaysia, the best-known example is the Islamic memorial stone at Pengkalan Kempas, Negeri Sembilan, dated to the 15th century. Inscribed on all faces of the stone, the scripts are in Kawi (old Javanese) and Jawi or Arabic.

The late examples of Indic-script Malay and earliest examples of Arabic-script texts represent a transitional period between Old Malay and Early Modern Malay. The earliest extant Malay inscription carved in Arabic script is the Terengganu Stone, dated 1303, found in Kuala Berang, Terengganu, in 1887. The text is a legal promulgation of Islam as the religion of the state, and provides the earliest evidence of the religion in the Malay Peninsula. But the language has a large number of Sanskrit terms, some of a very technical nature, which are now obsolete. The extensive use of Sanskrit vocabulary is a characteristic of Old Malay, and its grammatical system similar to modern Malay marks the text as a specimen of the transition from Old Malay towards Early Modern Malay. This transition accelerated in the late 15th century when Melaka assumed the role of pre-eminent trading port in the Southeast Asian region, and the Melakan empire reached its peak.

Early Modern Malay

By the end of the 15th century, Malay had begun to develop rapidly, not only as a language of trade and diplomacy, but also as a language used in the spread of Islam and Islamic literature. These developments radically changed the nature of the language: firstly, by allowing for the infusion of a massive vocabulary based chiefly on Arabic with additions from Persian and, later, Hindi; secondly, by introducing a new rhetorical style based on the Arabic model; thirdly, by admitting changes in grammar

---

682–1500 CE

Old Malay is characterized by extensive use of Sanskrit loan words and some affixes that are now obsolete.

Kedukan Bukit inscription, the earliest known Malay text, 682 CE.

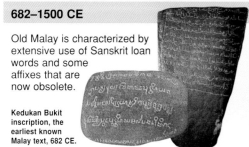

LEFT: The earliest known Malay inscription on the Malay Peninsula is the Terengganu Stone, dated 1303.

RIGHT: Pengkalan Kempas inscription, 1463–4, Negeri Sembilan.

1500–c.1850

Features of Early Modern Malay are the indigenization of Arabic loan words and changes in the affix system. Sentence word order fluctuates between 'verb-initial' and 'noun-initial'.

RIGHT: Letter in the Jawi script from the Raja of Kelantan and Tengku Sayid Abdul Rahman bin al-Habib Husain to W. Farquhar, 25 April 1822.

ABOVE: English translation of de Houtman's 1603 Malay handbook, 1614.

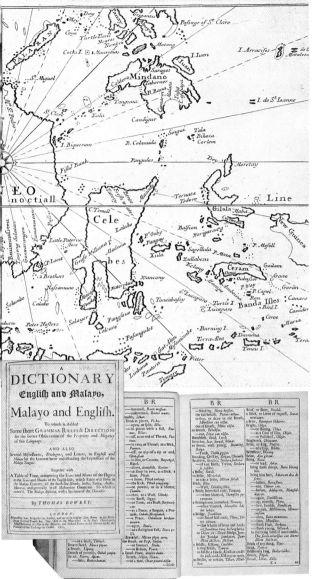

Late Modern Malay

By the beginning of the 19th century, Malay had developed into the major language of Southeast Asia, and the indispensable language of the Dutch and British colonial systems, as well as the chief language used to proselytize both Islam and Christianity.

By this time, Malay had absorbed many loan words from Arabic and Persian, and also from Portuguese and Dutch (see 'Characteristics of Malay'). These were incorporated in the standardized Malay dictionaries and grammars that appeared, together with a study of regional Malay dialects and codification of Malay literature. The 19th century also saw an expansion of Malay language educational systems and the use of Malay to disperse technological knowledge.

Malay became the indispensable language of contemporary political discourse as a result of its use in mass media, which began with the first Malay-language newspapers in both Arabic and Latin script. In the early 20th century, the independence movements in both British and Dutch colonies were fired by speeches and writings in Malay.

The Japanese Occupation of the Malay-speaking world during World War II (1942–5) hastened the pace of the nascent independence movements and the parallel use of the Malay language in Southeast Asia. The eventual birth of independent Indonesia on 17 August 1945 was later followed by Independence in Malaya on 31 August 1957.

Contemporary Malay

The constitutions of Malaysia and Indonesia both enshrined Malay as the national language, leading to efforts to draw the two dialects together through close co-operation. These efforts, coordinated by the Dewan Bahasa dan Pustaka (Institute of Language and Literature)—which was established to develop Malay language and literature, mirroring Indonesia's Balai Pustaka and Lembaga Bahasa dan Kebudaya-an—met with little initial success: an agreed spelling system, '*Ejaan Melindo*' was too impractical to be of use (see 'National language policy'). More practical steps were further thwarted in 1963 as a result of the Indonesian policy of *Konfrontasi*. However, with the normalization of relations in 1966, substantive steps toward standardization were taken which resulted in the adoption of a common spelling system in 1972. This had the additional effect of bringing order to the spelling system within Malaysia, where previous-ly a number of systems were in use.

Academic and translator Tan Sri Zainal Abidin bin Ahmad (1895–1972), better known as Za'ba, codified Malay grammar in the three-volume *Pelita Bahasa Melayu* published in 1941. He also modified the Jawi spelling system.

based on oral speech—for example, the shift of *akan* from a preposition to a suffix. These changes in language were matched by changing social conditions. One catalyst of this change was the capture of Melaka by the Portuguese in 1511. The zealous anti-Muslim policies of the Portuguese invaders led to the dispersal of Islamic specialists throughout the Malay Archipelago, accelerating the spread of Islam. The conquest of Melaka also caused the emergence of new regional entrepôts, modelled on the success of Melaka. As a direct consequence, in a relatively brief period, the Malay language became diffused more widely than it had been before.

c.1850–1957

Late Modern Malay incorporates numerous loan words from Dutch and English. The preferred word order is subject-verb-object.

LEFT: The first edition of *Bustan al-Katibin*, a book on Malay grammar by Raja Ali Haji, 1857.

RIGHT: Malay novels, such as Syed Sheikh Al-Hadi's *Hikayat Faridah Hanum* (1926), first appeared in the early 20th century.

After 1957

After Independence, strong political support for Malay resulted in Malaysia, Indonesia and Brunei setting up national language planning agencies involved in research and publication, as well as an international planning body which has unified orthography and terminology.

Third edition of the authoritative monolingual Malay dictionary published by Dewan Bahasa dan Pustaka.

Characteristics of Malay

For 1,300 years Malay has served as the chief language of diplomacy, advanced knowledge, politics and trade, making it the lingua franca of island Southeast Asia. With a straightforward sound system and user-friendly grammar, the language is easily learnt by speakers of other languages. It is also an adaptable language, having absorbed ideas and vocabulary from a variety of other languages.

The 'Latin of Asia'

When the first Europeans arrived in Southeast Asia in the early 16th century, they not only discovered new lands, but also new languages, among them Malay. By 1525, Antonio Pigafetta, who accompanied Magellan on his circumnavigation of the globe, had published Malay-Italian, Malay-French, and Malay-Latin word lists. Subsequent travellers to the archipelago continued to marvel at the Malay language, which they described as the 'Latin of Asia', 'like French in Europe', and measured its use and popularity 'as if [it was] the lingua franca of the Mediterranean'.

What was it about Malay that inspired these comparisons? Certainly in the 16th century, and probably for a millennium before, Malay was a prestigious written language that served as the chief language of diplomacy and religion, a role similar to that of Latin in Europe at that time. Laws and treaties were drawn up in Malay, theological treatises were written in Malay to explain Arabic texts, and like Latin, Malay was the language of advanced knowledge and international politics. Malay was also the language of contemporary literature: ancient stories were recast, reinterpreted and composed in Malay, and oral literature was performed in Malay, paralleling the role of French in European culture. More remarkably, Malay was also the chief language of trade. Not only were trading permits issued in Malay, but most of the international commerce of

Malay was used in commerce, such as in this trading permit issued to an English sea captain around 1602 (above), and international relations, such as this letter from Sultan Mahmud Shah of Johor and Pahang, dated 1811 (below).

16th-century Malay word list

In 1522, Italian tourist Antonio Pigafetta visited the island of Ternate in the Moluccas, and became the first European to compile a Malay word list. The list appeared in his book which has been translated into English with the title *First Voyage Around the World*.

Antonio Pigafetta (pictured here dining with Filipino chiefs) was one of only 17 men to return to Spain of the approximately 270 men who set out on the first circumnavigation of the globe.

Pigafetta's notation	Modern Malay equivalent	English word
Alla	Allah	God
naceran	nasrani	Christian
isilam	Islam	Islam
mischit	masjid	mosque
horan pandita	pendeta	wise men
mama ambui	emak	mother
anach	anak	child
saudala	saudara	brother
niny	nenek	grandparent
minthua	mertua	father-in-law
mi nanthu	menantu	son-in-law
horan	orang	person
poran poan	perempuan	woman
capala	kepala	head
lambut	rambut	hair
matta	mata	eye
idon	hidung	nose
bebere	bibir	lips
lada	lidah	tongue

Numeral classifiers

In Malay, a classifier is usually used between a numeral and the object being counted. For example, the phrase 'a dress' is expressed as *sehelai baju*, not the literal translation *satu baju*. As the classifier must match the intrinsic quality of the object in terms of size, shape and texture, there are several classifiers in common use, each applied to items of a particular shape or size. The following are some frequently used classifiers.

orang applies to people, e.g. *seorang Orang Asli* (an aborigine)

buah applies to large objects, e.g. *sebuah rumah* (a house)

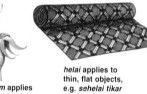

helai applies to thin, flat objects, e.g. *sehelai tikar* (a mat)

kuntum applies to flowers, e.g. *sekuntum bunga* (a flower)

batang applies to long or tall objects, e.g. *sebatang sungei* (a river)

biji applies to small objects, e.g. *sebiji manggis* (a mangosteen)

ekor applies to animals, e.g. *seekor gajah* (an elephant)

island Southeast Asia was conducted verbally in the language. No wonder Malay was marvelled at by Europeans, for this one language combined the social functions of three European languages.

Despite the deleterious impact of subsequent European colonialism, Malay has held its own and maintained or reclaimed the many roles it played 500 years ago. Its position as a language of advanced knowledge and politics has persisted in modern Southeast Asia; however, while it remains a language of commerce and literature, it has yielded some ground to English in both fields. Nonetheless, Malay has more than 200 million speakers and a vibrant range of diverse national cultures to support it.

Linguistic structure

The use of Malay has expanded at the expense of other regional languages, in part because of its linguistic structure. The sound system of standard Malay is straightforward, with a range of vowels and consonants often shared by speakers of other languages. Neither vowel length nor a heavy stress on the vowel changes the meaning of words, unlike in other regional languages such as Kadazandusun or certain Aslian languages which have complicated vowel systems, or Thai, Burmese and Chinese which use intonation to distinguish meaning.

Malay has 19 native consonants (including the semi-vowels) but in the course of its development, a number of consonants from other languages have entered the language through loan words, mostly from Arabic and English: *f, v, z, sh, kh*. Consonants are distinguished by place, manner of articulation, and voicing. Although Malay has hundreds of words of one, three, or four syllables, most Malay words have two syllables.

Malay phrases generally take the sequence head-modifier, the 'head' being the word which bears the meaning that is central to the mind of the speaker, whereas the modifier is filled by the word or phrase which tells more about the head. Hence, in *rumah besar* (literally 'house big'), and *sakit teruk* (literally 'ill serious') with *rumah* and *sakit* central to the mind.

In a geographical region of many word-order systems, Malay, with two basic sentence structures, has proven a language easily learned by speakers of other languages. It has also developed a rather detailed system of numeral classifiers, in a style similar to mainland Southeast Asian languages, allowing for ease in language intertranslatability (shifting from one language to another because structures are parallel). As a written language it appears in both the Roman (*Rumi*) and Jawi scripts (see 'The Malay written tradition'), with a common spelling system having been implemented in both Malaysia and Indonesia.

Wealth of vocabulary

Malay is a versatile language and its systems are open to enrichment from within the language itself (i.e. from the various dialects) as well as from other languages. Through its open lexical system it has managed to take in an extraordinarily high number of loan words. The languages which have

Malay spelling

The first standard Malay spelling system was formulated by a special committee appointed in 1904, and known as *Ejaan Wilkinson* after its chairman. This system was subsequently modified in 1924 by Zainal Abidin bin Ahmad (better known as Za'ba), a lecturer and translator at the Sultan Idris Training College: he thought the existing system did not reflect the way that the Malays pronounced their language. His system—known as *Ejaan Sekolah*—was implemented in the schools of Malaya, Singapore and Brunei, and remained the official spelling system until 1972. In that year, the Malaysia-Indonesia common system was implemented: a compromise between the two prevailing systems—English-based in Malaysia and Dutch-based in Indonesia. It resulted in the introduction of new graphemes (i.e. a letter or combination of letters representing a single phoneme). 'C' and 'sy' were introduced, neither of which existed in the previous systems: 'c' replaced 'tj' in Indonesia and 'ch' in Malaysia; 'sy' replaced the Indonesian 'sj' and the Malaysian 'sh'. Indonesia also agreed to accept the Malaysian graphemes 'j' and 'kh' for 'dj' and 'ch' respectively.

Formal talks between Malaysia (represented by Tun Syed Nasir, right) and Indonesia (represented by Ibu Roedjiat Moeljadi, left) to agree on a common spelling system began in 1966.

contributed the most loan words to Malay are Sanskrit, Arabic and English. The importance of Malay in intra-Asian trade has also brought in loan words from Persia and China. Portuguese and Dutch have contributed as a result of colonization. Arabic has had a particularly strong impact on Malay. Some Arabic words have been a part of Malay for so long that they have evolved to carry different meanings and pronunciations. Arabic remains a major force in the expansion of Malay vocabulary, as does English, with the annual inclusion of hundreds of English words, some by official declaration (e.g. scientific terminology) and others by popular demand (e.g. global pop culture).

In common with other major world languages, Malay constantly enriches and reinvents itself by absorbing ideas and terminology from the most convenient sources. This fascinated global travellers 500 years ago, and is no less astounding today.

Business signs in the town of Raub display the use of English vocabulary in Malay: *tuisyen* (tuition), *insurans* (insurance), *klinik* (clinic), and *agensi* (agency).

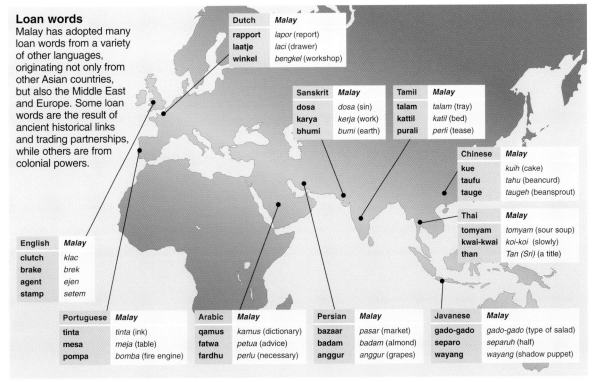

Loan words

Malay has adopted many loan words from a variety of other languages, originating not only from other Asian countries, but also the Middle East and Europe. Some loan words are the result of ancient historical links and trading partnerships, while others are from colonial powers.

Dutch	Malay
rapport	*lapor* (report)
laatje	*laci* (drawer)
winkel	*bengkel* (workshop)

Sanskrit	Malay
dosa	*dosa* (sin)
karya	*kerja* (work)
bhumi	*bumi* (earth)

Tamil	Malay
talam	*talam* (tray)
kattil	*katil* (bed)
purali	*perli* (tease)

Chinese	Malay
kue	*kuih* (cake)
taufu	*tahu* (beancurd)
tauge	*taugeh* (beansprout)

Thai	Malay
tomyam	*tomyam* (sour soup)
kwai-kwai	*koi-koi* (slowly)
than	*Tan (Sri)* (a title)

English	Malay
clutch	*klac*
brake	*brek*
agent	*ejen*
stamp	*setem*

Portuguese	Malay
tinta	*tinta* (ink)
mesa	*meja* (table)
pompa	*bomba* (fire engine)

Arabic	Malay
qamus	*kamus* (dictionary)
fatwa	*petua* (advice)
fardhu	*perlu* (necessary)

Persian	Malay
bazaar	*pasar* (market)
badam	*badam* (almond)
anggur	*anggur* (grapes)

Javanese	Malay
gado-gado	*gado-gado* (type of salad)
separo	*separuh* (half)
wayang	*wayang* (shadow puppet)

Regional varieties of Malay

Malaysia has at least 11 million first-language speakers of Malay, and a rich and diverse range of geographic dialects that developed historically as a result of both the physical landscape and socio-cultural diversity. These dialects often differ extensively, both in terms of phonology and, to a lesser extent, vocabulary. Nevertheless, and notwithstanding that speakers of some dialects may have strong regional accents, for the most part they remain intelligible to speakers of other dialects and standard Malay.

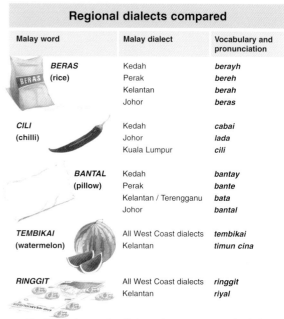

Regional dialects compared

Malay word		Malay dialect	Vocabulary and pronunciation
BERAS (rice)		Kedah	*berayh*
		Perak	*bereh*
		Kelantan	*berah*
		Johor	*beras*
CILI (chilli)		Kedah	*cabai*
		Johor	*lada*
		Kuala Lumpur	*cili*
BANTAL (pillow)		Kedah	*bantay*
		Perak	*bante*
		Kelantan / Terengganu	*bata*
		Johor	*bantal*
TEMBIKAI (watermelon)		All West Coast dialects	*tembikai*
		Kelantan	*timun cina*
RINGGIT		All West Coast dialects	*ringgit*
		Kelantan	*riyal*

TOP: Dikir Barat, a well-known east coast poetic tradition in which the chorus echoes the theme of the leader's song, uses Kelantan Malay.

ABOVE: Johor Malay is commonly used in Ghazal, the art of reciting romantic and religious verses in a singing style.

RIGHT: One of the three remaining villages on Tioman Island, off Johor's east coast, in which the Malay dialect spoken closely resembles Sarawak Malay.

Dialects of the Malays

Until the 19th century, almost all Malay speakers in the Peninsula depended for their livelihoods on its rivers and the sea. This, and the dense forests that covered the Peninsula which discouraged overland communication, have resulted in a geographic distribution of Malay dialects that traditionally paralleled the riverine topography, a different Malay dialect being spoken along each major river. Within each dialect, distinctive upriver and downriver sub-dialects are identifiable; there is an almost seamless gradation of small linguistic differences from one village to the next along the course of each river, with no strong lines of delineation. A similar situation is found along some stretches of coastline. A further explanation for the dialectal complexity of the language is that some of the Malay sub-groups have been present in the Peninsula for almost 2,000 years.

Excluding Indonesian Malay dialects used by certain immigrant communities, native speakers of Malay belong to nine dialect groups, seven on the Peninsula and one each in Sabah and Sarawak. Each dialect group is not a single homogeneous whole, but consists of several sub-dialects. Besides the native regional varieties of Malaysia, there are also varieties that have been brought from Indonesia and Brunei.

Shahnon Ahmad used the Kedah dialect in his novel *Ranjau Sepanjang Jalan* ('No Harvest But A Thorn').

The dialect groups with the largest number of speakers are Kelantan, Kedah and Johor, each with over a million speakers. The differences between these dialects are mainly phonological (i.e. words are pronounced differently), although some differences in vocabulary also exist. Speakers of one regional dialect are generally able to understand those of another. Kelantanese is an exception, however, primarily as a result of the characteristic non-voicing of many final nasal consonants in this dialect, affecting the quality of the preceding vowel. Examples include words in which the vowel 'a' precedes the final consonant, such as *makan* (eat), *makam* (mausoleum), both pronounced *makE'* in Kelantanese, and *malam* (night) and *malang* (unfortunate), both pronounced as *malE'*. Homonyms (words pronounced similarly but with different meaning) such as these are also created with the replacement of a final consonant 't' with a glottal stop, and of a final 's' with 'h'.

Each of the main dialects has various sub-dialects. However, these differ only slightly, mostly in terms of pronunciation. For example, in the Kedah dialect spoken on the Kedah plains, the final consonant 'a' is articulated towards the front of the mouth with an unrounded sound, whereas that in the eastern region of Padang Terap is more rounded.

Speakers of certain dialects are distributed over a large area, such as Kedah Malay which, despite being spoken in four different states, has relatively few sub-dialects (only six). This may be attributed to intensive rice cultivation which led to the breaking up of traditional village communities, and to the increased communication that resulted from the building of canals.

The Johor dialect is another widely distributed dialect, with speakers extending to both Melaka and Pahang, and a noticeable influence in Perak and Selangor, and even in the Riau-Lingga Archipelago and the areas around Medan and Pekan Baru on the island of Sumatra, all in Indonesia. This serves as a reminder of the hegemony of the Johor empire in the 17th to 19th centuries.

Of the Malay dialects spoken in East Malaysia, Sarawak Malay differs from that spoken in the Peninsula in terms of pronunciation, speech rhythm and to some extent, vocabulary. Sub-dialectal

Distribution of Malay dialects

Dialects spoken by Malays

Kedah	
Kelantan	
Terengganu	
Perak	
Pahang	
Johor	
N. Sembilan	
Melaka	
Selangor	

Source: Collins modified by Asmah

Malay dialects spoken by non-Malays

Temuan	
Baba	Orang Kanaq
Chitty	Orang Kuala
Jakun	Orang Seletar

0   100 km

Dialects of Peninsular Malaysia

Nine major dialect groups—spoken primarily by Malays—are present in the Peninsula, each related to a particular Peninsula state. Another five Malay dialects are spoken by relatively small groups of Orang Asli, mainly in small settlements spread over wide areas of the southern states, and two more by the Babas and Chitties of Melaka. The most obvious difference between the various dialects is pronunciation. Vocabulary also varies to a limited extent, but there is little grammatical distinction between the dialects.

Fishermen in Terengganu pushing their highly decorated boat ashore. Terengganu Malay is distinct from other Malay dialects as the letters 'm' and 'n' at the end of words are replaced with 'ng'.

INSET: Temuan Orang Asli speak Temuan Malay, which has some similarities to Terengganu and Kelantan Malay, as well as certain sub-dialects of Kedah Malay.

Malay dialects in Sarawak and Sabah

Sarawak Malay, is spoken throughout Sarawak in various sub-dialectal forms, although primarily around the towns of Kuching, Sibu, and Miri. Among these is the Saribas sub-dialect spoken in villages mainly along the Saribas and Lupar rivers, and close to Iban speaking areas. This has resulted in the borrowing of numerous Iban words. Brunei Malay is the first language of most Malays in eastern Sarawak, western Sabah (where it is a second language to Kadazandusun), Labuan and Brunei. Kedayan Malay, also known as Sabah Malay, differs from Brunei Malay only in a number of small sound changes. The immigrant Cocos Malay dialect is also spoken in eastern Sabah.

Malay dialect groups

	Core area of Sarawak Malay
	Peripheral area of Sarawak Malay
	Brunei
	Kedayan
	Cocos

0   100 km

Source: Wurm and Hattori

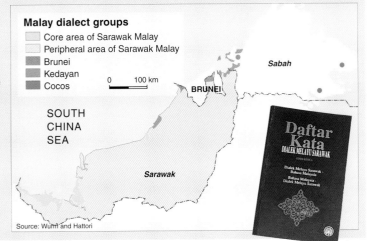

LEFT: Brunei Malays in Kampung Biau, Sipitang, Sabah, performing at a 'magunting' ceremony, celebrating a baby's first haircut.

RIGHT INSET: A Sarawak Malay wordlist published by Dewan Bahasa dan Pustaka.

variations are apparent between speakers from, for example, Kuching and Miri. A larger number of dialects are spoken in Sabah.

A dialect related to the Malay spoken along the Sarawak River near Kuching is spoken as the first language in the three remaining indigenous villages on Tioman Island off the east coast of the Malay Peninsula. However, the number of speakers of this dialect is declining as young people switch to the more dominant Johor Malay.

Dialects of the non–Malays

Of the 10 million non-Malay citizens of Malaysia, it is estimated that less than one per cent speak Malay as a first language. Of these, approximately 40,000 are Orang Asli—the remaining 80,000 or so Orang Asli speak Aslian (see 'Aslian languages')—amongst whom at least five Malay dialects are spoken: Orang Kanaq, Orang Kuala, Orang Seletar, Temuan and Jakun. Although little research has been done on these Malay variants, the number of speakers may be even greater given their wide distribution in small and discontinuous enclaves throughout Johor, Pahang, Melaka, Negeri Sembilan and Selangor.

Although technically a creole, the Baba dialect spoken by the Straits Chinese has a social parameter closely linked to the town of Melaka, and may therefore be considered a geographical dialect of Malay. This view is reinforced by another small Melakan group speaking almost the same dialect (again, technically a creole), namely the Hindu community of Chitty Malay speakers (see 'Creoles').

Lemang panas (glutinous rice cooked with coconut milk in bamboo), pronounced *lomang paneh* in the Negeri Sembilan Malay dialect, sold at the roadside near Banting in Selangor.

Social varieties of Malay

Social dialects are speech varieties that have evolved according to the social background of speakers, while registers are determined by social setting or function. Malay is characterized by both social dialects and registers. Contemporary Malay has only two major social dialects, but retains several special registers, including Royal Malay used for formal occasions and within royal families, and other specialized vocabularies for a variety of occupations, ranging from the archaic lexicon of shamans to that of new information technology workers.

William Marsden

In his 1812 *Dictionary of the Malayan Language*, William Marsden identified four varieties of Malay: *bhasa dalam* (courtly style), *bhasa bangsawan* (style of the upper classes), *bhasa dagang* (style of the merchants) and *bhasa kachuk-an* (mixed jargon of the bazaars). However, his classifications no longer accurately describe the social variation in modern Malay usage as there are now only two major social dialects of Malay: standard Malay and colloquial Malay.

Social dialects of Malay

Languages show considerable variation among different social groups and settings. People of different backgrounds often have their own ways of speaking. Language variation can be associated with class, gender, age and other social variables.

Speech varieties with identifying markers that belong to different social groups are called social dialects. Individuals from varying social backgrounds constantly adjust the way they talk to different situations. Speech varieties are determined by regularly recurring settings or function, and those with identifying markers are often called registers.

Previously, four primarily class-based varieties of Malay were identified, but currently there are only two major social dialects. The first, standard Malay (also known as formal Malay), is used in schools, universities, government administration and the media. Colloquial Malay, or a regional variant, is used in a wide range of situations, particularly less formal ones (see 'Contact languages').

Standard Malay is based on Johor-Riau Malay in terms of phonology, grammar and lexicon, due to the role played by the 17th-century Johor-Riau empire in spreading the Malay language, particularly through literature. In the late 19th century, the printing machine came to Singapore where

Royal Malay

Bahasa diraja (Royal Malay) is spoken by and to the nine sultans of Malaysia (previously Malaya), pictured above in 1957.

Bahasa diraja is a special register of Malay, used on formal occasions by both royalty and the commoners addressing them. It incorporates different words for everyday activities, terms of address and personal pronouns. For example, a sultan will refer to himself with *beta* (I), while non-rulers use *patik* (I) when speaking to the ruler, instead of the standard Malay *saya* (I).

English	Royal Malay	Standard Malay
arrive	*berangkat tiba*	*tiba*
approve	*berkenan*	*bersetuju*
come	*mencemar duli*	*datang*
die	*mangkat*	*meninggal dunia*
bathe	*bersiram*	*mandi*
send greetings	*berkirim sembah*	*berkirim salam*
permission	*limpah perkenaan*	*izin*
prince	*anakanda putera*	*anak laki-laki*
princess	*anakanda puteri*	*anak perempuan*
thank you	*junjung kasih*	*terima kasih*

Johor-Riau Malay was spoken, and the first Malay newspapers were published. When the British introduced Malay radio services in Singapore, it was Johor-Riau pronunciation that was used, and this practice was continued when Radio Malaya later opened branches in Kuala Lumpur and Penang, and subsequently changed its name to Radio Malaysia.

In 1988, the Dewan Bahasa dan Pustaka (Institute of Language and Literature) recommended an official pronunciation known as *bahasa baku* (uniform language) which focused on *sebutan baku* (uniform pronunciation) in an effort to standardize Malaysian Malay with Indonesian Malay. This was a 'spelling pronunciation', meaning that

Malaysia's first Prime Minister, Tunku Abdul Rahman, broadcasting in standard Malay in 1963.

people were supposed to pronounce words according to the way in which they were spelt. Though implemented in schools, sebutan baku was not well received as it sounded unnatural to speakers. In 1998, the government ruled that Malay pronunciation would be based on Johor-Riau Malay.

Colloquial Malay, the second major social dialect, is not formally taught, and is generally denigrated in the school system. It is, however, the form of Malay most often spoken in the home. It marks solidarity and equality of social standing, and may to some extent be associated with the uneducated class. It derives strength from its roots in the regional variants of Malay (see 'Regional varieties of Malay').

Features of colloquial Malay

The popular humour magazine *Gila-gila* appeals to many readers because it includes passages written entirely in colloquial Malay—widely understood and appreciated by many Malaysians. In the above cartoon panel, a grandmother talks to neighbours about her wayward grandson. Frequently used function words appear in a shortened (allegro) form: *itu → tu* (that), *tidak → tak* (not), *sudah → dah* (already). Transitive verbs never appear with a prefix—such as *buat* (do), *nasihat* (advise), *tampar* (slap), *suruh* (order); and discourse markers also differ from standard Malay, for example, *habis tu* instead of *sesudah itu* (after that).

The coronation of His Majesty the Yang di-Pertuan Agong

At his coronation, His Majesty the Yang di-Pertuan Agong (King or Supreme Sovereign) takes the Oath of Appointment, and (inset) the Prime Minister makes the Proclamation of Coronation, both in Royal Malay.

How to address a Sultan
The respectful Royal Malay welcome recorded below was extended to HRH the Sultan of Pahang by Universiti Malaya in 1985. It illustrates the deferential nature of the register.

A Royal Malay welcome
Mengadap Kebawah Duli Yang Maha Mulia,
Sultan Haji Ahmad Shah Al-Mustain Billah
ibni Al-Marhum Sultan Abu Bakar Riayatuddin Al-Muadzam Shah,
D.K.P. Sultan Pahang Darul Makmur,
Ampun Tuanku.

Tuanku Canselor
Ampun Tuanku beribu-ribu ampun
Sembah patik mohon diampun.

Patik memohon limpah kurnia Duli Tuanku menyembah maklum hasrat Senat Universiti Malaya mempersembahkan darjat akademik kepada Duli Yang Maha Mulia Sultan Pahang, yang telah berkenan mencemar duli ke kampus Universiti Malaya pada pagi ini.

Literal English translation
I present myself before Your Royal Highness,
Sultan Haji Ahmad Shah Al-Mustain Billah
ibni Al-Marhum Sultan Abu Bakar Riayatuddin Al-Muadzam Shah,
D.K.P. Sultan Pahang Darul Makmur,
My apologies, Your Royal Highness.

Your Royal Highness the Chancellor
A thousand apologies do I supplicate from Your Highness
Please accept the homage of your humble servant.

Your humble servant humbly supplicates for your great bounty to (hear her) inform Your Highness of the wish of the Senate of Universiti Malaya to humbly offer an academic degree to His Highness the Sultan of Pahang who has agreed to dirty the dust of his feet to visit the campus of Universiti Malaya this morning.

Code-switching is more common between colloquial Malay and English than standard Malay and English (see 'Contact languages').

Malay speakers who do not usually use standard Malay may, however, choose to use that social dialect in certain circumstances, such as when making formal political speeches or completing school assignments. Similarly, habitual speakers of standard Malay may at times switch to colloquial Malay in order to express collegiality.

Registers of Malay
A register refers to a language variety spoken during certain social situations. Among the numerous social registers of Malay, the best known is that relating to Malaysia's royal houses. When referring to the ruling sultans, for example, certain vocabulary items have to shift to this register, known as *bahasa diraja* (language of the rajah) or *bahasa istana* (language of the palace). The register is used in royal speeches and palace rituals, and in general sounds similar to classical Malay (see 'History of Malay'). In less ritualized settings, the rulers themselves prefer to speak English, or a regional Malay dialect, as do other members of the Malay élite.

In the past, a number of other registers also existed, for example taboo registers related to the spirit world. One extinct register, the 'camphor language', was used in the late 19th century by Malay-speaking Orang Asli on entering the jungle to seek trees bearing camphor. In the special setting of the deep jungle, standard words were replaced with a specialized vocabulary. Similarly, a different register was used when Malay shamans appeased local spirits

before the opening of new tin mines, notably in Perak, over a century ago. The variety of Malay registers demonstrate that to a greater extent than many other languages, choice of language in Malay must fit the situation, primarily as a mark of respect.

In contemporary Malaysia many new registers are identifiable, including a sports register with an exaggerated lexicon and an Islamic instruction register influenced by Arabic models. Highly technical registers are used in information technology manuals and trade journals. The jargon of counter-cultural groups, and many other special registers are used in certain situations. Malay, as with other living languages, is spoken in a dazzling array of subtle and specialized ways.

Occupational speech registers
Worker specialization in traditional industries led to the development of unique vocabularies. Several of these are still used today, such as those employed by Malay woodcarvers for technical terms specific to their craft, and by batik painters to describe aspects of their work such as styles, motifs, strokes and colours. Special registers in relation to rice farming were prevalent in many parts of rural Malaysia until as late as the 1970s. New registers continue to develop among workers in modern industries; this is particularly so among factory workers.

Factory workers use special speech registers, often as a mark of solidarity.

Workers harvesting rice in Kedah would once have used the traditional rice farming register.

Languages of Sarawak

Between 30 and 40 languages are spoken in Sarawak, Malaysia's largest state. Of these, at least 25 are indigenous languages, most of which may be grouped into 9 sub-families, all belonging to the Austronesian family. Some are more closely related to languages spoken outside Sarawak than to those spoken within the state. Several organizations are engaged in researching this complex language scenario. Sarawak is also home to a large number of speakers of Chinese; and English continues to play an important role in some speech domains.

Radio Times of Sarawak, published by the British colonial government, carried programme listings in English, Chinese, Malay and Iban.

Indigenous and non-indigenous

The largest indigenous language sub-family in Sarawak is Malayic, which includes Iban, the dominant ethnolinguistic group with some half a million speakers, as well as Malay and Selakau. Other language sub-families include Bidayuh (formerly known as Land Dayak), Melanau and Kajang. The Kayan, Kenyah, Kelabit and Penan languages may conveniently be grouped as 'Northern Sarawak languages' (see 'Northern Sarawak languages'). More distantly related languages also in the north of the state include Mirik and Bintulu, as well as Bisaya—which is more closely related to the Paitanic and Dusunic languages of Sabah than to any of the other Sarawak languages.

The only non-indigenous languages spoken widely as first languages in the state are those of the Chinese. The Chinese dialects spoken in Sarawak more or less replicate those of the Peninsula, but with a preponderance of Hokchiu (Foochow) and Khek (Hakka) rather than Hokkien or Cantonese (see 'Distribution of Chinese dialects'). The number of Indians in Sarawak is too small to constitute a speech community. English is spoken, but primarily as a second language.

Origins of language diversity

The complexity of Sarawak's languages is the result of group migration both across and

Language research

Several organizations have conducted and published research on the indigenous languages of Sarawak. Perhaps the best known of these is the Borneo Literature Bureau, which operated from 1959 until 1977, and focused on Iban. Other bodies that are still active include

The Borneo Literature Bureau Kuching office in the 1960s.

the Dewan Bahasa dan Pustaka (Sarawak Branch), the Sarawak Literary Society, the privately funded Tun Jugah Foundation, the Majlis Adat Istiadat Sarawak, the Yayasan Budaya Melayu Sarawak, and the Dayak Cultural Foundation.

Christian groups have also long been at the forefront of language research in Sarawak, and have published religious materials in many of the indigenous languages.

The Iban Bible, Bup Kudus, was temporarily banned by the government in 2003 due to concern that it might be misinterpreted by Muslims.

along many of Borneo's rivers. Following centuries of control by the Brunei sultanate, colonialism added to this web of languages by encouraging migration from China and by using English and Malay in the school and administrative systems. Migration is undoubtedly the reason that many Sarawakian languages have strong links to those spoken in Indonesian Borneo (Kalimantan).

KALIMANTAN

Source: Adapted from Wurm and Hattori

Iban, for example, is most closely linked to related variants spoken along the Kapuas River in Kalimantan. The closest relatives of the Kayan language are similarly found in Kalimantan (see 'Northern Sarawak languages'). Even the small Selakau group of western Sarawak speak a variant of Kendayan, a very large language group in northwest Kalimantan.

Multilingualism and classification

Many Sarawakians speak three or four local languages, as well as standard Malay and English. This multilingualism is a result of increased educational opportunities and improvements in transportation, aided by the mutual intelligibility of many Sarawakian language groups: itself a result of speakers learning indigenous languages other than their own, rather than any inherently close relationship between the various languages.

Reliance on broad cultural similarities as a basis for classifying Sarawak's

indigenous languages and the high level of multilingualism have impeded precise classification. Other classificatory difficulties have also arisen: for example the Malayic Selakau language is often mistakenly considered a Bidayuh language (see 'Malayic languages of Sarawak'). Similarly, Ngurik (also known as Murik), often considered a Kenyah language, shows a clear connection to Kayan.

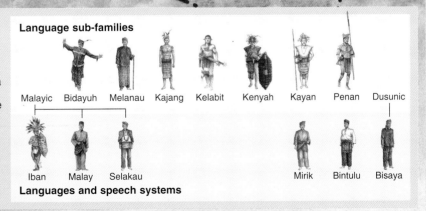

Uninhabited Area

Sarawak language speaker numbers

4.5% — 1.0%
26.3%
30.1%
5.6%
8.3% 24.2%

Languages and language groups	First-language speakers
Iban	586,548
Malay	472,173
Bidayuh	161,873
Melanau	109,882
Chinese	512,426
Northern Sarawak	87,472
Others	18,634
TOTAL	**1,949,008**

Note: The above figures, from the Population and Housing Census 2000, are based on ethnicity rather than language, and are thus only approximate. Specific information on languages was not collected. Census information for ethnicity is based on self-identification.

Indigenous languages of Sarawak

Some of the indigenous languages of Sarawak, such as Iban, Malay and Selakau, clearly belong to a language sub-family. Others, such as Kelabit, are sometimes referred to as languages, but are more correctly defined as language sub-families. Certain languages or speech systems, such as Mirik and Bintulu, have yet to be linked to any group.

Language sub-families

Malayic   Bidayuh   Melanau   Kajang   Kelabit   Kenyah   Kayan   Penan   Dusunic

Iban   Malay   Selakau

Mirik   Bintulu   Bisaya

Languages and speech systems

31

Malayic languages of Sarawak

Three identifiable Malayic languages are spoken in Sarawak. Of these, Iban and Malay are the most widely spoken languages, while Selakau is spoken only by a small minority. All three languages share a number of similarities, and Iban and Selakau in particular are further related to other Malayic languages spoken elsewhere in southwestern Borneo (West Kalimantan, Indonesia). Much research has been undertaken and published on the Iban language, with European linguistic interest stretching back to the mid-19th century.

TEMPAT TERKAWAL
PROTECTED PLACE
TEMPAT ENDA TAU DI-PAMSA
保護區

Notices often appear in several languages in Sarawak. Here, Malay is placed at the top, followed by English, Iban, and Chinese.

Defining Malayic languages

Malayic languages all belong to the Austronesian family of languages. They are categorized as Malayic by linguists working on the indigenous languages of Malaysia and Indonesia, based on the degree of their affinity with Malay, mostly from the point of view of their vocabulary content. For example, Iban is a Malayic language as it shares nearly two-thirds of its basic core vocabulary with Malay, whereas the Kadazandusun language spoken in Penampang, Sabah, for example, has only a 35 per cent similarity with Malay and is thus not considered a Malayic language. Malayic languages also share similarities in word and sentence formation. A Malay speaker will therefore find it easier to learn a Malayic language than a non-Malayic one.

Iban

Iban, the language with the largest number of speakers in Sarawak, is spoken as a first language by more than 580,000 people throughout the state, as well as by communities in Brunei and Sabah. As Iban is the dominant language in many parts of Sarawak, many people of other ethnic groups use it as a second or third language. Indeed, many Malays and Chinese are fluent speakers of Iban. An

As Iban traditionally had no true written form, Iban shamans (*lemambang*) used wooden tablets (*papan turai*) inscribed with symbols or pictures to remind them of procedures and verses to be chanted during rituals.

Similarities and differences: when did Iban and Malay split?

Linguists use a mathematical formula to determine the approximate number of years in the past that two related languages separated from one another, based on shared core (i.e. non-cultural) vocabulary. Iban and Malay share about 63 per cent of their core vocabulary. Linguists have used the formula to conclude that the two languages therefore separated about 1000 years ago. This time span may explain why certain similar words in each language have different meanings.

Different meanings: Iban and Malay

Iban	Meaning	Malay	Meaning
angit	fragrance	hangit	scorched smell
belut	earthworm	belut	eel
beram	rice wine mash	beram	rice wine
ibur	distressed	hibur	give comfort
kampong	deep forest	kampung	village

(After R.A. Blust, 1980)

Iban–Mandarin–English handbook has been published to assist the many Chinese studying Iban.

Several scholars have noted that Iban, although spoken by an ethnic group displaying a culture distinctly different from that of the Malays, is a particularly close relative of Malay within the Malayic group of languages. Nevertheless, the closest linguistic relatives to Iban are a number of languages and dialects spoken in the Kapuas River basin of Indonesian West Borneo (Kalimantan). Of these, a small number of speakers living in the lake region of the Kapuas basin identify themselves as Iban, while other nearby groups identify themselves differently yet speak variants which are mutually intelligible with Iban and could be considered Iban dialects. Yet other groups speak a variant which diverges so significantly from Iban that it may be considered a separate language. Collectively, Iban and its variants are referred to as 'Ibanic', and form a branch of the Malayic language group.

Within Sarawak itself, Iban is spoken with very little dialectal variation, although this apparent uniformity may represent under-reporting because no rigorous survey of Iban dialects has ever been conducted. Some authors have suggested that distinct Iban dialects were spoken in Sarawak by the

Iban in print

Since 1878, extensive texts of Iban oral literature have been published and studied. However, notwithstanding that Iban has been approved for instruction as a Pupils' Own Language (POL) in Malaysian schools since the 1980s, not many contemporary reading materials are available, with only a limited number of folk tales and novels produced to date. The novel *Putus Pengarap*, by Jantan Umbat, was finally published in 1987, some 15 years after it was written. The only monthly Iban-language bulletin to be published was *Pembrita* in Kuching during the early 1900s. Numerous Bible translations and religious books have, however, been made available in Iban.

Several extensive bilingual Iban dictionaries too have been published since 1900. Most of these are basic Iban–English dictionaries, including those by Howell and Bailey (1900), Scott (1956), Richards (1981), and Sutlive (1994). An Iban–Malay dictionary by Dewan Bahasa dan Pustaka (Institute of Language and Literature), Kuala Lumpur, was released in 1989. In addition, the Tun Jugah Foundation, based in Kuching, aims to publish an Iban-Iban dictionary in 2005. A study of Iban grammar by Asmah Haji Omar was published in 1981, adding further depth to the published research on vocabulary and phonology.

Key Iban works include Asmah's grammar study, Richards' dictionary and the novel *Putus Pengarap*.

Iban men from Batang Ai, Lubok Antu, wear traditional headdresses to perform a ritual sacrifice ceremony (*miring*) during the annual Gawai festival.

Iban-language textbooks, for both primary and secondary levels, have been developed for the teaching of Iban as a Pupils' Own Language (POL).

Balau, Sebuyau, Skarang and Buyau sub-groups. The Rimun speech variant certainly appears to diverge from the language's standard form.

Iban is both a complex and a flexible language, which makes use of a range of affixes to indicate the functions of nouns in a given sentence. Word order is often subject–verb–object, although other arrangements of sentence elements are used for grammatical and stylistic purposes. Iban has an extensive ritual vocabulary and is a language well known for its subtlety and expressiveness. Loan words from Sanskrit, Arabic, Malay and English are well integrated into the daily speech of Iban. Moreover, numerous loan words from Iban have found their way into the state's major Malay dialect, Sarawak Malay.

The expressiveness of the Iban language is well demonstrated in the 25 albums released by Iban recording artist Christopher Kelly.

Iban communities (at the time known as the 'Sea Dayak') vigorously resisted the expansion of British control of Sarawak during the Brooke era. As a result, their language received early Western attention. For example, Henry Keppel, the British naval officer who bombarded Iban villages along the Lupar and Saribas rivers, published some of the earliest vocabularies of Iban in his 1846 account of that gruesome military expedition. Christian missionaries also began their work among the Iban in the mid-19th century, and by the late 19th century a number of religious books had been published in the Iban language.

Malay

In terms of first-language speaker numbers, Malay is Sarawak's second-largest Austronesian language. Although some of the nearly 450,000 Malays counted in the 2000 census may speak other languages as their first language, their numbers are small. In addition, most non-ethnic Malays in the state speak Malay, as a second, third, or even fourth language. This situation is a result of the language's use in government administration, the education system, and the media.

A number of Malay dialects are spoken in Sarawak (see 'Regional varieties of Malay'). In eastern Sarawak, especially in Lawas and Limbang, and in some coastal areas near Miri, Malay

communities generally speak variants of Brunei Malay as their first language. The dominant Malay dialect, however, is Sarawak Malay. This dialect is chiefly spoken along the Sarawak River, by virtue of the state's capital, Kuching, being located on the river's banks. It is nevertheless widely spoken throughout the state, as a result of the significant role that has been played by the Sarawak River Malays in the government of the state since the Brooke administration of the 19th century. Indeed within the state, Sarawak Malay competes with standard Malay as an important language of wider communication (see 'Contact languages').

Selakau

With fewer than 5,000 speakers, Selakau (alternatively Silakau or Selako) is the Malayic language with the smallest number of speakers in Malaysia. It is spoken in villages near the Lundu River in western Sarawak. The Selakau people have often been grouped with nearby Bidayuh peoples, but this is an error based on a superficial comparison of roughly similar cultural practices. Rather, Selakau speakers in Sarawak comprise an 'outlier' group of the much larger Kendayan (Kanayatn) ethnolinguistic group, predominantly located in the neighbouring Indonesian province of Kalimantan Barat. Spread along the Selakau River and other river basins in Indonesia, especially that of the Sambas and certain tributaries of the Kapuas, the Kendayan probably number in excess of 100,000. The Kendayan and Selakau languages are mutually intelligible.

In the 1960s, anthropological linguist A. Hudson demonstrated the close relationship between the Selakau and Malay languages, which exists despite numerous cultural differences. Earlier authors had also remarked on the similarity in grammar between the two, especially in the system of affixes. Nonetheless, Selakau has undergone distinctive sound changes which make it unintelligible to speakers of Malay. At the same time, Malay has shed some of the complex morphology used to mark Selakau syntax, further distancing Malay from Selakau.

Very few publications are available on the Selakau language as it is spoken in Malaysia. One notable exception is Sipol Strassman's Malaysian-Selakau word list, published in 1992.

Fajar Sarawak was the first Malay-language newspaper to be published in Sarawak. It ran from February to June 1930.

Sarawak Malay is spoken in settlements along the Sarawak River, which runs through the state capital, Kuching.

Selakau wedding ceremony. The ceremony is similar to that of the Bidayuh, except that it is conducted in the Selakau language.

Malayic vocabulary in Sarawak

Iban	Malay	Selakau	English
bilik	bilik	biik	room
lalat	lalat	aat	fly
jalai	jalan	jaatn	travel
makai	makan	makatn	eat
laban	lawan	lawatn	fight
malam	malam	maapm	night
apai	bapa	apak	father
indai	emak	inuk	mother
sida	mereka	ia	they

Bidayuh, Melanau and Kajang sub-families

Bidayuh speakers form the second-largest indigenous ethnolinguistic group in Sarawak. Their concentration near the state capital, Kuching, led to Bidayuh being the subject of early study. Speakers of the smaller Melanau language sub-family mainly live at the mouth of Sarawak's longest river, the Rajang, while Kajang is spoken further inland. Much research remains to be done on these sub-families.

The term 'Land Dayak'
In the early colonial era, Westerners recognized two indigenous groups and gave them names based on superficial characteristics. At that time, some Iban groups, especially along the Saribas and Lupar rivers, were allied with local Malays and fought side-by-side with

Catholic prayer book in the Bukar-Sadong Bidayuh speech system.

Bidayuh

Sarawak's second largest indigenous language sub-family, after Malayic, is Bidayuh (formerly known as 'Land Dayak') with approximately 135,000 speakers. All of the several recognized Bidayuh speech systems in Sarawak are within 75 kilometres of Kuching. As a result of the proximity of this area to the administrative capital, Bidayuh speech systems were among the first to be studied by government officials and missionaries as early as the mid-19th century. Nevertheless, this distinctive sub-family remains poorly described, partly because many related Bidayuh

speech systems exist in West Kalimantan (Indonesian Borneo), where documentation is minimal.

One interesting characteristic of Bidayuh speech systems is the phenomenon of final nasal preplosion. This term describes the 'stretching' of final nasal consonants, *-m*, *-n* and *-ng*, into clusters beginning with a stop consonant, *-bm*, *-dn* and *-gng*. This usually happens whenever the last syllable does not begin

Four Bidayuh speech systems

Lara'
Near the Indonesian border, the village of Pasir Tengah is home to Lara', the most divergent Bidayuhic language in Sarawak. Fewer than 2,000 people are reported to speak this language in Sarawak, which has been analysed as a dialect of Bekati', a larger Bidayuhic language widely spoken across the border in Indonesian West Kalimantan. However, it appears that many Lara' speakers in Sarawak are switching to the Malayic Selakau language spoken by their neighbours in the same district (Lundu'). There are no known publications in the Lara' language.

Bau-Jagoi
Another complex of dialects is named after the town of Bau and the nearby mountain, Jagoi. Except for the isolated Lara' language, this is the westernmost Bidayuhic language in Sarawak. Some short word lists and a phrase book provide only limited information about this language. Singai (also known as Singhi) is a somewhat divergent dialect of Bau-Jagoi; a vocabulary of this dialect, compiled about 1900, was published in 1956. Further research in 1969, based on a statistical comparison of a limited vocabulary, supports the theory of a Bau-Jagoi cluster of closely related dialects. However, it is likely that the Bau-Jagoi language is more closely related to Biatah than to other Bidayuh languages.

There is some concern that Bau-Jagoi and other Bidayuh languages are in a slow decline, gradually being replaced by Malay and English.

Biatah
In the mid-19th century, an Anglican mission was established in Quop (Kuap), a Biatah-speaking village south of Kuching and by 1861 Rev. W. Chalmers had published a trilingual dictionary of English, the Kuap variant of Biatah and Sarawak River Malay. This variant, which he called 'Sentah', is now called Siburan and has become the chief, 'standard' dialect of Biatah. Most publications in Biatah, including Bible translations and other religious books, are published in the Siburan dialect. According to P. Kroeger, at least three other Biatah dialects can be identified: Penrissen, Lower Padawan and Upper Padawan.

ABOVE: Bidayuh women in Kampung Semban speak a variant of Biatah.

RIGHT: Chalmers' 19th-century vocabulary of 'Sarawak Dayaks' was of a Biatah dialect.

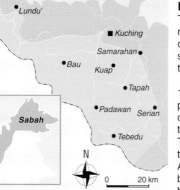

Bukar-Sadong
This Bidayuh language comprises a number of mutually understandable dialects, and is spoken in the area surrounding the town of Serian, to the southeast of Kuching.

Although between 1954 and 1972 several linguistic and anthropological studies were carried out on the Bukar-Sadong language and the culture of its speakers, including Topping's 1969 language survey, there have been few studies since. A Catholic catechism and prayer book, *Pisaya inya Kristen*, was, however, published in 1999.

ABOVE: New rice ceremony at Kg Sebambau, near Serian.

BELOW: A Bukar-Sadong-speaking woman weaving a traditional basket.

Bidayuh Gawai greetings card from the town of Bau.

Comparative vocabularies

Bukar-Sadong	Biatah	Bau-Jagoi	Lara	English
sihip	nok	nuak	nucur	drink
kəpikn	kəjit	kojit	rajak	ear
bihis	sinit	sonot	sunut	black
umoʔ	piʔidn	piʔidn	paitn	water
ajuu	punok	punuok	rutuk	back

(After Kroeger 1994; Topping 1969.)

them on sea-going vessels which made daring raids on coastal ships and forts. These sea-going non-Malays were simply referred to as 'Sea Dayaks'. The indigenous people in the Kuching area did not go to sea and were thus named 'Land Dayaks'.

The Iban are no longer referred to as Sea Dayaks, so the usefulness of the term Land Dayak is dubious. As many of Sarawak's indigenous peoples live in interior areas far from the sea, they are all 'land' people. The term 'Bidayuh' is now used for the groups formerly named Land Dayak. Bidayuh is based on a widespread term in that sub-family of languages (*bi-dayeh* meaning 'people of the interior'). Linguistically, the entire language group, which includes several languages in Sarawak and West Kalimantan, is known as Bidayuh, in parallel to other groups such as Malayic.

ABOVE LEFT: Shaman conducting a ritual as part of the Bidayuh Gawai Pangah festival.

RIGHT: 'Land Dayaks' photographed c. 1900 by Charles Hose, district officer of Sarawak's Baram region.

with a nasal. So, for example, *barim* (blue) is pronounced *baribm*, *butan* (coconut) becomes *butadn* and *bandung* (tapioca), *bandugng*. *Maan* (eat), on the other hand, is pronounced *maan*, and *kinyam* (feel), *kinam*. Most Bidayuh speech systems show this special pronunciation feature to some degree, although details may vary. It also occurs in other languages in western Borneo, including Selakau—which is not related to Bidayuh (see 'Malayic languages of Sarawak'). In Indonesian West Kalimantan, even Malay dialects and some Iban dialects have the same sound change.

There is some concern that Bau-Jagoi and other Bidayuh speech systems are in slow decline, gradually being replaced by Malay and English, especially in urban areas. However, there is evidence to suggest that at least in home and family situations Bau-Jagoi is holding its own.

Melanau

Stretching northward from the Rajang River delta as far as the Balingian River are villages and hamlets of Melanau speakers, with close linguistic relatives as far as Kanowit up the Rajang. Known to Brunei Malays as early as the 16th century as Melanau, Milano or Lemanau, the Melanau-speaking villagers had come to terms with the demanding environment of the vast delta swamps of the Rajang. Unlike many groups in Sarawak, the Melanau depended on sago palm, not rice, as their food staple. Traditionally, they built very high, sturdy houses to survive tidal floods and attacks from other ethnic groups. By the early 19th century, many had converted to Islam. However, although most Melanau speakers are now Muslims, some still retain traditional beliefs and a further minority have become Christians.

Notwithstanding their religious differences, all Melanau speakers are bilingual in their own language and Malay, and Melanau has been heavily influenced by Malay. However, in Melanau villages, especially in the Igan area, Melanau remains the dominant language; even Malays resident in Igan speak Melanau with their neighbours.

There is a high degree of mutual intelligibility amongst the various geographically distinct Melanau speech systems, probably due to the extensive communication network provided by the many channels, rivers and canals in the area.

While a number of 19th-century word lists of Melanau are available, no modern dictionary has been published to date. Linguist Robert Blust has provided a brief sketch of the morphology and phonology of Mukah dialect, which indicates the complexity of the Melanau affix system as well as a range of registers distinguished by generation. Melanau publications are few in number, and include a Bible translation and prayer books, for example *Sebiang Adat Kristian* in the Melanau Dalat speech system.

Kajang

At one time classified as a branch of the so-called Melanau-Kajang group, Kajang refers to a number of speech systems used by small ethnic groups, mostly in disconnected settlements on the upper reaches of the Rajang River. Included among these are the Lahanan, Kejaman and Ukit speech variants. Although documented as long ago as the 19th century, very little information is available, except for some very brief word lists.

Since the early 1900s, many speech systems previously found along the upper Rajang River have become extinct. Others, such as Kejaman, have undergone striking sound changes. All have been heavily influenced by Kayan, the major language of inter-ethnic communication in that region of the Rajang. Other more pervasive languages are also used in these communities. For example, a typical Catholic church service in a Kejaman village might consist of hymns sung in Malay, prayers said in Iban, Bible readings in Kayan, and instruction given in Kejaman. There is real concern that the minority Kajang speech systems are under considerable social pressure with a strong likelihood of language loss in the next few generations.

An extinct Kajang language

In 1901, D. Bailey reported that the Sru people near Seratok on the lower reaches of the Rajang numbered only 36, after the warfare and diseases of the 19th century. A few other members of the Sru had already become Muslims and adopted a Malay identity. In the same year, another official, F. de Rozario, classified the Sru people as relatives of the Ukit group in the upper Rajang. Bailey's word list of only 140 entries survives as a record of the Sru language.

English	Sru
live	*murip*
tongue	*jila*
blood	*da*
give	*be(h)*
rice	*bas*
fire	*apoi*
liver	*atoi*
stand up	*tiga*
hair	*rebok*
water	*danum*
drink	*ip*
tooth	*tugau*
run	*maliba*

Kajang-speakers, including Kejaman-speakers, in traditional costume, in the upriver town of Belaga, led by an elder playing an *engkurai* wind instrument.

Fishermen at the wharf in Mukah: the Mukah speech system seems to have attained a position of prestige among the Melanau variants.

Northern Sarawak languages

Several distinct minority Austronesian language sub-families and speech systems are spoken in north Sarawak. Whilst fieldwork has provided the basis for describing and classifying the numerous languages in northeastern Sarawak, more research is needed to resolve disagreements about the inter-relationships of these languages and dialects. Migrations, fusions, separations and complex naming practices have all made the task difficult.

Much of northern Sarawak, including the Bario Highlands, above, remains relatively isolated, with few road links. Access is primarily by river or air.

Naming traditions

The use of teknonyms (i.e. name of a parent based on the name of his or her child) and necronyms (i.e. name adopted after the death of a relative) is widespread in northern Sarawak. In 1882, Hugh Low commented on this practice during his trip to the upper Rajang basin.

'Laki Bato Dian is the son of Laki Dian Bato and the father of Oyong Dian Bato. His own name is Bato, his father's Dian; this is why he is called Bato Dian. Laki implies that he is a grandfather; Oyong before a name denotes the death of the first born; Akam the death of some other child; Haval implies on the part of a man the loss of a wife or sister; Balo on the part of a woman the loss of a husband or brother; Hiat on the part of man the loss of a brother; on the part of a woman the loss of a sister.'

Low's description is still accurate today.

Three generations of Kelabit speakers at home in the Bario highlands.

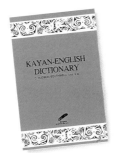

Southwell's Kayan-English dictionary was the first, and remains the only, to be published.

Kelabit

Speakers of the Kelabit sub-family (previously known as the Kelabit-Lundayeh or Apo Duat group) traditionally live in eastern Sarawak as well as adjacent areas of Sabah, Indonesian East Kalimantan and the Temburong district of eastern Brunei. The sub-family comprises more than 12 identified speech systems, many displaying a high level of mutual intelligibility. Of these 12, two major speech variants are recognized: Lun Bawang or Lundayeh, spoken along the north eastern edge of Sarawak, and Kelabit, which has its homeland in the Baram highlands, especially the Bario plateau, though some groups live across the border in Kalimantan, Indonesia.

An unpublished 3,000-word dictionary of Lun Bawang compiled in the 1950s by C. H. Southwell was used by the team of specialists who translated the entire Bible (*Bala Luk Do'*) into the language in 1982. In addition, a Kelabit–English vocabulary of similar size was published by R. Blust in 1993, with preliminary notes on Kelabit's morphophonological features.

All these languages are undergoing rapid change and play a reduced role in contemporary Malaysia. With increased access to education after 1946, migration from remote settlements to cities has become very common. There are an estimated 5000 speakers of the Kelabit speech system in Sarawak, of whom approximately 1000 live in the coastal town of Miri. With the increasing number of speakers residing in urban areas, there is a likelihood that the first language of the next generation will be either Malay or English.

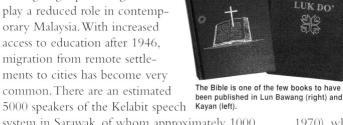

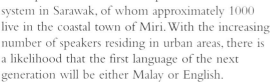

The Bible is one of the few books to have been published in Lun Bawang (right) and Kayan (left).

Kayan

The Kayan language is spoken in remote riverine communities spreading out from the Usan Apau plateau into both Malaysia and Indonesia. In Sarawak, most Kayan communities are found in the upper reaches of the Rajang and Baram rivers. In the 2000 census some 25,000 Malaysian citizens in Sarawak identified themselves as Kayan.

An extensive Kayan-English dictionary by C. H. Southwell was published in 1980 and R. Blust wrote a grammatical sketch of the Uma Jaman

Orang Ulu

Although some groups along the Baram River have used the term 'Orang Ulu' (upriver people) loosely for geographic self-reference, it has become a shorthand phrase for any indigenous group other than the dominant Iban, Malay, Bidayuh and Melanau ethnolinguistic groups. However, this use of the term has neither a linguistic justification nor a solid cultural basis. Even the implied geographic reference is misleading, as it includes groups who often live great distances from upriver areas, such as the Bisaya. While there may be some political benefit for the smaller groups to rally together under this broad term, it should not be used arbitrarily for purposes of description or classification.

variant in 1977. The Bible and other Christian books, such as the hymnal *Buhup Nyanyi*, have been translated into Kayan and are widely distributed.

Along some parts of the Rajang and Baram rivers, Kayan functions as a language of wider communication among groups speaking different, unrelated first languages (see 'Contact languages'). The Kayan language has a high degree of uniformity, reflecting the relatively recent migration of its speakers from the Usun Apau plateau.

Many linguists mistakenly consider Kayan speech variants to be related to the Kenyah language sub-family. One example is Ngurik (also known as Murik), spoken in two longhouses on the Baram River (population 359 in 1970), which has been mistakenly classified as being a member of the Kenyah sub-family, probably as a result of cultural rather than language affinities.

Most Kayan speakers, such as these hunters, continue to live upriver in relative isolation.

Kenyah and Penan

Some 24,000 Kenyah speakers, and approximately 12,500 Penan speakers, mostly reside in the upper reaches of the Rajang and Baram rivers, which almost meet in the highland plateau of Usun Apau, an area also inhabited by the speakers of Kayan. Large communities of Kenyah also exist in eastern Borneo (Indonesia), giving rise to continuing transborder travel and communication along historic migration routes. Kenyah communities moved into the interior of northeast Sarawak many generations ago, accounting for the large number of Kenyah dialects and obvious differences among them, in contrast to Kayan's rather high level of uniformity.

The Kenyah people themselves recognize a large number of speech system variants, but the names given to these are sometimes based on clan groupings and traditions of settlement history rather than clear linguistic boundaries. The variants include Leppo' Tau, Leppo' Jingan, Leppo' Ke', Badeng and Sebop, spoken on the Tinjar River (a Baram tributary). Many Kenyah also speak fluent Kayan and other languages, but Kenyah nevertheless serves as a language of wider communication in areas such as the uppermost Baram River.

Some radio programmes are broadcast in Kenyah, and the language is also used in church services. The New Testament (*Kitap Tuket Mading*) has been available in Kenyah since 1978. In addition, a typescript vocabulary of Kenyah by A. D. Galvin has been in circulation since 1967 and many studies of oral traditions have appeared, most notably V. K. Gorlinski's work on Kenyah (Leppo' Tau) poetry and song forms in Long Moh and Long Mekaba, on the Baram River.

There has been a long-term association between many Penan groups and Kenyah villages. This relationship is reflected in the similarities that exist between the Penan and Kenyah speech systems. A wide range of materials, including Bible extracts

Kenyah leader Dato Temenggong Oyang Lawai Jau (1894–1974) was known to give speeches that lasted up to six hours in the longhouses he visited.

(*Surat Tuhan Jaji' Bu'un*) (1974), hymnals, and primers with a religious focus (*Tebara' Tong Tuhan Yesus*) (1997) have been published in Penan variants.

Other language communities

Many other languages are spoken in Sarawak. Four related speech systems, each with a small, declining number of speakers, have been identified in the Lower Baram area: Mirik (spoken in Miri), Berawan, Narom (spoken in a village near the town of Marudi), and Kiput. Like English, but unlike most other Malaysian languages, all four Lower Baram speech systems mark the tense of verbs. This is done with vowel changes. For example, in Kiput, *tupeh* means 'is pounding' whereas *tipeh* means 'pounded'. Other sound and lexical innovations connect these minority languages to each other and other North Sarawak speech systems.

The number of speakers of another language, Bintulu, has increased in contrast over the course of the last century. It is chiefly spoken by Muslims in the coastal town of Bintulu and in river settlements in northeastern Sarawak, together with a number of Penan groups in some of these areas who have adopted the language. Some linguists and many Sarawakians may consider it a Melanau variant, but lexical evidence suggests strong differences between Melanau and Bintulu.

Bisaya is more closely related to Sabahan languages than to those of Sarawak. Speakers are found in both states, and Brunei as well. The Bisaya language spoken in Sarawak belongs to the Dusunic language group, the largest ethnolinguistic group of Sabah (see 'Dusunic languages of Sabah'). Spoken chiefly in Limbang in eastern Sarawak, there are also Bisaya communities in Lawas and Brunei.

Relatively few of the Penan ethnolinguistic group remain nomadic.

Special registers

Berawan prayers

Long Teru on the Tinjar River, in the Baram area, was the last community in which the traditional belief system of the Berawan-speaking ethnic group was practised. Until recently, features of the Kayan and Kenyah religious system reported in the 19th century prevailed. As with many ritual speech systems, prayers and incantations reflected borrowings from other languages, yielding a highly literary and solemn speech register.

Complex ritual prayers were performed in Long Teru until the mid-20th century.

Kenyah sung poetry

The Leppo' Tau Kenyah of the upper Baram river use a distinct register of their language, *ipet*, to versify. This way of speaking occurs in two genres of sung poetry: *isiu belian* (song language) and *isiu bali* (spirit language). The register links various synonyms or near-synonyms, many borrowed from other dialects and languages.

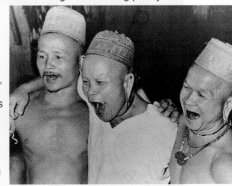

Ulu Baram Kenyah men singing poetry during the Gawai festival, during which *tuak* (local rice wine) is consumed.

Languages of Sabah

Some 50 languages are spoken in Sabah of which 33 are indigenous to the state. Most of these are Austronesian languages belonging to the Dusunic, Murutic, Paitanic, Sama-Bajau and Malayic language groups. Other isolated tongues are also spoken; however, the main non-Austronesian languages are Chinese and English, although first language speaker numbers of the latter are small. Several organizations research and publish information on the indigenous languages.

Sabah's Austronesian languages

Languages from five Austronesian language groups are spoken in Sabah. The most complex of these is the Dusunic group with 13 languages including Central Kadazandusun, the Sabah language with the largest number of speakers. The next most complex language group is Murutic, of which Tagal is the most widely spoken language. The Paitanic language family contains five languages spoken by groups along Sabah's eastern rivers. Muslim speakers of Paitanic languages are often called Orang Sungai (river people). The Sama Bajau language group has six languages, with speakers on both the east and west coasts of Sabah, amongst whom are recent immigrants from islands such as Jolo in the southern Philippines.

Malayic languages are also spoken in Sabah. Brunei Malay and Kedayan Malay—which differ to some extent from standard Malay in both vocabulary and phonology—are spoken near the Sarawak and Brunei borders. More recent immigrants from the Cocos Islands and Indonesia speak other forms of Malay. Iban is also spoken, near Tawau, by immigrants who arrived from Sarawak in 1954.

Reflecting the linguistic diversity of the state, the *New Sabah Times* daily newspaper, with a circulation of some 20,000, is published in three sections: English, Malay and Kadazandusun (Dusunic language).

Ethnolinguistic complexity

In the 18th century, the numerous ethnic groups of Sabah were broadly divided into two groups—largely animistic interior peoples and a number of mobile, predominantly Muslim, coastal communities. Although some intermarriage did occur, there was generally little contact between the two communities. This stemmed from Sabah's physical geography keeping inland groups apart from much outside influence, while its position on the ancient Southeast Asian trade route led to seafaring groups settling along the coast. The complexity of Sabah's ethnic groups is such that great cultural variety often exists between speakers of languages within the same language group.

Additional complexity derives from the common practice of intermarriage between indigenous and non-indigenous groups. Many of the offspring of such marriages claim to be indigenous. This has led to the classification of new ethnic categories, for example that of 'Sino-native', reflecting the extent of mixed marriages between the Chinese and indigenous peoples. Ethnic boundaries remain fluid.

The ethnic groups that inhabit fishing villages such as this in Semporna (below left) are distinct from inland groups, such as the Lundayeh, seen here collecting ferns as food (below right).

Classifying Sabahan language groups

The number and distribution of speakers of the Sabah language groups vary widely, and remains relatively fluid. Precise measurement is made difficult by differences in ethnic and linguistic terminology. It is nevertheless clear that some languages are spreading in terms of speaker numbers and domains of language use. Standard Malay is one such, as it is used in education, administration and as a language of wider communication. Other languages, meanwhile, are declining. Still, many Sabahans speak a third or even fourth language in addition to their first language and Malay.

Tamu besar (large markets) are a meeting place for speakers of the many different Sabah languages.

Speaker numbers
Sabahans speak first languages from at least eight language groups.

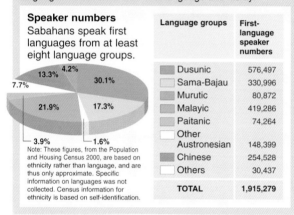

30.1%
17.3%
21.9%
13.3%
4.2%
7.7%
3.9%
1.6%

Note: These figures, from the Population and Housing Census 2000, are based on ethnicity rather than language, and are thus only approximate. Specific information on languages was not collected. Census information for ethnicity is based on self-identification.

Language groups	First-language speaker numbers
Dusunic	576,497
Sama-Bajau	330,996
Murutic	80,872
Malayic	419,286
Paitanic	74,264
Other Austronesian	148,399
Chinese	254,528
Others	30,437
TOTAL	**1,915,279**

Several other distinct Austronesian languages are spoken. One of these, Iranun, is spoken along certain parts of the coast and is related to languages of the southern Philippines. Many Iranun speakers claim descent from groups that fled volcanic eruptions in that area around 1630. Suluk, a trade language, is similarly spoken on the coast by both long-term residents and more recent Tausug settlers from the Sulu islands. Lundayeh (Lun Bawang) language speakers, who live in southwestern Sabah, migrated several decades ago from Kalimantan, and are also found in Sarawak. Two further languages not closely related to other Sabah indigenous languages are Bonggi (on Banggi and Balambangan islands) and Ida'an-Begak (near Lahad Datu on the east coast).

Non-Austronesian languages in Sabah

A number of non-Austronesian languages are also spoken in Sabah. Amongst these, only Chavacano, a Spanish creole originating from the southern Philippines and used by a tiny community of speakers in Semporna, has origins near Sabah (see 'Creoles'). The Chinese dialects are the most widely spoken non-Austronesian languages. Chinese economic migrants were amongst the earliest to arrive in Sabah in large numbers. Initially, in the 17th and 18th centuries, their presence was linked to the China-Sulu trade. Subsequently, greater numbers were brought in by the British North Borneo (Chartered) Company to develop plantations. Today it is the Khek (Hakka) who form the largest

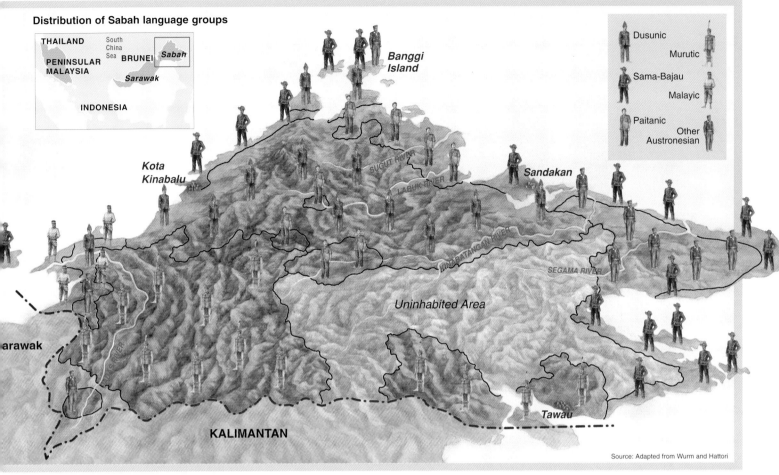

Distribution of Sabah language groups

THAILAND
South China Sea
PENINSULAR MALAYSIA
BRUNEI
Sabah
Sarawak
INDONESIA

Banggi Island

Kota Kinabalu

SUGUT RIVER
LABUK RIVER

Sandakan

KINABATANGAN RIVER

SEGAMA RIVER

Uninhabited Area

Sarawak

Tawau

KALIMANTAN

Dusunic
Murutic
Sama-Bajau
Malayic
Paitanic
Other Austronesian

Source: Adapted from Wurm and Hattori

Chinese language group (see 'Distribution of Chinese dialects'). English, too, is spoken in Sabah, and has become a first language among certain groups in urban areas. It is also used in a number of important speech domains, including newspapers.

As is the case in Sarawak, the traditional pattern of language distribution continues to alter as a result of education, use of the national language, media impact, and demographic change.

Research into Sabah languages

Several organizations continue to undertake research into the languages of Sabah. As early as the 1950s, Kadazandusun was taught in selected mission schools in the state, and in 1958 the first Dusunic language dictionary was published. Dictionaries of Coastal Kadazan and Central Dusun followed in the 1990s.

One of the most active language organizations in Sabah is the Kadazandusun Language Foundation. Established in January 1996 as a non-profit-making body, it has built on work by the Summer Institute of Linguistics (SIL) and the Kadazan Dusun Cultural Association, and aims to preserve, develop and promote the Kadazandusun language. The foundation successfully re-established Kadazandusun as a language of education, with its introduction in 15 primary schools in 1997. This, however, is on a trial basis with the language being taught outside school hours. It is hoped that eventually Kadazandusun will be taught at secondary level and be included in public examinations; this will require

teacher training. Kadazandusun language classes are also available at Universiti Malaysia Sabah, where a Kadazan Dusun Chair has been endowed, although this is not restricted to merely linguistic research on the Kadazandusun.

The Malaysian branch of SIL, established in Sabah for over 25 years, undertakes research on the indigenous languages, much of which is published by the Sabah Museum. The Persatuan Seni Budaya Bajau, Sabah (Bajau Cultural Society, Sabah) funds and supports conferences on the Bajau languages and culture, has funded the publication of a Bajau dictionary, and actively collects Bajau oral literature.

Governmental bodies are also active. The Sabah Museum includes materials on the indigenous languages in both its exhibitions and its journal, and has published a series of folk tales in the various languages together with Malay and English translations. There is a substantial body of literature in the Kadazandusun language available in the Sabah State Library; and while the Sabah branch of the Dewan Bahasa dan Pustaka (Institute of Language and Literature) primarily promotes the use of the national language, Malay, it also conducts research on the state's indigenous languages.

An adult literacy class (above) and five-language phrase book (right), organized and published by the Kadazandusun Language Foundation.

A Pocket KADAZAN-MANDARIN-ENGLISH-MALAY-BAJAU Phrase Book

Inggou bo no?
Ni hao ma?
How are you?
Apa khabar?
Ian abar?

CHRISTINA JOHN LUAN

Dusunic languages of Sabah

Part of the Austronesian language stock, the Dusunic language group—comprising 13 languages, and an even greater number of dialects—is the largest language group in Sabah, with communities of speakers spread across much of the northern and central parts of the state. The languages exhibit a great deal of diversity, yet speakers recognize the unity in their language group and ethnicity. A standard language, 'Kadazandusun', is now taught in some schools.

Dusunic language speakers

Source: Wurm and Hattori

Villagers from Kampung Karanaan, Tambunan listening to a broadcast in Kadazandusun on Radio Malaysia in the 1960s. Sabah's Radio Six broadcasts in Sabah languages other than Malay.

Classifying the Dusunic speakers

The classification of the ethnolinguistic groups that constitute the speakers of the Dusunic sub-family of languages is problematic. For example, many Dusunic groups, including those in the northern Kudat Division and some in the south, refer to both their language group and ethnicity by the autonym *Momogun*, which probably originally meant 'local people'. However, some of these groups also use the term *Dusun*—which in Malay means 'orchard'—to identify their own language when they are speaking Malay or English. The term 'Dusun' is also used by most of the Central Dusun people to refer to themselves, and—confusingly—has also long been used by outsiders to refer to the Dusunic peoples and languages as a whole.

The Rungus (*Momogun*) people, in the Kudat division, view themselves as distinct from the other Dusunic groups. They do not usually identify themselves as Dusun, although they recognize the relationship between their respective languages.

The term *Kadazan* traditionally referred only to the people and language of the Penampang and Papar districts, also called Coastal Kadazan. It is likely to have originally meant 'people'. In recent times, the term has been adopted by other groups, such as the Labuk-Kinabatangan Kadazan. Confusingly, it has also at times been used synonymously with 'Dusunic'. Furthermore, various combinations of the terms 'Kadazan' and 'Dusun' have been used to describe the Dusunic group of languages, including the commonly used adjoined term 'Kadazandusun'.

Language variety

Within the Dusunic language family there are some 13 separate languages of which many have more than one dialect. Central Dusun, by far the most widely spoken Dusunic language, has a large number of dialects, some of which, such as the Sugut Dusun and Minokok dialects, may be distinct enough to be classified as separate languages.

Notwithstanding that Coastal Kadazan has far fewer speakers than Central Dusun, the early educational opportunities that existed in the Coastal Kadazan speaking area during the colonial period led to its becoming the major Dusunic language used in Sabahan newspapers, and so it remains.

The term 'Kadazandusun' is used to refer to the 'shared' or 'standard' language taught in selected schools since 1997 (see 'Language policy in action'). Coastal Kadazan and Central Dusun had earlier been taught in a number of mission-run primary schools and Native Voluntary Schools (NVS) from the mid-1950s until the late 1960s. However, the 'standard' language is based on Bundu and Liwan, two dialects of Central Dusun (referred to conjointly as Bunduliwan), and is enriched by other Dusunic languages. A Terminology Development Panel equips the standard language with new terminology, especially terms relating to the sciences and mathematics.

The Dusunic languages have borrowed from other languages. Coastal Kadazan has borrowed most heavily from English, due to early contact with missionaries. It has also borrowed Chinese words, such as *sikang* (spoon), which in Central Dusun is *sudu*', similar to the Malay *sudu*. Other Dusunic languages have borrowed some from English in the past, but now borrow mainly more from Malay.

The genetic relationships among the Dusunic languages are still uncertain. The Lotud language is somewhat distinct from other Dusunic languages, and it is possible that Bisaya and Tatana form a subgroup within the Dusunic group.

Distinctive features

Many Dusunic languages require all nouns to begin with a consonant. Thus, root-words starting with a

Origin of the Dusunic peoples

Most Dusunic peoples share a similar legend as to their origin, which they trace to living near a large *nunuk ragang* (red fig) tree. The Labuk-Kinabatangan Kadazan and the Kuijau people claim the tree was located in a village formerly called Tampias (now renamed Nunuk Ragang) about 40 kilometres west of Telupid. A large tree in the vicinity, that may have been the tree in question, is said to have been felled in 1975. However, more linguistic research is required to lend scientific support to the legend.

Oathstones

In the absence of an indigenous Dusunic writing system, oathstones were traditionally used to signify agreements and allegiances.

The Keningau oathstone, bearing an inscription in Malay, was inaugurated in 1964 on the first anniversary of the Formation of Malaysia. It marked the exchange of reciprocal oaths between the Sabahan people and the Federal Government.

The Nunuk Ragang monument, in the shape of a giant tree stump, marks the site of the Dusunic peoples' legendary origin.

Dusunic ethnolinguistic diversity

1. Coastal Kadazan speakers participating in a rice-wine drinking ceremony, **2.** Lotud ladies meeting and **3.** a Rungus family speak distinct but related Dusunic languages.

vowel automatically have a 't' added to them. In some Dusunic languages, this 't' is fossilized, meaning that it is permanently attached to the roots; while in others, it is only sometimes added. This 'moveable t' serves to distinguish various Dusunic languages from one another. For instance, the Lotud words *ulun* (person) and *ulu* (head) remain the same as their respective root-words, whereas in Central Dusun

these words become *tulun* and *tulu* instead. Furthermore, the moveable 't' does not exist in the related Paitanic or Murutic languages.

Another distinctive feature of certain Dusunic languages is that they have a pair of sounds, 'v' and 'z', which are substituted by 'w' and 'y', or 'v' and 'j' in other Dusunic languages. Thus, the words for 'housing cluster' in Rungus, Kimaragang, and Labuk-Kinabatangan Kadazan are *kavalazan*, *kawalayan* and *kavalajan*, respectively. However, it should be noted that even where two Dusunic languages use the same consonants, this should not be considered an indicator of linguistically similarity. Conversely, dialects of the same Dusunic language may use different sets of consonants.

All of the Dusunic languages have a rich morphology, or system of affixation, including prefixes, suffixes and infixes. There are in fact so many affixes that in some cases a single root-word, when combined with various combinations of affixes, can yield over fifty different words.

1. Kadazan Dusun-Malay-English dictionary published by the Kadazan Dusun Cultural Association (KDCA) in 1995.
2. *Learn to Speak Kadazan*, compiled by the KDCA and Summer Institute of Linguistics.
3. One of several trilingual phrasebooks published by the Sabah Museum.

Kadazan marriage negotiations

The Coastal Kadazan conversation recorded below, in the Penampang or Kadazan Tangaa' dialect, illustrates well the allegorical nature of the language.

It is typical that when a young man's mother is interested in pursuing marriage negotiations with the family of a young woman, she and her companions will visit the young woman's mother in order to arrange for a more formal social visit. If the latter's family feels positive about the proposed union, they will consent to

this later meeting. Otherwise, they may say, '*Hogoson po dati, tu omuhok po iho tanak dagai*' ('There's no need to come, because our daughter is too young'). The boy's family will understand this response to mean that the girl's family does not wish to pursue negotiations, regardless of the young woman's age.

A Tambunan Kadazandusun couple feed each other with rice during their wedding ceremony, which traditionally lasts several days.

Bride's mother (BM):
Ta. Nokoikot kou no.
Oh! So you've come.

Groom's mother (GM):
Oo'. Mooi zikoi pikiinggat diozu.
Yes, we've come to chew betel leaf with you.

BM: *Oonu no kozo o pinanau diozu do nokoikot do doiti' do baino?*
What is the reason you have come here today?

GM: *Nokoikot zikoi doiti' tu' kivaa do bunga' diozo di kaanangan dagai do mogkotu'.*
We have come because you have a flower we'd like to pluck.

BM: *Id nomboo dati' iso' diho' bunga' do komozon diozu?*
Which flower is it that you are referring to?

GM: *Ba. Id nomboo po vagu' nga' I piintangaan?*
Ah. Which one but the middle one?

BM: *Iisai o mogkotu' dino?*
Who wants to pluck it?

GM: *I tanak dagai do totuo no kozo.*
Our eldest child.

At a second marriage negotiation visit in Penampang, dried palm leaves are used to count out the bridewealth price.

BM: *Ta. Ingkuo dii dati' gia do poimata' po kozo iho'? Au' po navahad.*
My! How is it possible with one so immature. (She) hasn't even blossomed yet.

GM: *Ba. Sundung tuu do ingkaa, nga' miho i' do tudukan do tiinu'.*
Yes, but although that is true, she can be taught to learn things.

BM: *Au' zou nokoiho, tu' mogiuu'uot podii gia.*
I don't know, because we have to discuss it first.

GM: *Aiso i' motuu gia o sanganu dosido?*
There isn't anyone else who has spoken for her?

BM: *Aiso i' bo, tu' iisai nodii gia mimang tu' aiso i' toihahaan?*
No, because who would want someone who doesn't know anything?

GM: *Ba. Ingkaa no. Koikot zikoi do doiti' do mooi pokiakan diozu do duvo po minggu' mantad baino.*
All right. We'll come here to eat and negotiate with you in two weeks.

BM: *Ba. Ingkaa no.*
All right.

Sama-Bajau, Murutic and Malayic languages of Sabah

The next most widely spoken languages in Sabah, after the Dusunic languages, are those from the Murutic and Sama-Bajau language groups. As many as thirteen Murutic languages are spoken by inland peoples, and six Sama-Bajau languages by mainly Muslim groups along the east and west coasts. Malayic first language speakers include Ibans, originally from Sarawak, and speakers of four distinct Malay dialects.

Distribution of Murutic, Sama-Bajau and Malayic language speakers

Sama-Bajau
○ East Coast
■ West Coast
Murutic
Malayic (excluding standard Malay)

0   50 km

Sabah

Gana
Beaufort Murut
Keningau Murut
Bookan
Kedayan Malay
Paluan
Tengara
Cocos Malay
Okolod
Sembakung
Timugon
Tagal
Iban
Kalabakan
Okolod
Selungai Murut
Serudung
Serudung

Source: Wurm and Hattori

Sama-Bajau languages

The term Sama-Bajau refers to a distinct group of languages. Some confusion has, however, arisen in the use of the term, as historically the Bajau people referred to themselves as Sama, whereas outsiders referred to them as Bajau. Today, many Sama-Bajau speakers themselves use the term Bajau or Bajau/Sama in this way. Furthermore, the term 'Bajau' is now often used—often for political reasons as a result of the relative prestige of Sama-Bajau speakers—as a generic term to encompass a number of different languages, some of which belong to the Sama-Bajau group (for example, West Coast Bajau and Yakan) and some of which do not (these include Iranun and Suluk).

The Sama-Bajau language sub-family has the second largest number of speakers in Sabah after the Dusunic languages, with a Sama-Bajau-speaking population of around 300,000. Many more speakers are found outside Sabah, to the extent that the

Sama-Bajau group as a whole is in fact larger than even the Dusunic group. Also, while the other three major language sub-families in Sabah (Dusunic, Murutic and Paitanic) have their homeland in northern Borneo, the Sama-Bajau group as a whole is widely dispersed across insular Southeast Asia, and its homeland remains unconfirmed. However, Sama-Bajau language speakers certainly represent a later wave of migration to Sabah than those of these three other groups, with evidence that they may have been in northern Borneo since the 16th century.

The main Sama-Bajau languages spoken in Sabah are: West Coast Bajau, Kagayan (also called Mapun), Bajau Balangingi, Central Sama, Southern Sama, and Yakan, each constituting a definite language community. The last five of these languages may loosely be classified as East Coast Bajau, although speakers are also found on the west coast. Only West Coast Bajau is primarily spoken in Sabah. The East Coast Bajau languages are mainly spoken in the southern Philippines, but they all have large numbers of speakers in Sabah.

West Coast Bajau speakers live along the Sabah coast from Kuala Penyu in the southwest to Terusan in the Labuk-Sugut District. It has been suggested that the language comprises a geographical dialect continuum with speakers able to understand dialects in adjacent areas, but finding difficulty in understanding those further away, and sometimes finding those furthest away completely unintelligible.

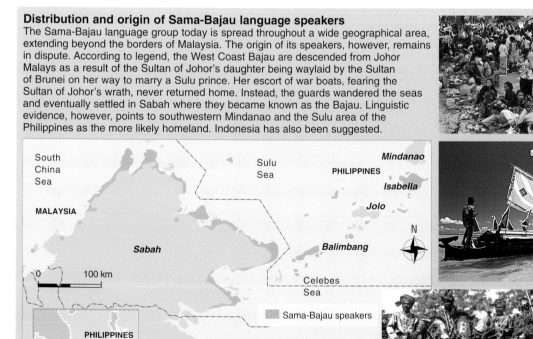

Distribution and origin of Sama-Bajau language speakers

The Sama-Bajau language group today is spread throughout a wide geographical area, extending beyond the borders of Malaysia. The origin of its speakers, however, remains in dispute. According to legend, the West Coast Bajau are descended from Johor Malays as a result of the Sultan of Johor's daughter being waylaid by the Sultan of Brunei on her way to marry a Sulu prince. Her escort of war boats, fearing the Sultan of Johor's wrath, never returned home. Instead, the guards wandered the seas and eventually settled in Sabah where they became known as the Bajau. Linguistic evidence, however, points to southwestern Mindanao and the Sulu area of the Philippines as the more likely homeland. Indonesia has also been suggested.

South China Sea

MALAYSIA

Sabah

0   100 km

Sulu Sea

Mindanao

PHILIPPINES

Isabella

Jolo

N

Balimbang

Celebes Sea

Sama-Bajau speakers

PHILIPPINES
MALAYSIA
INDONESIA

Right top: Sunday *tamu* (indigenous market) at Kota Belud in northern Sabah during the 1960s attended by a potpourri of indigenous people, including the West Coast Bajau.

Right centre: Ceremonial lepa boat used by the East Coast Bajau-speaking Bajau Laut (Sea Bajau).

Right: Originally a coastal fishing people, some West Coast Bajau speakers have become acclaimed horsemen.

Structurally, the Sama-Bajau languages are similar to other western Austronesian languages in that use is made of affixes, and reduplication is employed. Much research remains to be done on syntax.

The Murutic peoples and languages

According to the 2000 census, over 80,000 Sabahans classified themselves as Murut. However, caution should be exercised with the terms 'Murutic' and 'Murut' as they are sometimes mistakenly applied to a variety of ethnic groups that share cultural similarities even if they are not speakers of the well-defined Murutic language sub-family.

Thirteen Murutic languages are spoken in Sabah, some in the interior, near the state's southern border, others to the southeast near Tawau. Murutic languages are also spoken in Sarawak and Kalimantan (Indonesia). The largest and most homogeneous of the Murutic languages in Malaysia is Tagal, which is spoken throughout southwestern Sabah. The Tagal people live on five major river watersheds—the Maligan, Padas (Tomani), Talakosong, Tagal and Salalir—an area of mountainous terrain and largely impassable rivers.

Of the other Murutic languages, small groups of Okolod speakers are found to the southeast and east of the Tagal, in an area spanning the borders of Sarawak and Kalimantan. South and southwest of the Tagal areas, spanning the border with Kalimantan, are the Sembakung Murut and Selungai Murut speakers, named after the rivers along which the people live.

Trilingual phrase book facilitating communication in the Timugon Murut language.

The speakers of Timugon, the second most widely spoken language, inhabit a small, well-defined area north of the Tagal. More than half of the Timugon villages are on the western bank of the Pagalan River, which runs south through the fertile Tenom Valley. The others live on the eastern side of the Padas River, which flows from the south. Their neighbours to the east are the Paluan who live in the hilly area above the Padas River.

To the northeast of the Timugon area is the Keningau district, where there is much linguistic variety, including several Murutic languages. These include speakers of Keningau Murut, Gana and the Bookan (Baukan) Murut. Further to the east, Beaufort Murut is spoken. Several other Murut languages are spoken in southeastern Sabah. Among them are Kalabakan, Serudung and Tengara.

Unsurprisingly, Murutic languages which are geographically close seem to exhibit a higher level of similarity than more distant languages. Various researchers have suggested a broad ethnolinguistic division between Lowland Murut (Bookan (Baukan), Keningau and Timugon) and Highland Murut (Paluan and Tagal). The suggested subdivisions are based on lexical and phonological data taken from a statewide language survey in 1978–81 that made an extensive comparison of word lists.

Since the early 1900s there have been various attempts to classify the Murutic-speaking peoples. Unfortunately, several discrepancies between them are apparent. In particular, the Lundayeh (Lun Bawang) speech variants, spoken mostly in Sarawak, were once mistakenly classified as Murutic. It is now however clear that they are not. Neither is Tidong, which is in fact a separate group of speech variants, whose speakers have traditionally lived close to the Murut of east Sabah. On the other hand, Gana is a Murutic language, although its speakers refer to themselves as Dusun as a result of their geographical proximity and cultural affinity to that group.

Malayic languages

In Sabah, there are two main Malayic languages, Iban and Malay. Although there is a community of Iban speakers near Tawau on the east coast of Sabah, the majority of Iban speakers live in Sarawak (see 'Malayic languages of Sarawak'). The language used in Sabah does not differ from that in Sarawak.

As with the rest of Malaysia, standard Malay is used as the medium of instruction in schools and is commonly spoken as a second language by non-Malays. However, other local dialects are also spoken in Sabah (see 'Regional varieties of Malay'). These include Brunei Malay, Kedayan Malay, Cocos Malay, and Banjar Malay. Brunei Malay is primarily spoken in Brunei, Labuan and eastern Sarawak although a large number of speakers live in southwestern Sabah. Kedayan Malay is closely related to Brunei Malay, but is nevertheless distinct. A small Banjar Malay community exists near Tawau in Sabah, although this dialect is more widely used in south Kalimantan, Indonesia. Cocos Malay is spoken by two communities in eastern Sabah, near Tawau and Lahad Datu (see 'Creoles').

Tengara Muruts at the headwaters of the Kinabatangan River in 1935.

'Sumardi goes to the Hospital', a booklet in Tagal Murut and Malay published by the Museum and Archives of Sabah, with the cooperation of Summer Institute of Linguistics, in 1989.

Jumping on the *lansaran* (springy platform) to reach a *singkowoton* (trophy) suspended above, is a traditional Murut entertainment, accompanied by singing, chanting and cheering.

Sabah Malay women in Kota Belud giving a traditional welcome with *kompang* (drums).

Paitanic and other Austronesian languages of Sabah

At least five Paitanic languages are still spoken in northeastern and central Sabah. Among the least known Sabahan languages, their distribution provides interesting evidence of the movements of their speakers. Some ten other Austronesian languages—which do not belong to the state's five major language groups—are spoken in Sabah, although for seven of these languages the majority speakers live outside Sabah.

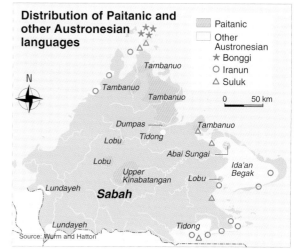

Distribution of Paitanic and other Austronesian languages

- Paitanic
- Other Austronesian
- ★ Bonggi
- ○ Iranun
- △ Suluk

Tambanuo
Tambanuo
Tambanuo
Tambanuo
Dumpas
Lobu — Tidong
Lobu
Abai Sungai
Upper Kinabatangan — Lobu
Ida'an Begak
Lundayeh
Sabah
Lundayeh
Tidong

N
0   50 km

Source: Wurm and Hattori

TOP: Tambanuo villagers in Kampung Lobang Buaya, gathered on the verandah of the headman's house to greet visitors.

ABOVE: Tambanuo speakers in Kampung Lobang Buaya performing the *morunsai*, the art of circular dancing and singing using an improvised call-and-response technique between the male and female performers.

Paitanic languages: dispersed yet distinct

This group of languages is named after the Paitan River which flows through one of the Paitanic areas. An early identification of the group was made after a statewide survey of Sabahan languages, completed in 1981, which involved extensive comparison of word lists and speech samples. The survey revealed linguistic affinity among geographically dispersed groups in isolated environments.

Five Paitanic languages—Dumpas, Tambanuo, Upper Kinabatangan, Lobu and Abai Sungai—are spoken in the Labuk-Sugut and Kinabatangan districts along several major rivers as well as in the Pitas District, west of the Witti Range in the Keningau district, in an isolated area of the Ranau district, and along the Segama River in Lahad Datu district. In addition, large groups of Paitanic speakers who have moved from these areas to the market towns of Beluran, Bukit Garam and Sandakan have maintained their linguistic and ethnic identity and often live together in the same neighbourhoods or hamlets.

Linguistic characteristics other than solely lexical items mark the Paitanic languages as a distinctive group. For example, most Sabah languages use vowel harmony: as a root word is affixed, the vowels in the

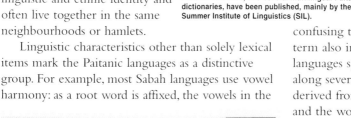

Paitanic folk tales, and several multilingual Paitanic dictionaries, have been published, mainly by the Summer Institute of Linguistics (SIL).

original root and the affix become the same; therefore, the root *ondom* (remember) plus the affix *an-* results in *andaman*, rather than *ondoman*. By way of contrast, the Tambanuo language does not have vowel harmony, but has a process of vowel neutralization. For example, *alap* (take) when combined with the suffix *an*, becomes *olapan*. The distinction between 'a' and 'o' is neutralized, or lost.

Paitanic languages also exhibit a highly complex system of verbal affixation in their grammar. A single root-word can be affixed in 50 or more ways to form new words with a range of different meanings and functions.

The five Paitanic languages

Tambanuo—spoken along the Sugut, Paitan, Kaindangan, Tengkarasan and Kanibungan rivers in northeastern Sabah—is the Paitanic language with the largest number of speakers (approximately 20,000). Though Orang Sungai (river people) is a well-known and descriptive ethnonym for this group, it is confusing to use it as a language name since the term also includes speakers of several different languages spoken predominantly by Muslims residing along several of Sabah's rivers. The label Tambanuo is derived from an archaic personalizing prefix *tom-* and the word *wonuwo*, which means 'world' or 'large area'. Tambanuo has long been in use as a trade language in parts of northeast Sabah; even Chinese and other merchants in the area learn to speak it.

The second largest Paitanic language, Upper Kinabatangan, is spoken by some 6,000 people residing at the upper reaches of the Kinabatangan River, and comprises a group of very closely related dialects. Officially known as Orang Sungai, the speakers of this language use neither that term nor the term Upper Kinabatangan to refer to themselves or their language. Instead, they refer to themselves by the names of their dialects, such as Kalabuan, Makiang, Sinabu, Milian, Sinarupa, Kuamut and

Traditional isolation

Many of the areas in which the Paitanic languages are spoken are isolated, surrounded by thick jungle and rugged terrain. This was even more so the case in the past before construction of roads into and within these areas. Some areas, particularly on the Kinabatangan River, are now promoted as eco-tourism destinations.

Orang Sungai fisherman on the Kinabatangan River.

Both the Orang Sungai (pictured here) and the Ida'an are involved in the collection of birds' nests.

Dusun Segama. Among these dialect groups, only the Dusun Segama have left the Kinabatangan area and now reside on the Segama River in the Lahad Datu district. Although this dialect has diverged somewhat from the others, Dusun Segama speakers still acknowledge the Kuamut area on the Kinabatangan River as their homeland, and continue to retain a high level of understanding of Upper Kinabatangan.

Closely related to the Upper Kinabatangan language is the Lobu language which has two dialects, Lobu and Rumanau, spoken in three distinct locations by a population of some 2,800. The Rumanau dialect group reside near the Upper Kinabatangan language areas east of the Witti Range, while another of the groups, who refer to themselves as Lobu (literally 'people'), live to the west of the Witti Range in the Keningau district. As newly built roads from their area to Keningau town have improved access to the town, these people now identify themselves with the Murutic and Dusunic groups of Keningau rather than with the more closely related Paitanic peoples of the Kinabatangan River area, though they still reside on tributaries of the Kinabatangan River. The third group resides in a remote area of Ranau district, and has largely dispersed as a result of intermarriage with the dominant ethnolinguistic Dusun group of the area.

Abai Sungai is spoken in a single village of about 500 people at the estuary of the Kinabatangan River. During the statewide language survey of 1978-81, these villagers were found to be actively assimilating Malay into their language. This may account for the classification of Abai Sungai as a language separate from other Paitanic languages. The fifth Paitanic language, Dumpas, is also spoken by approximately 500 people.

Other Austronesian languages

Besides the Paitanic languages, and those of the four indigenous language groups (see 'Dusunic languages of Sabah', and 'Sama-Bajau, Murutic and Malayic languages of Sabah'), at least ten other Austronesian languages are spoken, some by very few speakers. Three of these languages are found exclusively in Sabah, Ida'an, Bonggi, and Iranun (Illanun). The majority of speakers of seven of the languages live outside Sabah: Suluk (Tausug) and Molbog are primarily spoken in the Philippines; Lundayeh (Lun Bawang) in Sarawak; Bugis and Wolio in Sulawesi, Indonesia; Javanese in Java, also in Indonesia; and some 25,000 Tidong speakers, scattered throughout villages in the southeast, form part of a larger group centred in eastern Kalimantan.

Two of the very few published works in the 'other' Austronesian languages.

TOP: A Suluk man with his boat on Mabul Island, a popular diving spot situated close to the more famous Sipadan Island.

ABOVE: Lundayeh women preparing a meal in the kitchen of a longhouse near the border with Sarawak.

Minority Austronesian languages exclusive to Sabah

Two Bonggi speakers at Kampung Pangkalan Darat on the east coast of the northern island of Banggi.

Bonggi
Bonggi is spoken by about 1,400 people on the islands of Banggi and Balambangan off the northern coast of Sabah. The language appears to be remotely related to some of the languages spoken on Palawan Island in the southern Philippines. One difference between Bonggi and other Sabah languages is the sound system. Whereas other Sabah languages have a plain 'm', 'n', and 'ng' at the end of a word, Bonggi often has 'bm', 'dn', and 'kng'. For example, the Malay terms *garam* (salt) and *kangkung* (edible water-convolvulus) are pronounced *garabm* and *kangkukng* in Bonggi, a feature also found in the Selakau language of Sarawak.

Iranun
Closely related to the Magindanao and Maranao languages of Mindanao, the Philippines, Iranun is spoken by nearly 14,000 people in Sabah.

Girls in traditional Iranun costume, Kota Belud.

Members of the Begak, an Ida'an ethnolinguistic sub-group, in traditional dress at the annual Sabah Fest.

Ida'an
The Ida'an language is spoken by more than 5,000 ethnic Ida'an Begak in the Lahad Datu, Kinabatangan, and Sandakan Districts. They are known to have lived in the area, where they have been involved in the collection of much sought-after birds' nests, since at least the 15th century.

Aslian languages

The Aslian languages, belonging to the Mon-Khmer branch of the Austroasiatic stock, have the longest association with the Malay Peninsula of any languages. Linguists adopted the label 'Aslian' in the mid-1970s when the mutual relationship between these languages was identified. The name was chosen because the languages are spoken by Orang Asli, the aboriginal or indigenous minority peoples of the Peninsula. Today, many of the Aslian languages are endangered. Some have already disappeared.

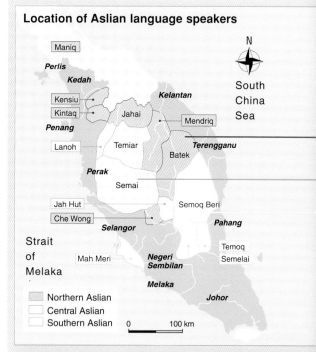

Location of Aslian language speakers

Maniq
Perlis
Kedah
Kensiu
Kintaq
Penang
Lanoh
Perak
Jah Hut
Che Wong
Strait of Melaka
Mah Meri
Jahai
Temiar
Semai
Selangor
Negeri Sembilan
Melaka
Kelantan
Mendriq
Batek
Semoq Beri
Pahang
Temoq
Semelai
Johor
Terengganu
South China Sea
N

Northern Aslian
Central Aslian
Southern Aslian
0   100 km

Three Temiars from northern Pahang photographed in 1934. Today, Pahang is the state with the largest Orang Asli population.

Origin of the Aslian languages

Linguistic evidence suggests that the Aslian languages originally appeared on the western side of the main range of mountains, probably in the Perak valley, and only later spread eastwards into Kelantan, Terengganu and Pahang. Today, Pahang is home to the greatest Aslian linguistic diversity, and it seems likely that the area around the mountain Gunung Benom was a particularly significant region of secondary Aslian dispersal (see 'Aslian: characteristics and usage').

Further evidence for these theories is provided by archaeological finds: ancestral Aslian languages were probably spoken by the people who made the prehistoric tripod pottery vessels excavated on the western side of the Malay Peninsula, dating from around 1700 BCE until the first millennium BCE.

During the past three millennia the Aslian sub-family of languages has divided into three or four main sub-groups—Northern Aslian (or Jahaic), Central Aslian (or Senoic), and Southern Aslian (or Semelaic)—each containing a number of distinct languages. Jah Hut, usually classified as a Central Aslian language, may yet prove to constitute a distinct sub-group.

The precise relationship of the Aslian languages to other Mon-Khmer languages remains unclear, as few of the latter have been studied in detail. However, the one to which they appear most closely related is Mon, the classical inscriptional language of central and south Thailand and south Myanmar. Mon-Khmer comprises a northern sub-group that includes minority languages spoken in Myanmar, Thailand, Laos, Vietnam and southwest China, as well as an eastern sub-group comprising Khmer and Vietnamese, along with unwritten minority languages spoken in Cambodia, Laos and Vietnam. Aslian and Mon, together with the Nico-barese languages, spoken in the Nicobar Islands in the Indian Ocean, may constitute a southern sub-group within Mon-Khmer.

Research into Aslian

Interest in Orang Asli languages was pioneered by the Austrian scholar Wilhelm Schmidt (1901) and the Englishman C. O. Blagden (1906). The colonial administrator R. J. Wilkinson (1910) subsequently discovered a number of languages unrecorded by Blagden. Research then lapsed until the 1960s and 1970s, when new studies were produced by Gérard Diffloth (Semai, Jah Hut), Geoffrey Benjamin (Temiar) and Asmah Haji Omar (Kintaq). Diffloth coined the term 'Aslian' in 1973 to refer to the Mon-Khmer languages of Peninsular Malaysia and southern Thailand. Since the late 1990s there has been a renewal of scholarly interest in these languages, with studies by Malaysian, Thai, Australian, American and European researchers. A bibliography of Orang Asli studies published in 2001 lists no fewer than 106 publications on Orang Asli linguistics, the majority of which deal with Aslian languages. Nicole Kruspe's 500-page *A Grammar of Semelai*, published in 2004, is the most detailed study to date of any Mon-Khmer language.

Researcher Duncan Holaday checking a transcription of the Jah Hut language with Dollah bin Hok.

Labelling and classifying Aslian languages

Individual Aslian languages are usually referred to by the ethnic label of the people who speak them: for example, the language spoken by the Semais is known as Semai. However, these ethnic-based names are not always an accurate guide to the linguistic situation. For example: Kensiu and Kintaq are the names of distinct social groups, but are dialects of the same language, as are Mah Meri,

The Aslian languages separated at a relatively early stage from other branches of Mon-Khmer and have retained many conservative phonological and lexical features which provide important evidence in uncovering the earlier history of mainland Southeast Asia and the reconstruction of the ancestral Proto-Mon-Khmer language.

Extinct languages

Several Aslian languages are already extinct, for example Wila' (alternatively Bila' or Lowland Semang), recorded as having been spoken on the Province Wellesley coast opposite Penang in the early 19th century, and the Ple-Temer tongue, previously spoken near Gerik in northern Perak. The puzzle of Kenaboi, spoken in Negeri Sembilan until the late 19th century, has yet to be solved. Analyses show that the 240 recorded Kenaboi words (once thought to be unrelated to any other known language) betray a strange mixture of Malay and wider Austronesian, as well as Mon and Aslian, elements. It may well have been a taboo jargon used during forest expeditions (see 'Social varieties of Malay').

Endangerment and survival

Since they are spoken by small numbers of people, all Aslian languages are endangered to some degree. This results from speaker deaths and linguistic assimilation with the Malay community. The degree of endangerment varies, however. The least endangered is probably Temiar, a language that shows little dialectal variation and is mutually comprehensible

The diagrams below show in simplified form the genetic relationship between the various Aslian languages (dotted lines represent undetermined relationships) and the population figures for each group of speakers.

Northern

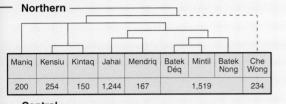

Maniq	Kensiu	Kintaq	Jahai	Mendriq	Batek Déq	Mintil	Batek Nong	Che Wong
200	254	150	1,244	167	1,519			234

Central

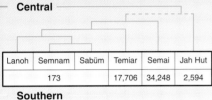

Lanoh	Semnam	Sabüm	Temiar	Semai	Jah Hut
173			17,706	34,248	2,594

Southern

Semoq Beri	Semelai	Temoq	Mah Meri
2,348	5,026		3,503

Population figure source: COAC calculations from JHEOA data, 1999.

Besisi, and Betisék, referred to here solely as 'Mah Meri'. On the other hand, ethnic labels such as 'Batek' or 'Lanoh' each cover speakers of three languages. Further confusion arises from the use of different labels to refer to the same language: both 'Sengoi' and 'Senoi' have been used to refer to Semai, and 'Senoi' is also used by some for the Temiar language.

throughout a growing population living over a wide area. Surrounded on all sides by speakers of other Aslian languages, it has become something of a lingua franca among them. Temiar is also a language of radio broadcasting.

On the other hand, the tiny speech communities of the Northern Aslian languages are not necessarily about to disappear either. Their small numbers have been maintained for centuries by special social processes aimed at adjusting their population structure to the requirements of nomadic foraging. They have usually preferred to marry non-relatives living some distance away, so that any one settlement contains speakers of many different dialects. Moreover, they have always been in close contact with outsiders, and they learnt long ago how to maintain their distinctive ways of life and languages in the face of cultural and linguistic traditions other than their own.

However, the majority of Aslian speakers, who are mostly farmers, display a very different pattern of dialect differentiation, as a result of their sedentary way of life. Semai, for example, which has the largest number of speakers among the Aslian languages, is split into around 40 divergent valley-based dialects, which are not all mutually intelligible. As a result, Semai as a whole is not necessarily assured of long-term survival. Each Semai dialect has relatively few speakers, and some kind of language standardization may be necessary to commit it to writing and ensure its continued existence. (Semai is a language of broadcasting, however, which should aid its survival.) More endangered are Mah Meri, and (perhaps) Semelai, since some of their speakers have long been shifting to the use of Malay.

In the process, they have become linguistically more similar to their Orang Asli neighbours, the Jakuns and the Temuans, both of whom speak variants of Malay.

TOP: A combination of pictures and Malay is used to explain the consequences of a development project to speakers of different Aslian languages. While Aslian languages are spoken within their respective speaker communities, communication between the different groups is often in Malay.

ABOVE: Semai teenagers at a wedding *joget* (dance) in Kampung Sungai Genting, Chenderiang, show the effects of changes in Orang Asli traditional life; they act, and speak, like 'mainstream' Malaysians.

The Orang Asli

In 2000, there were approximately 133,000 Orang Asli (a Malay term meaning 'original people') in Peninsular Malaysia. The largest populations are found in Pahang (approximately 47,000) and Perak (approximately 40,000), but there are smaller populations in all the other states except Perlis. The Orang Asli were originally classified by anthropologists—and still are by the Jabatan Hal Ehwal Orang Asli (Department of Orang Asli Affairs, or JHEOA)—into three main categories: Negrito, Senoi and Aboriginal (or Proto-) Malay. However, this classification does not correspond to the way in which the Orang Asli refer to themselves, nor does it correspond to the classification of the Aslian languages into Northern, Central and Southern.

Semai woman in Sungai Sioi, near Tapah in Perak, harvesting hill rice on a swidden site.

Some 80,000 Orang Asli speak Aslian languages; the remainder speak Malay dialects (see 'Regional varieties of Malay'). Aslian-speakers consist variously of large, medium-sized and small speech communities, reflecting the different modes of life pursued over the centuries and even millennia by the various groups. These different modes have themselves profoundly affected the sociolinguistic profiles of the various Aslian languages.

Often erroneously regarded as nomadic, the majority of Orang Asli are, and have always been, swidden farmers. Indeed, they move around not much more than Malay settlers did until relatively recently. Through various policies implemented by the JHEOA, the government has caused many Orang Asli to live in or close to urban settlements. As a consequence, many are becoming more fully integrated into mainstream Malaysian society. Nevertheless, the Orang Asli remain one of the most marginalized and impoverished ethnic groups.

ABOVE LEFT: Batek youth (right) preparing blowpipe darts in the jungle of Taman Negara, Pahang.

ABOVE RIGHT: Jah Hut elders in Kampung Pian, Kuala Krau, Pahang, making a winnowing tray from rattan.

BELOW: Temoq mother and children at home in Kampung Embun, Maran, Pahang.

Aslian: characteristics and usage

The grammar and vocabulary of the Aslian languages are as rich, subtle and elaborate as those of other languages. They all possess a larger number of phonemes—meaningfully distinctive sounds—than Malay, and employ sophisticated grammar. While the languages lack an indigenous written tradition, efforts have been made to record and preserve them. The languages are used to a limited extent in the media, and education in the Semai language has been introduced in a small number of schools.

Gunung Benom (*gunung* is Malay, and *benom* Mon-Khmer, for mountain) is over 2000m in height

Writing Aslian
The best method of writing Aslian is derived from the long-established International Phonetic Alphabet. A selection of the characters used is given below.

Symbol	Sound
c	*ch* in the English *chew*
ɲ	*ny* in the Malay *nyata*
ŋ	*ng* in the English *singer*
ʔ	*k* in the Malay *duduk*
k	*k* in the Malay *makan*
a	*a* in the Malay *makan*
ɛ	*e* in the English *get*
ə	*e* in the Malay *betul*
ɔ	*au* in the (British) English *taught*
ā, ō etc.	nasal vowels
ɔɔ, uu etc.	long vowels (Temiar, Semai)
pʰ, tʰ etc.	aspirated stops (Semelai)

What are Aslian languages like?
The Aslian languages have complex sound systems, and this has led to the emergence of a variety of different ways of writing the languages. Some special features of Aslian pronunciation are particularly notable. In most Aslian languages, the final syllable is strongly stressed, and in several Aslian languages certain consonants are pronounced in a distinctively split manner when they occur at the end of a word, for example the Temiar word *kabm* (bite) for *kab*. This feature is of historical interest as it is also found in certain minority languages spoken in Johor, Sumatra and Sarawak, unrelated to Aslian. Also, unlike Malay, the voiced stops *b*, *d*, *j*, and *g* can occur at the end of a word, such as the Temiar *gabag* (sing); the same is true of the consonants *ɲ* and *c*: Jahai *pɔɲlɔɲ* (to sing); Jah Hut *bɲahec* (fear).

Aslian consonants are otherwise generally similar to those of Malay. All Aslian words begin with a consonant. Those that might seem to begin with a vowel actually have an initial 'catch-in-the-throat', the glottal stop symbolized by the character *ʔ*. In most Northern and Central Aslian languages, words end in consonants too, occasionally not released audibly. Indeed, words that sound as if they end in a diphthong (*-oi*, *-au*, etc.) actually end in the consonant *y* or *w*. For example, Senoi Praaq (fighting people), the title of the Orang Asli para-military regiment, should strictly be written *Sɛnʔɔɔy Pɔrak*.

The influence of Aslian
Several words in the Malay lexicon are Mon-Khmer words, and therefore presumably from Aslian. These include *ketam* (crab) and *lang* or *helang* (eagle or hawk). Another word no longer found in Malay, but recorded in Bowrey's 1603 'Malayo' dictionary, is *komon* (nephew).

There are also a number of place names throughout the Peninsula that are Aslian or Mon-Khmer in origin. The best known is (Gunung) Benom in Pahang. *Benom* is a widespread Mon-Khmer word for mountain or hill, as in the Cambodian capital, Phnom Penh.

Each Aslian language has its own distinctive features, although there are a number of commonalities. Some of these are distinctive of the Aslian sub-family of languages. For example, although monosyllabic root-words are frequent, many root-words have two syllables, with a full vowel in the first syllable, such as the Mintil *kanit* (small) and Semai *sumaac* (to boil over). Such words are unusual in the Mon-Khmer family of languages, and have been lost entirely amongst its northern members, which have long been in contact with monosyllabic languages of other language families. More common, and more typically Mon-Khmer, are one-and-a-half-syllabled root-words such as *bihiip* (blood, pronounced *bhiip*) in Semai. Longer words appear too, although these usually contain more than one morpheme (an indivisible meaningful unit).

Expressives
Expressives are a special class of words that form an essential part of Aslian speech. They constitute a distinct lexical type, neither noun nor verb, adjective or adverb, with a semantics and traceable Mon-Khmer etymology of their own.

They describe a diversity of things and concepts: noises, colours, light patterns, shapes, movements, sensations, emotions, and aesthetic feelings. All are based on nature and other familiar things seen and known in the jungle where the speakers traditionally live.

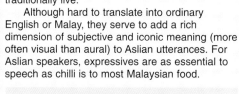

Sɔɲsulɔɲ may be roughly translated as 'the odd appearance of a snake's head, sharp yet not pointed, rounded-off, yet not round'.

Although hard to translate into ordinary English or Malay, they serve to add a rich dimension of subjective and iconic meaning (more often visual than aural) to Aslian utterances. For Aslian speakers, expressives are as essential to speech as chilli is to most Malaysian food.

Single-word Semai expressives

sɔpsɔrajãāp	'many tears falling in large and fast flow'
sɔpsɔrijãāp	'many tears falling, making many slow rivulets'
rɔɲruhɔɔɲ	'the appearance of teeth attacked by decay'
kɔckɔmrɔʔɛɛc	'short, fat arms'

The Semai language has a particular term, *cɔwcɔmrɔhaaw*, for the sound made by a waterfall, such as this at Ulu Tenlop, Tapah.

The Temiar verb
The Temiar verb paradigm is one of the most elaborate and productive among the Mon-Khmer languages. Temiar root-words comprise one, one-and-a-half or two syllables, (e.g. *gɔl* 'to sit', *sɔlɔg* 'to sleep', and *halab* 'to go downstream', respectively). The main inflectional device is incopyfixation, a partial reduplication, in which the final consonant of the root is copied to an earlier position in the word as an infix. A further inflection in Temiar is the infix *a* which is used in verbs where the subject is thought of as undergoing his or her own action.

sɔlɔg 'to sleep'

sɔlɔg	'sleep' (viewed as a completed act)
sɛglɔg	'sleep' (viewed as an incomplete act)
bɔ-sɛglɔg	'currently sleeping'
sɛnlɔg or *sɛnɛglɔg*	'a sleeping'
salɔg	'fall asleep' (uncontrolledly)
bɔ-salɔg	'currently falling asleep'
sɔnalɔg	'a falling asleep'
sɛrlɔg	'put (someone) to sleep' (viewed as a completed act)
sɛrɛglɔg	'put (someone) to sleep' (viewed as an incomplete act)
ba-sɛrɛglɔg	'currently putting (someone) to sleep'
sɛrɛnlɔg	'a putting (of someone) to sleep'

Affixation

Word formation in the Aslian languages is based on the addition of prefixes and infixes (an affix in the middle of a word) to the root-word; suffixes only occur in recent borrowings from Malay. The infix *n* is especially striking in the range of meanings it carries in the various languages.

The effect of the infix *n*

Language	Root-word	Root-word with infix added
Jahai	*makɔʔ* 'egg'	*mənakɔʔ* 'eggs' (in counting)
Kentaq	*ʔilay* 'to bathe' (perfective)	*ʔənlay* 'to bathe' (imperfective)
Temiar	*cɛbciib* 'go'	*cɛbniib* 'a going'
Semai	*bah* 'uncle' (in direct address)	*mənah* 'uncle' (referential)
Semelai	*sudu?* 'spoon'	*snudu?* 'spoonful'
	sma? 'person'	*snma?* 'kind of person'

Generally, however, Aslian languages are phonologically conservative, retaining several features that have been lost by other languages: 'original' long vowels (Central Aslian only), and full consonantal and vocalic systems. As with Mon–Khmer in general, Aslian languages are characterized by some of the 'fullest' phonemic systems in the world.

Each of the Aslian languages has to some extent reacted to the dominant position of Malay. Borrowing from Malay appears highest among the smaller nomadic population groups, while among the large Orang Asli farming populations the rate is generally much lower due to their relatively remote situation and higher degree of self-sufficiency. Exceptions among this latter group, however, are the Southern Aslian languages, as their speakers favour trade links with Malays and others downriver.

Aslian usage

Aslian literature consists mainly of an oral tradition with little published in the original languages (see 'Orang Asli oral traditions'). There is little indication of any sustained literacy campaign to popularize Aslian tongues. Nevertheless, a number of organizations have published materials for readers of the Aslian languages.

Since 1959, some Aslian languages have been used by Radio Malaysia on Radio Seven. Initially broadcast for only half an hour per day, transmission has since 2001 been for nine hours every day. News, interviews, magazine-type programmes, and dramas are broadcast in Semai, Temiar, and the Malayic Orang Asli languages, Jakun and Temuan (see 'Regional varieties of Malay').

Late-night community discussion among the Semai of Baretchi, Ulu Tenlop, conducted in the group's distinctive dialect.

Aslian grammar and vocabulary

The elaborateness, richness and subtlety of the Aslian languages are evident in Aslian storytelling and religious songs.

Recorded in southern Kelantan in 1964, the extemporised Temiar song presented below is sung by a shaman, although the words are ostensibly those of a spirit-guide. The use of *yaar* (he and I), a dual-number pronoun, emphasizes their mutual cooperation as teacher (the spirit-guide) and pupil (the shaman). Distinctive dual-number pronouns are found in all Northern and Central Aslian languages (alongside singular and plural forms), and extensive use is made of them particularly in stories and songs.

Semai is taught at a limited number of schools for Orang Asli children, such as this in Kampung Sungai Senta, Perak.

As is typical of Aslian religious lyrics, several Malay words appear. *Guru* (teacher), *tamu* (guest), or perhaps *temu* (meet)), and *muncung* (snout) have been altered by imposing Aslian morphology or changing the word-class to become *gənuruuʔ* (teaching), *tənamuuʔ* (wreath, i.e. where the spirit is made a guest of the people), and *muɲcoɲ* (to stick out). On the other hand, the noun *sənaɲ* (remnants) has nothing to do with the similar sounding Malay adjective *senang* (at ease), but is a pure Temiar word formed from the verb *sak* (to wither) by the infixation of *n*.

Although the language of this song text is highly allusive and poetic, the sentence structure is very similar to that of everyday Temiar conversation. To some extent, it can stand as a typical example of Aslian language patterns. But each Aslian language has its own syntactic features.

Sentence organization: a Temiar song

Samɔh dalam baley, ʔim-ʔintey cə-yaar gənuruuʔ.
Behold inside house, I-INTENTIVE-glance PARTICLE-he-and-I teacher+n.
(Behold within the house, I will glance at us two as we engage in mutual teaching)

Ma-lɔɔʔ tənamuuʔ ləbagʔ? Gabag tɛrman!
To-where wreath *lebag*? Sing CAUSATIVE+play
(Where is the wreath of *lebag* flowers? Sing, make play!)

Samɔh sənaɲ kəwaar
Behold wither+n palmleaf,
(Behold the remnants of last time's palm whisk)

pɛnsaar molaɲ.
CAUSATIVE+n+hurry barkcloth headdress.
(but hurry forward with the new barkcloth headdress.)

Samɔh la-gɛlgəlɛɛl. Na-muɲcoɲ ʔayaap.
Behold *lah*-EXPRESSIVE. It-snouts Ayam.
(Behold the fine singing. Gunung Ayam rises up)

Rɛʔ-doh yaar guruuʔ. Yəəh, ma-lɔɔʔ...?
Like-this he-and-I teacher. Oh, to-where...?
(Like this are my shaman and I. Oh, where...?)

A trilingual dictionary published by the Jabatan Hal Ehwal Orang Asli (JHEOA) (Department of Orang Asli Affairs).

Formal education in the Aslian languages is only available to a relatively small number of Orang Asli. This includes some Semai-language kindergartens. Government schools for Orang Asli children use Malay as the medium of instruction. Nevertheless, 12 primary schools have been selected to teach Semai as a Pupils' Own Language (POL) (see 'Language policy in action'). However, in 2003, only seven schools, five in Perak and two in Pahang, had commenced teaching because of a lack of trained teachers. All Semai language teachers are themselves Orang Asli. Teaching aids and additional resources are being developed. At present the language is not formally examined.

Pioneer Orang Asli pop group

Jelmol, a group of Temiar and Semai Orang Asli singers, has recorded two commercial pop albums, *Asli* (1999) and *Emas Permata* (2000), which include tracks in Temiar (the other songs are sung in Malay). They are regularly broadcast on Radio Seven.

Jelmol (Temiar for 'mountain') have sold over 25,000 copies of *Asli*, their first album.

Origins of Chinese dialects

Speakers of the Chinese dialects form the second-largest speech group in Malaysia after Malay. This is the result of long-standing historical links with China, culminating in Chinese immigration on a vast scale in the late 19th and early 20th centuries. The majority of these immigrants were from southern China and spoke one of nine Chinese dialects. Despite the growing use of Mandarin over the last 40 years, these same original dialects still retain their importance.

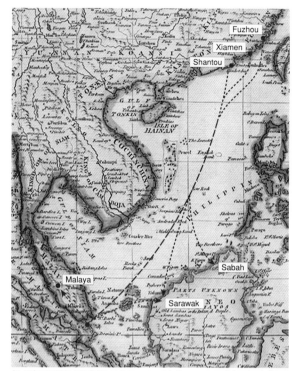

An estimated 835,000 Chinese (known as *sinkeh* or new guests) emigrated to what is now Malaysia between 1851 and 1925, having departed from ports in southeastern China.

Founded in 1816 by the London Missionary Society, the Anglo-Chinese College, Melaka, included Chinese literature among the subjects on its curriculum.

Springboard to China

In the early 19th century, Penang and Melaka played important roles in the spread of Western ideas through the Chinese language. In 1807 and 1809, 11 Chinese seminarians from Sichuan and Fujian arrived in Penang to continue their study of Roman Catholic theology. In 1810, the College General was established to train Catholic priests for missionary activity in China.

In 1818, even before the British gained permanent possession of Melaka, the Anglo-Chinese College was established by the London Missionary Society, a Protestant organization focused on the conversion of China. Since China was still closed to the West, Melaka was the chosen staging ground. Besides preparing missionaries, Melaka was the centre for publishing in Chinese. In 1823, the world's first translation of the Bible into Chinese was published in Malaya.

Early contacts with China

Chinese officials and Buddhist pilgrims travelling to and from India were the main visitors to Southeast Asia before the 10th century CE. From the 12th century, when overland routes across China were closed, maritime trade increased. Luxury goods from Southeast Asia, such as spices and rhinoceros horn, were traded for Chinese ceramics by imperial-sponsored and private-trading convoys. The monsoons made long stays inevitable and colonies of Chinese traders formed in Malayan ports.

Relations between China and the Malay Peninsula grew stronger after the founding of Melaka at the end of the 14th century. Chinese Admiral Zheng He (Cheng Ho)'s naval mission to Melaka in 1405 resulted in the declaration of Melaka as a Chinese protectorate and provided security from the expanding Thai kingdom to the north. Chinese traders became frequent visitors to Melaka, and established a permanent enclave in the multiethnic entrepôt. It was during this period that the Straits Chinese, descended from Hokkien fathers and Malay-speaking mothers, became established (see 'Creoles'). As a small minority, they integrated with the majority Malay population to a greater degree than the

later waves of Chinese immigrants. The Hokkien-influenced Malay creole developed by them was not only spoken among themselves, but for a time during the 18th and 19th centuries was the main language of inter-ethnic communication.

Migration in the 18th and 19th centuries

The number of Chinese in what is now Malaysia further increased in the 18th century, particularly on the east coast of the Peninsula; in Kelantan they engaged in gold-mining and in Terengganu they grew pepper. However, it was the large-scale migration that occurred from the mid-19th century which cemented the place of the Chinese dialects in the Malaysian linguistic tapestry.

These Chinese immigrants worked in tin mines, gambier and pepper plantations and, later, rubber estates. With the building of roads and railways under British rule, the Chinese began to spread throughout the whole Peninsula, opening shops in every town and becoming involved in market gardening and plantations. Many provided essential services as tailors, tinsmiths, coffin makers, shoemakers and carpenters. Others became financiers to Malay sultans and British businessmen. However, they were primarily only sojourners, who worked to accumulate savings with which to return to China.

As the majority of this wave of Chinese immigrants were uneducated, and the use of Mandarin was not widespread (it became the Chinese national language only early in 1924), they communicated in their own local Chinese dialect. However, as the Chinese dialects spoken in the Peninsula are often mutually unintelligible, communication between members of different Chinese dialect groups was often in Malay. Indeed,

Chinese–Malay vocabulary

Chinese traders and officials collected word lists of Malay which were stored in the Imperial archives until the archival scribe of the Ming dynasty, Yang Lin, compiled a Chinese–Malay vocabulary in 1560. In 1877, Lin Hengnan published a Malay dictionary, *Tong Yi Xinyu* (Chinese-Malay New Words). A revised edition with the new title *Hua-Yi Tongyu* (Chinese-Malay Words) was published in 1883. Subsequently, numerous bilingual dictionaries have been published.

In multilingual Malaysia, Chinese has been influenced by both Malay and English, with the adoption of words from both of these languages. Similarly, Chinese has influenced Malay (see 'Characteristics of Malay').

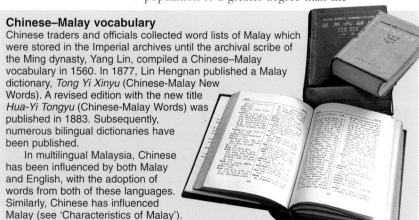

Some of the numerous Chinese-Malay dictionaries that have been published. Modern editions generally include the romanized Pinyin spelling of Chinese words as well as ideographs.

Chinese dialect homelands

Linguist Yuan Jiahua has shown that in China, Chinese dialects belong to seven major dialect groups. Chinese immigrants to Malaya traditionally spoke dialects belonging to only three of these: Min, Yue, and Kejia. Modern Standard Chinese, or Mandarin, has a more recent local history.

Min dialect group

Koh Seang Tat (seated second row, fourth from right), an eminent Penang businessman, with his family in the early 20th century. He was the great-grandson of Koh Lay Hwan, who emigrated from the Hokkien (Fujian) province of China to Kedah in the late 18th century.

Hokkien
Hokkien is the Xiamen (Amoy) variant of the Min dialect group, which is itself a member of the Min 'supergroup' of dialects which are spoken in the Chinese provinces of Fujian, Eastern Guangdong and Hainan as well as in some parts of Taiwan.

Hokchiu (Foochow), Henghua and Hokchia
These are three further variants of the Min dialect group. *Hokchiu* is the Hokkien word for Fuzhou (Foochow). It is mainly spoken in Fuzhou, the provincial capital, and the adjoining Minhou Special District. Henghua (Xinghua) is spoken in the Henghua district between Fuzhou and Amoy, and Hokchia in the Fuqing district just south of Fuzhou.

Teochew
Teochew, pronounced *Chaozhou* in the Pinyin system, is the Shantou (Swatow) variant of the Min dialect group. The Teochew in Malaysia can trace their roots to the banks of the Hanjiang River in east Guangdong.

Hainanese
Hainanese is a Min dialect variant spoken in Malaysia by Chinese who originated from Wenchang district in the northeast of Hainan Island. Formerly part of Guangdong, Hainan is now a separate province.

Yue dialect group
Cantonese
Cantonese is the colloquial term for the Guangzhou (Canton), Hong Kong variant of the Yue dialect group. *Yue* is the simplified name for Guangdong, although the language is not confined to that province. Malaysian Cantonese speakers mostly originate from the Pearl River Delta.

Kwongsai
The Guangxi variant of the Yue dialect group, *Kwongsai* is the Cantonese name for Guangxi. It spoken in south Guangxi, the ancestral homeland of the Malaysian Kwongsai.

Kejia dialect group
Khek (Hakka)
Khek refers to the Kejia group of dialects (pronounced 'Hakka' in the local dialect); *Khek* is the Hokkien pronunciation of Kejia. It is linguistically distinct from the Min and Yue dialect groups. Khek speakers in Malaysia mainly originated from east Guangdong and the Yongding district in the west of Fujian province.

Northern dialect group
Mandarin
This is the standard Beijing variant of the Chinese language. Used traditionally by officials, it was selected as the national standard in China in 1924.

Source: Wurm and Li, 1987

Isabella Bird, visiting the mining boomtown of Taiping in 1879, remarked that '*five dialects of Chinese are spoken, and Chinamen constantly communicate with each other in Malay, because they can't understand each other's Chinese*' (see 'Malaysia in foreign literature').

It was in the 19th century that the numerous communal organizations, such as *kongsi* (clan or common-origin associations) and *hui* (benevolent societies) became established, often with membership drawn from speakers of a single Chinese dialect. Linguistic division was further maintained by the trend in urban areas of speakers of a common dialect to specialize in a particular trade or service, and all to set up business in the same street (see 'Distribution of Chinese dialects'). As a result of the relative independence of the Chinese community, Malay and later British officials often learnt to speak Chinese, and indeed were encouraged to do so.

The 20th century and the rise of Mandarin
Only after World War I did substantial female Chinese immigration begin. This signalled a change among the Chinese from a transient to a settled population. However, as marriage between speakers of different dialects was discouraged until quite recently, very little inter-dialect socialization resulted.

Although most Chinese continue to speak their original southern Chinese dialects as a first language, use of Mandarin is increasing. It is now perceived to be the Chinese lingua franca, both in Malaysia and worldwide. Its growth in Malaysia may partly be attributed to the influence of Chinese schools, where it is used as the medium of instruction.

Common-origin associations
In the 19th century, new immigrants mostly associated with speakers of their own dialect as Mandarin was only adopted as the common language of China early in 1924. Nearly all immigrant Chinese were persuaded to join *kongsi*—known to the British administration as 'secret societies', although they were not in fact secret—whose membership was predominantly drawn from the speakers of the same dialect. Originally formed as cooperatives to start business ventures, the kongsis expanded to provide housing, training, employment, religious facilities and education to new arrivals. The kongsi became tightly knit communities which ensured the continued use of the various Chinese dialects.

The principal common-origin associations were the Guangdong Association for Cantonese speakers, Fujian Association for Hokkien speakers, Teochew Association and Hakka Association. The ongoing, although diminishing, role of these and other similar organizations has helped ensure the continuance of the various Chinese dialects in Malaysia.

The Kuching Hainan Association building in Kuching, Sarawak.

Distribution of Chinese dialects

After China and Taiwan, Malaysia has the largest population of Chinese speakers in the world. The waves of Chinese migration into Malaysia from southern China from the mid-19th to early 20th centuries have created an incredibly complex pattern of distribution of the Chinese dialects. This is to some extent due to the economic pursuits undertaken by the different speech groups. Over the years, the dialects have evolved in Malaysia and become localized.

The former Straits Settlement of Penang, in which the Hokkien dialect predominates, is the Malaysian state with the highest density of Chinese speakers. They form nearly half of the state's total population.

Many Malaysian Chinese are descended from Chinese labourers such as these. Here seen probably leaving from Xiamen (Amoy) for Singapore and Malaya in the late 19th or early 20th century.

Patterns of size and distribution

The number of Chinese, and by inference Chinese speakers, has increased from 2,667,452 (for Malaya, Sarawak and Sabah) in 1957 to 5,365,846 in 2000, comprising 26 per cent of the total Malaysian population. During this period, certain dialects have thrived; in particular Hokkien, the most widely spoken dialect, with speaker numbers rising from 740,635 in the Malay Peninsula in 1957 to 2,020,868 in Malaysia in 2000. While the number of speakers of some dialects, such as Khek (Hakka), remained static during the 1990s, the number of Hokkien speakers increased. There has been a decline in the number of Kwongsai speakers since Independence; from 69,122 (Malay Peninsula only) to only 51,674 in 2000. This may be partly due to cultural and linguistic identification by this group with the larger Cantonese-speaking community.

The four major Chinese dialects spoken in Malaysia are Hokkien, Khek, Cantonese and Teochew. Speakers of these and the other Chinese dialects are not evenly distributed throughout the country. Whereas Hokkien and Teochew speakers are more numerous in the northern and southern regions of the Peninsula as well as along the coast, Cantonese and Khek speakers are more populous in the central inland regions. This pattern is a result of the chain migration of Chinese to Malaysia and the different occupations in which members of each dialect group were traditionally engaged. Although a small minority elsewhere in the country, the Hokchiu (Foochow) community predominates in Sarawak. Some 85 per cent of the Chinese speaking population reside in urban areas, and different Chinese dialects dominate the various towns and cities, even those relatively close to one another.

Regional linguistic differences

With the stabilization of the distribution pattern of Chinese speakers, as early immigrants settled permanently and raised families, each of the dialects has to some extent become localized. Hokkien, the most widely distributed dialect, is the most localized as a result of long-term interaction with the Malays and other local ethnic groups. Regional differences in loan words may occur among speakers of the same Chinese dialect.

In the most northerly Peninsula states, Hokkien and Teochew each have variants that incorporate more loan words from English and Malay than their corresponding southern variants. For example, *ni* (from the Malay *ini* (this)), *tu* (from the Malay *itu*

Geographical distribution of the Chinese population

Perlis 19,308 9.9%
Kedah 224,435 14.5%
Kelantan 44,545 3.5%
Penang 549,497 46.3%
Terengganu 24,007 2.8%
Perak 618,972 31.9%
Pahang 206,973 17.5%
Labuan 9,025 15.9%
Sabah 254,528 13.3%
Selangor 1,161,917 30.8%
Johor 825,002 33.5%
Kuala Lumpur 536,777 43.5%
N. Sembilan 207,661 25.9%
Melaka 170,774 29.1%
Sarawak 512,426 26.3%

+ Density of Chinese population -

The total Chinese population of each state is given in bold figures, together with the percentage of the state's total population that this comprises.

0   100 km

N

Number of speakers of each dialect by state

	Hokkien	Khek	Cantonese	Teochew	Hokchiu	Hainanese	Kwongsai	Others
Johor	415,012	139,577	97,408	91,111	11,442	28,371	7,954	34,127
Kedah	101,199	23,668	24,626	61,526	1,440	3,628	731	7,617
Kelantan	29,835	3,580	5,567	999	130	1,566	228	2,640
Melaka	81,424	32,375	17,150	11,092	834	11,151	544	16,204
N. Sembilan	63,940	62,463	55,447	4,330	5,402	7,924	2,293	5,862
Pahang	59,058	37,554	61,820	10,701	3,131	7,503	19,629	7,577
Perak	154,216	133,767	201,642	60,312	28,251	9,877	11,688	19,219
Perlis	9,273	4,062	1,839	2,842	62	442	320	468
Penang	297,605	39,605	64,505	122,681	3,298	10,775	579	10,449
Sabah	33,819	147,551	31,229	11,549	5,154	6,652	470	18,104
Sarawak	68,935	161,552	29,434	38,120	178,261	7,675	382	28,067
Selangor	505,504	203,998	289,455	58,465	9,376	27,203	4,444	63,472
Terengganu	11,428	2,186	4,078	1,005	141	3,124	154	1,891
K. Lumpur	185,062	98,926	182,909	22,259	4,161	14,849	2,246	26,365
Labuan	4,558	1,990	885	288	471	305	12	516
TOTAL	2,020,868	1,092,754	1,067,994	497,280	251,554	141,045	51,674	243,046

Note: For each state, red, blue and green figures indicate the three dialects with the most speakers.

Source: Population and Housing Census 2000.

A complex state

The distribution of the Chinese dialects within Perak is particularly complex. Hokkien prevails in the north and the coastal region, although Khek (Hakka) is popular in Selama and Sungai Siput as well as other smaller townships. Cantonese is the common language in urban centres along the North-South highway from Ipoh to Tanjung Malim. Hokchiu dominates near Sitiawan.

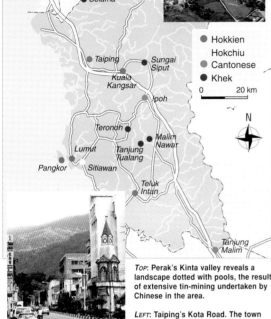

● Hokkien
Hokchiu
● Cantonese
● Khek

0   20 km

N

TOP: Perak's Kinta valley reveals a landscape dotted with pools, the result of extensive tin-mining undertaken by Chinese in the area.

LEFT: Taiping's Kota Road. The town grew from a 19th-century Chinese tin-mining camp.

(that)), *pula* and *pun* (Malay for 'also'), *tapi* (from the Malay *tetapi* (but)), and *takkan* (from the Malay *tidak akan* (will not)) are used by Hokkien speakers in Perlis, North Kedah, and Penang. In Kelantan, Thai as well as Malay loan words are found in the local Hokkien dialect, which may be classified as a creole (see 'Creoles').

Sarawakian Chinese

Hakka Chinese were the earliest Chinese immigrants to Sarawak. Until 1980, Khek was the most widely spoken Chinese dialect in Sarawak. It was then surpassed by Hokchiu (Foochow). The Hokchiu community, originally based in Sibu, expanded to open up new frontiers including Sarikei, Kanowit, and Kapit, and then spread to Bintulu, Miri, Kuching, and other towns.

Different Chinese dialects dominate in different towns. In the capital, Kuching, where the Chinese form a larger proportion of the population than any other town, Hokkien prevails, but Khek is also popular. In northern Sarawak, the Hokchiu dialect is more common. It forms the main dialect in Sibu and Bintulu, while Khek and Mandarin are popular in Miri. Hokkien is the most widely used dialect in Kapit, further inland.

Sarawakian Chinese praying during the Chinese New Year festival.

The dialect-occupation link

Most of the Chinese who laboured in tin mines in the late 19th and early 20th centuries were Khek (Hakka).

The distribution of Chinese dialects in Malaysia can to a large extent be explained by the dialect-occupation nexus; that is the settlement of speakers of particular dialects according to their economic activities during the colonial period.

Nineteenth-century Chinese immigrants had no single common dialect and were mostly uneducated. They thus tended to cluster themselves according to their ethno-linguistic group, which usually corresponded with their place of origin, and worked with or for relatives or members who spoke the same dialect. Speakers of a single dialect usually settled in one area and concentrated on economic activities in which some members had already proved successful.

Specialization was such that certain occupations or trades became associated with speakers of particular dialects: bicycle dealers with Henghua; herbalists with Khek; chefs with Hainanese and coffee-shop operators with Hainanese and Hokchiu (Foochow). Rapid modernization of the Malaysian economy has, however, led to a weakening of the dialect-occupation link in recent times.

Traditional trades and occupations of the various dialect groups

Hokkien	Urban traders, shopkeepers, tailors, the banking and rubber industries
Cantonese	Carpenters, miners, blacksmiths, cobblers, artisans, jungle clearing, tin industry, commerce and gold shops
Teochew	Fishing and rice trading, grocers
Khek	Herbalists, tin mine labour, rubber estates, construction and commerce, especially pawn shops
Hainanese	Chefs and cooks, domestic servants, shopkeepers, food establishments, the hotel industry and owners of small rubber estates
Henghua	Bicycle dealers, taxi and bus drivers
Hokchiu	The banking, finance, and timber industries, hardware and coffee shop operators, bus drivers

1. A large number of Khek (Hakka) are involved in the construction industry. 2. Hainanese continue to be associated with food establishments. 3. Gold shops are often owned and operated by Cantonese. 4. Another trade commonly associated with the Khek is that of herbalist.

Use of Chinese

The Chinese dialects spoken in Malaysia have become localized or 'Malaysianized', and are widely used by the Malaysian Chinese in numerous social contexts. While generally speakers still identify themselves in terms of their principal dialect, there is an increasing trend towards the use of Mandarin, to a large extent as a result of its use as a medium of instruction in the local education system. Speakers of the various dialects are in any case united by a common writing system. This has facilitated the publication of Chinese materials.

Shopfronts in Chinatown, Penang, demonstrate the importance of the Chinese language to the Malaysian Chinese community.

Choice of dialect

The family remains the most important institution for perpetuating a language or dialect and, hence, identity. At home, children usually learn one Chinese dialect, which is either the common one of the area or that of one (or both) parent(s). If their home language is not the same as the local one, then children are likely to also learn the latter from their neighbourhood peers and playmates. Generally, however, the local dialect is spoken within the family too, so that, for example, in an area where Hokkien is spoken by the majority, that dialect will be adopted even in households in which it is not the traditional dialect of the parents. In families where both husband and wife were educated in Chinese-medium schools, Mandarin is often chosen as the home language. In some southern areas of the Malay Peninsula, Mandarin has long been adopted as the preferred dialect.

English-speaking ethnic Chinese families also exist, particularly in urban centres, because of the long-established and pervasive influence of English education. However, in these families, a Chinese dialect, most probably the local variant, is often learnt and spoken too.

As the Chinese population of Malaysia is widely distributed and significant in size, it is often possible (and, indeed, necessary) to learn another Chinese dialect outside the home, often in the workplace or marketplace (see 'Distribution of Chinese dialects'). However, speakers of one of the major dialects (Hokkien, Khek, Cantonese or Teochew) who do not venture out of their local neighbourhoods for education or employment tend to be limited to one Chinese dialect. This is the case for example with most Cantonese speakers in Kuala Lumpur, and Hokkien speakers in Alor Star.

The Chinese dialects spoken in Malaysia have over the years become localized, as is apparent from the use of Malay and English loan words (words adopted from another language). Words from other Chinese dialects are also injected, depending on the educational and cultural background of the speaker.

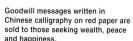
Chinese opera troupes stage performances in Hokkien, Cantonese and Teochew.

Goodwill messages written in Chinese calligraphy on red paper are sold to those seeking wealth, peace and happiness.

Mandarin, too, has been localized, as a result of the influence of the other Chinese variants spoken in Malaysia, rather than of Malay. Such dialectal influences on Mandarin are regarded as mispronunciation, and, like the use of loan words, are discouraged in teaching at school.

Mandarin education

Malaysian Chinese have become increasingly integrated linguistically, firstly because of a common writing system and secondly because Mandarin has become a lingua franca and spoken standard. In addition to the family, schools, particularly those that use Mandarin as the medium of instruction, constitute another powerful means of transmitting Chinese language, world-view and culture.

Mandarin is taught at both primary and secondary levels and classical Chinese is included in the secondary curriculum. The Pinyin system of Romanization is used in teaching pronunciation, and Chinese characters are taught in the simplified form. Students in Malay-medium primary and secondary schools, irrespective of their ethnic origin, may take Mandarin as a subject. Proficiency in Chinese can be

Members of the Malaysian Chinese Writers' Association greet each other in Mandarin and other Chinese dialects at a literary award night.

Conversational Chinese

Code-switching (the direct use of words from other languages in the language one is speaking) is common among speakers of the various Chinese dialects. Both Malay and English words are often employed in conversation, and the various Chinese dialects themselves are also used interchangeably.

evaluated in public examinations at various levels. Many students also practise using the writing brush, although Chinese calligraphy is not examinable. The study of Mandarin enables students to appreciate Chinese literature and to specialize in Chinese at the tertiary level. At this level, the Chinese Studies Department at Universiti Malaya offers courses for students aspiring to specialize in Mandarin, as well as Chinese literature, culture, history and philosophy. Other government and private universities and colleges also offer various levels of Mandarin study.

Chinese dialects in the media

The mass media contribute to the continuity of the Chinese dialects in Malaysia. Several daily newspapers, periodicals and magazines are published in Mandarin. Others, together with movies and music, are imported from China and Taiwan.

Both state-run and privately owned radio and television stations air various Chinese programmes. Most Chinese programmes on government radio stations are broadcast in Mandarin. In the early 1980s, television dramas and films were mainly imported from Hong Kong and were in Cantonese. However, from the late 1990s, with the advent of ASTRO, the Malaysian satellite television network, a wider selection of Chinese programmes has been aired, in Mandarin and Hokkien as well as Cantonese. Television news, however, is only broadcast in Mandarin. Some television dramas have been produced locally in Cantonese, and dubbed into Mandarin for export to overseas markets including Taiwan. In 2003, TV2—one of two state-run television channels—began to dub into Mandarin all productions in other dialects.

Many dialects, one script

The Chinese script, which dates back more than 5,000 years, traditionally comprised many more characters or ideograms than the simplified form used today. Each of the thousands of characters represents a meaning as well as a sound (usually one

syllable), which is pronounced differently in each of the Chinese dialects. With so many characters to learn, it can take many years for a Chinese speaker to be able to read Chinese text competently. Indeed, many Malaysian speakers of Chinese, primarily those who were not educated at Chinese-medium schools, are unable to read Chinese.

This Chinese character can be translated into English as the word 'heart'. As is typical of Chinese characters, it is pronounced differently in the various dialects: *xin* in Mandarin, *sim* in Hokkien, *sum* in Cantonese, and *xim* in Khek.

The importance of numbers

To Chinese speakers, numbers have a significance that extends beyond the mathematical. This is often attached to similarities in their pronunciation, particularly in Mandarin and Cantonese, to other value-laden words.

Significant numbers for Chinese speakers

Number	Mandarin word	Meaning
2	(*er*)	Chinese culture places high value on even numbers. Sequentially the first such number, two is believed to be lucky.
3	(*san*)	'San' sounds very similar to the word 'sheng' (grow) in Mandarin, and in Cantonese, 'sum' (three) sounds even closer to 'sang' (grow). The number is thus viewed as representing prosperity.
4	(*si*)	Despite being an even number, this number is avoided—particularly by the Cantonese and Hokkien—as it sounds like the word for 'die'.
8	(*ba*)	The most revered number, it is both even and the multiple of two even numbers. Furthermore, in Cantonese it is pronounced 'fatt', which also means 'make a fortune' in that dialect—a linguistic similarity that has influenced speakers of the other dialects too.
9	(*jiu*)	As the largest single digit number, nine is popular with Chinese speakers. In both Mandarin and Cantonese, the number is homophonic with 'forever'; couples therefore often choose to marry on 9 September, being the 9th month.

Lift buttons, showing the practice of renumbering floors 4, 14 and 24 as '3A', '13A' and '23A'.

ABOVE: The name of an office block at number 138, Jalan Ampang, Kuala Lumpur, incorporates those auspicious digits.

RIGHT: The double-happiness symbol displayed during Chinese weddings comprises two ideograms for 'happiness'.

Chinese schools

The first record of Chinese education is the establishment in 1815 of a Chinese school by the London Missionary Society in Melaka. The few other early schools taught in the local Chinese dialects. Mandarin education was spurred by the exile to Malaya in the 1880s of two members of Chinese Emperor Guangxu's Cabinet, who pressed the local Chinese community to expand the availability of education. The intellectual upsurge that occurred in China in 1919, known as the May Fourth Movement, served as a further spur to local Chinese-language education. Local community-funded Chinese schools continued to grow in number, despite temporary setbacks during the economic depression of the 1930s and the Japanese Occupation from 1941 to 1945. In 1961, with the enactment of the Education Act, the government began to provide primary education using Mandarin as the medium of instruction in national-type (Chinese) schools, a situation that has continued. Although the majority of pupils attending these schools are Chinese, non-ethnic Chinese children account for some 10 per cent.

There is no regular government funding for Chinese secondary schools, so most Chinese-educated primary pupils continue their education at Malay-medium schools. There are, however, some 60 independent secondary schools. Community involvement continues through statutory Parent-Teacher Associations and often boards of school managers who enlist the help of the community to raise funds.

TOP LEFT: The modern Lai Meng Sekolah Rendah Jenis Kebangsaan (Cina) (Chinese National-type Primary School) in Kuala Lumpur.

LEFT: Part of the Tan Kongsi, or clan house, in Penang was occupied by a typical pre-Independence Chinese-medium school.

ABOVE: A class in progress at the Tan Kongsi in 1954.

Chinese school numbers

Year	Total
1815	1
1920	494
1922	392
1930	738
1931	646
1946	1078
1957	1342

Year	Primary schools	Secondary schools
1997	1281	60
2003	1286	60

Source: Ministry of Education and Kua Kia Soong

An illustrated Chinese primary school text book.

Indian languages

Contacts between the Malay World and the civilizations of India began more than 2,000 years ago. By the 4th century CE, Sanskrit and other languages spoken in India were having a substantial impact on the Malay language through trade and cultural links. Major migration from India to the Malay Peninsula began in the late 18th century, peaked around 1920, and resulted in an Indian community speaking many languages. In recent times the dominance of Tamil has increased.

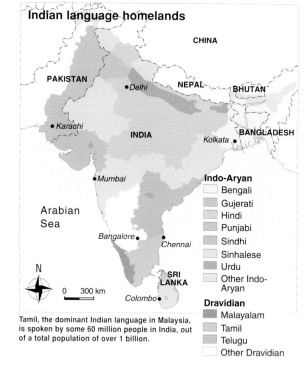

Indian language homelands

Tamil, the dominant Indian language in Malaysia, is spoken by some 60 million people in India, out of a total population of over 1 billion.

Indo-Aryan
- Bengali
- Gujerati
- Hindi
- Punjabi
- Sindhi
- Sinhalese
- Urdu
- Other Indo-Aryan

Dravidian
- Malayalam
- Tamil
- Telugu
- Other Dravidian

A long history

As early as 200 BCE, Indian pottery and beads already formed part of the trade system in mainland Southeast Asia. Indian traders and religious specialists have visited the ports and shrines of Kedah since the 4th century CE, if not earlier. The earliest evidence of Indian languages can be found in Sanskrit inscriptions discovered in Borneo dated to 400 CE.

The intensive contact between the Malay and Indian languages is evidenced by the large number of Sanskrit, Hindi and Tamil loan words used in modern Malay (see 'Characteristics of Malay'). When Westerners first arrived in Melaka in the 16th century, they found a large community of Gujerati merchants and other groups from Bengal, Golconda, Malabar and Coromandel. Although the imposition of European colonialism weakened these ancient links, it did not completely sever them. Even as late as the 18th century, Indians served as court officials and interpreters in the Perak sultanate.

The establishment of a British colony in Penang in 1786 led to a rapid increase in speakers of Indian languages in Malaya. Because Penang was under the jurisdiction of the British commercial and colonial system in India, much of the British army in Malaya comprised north Indian recruits. These soldiers had an impact on the development of Penang island's urban culture, and, as the British endeavour

Muslim Sepoy soldiers from north India served in British colonial Penang from 1786.

expanded, Indian communities of soldiers, police and clerks spread to almost all the towns and cities in the Malay Peninsula.

At the end of the 19th century, British officials and capitalists organized the massive migration of south Indians to Malaya to work as labourers on newly established rubber estates and to build the roads, railways and other public works necessary for the development of an export economy.

This massive movement of south Indians to Malaya peaked between 1911 and 1921, when the average growth of the Indian population in the Malay Peninsula alone was 6.1 per cent each year, mostly through immigration. By 1921, Indians constituted more than 15 per cent of the total population of Malaya. Although the proportion of Indians in the general Malaysian population has subsequently declined, Indians remain the second

Malaysian Indian distribution

Most Malaysian Indians live on the west coast of the Peninsula, where the first rubber plantations were located on which the majority of early Indian immigrants worked. Since the 1990s, Indian plantation labour has increasingly been replaced by foreign workers.

Malaysian Indian population

Group	Population
Tamil	1,405,215
Sikh/Punjabi	56,378
Telugu	38,993
Malayali	35,809
Pakistani	11,313
Bangladeshi	2,951
Sinhalese	1,641
Other Indian	41,477
Total	**1,593,777**

Source: Population and Housing Census 2000.

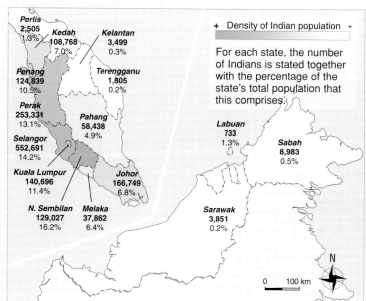

+ Density of Indian population -

For each state, the number of Indians is stated together with the percentage of the state's total population that this comprises.

Perlis 2,505 1.3%
Kedah 108,768 7.0%
Kelantan 3,499 0.3%
Penang 124,839 10.5%
Terengganu 1,805 0.2%
Perak 253,331 13.1%
Pahang 58,438 4.9%
Selangor 552,691 14.2%
Labuan 733 1.3%
Sabah 8,983 0.5%
Kuala Lumpur 140,696 11.4%
Johor 166,749 6.8%
N. Sembilan 129,027 16.2%
Melaka 37,862 6.4%
Sarawak 3,851 0.2%

Top: European planters like Henri Fauconnier, shown in 1910, learned Tamil in order to communicate with their workforce.

Above: Since the 1950s, many Indians have migrated from plantations to cities, which offer greater economic opportunities.

largest minority group after the Chinese (see 'Distribution of Chinese dialects'). In 2000, Indians constituted 7.6 per cent of the total population.

Although the Indian population of Malaysia is a multilingual group, speaking at least ten different languages belonging to two distinct language families, 88 per cent of Malaysia's Indians speak Tamil as their first language. Two other South Indian (Dravidian) languages are also spoken: Telugu and Malayalam. Most of these speakers also speak Tamil as a second or third language. The Telugu community has traditionally been concentrated in Teluk Intan, Perak, and certain parts of Kedah and Johor. The Punjabi-speaking population of Malaysia comprises only 4 per cent of the total Malaysian Indian group; other languages, such as Sinhalese, Sindhi, Gujerati and Bengali are spoken by even smaller communities.

Written in both the Punjabi and Roman scripts, a sign points the way to a Sikh temple (*Gurdwara*).

Education

All the Indian languages spoken in Malaysia are taught privately at home, in temples, and by the associations of each ethnolinguistic group.

The Appar National-type Tamil Primary School in Kuala Lumpur is one of the relatively small number of Tamil-medium schools located in urban areas.

Tamil is used as the medium of instruction in designated schools (see 'Tamil'). As there are no Tamil-medium secondary schools in Malaysia, pupils from these schools are channelled to national Malay-medium secondary schools. Here, students are able to continue to study Tamil as an optional subject under the Pupils' Own Language (POL) programme (see 'Language policy in action'). These classes are also available to those students who have not attended Tamil primary schools.

In the past there were as many as 50 Telugu-medium primary schools, however only two remain, both attached to Tamil schools in Bagan Datoh, Perak. These too are likely to close in the near future as a result of low student numbers. Telugu does, however, continue to be taught as a POL in certain schools in Kedah, Negeri Sembilan and Perak and until the 1990s, it was offered as a subject in public examinations, but this is no longer so. Punjabi, on the other hand, is still offered as a subject for the Penilaian Menengah Rendah (PMR) examination, despite not being taught in any government schools. There is, however, one private Punjabi school in Sentul, Kuala Lumpur.

Languages in action

All of these languages still serve as first languages and are also used as a means of communication and expression in religious meetings and prayers, and at cultural functions. Languages such as Telugu and Malayalam are used in weddings and other ceremonies of the group concerned. If a cultural show is staged by the members of an Indian community, the songs and dialogues are in their language, but the compere often speaks in both English and the Indian language, or in English exclusively, depending on the audience and environment. Sanskrit mantras are also used for prayers, particularly in temples.

Works in Tamil are published extensively in Malaysia, including journals, novels, short stories and poetry. Locally published materials in the other Indian languages are rare, although a small number of magazines and newsletters are printed in Punjabi. Nevertheless, Malaysian Indians are able to obtain materials from India. Other than Hindi movies, the main Indian language on Malaysian television is Tamil. Satellite broadcaster Astro transmits an Indian-language television channel, and two Indian language radio stations. Radio Television Malaysia's (RTM's) Radio Six also provides a 24-hour Indian language service, primarily in Tamil but with allocations for Malayalam and Telugu, as well as Hindi songs.

The First International Conference of Tamil Studies was held in Kuala Lumpur in 1966. Other Indian language conferences have since been held.

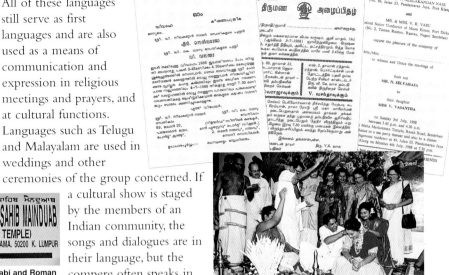

TOP: Trilingual Malayali wedding invitation printed in Malayalam (left), Tamil (centre) and English.

ABOVE: The ceremony at a Malayali wedding is conducted in both Sanskrit and Malayalam.

Programme cover from the 6th International Tamil Language Studies Conference, held in Kuala Lumpur in 1987.

Indian movies in Malaysia

Tamil movies, imported from India, have since the 1960s been the most popular type of Indian film with Malaysian cinema-goers and are played in a number of cinemas throughout the country. In the past cinemas playing only Indian films were common, and while their number has declined drastically over the years, cinema complexes continue to show Indian movies. Hindi movies too, are shown, and on television are given more airtime than Tamil films, as they are also popular with the larger Malay audience, and are broadcast with subtitles in Malay.

A limited number of Tamil films and dramas continue to be produced locally, including those by producer and director Sugan Panchatcharam, also renowned for his Malay television dramas.

TOP: The Coliseum cinema, built in 1920, continues to show both Hindi and Tamil movies.

ABOVE: Locally published Indian movie magazines printed in Tamil, Malay and English, are read by Indians and Malays.

LEFT: Sugan Panchatcharam directed the film *Naan Oru Malaysian* ('I am a Malaysian')

Tamil

With over a million speakers, Malaysia has the third-largest Tamil-speaking population in the world after India and Sri Lanka. Although many Tamils are descended from immigrants who arrived in the late 19th and early 20th centuries, the links between the Malay Peninsula and the Tamil homeland in southern India are ancient and continuous. This is reflected in the many Tamil loan words in Malay. Today, Tamil is the first language of the second-largest minority group in Malaysia, and maintains an important role in education, religion and the mass media.

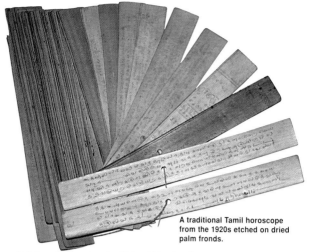

A traditional Tamil horoscope from the 1920s etched on dried palm fronds.

The logo of the Kuala Lumpur Tamil Youth Bell Club incorporates the club's motto '*uyarv:om*' ('we progress') at the top.

Tamil heritage

Tamil, the most widely distributed Dravidian language, has a large homeland in the Indian state of Tamil Nadu, and significant numbers of speakers overseas. Among the Dravidian languages, Tamil has the oldest literary heritage dating back to the *Tolkappiyam*, a comprehensive grammar book, written in the 3rd century BCE. The present Tamil script has long been in use, appearing in 7th-century inscriptions in India. For more than a thousand years, initially as a result of intra-regional trade, Tamil has contributed to the enrichment of the Malay language. A number of Tamil loan words are found in the contemporary Malay lexicon, including *kapal* (ship), *katil* (bed), *kedai* (shop), *ketumbar* (coriander), *kolam* (pond), *nelayan* (fisherman), and *peti* (box).

Tamil as used in Malaysia

The Tamil language has a 30-letter alphabet: 10 vowels, two diphthongs and 18 consonants. Some of these characters represent more than one sound, depending on their placement. For instance, the character '**க**' is pronounced 'k' where it occurs as the initial letter in a word, but elsewhere as either 'g' or 'h'. Tamil is diglossic, meaning that the written and spoken languages differ.

Tamil is agglutinative; that is, words are formed by the addition of affixes to root-words. Suffixes are by far the most predominant form of affix. Tense is indicated by the addition of suffixes to verb stems. Auxiliaries are always placed after the main verb, and adjectives are always placed before the nouns that they qualify. Tamil is an 'SOV' language, that is, sentences are formed so that word order is subject-object-verb. Tamil contains a large number of Sanskrit words, for example *pa:dam* (foot, related to the Latin-derived English word, pedal).

Malaysian Tamil differs from that spoken in India and the rest of the world. One difference is that in India, a large number of Tamil dialects exist, whereas in Malaysia there is little dialectical difference. Another feature of the

'Malaysianization' of Tamil is the borrowing of linguistic elements from Malay. This phenomenon may have arisen for a number of reasons, including necessity (such as the names of fruits and vegetables found only in Malaysia), the comparative ease of expression in Malay, the lack of equivalents of similar strength in Tamil, or purely as a matter of choice. The words so borrowed mainly refer to common

Brickfields: a traditional Tamil centre

Named after the brick kilns established by Kapitan China Yap Ah Loy, following the 1881 fire which razed most of Kuala Lumpur, Brickfields is one of three areas in Kuala Lumpur which traditionally had a heavy Tamil concentration: the others being Sentul and Kampung Pandan. Tamils came to the area mainly because of the construction of government staff quarters for middle-ranking civil servants, the creation of a housing colony for Kuala Lumpur Sanitary Board labourers, and the establishment of the Malayan Railways headquarters.

Ceylonese Tamils were among the first to arrive at the turn of the 20th century to clerical jobs in the railways and brick-built houses known as the Hundred Quarters. They built the first Hindu temple—the Sri Kandaswamy Kovil—in 1909 and, with Indian Tamil assistance, they established the Vivekananda Ashram, a centre for cultural and charitable activities in 1904. Tamil labourers arrived soon after. They occupied tiny quarters, known as

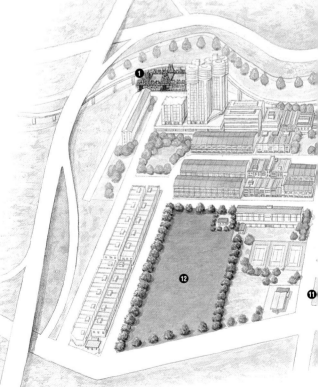

Malay loan words in Malaysian Tamil

Malay	Malaysian Tamil	Original Tamil	English
sarung	**saron**	kaili	sarong
bakul	**vakulu**	ku:tai	basket
campur	**campo:ru**	ce:r	mix
pasar	**pasa:ru**	cantai	market
kelambu	**kla:mbare**	kosuvahi	mosquito net
atap	**a:tta:ppu**	kurai	roof

Pronunciation: *a:* as the 'a' in 'father'; *e:* as the 'ere' in 'where'; *o:* as the 'aw' in 'thaw'; *u:* as the 'ou' in 'you'.

items, acts and descriptions involved in everyday life. They are treated as Tamil words for the placement of applicable suffixes and are generally pronounced with lengthened vowels.

In India, on the other hand, there is a far greater level of borrowing from English. This has not been the case in Malaysia. The reason for borrowing differs too: in India words are adopted to hide caste or regional identity, whereas Malaysian Tamil is spoken within a single speech community.

Tamil schools

The first Tamil-medium schools in the Malay Peninsula were established in the 19th century by missionary bodies. Government schools were founded in 1900, in Perak and Negeri Sembilan. Although some estate owners also set up schools in order to attract labour, it was not until 1912 that the establishment of schools on estates became compulsory where there were at least 10 eligible children; annual government grants were later made to these schools. By 1930, 333 Tamil primary schools

were operating in the estates. Training for Tamil teachers began in 1937. However, as the government at that time did not provide Tamil schools for the children of its own urban employees, many attended English-medium schools.

The situation improved after World War II. However, Tamil secondary schools have never been introduced, although Tamil pupils can continue their education in Malay-medium secondary schools subject to a one-year transition course. In 2003, the government selected 25 schools at which the learning of Tamil by non-Indian pupils and non-Tamil speaking Indians as an additional language has been encouraged, together with Chinese and Arabic.

Tamil language and literature are also offered at tertiary level. Universiti Malaya provides courses on Indian literature and culture using Tamil as the medium of instruction, and in 2000 started a degree programme in Tamil linguistics.

The name of the annual Thaipusam festival, celebrated by predominantly Tamil-speaking Hindus, is derived from the Tamil words *thai* (the month of the Tamil calendar in which the festival falls) and *pusam* (a star in the Tamil zodiac, the appearance of which coincides with the full moon).

the 'Coolie Lines', along Jalan Berhala on the site of the present day Palm Court condominium. Their presence led to the city fathers building a toddy (a sour alcoholic drink made from fermented coconut sap) shop nearby. The preponderance of Tamils in the area also led to the then Lido Cinema becoming synonymous with Tamil movies.

Tamil Christians established the Evangelical Lutheran Church in 1924, while Tamil Methodists later set up a church along the same road. These two churches and the local Catholic church continue to conduct services in Tamil.

Enclaves of Tamil language and culture such as Brickfields are gradually making way for modern business and residential centres, such that they may be lost entirely.

ABOVE: Built to house immigrant Tamil workers at the turn of the century, the Hundred Quarters have changed little since.

ABOVE RIGHT: The Vivekananda Tamil-medium Primary School, which opened in 1914, now shares its compound with the Malay-medium Vivekananda Secondary School.

LEFT: The Vivekananda Ashram centre, in front of which stands a statue of the north Indian Hindu saint, Swami Vivekananda.

CENTRE RIGHT: One of Brickfield's many Tamil restaurants, with a signboard in Malay, Tamil and English.

BOTTOM RIGHT: Sri Kandaswamy Temple remains a Ceylonese Tamil Hindu temple.

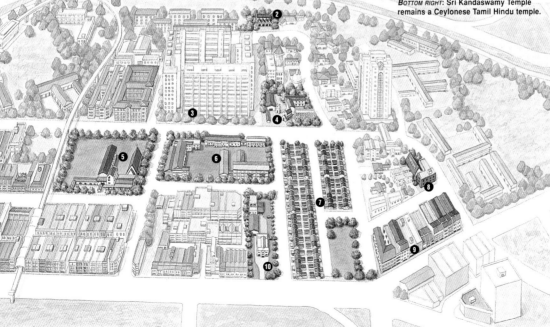

KEY:
1. Sri Kandaswamy Hindu Temple.
2. Temple of Fine Arts, centre for Tamil and other Indian performing arts.
3. Palm Court condominium, site of the former 'Coolie Lines'.
4. Our Lady of Fatimah Catholic Church.
5. Tamil Methodist Church.
6. Vivekananda Primary School and Secondary School.
7. The Hundred Quarters and field.
8. Zion Evangelical Lutheran Church.
9. Tamil shops and restaurants.
10. Vivekananda Ashram cultural centre.
11. Site of the Lido Cinema.
12. The Keretapi Tanah Melayu field, formerly the Malaysian Railways Recreation Club, of which Tamils formed the majority of members until its closure in the 1990s.

English

Malaysia is among the top ten English-speaking countries of the world in terms of speaker numbers. The status of English is tied to local history and to the language's embodiment as a symbol—a different symbol for different groups. Although a large number of Malaysians speak English, very few do so as their first language. Most speak colloquial Malaysian English, influenced by the grammar, vocabulary and pronunciation of the vernacular languages.

Commemorative plaque in Melaka written in the formal 19th-century English of the British administration.

Early influence

In 1811, Ahmad Rijaluddin, a Malay language teacher to British merchants, included English words in *Hikayat Perintah Negeri Benggala*, a report of his visit to Calcutta. Few survive in modern Malay.

English loan words in Ahmad's Hikayat	
English	**Malay**
adjutant	ajuten
admiral	hatmiral
judge	jerji
company	kampeni
council	kamsil
country	kateri
commander	kemendur
colonel	kernal
coachman	kucmin
lieutenant	leftan
platoon	palatan
frigate	pereget
pinnace	pinas
police	polis
soldier	sojar
troop	turub

History

British traders from India were active in Kedah and Perak in the 17th and 18th centuries, but only after an English settlement was founded on Penang in 1786 did the English language gain a foothold. The first English language school, Penang Free School, opened in 1816, but English loan words had found their way into Malay literature even earlier.

In the 19th century, access to English language schools in the Malay Peninsula, first founded by Christian missionaries, reflected divisive British colonial policy. In particular, very few Malays had access to English-language education in towns. Even in 1968, more than 65 per cent of pupils in English secondary schools were Chinese or Indians.

With the need for more English speakers to maintain the administrative and commercial system, English language education was offered to the Malay élite at the Malay College at Kuala Kangsar, founded in 1905. By the 1940s, English-medium schools were perceived as an effective way of preventing the growth of communalism. However, many Malay nationalists viewed English as a colonial language used to suppress their rightful aspirations.

Thus, after Independence in 1957, Malay was made the sole national language. English was retained as a second official language for the next 10 years to ensure a smooth transition from English to Malay. In fact, the position of English in some ways strengthened during those years. For example, in 1957 enrolment in English-medium secondary schools was 48,235 but by 1967, it had soared to 349,121. Tertiary institutions provided further incentive for English study.

In 1970, the implementation of the National Education Policy drastically reduced the role of English. From 1982, all government English-medium secondary schools became Malay-medium schools (although English was still taught as an individual subject), by which time the university system had also switched to the Malay medium.

However, concerns that English language competency amongst young Malaysians had declined led to the re-introduction of English as the medium of instruction for the teaching of mathematics and science in all schools, in 2003.

English-language (*Bahasa Inggeris*, in Malay) courses are popular throughout the country.

Contemporary English

Outside the educational setting, Malay has replaced English in many fields. Virtually all government offices are exclusively Malay-language-oriented. The vast majority of Malaysians, and particularly those under 40, can speak, read and write Malay. More Malay newspapers are sold than English ones.

However, the increasing importance of English as a global language and Malaysia's commitment to a global economy has meant that the position of English, while reduced in some fields, overall remains strong. It is still indispensable in higher education; although in public universities lectures and tutorials are mostly conducted in Malay, reading materials are largely in English. Further, the numerous private universities and colleges established from the 1990s onwards offer tertiary education in English.

Malaysia's corporate world is mainly English-speaking, and English-language competence remains a prerequisite for many careers, not only professional and governmental, but also in areas such as popular entertainment (see 'Language policy in action').

While the number of English speakers has increased dramatically since Independence in 1957, there has been much discussion about the quality of their English, with many people claiming the standard of English spoken in the country has fallen. Nevertheless, the percentage of Malaysians who are competent, proficient speakers of English has increased. To a large extent this is due to the fact that almost all Malaysians now have access to English

Malaysian English

English is spoken by many Malaysians as a second (or third) language. Colloquial Malaysian English includes grammatical features and word order influenced by Malay, Chinese and Tamil. Verb–subject agreement is often ignored, as are tenses, as Chinese and Tamil do not have such grammar rules. As for pronunciation, the final consonant is often dropped (for example, 'want' is spoken as 'wan'). A generous addition of Malay and Chinese words enhances the lexicon of this indigenized variety of English. Traditional English morphology is often reduced, with inflectional and aspectual affixes deleted. Sentence inversion is often dispensed with and sentences become elliptical.

Malaysians not proficient in this form of English usually speak pidgin English, a variant normally heard in shopping areas in cities and larger towns. This form of speech has a vocabulary that is mostly English with a mixture of words from other languages, particularly Malay. The grammatical rules of pidgin English are much influenced by Malay and speakers have no regard for tenses, number or gender. The pronunciation and intonation may be akin to Malay, Chinese or Indian, depending on who speaks it.

Most tourists can understand the Malaysian English spoken by traders in Kuala Lumpur's Petaling Street.

Standard English	Malaysian English
How can you be like that?	Where can like that one?
How did you get here?	By what you come ah?
I got here by taking a taxi.	Taxi lah! What else!
Do you want this or don't you?	You wan this a not?
You are very fussy.	You ah! So fussy one lah!
You are very rich.	Wah! You so rich ah!
Will you please come over here?	Come lah!
It's very cheap.	Ai yah! Very cheap only!
I'm going home.	I'm going back now.
I'm taking her to the airport.	I'm sending her to the airport.
Switch on the light.	On the light.
It's my day off.	It's my off-day.
What shall we do?	So how?
Should we wipe our faces?	Mop the face is it?

English in Sabah and Sarawak

Students during an English-language class at Gaya College, Sabah in 1966.

The Malaysian English spoken in Sabah and Sarawak differs from that used in Peninsular Malaysia. The former follows the intonation of the indigenous languages prevalent there including, for example, the neutralization of the pronunciation of consonant clusters.

Standard pronunciation	East Malaysian pronunciation
stop	setop
big	beg
go	go (with a wide open 'o')
office	ufis

from primary school, if not earlier. It may also be attributed to the popularity of English-language music, television and films, which have led to some Americanization of the English spoken in Malaysia.

Varieties of English

English in Malaysia has been categorized into three levels: the acrolect, the mesolect and the basilect. The acrolect is the variety that is near-native, and not many Malaysians fall into this category. Only those educated in core English-speaking countries from early schooling up to university may be found to speak the acrolect variety. Although considerable prestige is given to speaking such English, only a tiny percentage of Malaysians are proficient in it.

Most academicians, professionals and other English-educated Malaysians speak mesolect English. Malaysian English (ME) belongs to the mesolect. It is Malaysian English that is used in daily interaction.

English words in Malay

Numerous English words have been incorporated into the Malay lexicon, with only minor changes in spelling.

The Malay translation of 'ticket counter' is easily recognizable on a sign in Kuala Lumpur's Sentral train station (top). The Malay word for 'taxi' is 'teksi' (above), and for 'post', 'pos' (right).

This variety has much in common with the English spoken in the other former British colonies of Asia. But in Malaysian English, both the lexicon and the grammar show the influence of Malaysia's local languages, especially Malay and Chinese variants.

Sociolinguists have divided ME into ME I and ME II. The higher of these, ME I, is the colloquial form of English that Malaysians use with one another. It reflects some use of correct grammar, but with many local features, especially from Malay. ME II is the pidginized Malaysian variety of English. Pronunciation is often modified by the influence of the speaker's first language. Some grammatical particles are borrowed directly from local languages. For instance, *la* and *a*, from either Malay or Chinese, have a wide range of functions in Malaysian English. Even English particles often have a range of syntactic functions; the role of 'also' in Malaysian English marks concessive clauses as in 'sit all day also no fish' meaning 'even if you sit all day, you won't catch any fish', and universal quantification: 'Which way also can?' meaning 'Can I take another route?'

Many Malaysians speak English only as a language of wider communication, with little training in the language, and consequently a reduced vocabulary. In some cases, this ad hoc use of English may even be considered a pidgin English, especially when some native English speakers claim they are unable to understand it. In fact, many speakers adapt their speech variety to the social setting, sliding back and forth from formal English to Malaysian English, and even to pidgin English when necessary. The frequency of code-switching from Malay, Tamil or Chinese to English is facilitated by the wide range of English varieties from which to choose (see 'Language usage').

English pronouns in Malay conversations

The egalitarian English personal pronouns 'I' and 'you' often replace the Malay terms due to the complicated system of Malay pronouns, which vary according to the status of both the speaker and the person being addressed as well as dialects, leading to a very wide choice of terms. In Malay, the use of personal pronouns is even unacceptable in certain instances, especially when addressing a person senior to oneself. Thus, particularly among friends, the more neutral English pronouns are very popular. The question of status is eliminated, and there are no difficult choices to be made.

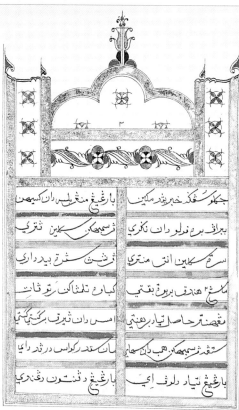

1. A copy of the *Hikayat Patani* (History of Patani) dated 1783, folded accordion-style.

2. Double illuminated frontispiece of a copy of the narrative poem *Syair Ken Tambuhan*, in the collection of the library of Leiden University, the Netherlands.

3. *Hukum Jenayah Karangan Sheikh Abdul Rauf Fansuri* (Criminal Law by Sheikh Abdul Rauf Fansuri).

4. Illuminated page from *Hikayat Nabi Mikraj* (Story of the Prophet's Ascension to Heaven).

5. Opening page of the *Aqa'id of Al-Nasaf*, the oldest surviving Malay manuscript, dating from 1590.

6. Stories from the Malay literary classic *Hikayat Hang Tuah* feature in a 1953 edition of *Majalah Comic Melayu* (Malay Comic Magazine).

LITERARY HERITAGE

In the absence of an indigenous written tradition, oral literature thrived and continues to survive among the indigenous peoples of Malaysia: the Malays, Orang Asli and numerous Sarawak and Sabah groups. The oral tradition encompasses a wide range of genres from folk tales to legends, romances to epics, and poetry to proverbs. The Malay oral tradition was influenced by early Indian epics such as the *Mahabharata* and the *Ramayana*. Originally confined to the Sanskritic tradition, this Hindu influence later included other traditions, such as those of southern India including the *Hikayat Mara Karma*, *Hikayat Pancatenderan* and *Hikayat Gul Bakawali*, which became part of the Malay literary heritage. The Panji cycle from Hindu Java was another source for Malay romantic tales. Malay poetry too, was—and remains—highly developed with a large number of forms. Some of these are still popular, and use of the *pantun* in particular has even spread to other languages.

The Chinese and Indian communities who later emigrated to what is now Malaysia brought with them long-established written traditions from their homelands, but only began to write locally produced works in the 19th century (see 'Modern Literature'). Among the Malays, the written tradition commenced with the advent of Islam in the Peninsula—at the latest by the 15th century—and the adoption of the Arabic-based Jawi script. This tradition was influenced not only by the pre-existing indigenous oral tradition, but also by newer sources from the Muslim world. Works produced ranged from theological literature and works on governance and legal digests, to romances, moral anecdotes, popular tales of the Islamic prophets, and animal tales, and were written in a variety of styles from the religiously scholarly to the popular Hikayat form.

The Malay sultanates produced their own literary tradition, as scribes were employed to record the significant events of the time. These histories were later copied and recopied, with subsequent scribes both adding to and subtracting from the original texts. The celebrated *Sulalatus al-Salatin*, popularly known as the *Sejarah Melayu* (The Malay Annals), may have had a core recorded during the Melaka period (1401–1511), but it is said to have been rewritten in 1536 and revised in 1612. Elements of this work were used and expanded upon in the landmark *Hikayat Hang Tuah*. Both of these works have been nominated as world heritage items under the United Nations Educational, Scientific and Cultural Organization (UNESCO) 'Memory of the World' programme.

Dharmawangsa and Krishna transformed into giants in a scene from a Wayang Kulit performance of a story from the epic *Mahabharata*.

Malay oral traditions

Until the 20th century, written Malay was mainly confined to a limited circle. The literature of the majority of the population, beyond the royal courts, was preserved in the oral tradition. The spread of formal education marked a decline in the role of this tradition. However, a rich variety of genres, both sung and spoken, had already emerged, some of which have been preserved to the present day.

Professor Sweeney's book records the oral works of Mat Nor, a Tok Selampit (storyteller who plays the rebab while reciting his tales) in Kelantan (inset).

Endurance of oral tradition

The oral tradition has survived, and even thrived, among certain segments of Malay society, where it has now for decades existed side by side with the written tradition, and more recently with more modern electronic media. The traditional oral culture has been retained in rural communities and, to a much more limited extent, also in urban centres. It continues to prosper in particular among rural Malays engaged in agrarian or maritime economic activities. The tradition not only serves to provide entertainmen,t but also has a ritual and cere-monial role, thereby helping to ensure the stability of communal life. In addition, myths and legends (see 'Malay myths and legends') legitimize traditional customs and beliefs.

Malay folklore

Malay folklore continues to be passed on through the oral tradition. In Kelantan, the oral tradition remains comparatively strong among the rural Malays despite the objection of Islamic author-ities who deem certain traditional practices and observances to be at odds with the religion. These practices, which may be classified as behavioural traditions, nevertheless survive, albeit often in a somewhat altered form, as they are enmeshed in the life-rhythm of the rural population.

Ceremonies and rituals traditionally mark the beginning of the planting season, and the fishing period. Many Malays believe in the concept of the rice soul (*semangat padi*). The pre-planting rituals

Certain forms of oral traditions are no longer practised. These include *puja pantai* ceremonies conducted by Malay fisherman to appease the spirits and ensure a bountiful catch.

The Malay oral tradition is preserved in ceremonies such as engagements and marriage negotiations, where *pantun* are often recited.

Oral traditions in ritual
Oral traditions are perpetuated in Malay rituals, such as the curing ritual known as Main Puteri, shown here. The shaman (centre, holding the tray) invokes the spirit that is causing the patient's illness so that he may offer appeasement. He recites *mantera* in archaic Malay, often unintelligible to listeners. Similar ceremonies are also conducted prior to performances such as Mak Yong, Menora and Wayang Kulit.

express the farmers' concern to preserve the continued well-being of this rice soul. Rituals such as *puja pantai* or *menyemah hantu laut* were tradition-ally performed by fisherfolk to ensure a bountiful catch as well as their safety at sea.

Various harvest observances reflect a feeling of gratitude and joy. Thanksgiving rituals featuring both Islamic elements and inherited traditions are presided over by a shaman (*pawang*). These include various forms of traditional performance, such as shadow play (Wayang Kulit), folk theatre (Mak Yong and Menora) and dancing, as well as traditional pastimes including kite-flying (*main wau*), top-spinning (*main gasing*) or drum-beating (*main rebana besar* or *keretok*). Malay villagers in other states also traditionally observed post-harvest rituals and celebrations, including Belotah in southern Perak, Joget Lambak and Dondang Sayang in Penang and Melaka, Tari Endang in Ulu Tembeling, Pahang, and Main Balai in Ulu Dungun, Terengganu.

Verse forms

The majority of oral traditions comprise rhyming verse. Although many such traditions have been lost over the course of the 20th century as a result of increasing literacy, one form—the *pantun* (see 'Traditional Malay poetic forms')—remains popular. The pantun is utilized in various ways, such as

Oral traditions are central to Wayang Kulit performances, both in the rites preceding a performance and in the repertoire of the puppeteer.

Stories for the Menora, a dance-theatre form derived from the name of its heroine, are handed down through oral transmission.

Mak Yong, an ancient Malay dance-theatre form associated with the Kelantan royal court, incorporates formal as well as improvised spoken text.

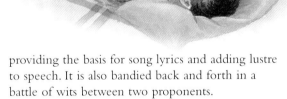

providing the basis for song lyrics and adding lustre to speech. It is also bandied back and forth in a battle of wits between two proponents.

Similarly, *perbilangan* are two-line proverbial sayings which rhyme internally and finally, such as '*Siakap senohong gelama ikan duri/Bercakap bohong lama-lama mencuri.*' ('Giant sea perch, large threadfin, jewfish and sea catfish/Telling lies will eventually lead to stealing.')

Nursery rhymes are also popular, especially those which teach limb movements: 'Pok Amai-Amai' encourages clapping, and 'Itu Bulan, Itu Bintang' teaches a baby to point.

Repertoire of stories

The repertoire of oral stories in Malay, recounted and preserved by professional storytellers, consists of a varied collection for different occasions and audiences. Indigenous animal tales, while primarily for entertainment, also included explanations of the origin of various things in the everyday Malay landscape, particularly the forest; for example how the python lost its poison, and how the tiger acquired its stripes. The best-known animal story is that of Sang Kancil, the wily mouse deer.

Romances, or rather, fairy tales, also feature prominently. Structurally, these are similar to the folk rendition of the Hindu epics such as the *Ramayana* and *Mahabharata*, dwelling on the adventures of royal heroes with wondrous powers who overcome all kinds of obstacles (see 'The *Ramayana*' and 'The *Mahabharata*'). Audiences become enthralled by the vivid and picturesque descriptions of the characters, the grandeur of the festivities and the action-packed battles. Stock phrases and poetic expressions punctuate the stories at crucial and dramatic points. The recitation of a single romance traditionally took two or three nights. Romances of local provenance include *Malim Deman*, *Anggun Che Tunggal*, *Raja Dewa* and *Terung Pipit*. The humorous stories of Pak Belalang, Pak Kadok, Si Luncai, Lebai Malang, Pak Pandir, Abu Nawas or Mat Jenin have parallels in stories from India and the Middle East, but the metamorphoses undergone by their characters and settings from the original form make them truly local. The Panji stories (see 'Panji romances'), too, are romances, and also feature in the Malay oral tradition. Other tales may have originated from Sumatra, such as the *kaba* (a Minangkabau oral performance tradition of west Sumatra) in *Hikayat Putri Bongsu dan Malim Deman*.

A scene from a Sang Kancil tale: the mouse deer tricked a vain, foolish tiger into wearing a python, believing it was King Solomon's prized belt.

Storytelling styles

The art of storytelling was an important part of traditional Malay entertainment. Professional raconteurs were called *penglipur lara* (soother of woes), but were also known by specific names in various localities. Storytellers who survived until the mid-20th century included those known as Awang Batil in Perlis, who recited tales while tapping rhythmically on a metal bowl (*batil*); Tok Selampit in Kelantan, who provided music accompaniment on the rebab (a stringed instrument) while telling stories; and the melodious Tukang Cerita (storyteller), who recounted long tales lasting two or three nights in Ulu Tembeling, Pahang, and Ulu Dungun, Terengganu.

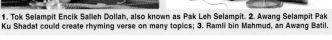

1. Tok Selampit Encik Salleh Dollah, also known as Pak Leh Selampit. 2. Awang Selampit Pak Ku Shadat could create rhyming verse on many topics; 3. Ramli bin Mahmud, an Awang Batil.

Orang Asli oral traditions

In the absence of indigenous writing systems, oral traditions have played an important role in transmitting cultural values and norms, as well as indigenous knowledge within each of the Orang Asli communities of Peninsular Malaysia, and continue to do so. These traditions include myths, legends, origin stories, and oral histories. All of these are, for the Orang Asli, records of actual events. Each group has its own versions, although there are many common themes and shared elements.

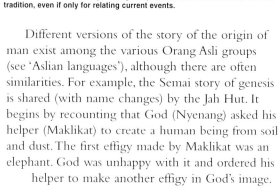

A community gathering in Kampung Poh, Bidor, Perak to disseminate news of land encroachment. Such gatherings help ensure the continuation of the oral tradition, even if only for relating current events.

The late Batin Long, formerly headman and shaman of the Jah Huts in Kampung Pian, Kuala Krau, was renowned as a storyteller.

Storytellers

Among the Orang Asli, it is the community elders and shamans who carry on the oral literary tradition. Prior to the mid-1950s it was common for the elders to narrate these traditions to their children before they went to bed. These stories served not only to captivate the minds of the storytellers' young audiences, but also to imbue them with socio-cultural values.

Stories were, and to a more limited extent still are, also told by shamans to their followers as part of the process of learning to become a shaman. Shamans must know a vast amount of orally transmitted knowledge, particularly that concerning illness, including stories, ritual songs, spells and charms, prohibitions, taboos, customs, and values, as well as ethics and morals.

Many Orang Asli continue to make a living selling jungle produce such as bamboo. Their stories reflect this continuing close relationship with the natural environment.

Origin tales

In particular, a shaman is required to know the origin stories of mankind, animals, plants and geographical features. A shaman must also know the origin tales of supernatural beings. These are believed to be the source of illnesses; a person will become ill if his or her soul is captured, or body penetrated, by a supernatural being, and is healed when a shaman curses that being.

Jah Hut shaman and storyteller Batin Long's depiction of Bes Ta'on, one of the *bes* (illness-causing spirits).

Different versions of the story of the origin of man exist among the various Orang Asli groups (see 'Aslian languages'), although there are often similarities. For example, the Semai story of genesis is shared (with name changes) by the Jah Hut. It begins by recounting that God (Nyenang) asked his helper (Maklikat) to create a human being from soil and dust. The first effigy made by Maklikat was an elephant. God was unhappy with it and ordered his helper to make another effigy in God's image. Once the man-like effigy was completed, God asked Maklikat to carry a soul (*kloog*, literally 'breath' in Semai) to it, to give it life. This Maklikat did, carrying it in his closed hand, but out of curiosity since he could not feel anything in his hand, and wanted to see what he was holding—he opened his fingers to look inside, thereby allowing the soul to escape. The lost soul became the father of evil and, having been born before, and being invisible to, humans it remains superior to them. It is for this reason that a shaman has a difficult task in protecting human beings from evil spirits.

Stories also serve to inform about the origins of certain basic values and customs. The Batek people, for instance, believe in equality among all earthly creatures. Their society draws its egalitarian inspiration from the story of superhuman beings called *hala'* and the creation of mankind and other living creatures, wherein the earth was inhabited by

The Tale of Pak Pandir
The comic character of Pak Pandir appears in both Malay and Orang Asli folklore, as a Malay in the former, and an Orang Asli in the latter.

Pak Pandir lived deep in the jungle. One day, at the request of his pregnant wife, he tried to catch a hornbill.

The bird was so large that it flew away with him, until he lost his grip and fell onto a Raja's palace.

The Raja thought Pak Pandir might be a super-human, but first set him three tasks as a test. The first was to bring him a buffalo.

Pak Pandir admitted he did not know what a buffalo was, so the Raja informed him that it ate grass. Misunderstanding, Pak Pandir returned with a grass cutter.

Asked to bring a white-capped imam and a bearded religious teacher, Pak Pandir mistakenly brought a pipit bird and a goat.

the hala' before the first human was created. The immortal hala' neither ate nor grew old. Even when the first human beings were created, many hala' still lived on earth in human and animal form. The story recounts that it was the hala' who created food for human beings, in particular the wild yam, the Batek staple food. Indeed, these tubers were once hala'. After man was created, some of the *hala' asal* (original hala') noticed that there was nothing for humans to eat. So they ordered other hala' to become tubers. These hala' left their human bodies behind, and sent their shadow-souls to earth into newly formed tuberous bodies. However, after a while, these hala' began to miss their relatives, and cry, so they sent their shadow-souls up to the sky, leaving the tubers behind.

Moral and cultural tales

Moral lessons often feature in Orang Asli myths. One such lesson—of the apparently worthless being highly valuable—is popular among the Semai and the Temiar. This is the tale of Bah Lujch, the last child of a family. Inferior to his brothers and sisters, and afflicted with a skin disease, Bah Lujch felt victimized and left his family. He went on to learn healing skills and other indigenous lore, and returned to use these to save his arrogant brothers and sisters.

The oral tradition also explains the existence of cultural traits. For example, a story that is to a large extent shared by several of the Orang Asli sub-groups seeks to explain why the Orang Asli and the Malays are distinct despite their many similarities. In the Semelai version God (Tohan), in attempting to create man, accidentally created two males who lived in harmony relying for food on game, particularly wild boar meat. On a number of occasions, as the elder brother handed over a piece of meat to his sibling, the meat fell to the ground. The brothers thus concluded that God had forbidden the younger brother from eating boar. The younger brother, worried that he would starve, therefore went to look for new sources of food. He brought with him a letter from God that became the source of ritual power and the key to new knowledge (*kepanayan areh*). Sometime later, he adopted Islam and became a Malay. His elder brother remained a Semelai.

Humorous stories

While primarily for entertainment, comical tales often contain both philosophic and moral elements. In the story of Pet, for example, the moral is that people should not underestimate small threats; indeed the monkeys in the tale (there being a sufficiently large number of them) are portrayed as constituting a serious threat to human life. Such tales are similar to Malay folklore; there has even been some borrowing and customization of Malay characters, such as Pak Pandir.

Oral histories

The Orang Asli usually recount their history in the form of legends, and focus in particular on the hardships faced by the Orang Asli community. One such history relates to the war (known to the Semai as *praaq sangkil*) between the Semai and Malay (specifically, the Rawa from Sumatra) slave raiders that occurred prior to the intervention of the British in Perak. At first, the Semai managed to hold off the raiders. However, they returned in greater numbers, forcing the Semai to flee and break up into smaller groups to avoid detection. While running away from the raiders, the Semai prohibited couples from having children, and any that were born were killed, as their crying would attract the attention of the raiders. This oral history explains why the Semai live in small groups scattered across most of Perak. It also helps explain why the total population of Semai, and indeed of the Orang Asli as a whole, is very small, despite the community having populated the Peninsula for several thousand years.

Other oral histories relate Orang Asli life from pre-colonial times through the colonial era, Japanese Occupation and Malayan Emergency, and their involvement in nation building to the present day.

Functions of the oral tradition

ABOVE: The creative Orang Asli oral tradition is used for both entertainment and ritual purposes. Semai folk in Kampung Kuala Tual, Pahang, enjoy listening to an elder narrating some of his past exploits.

RIGHT: A Jah Hut shaman (right) performing the *benisoy* healing ritual on an infant. He is holding a small statue with which he captures the evil spirit causing the disease, and which he then discards in the river.

Folklore characters are often portrayed by Mah Meri craftsmen in wood carvings.

Finally—having been misled by the villagers—he returned with a tiny seluang fish instead of a tapah fish. The Raja's rage became uncontrollable.

The Raja sentenced Pak Pandir to death by having his head peeled, and left him in a chicken coop overnight so the chickens would peck his brain.

As he was innocent, Pak Pandir miraculously recovered by the morning. The Raja apologized to him and offered his daughter's hand in marriage.

Pak Pandir declined, summoned the hornbill, and returned to his village. As soon as he arrived home, his wife gave birth.

Oral traditions of Sarawak

Other than the Malays and Melanau, who adopted the Arabic script upon conversion to Islam, the indigenous peoples of Sarawak never developed writing. Thus all literature was oral, and this formed the basis of their cultural practices. Similar themes are found throughout the oral literature of the various ethnic groups: the relationship of the people to their past, particularly their ancestry, and the spirit world, especially its influence on food production and health. Rituals often accompany the recitation of oral literature.

ABOVE LEFT: Paddy planting ceremonies such as this honour Pulang Gana.

ABOVE RIGHT: Victors of a contest to find the young Iban man most worthy of representing the warrior-hero, Keling.

Iban tales

Iban myths comprise narratives about the Iban pantheon, spirits and cultural heroes, and provide the Iban with a sense of their past and heritage. Iban *jerita tuai* (ancient tales or myths) are normally prose narratives, although some are recited in poetic form known as *pengap* (or *timang*) at rituals or ceremonies. Iban creation myths and stories of cultural heroes explain the origin of landscapes, rice cultivation and customs and traditions. They also provide an explanation as to why certain customs are observed or rituals held, especially those relating to the agricultural cycle, the establishment of longhouse communities, communication with other groups, and regulation of community life.

During Gawai Batu, a ritual to inaugurate a new planting season, the earth spirit Pulang Gana is invoked with sacrifices and offerings made in his honour. Nevertheless, the myth attributes the origin of rice and other plants to other spirits, such as Simpang-Impang, Siti Permani, or the offspring of the god Petara and his wife Seti Awa. The myths of another deity, Singalang Burung, provide the Iban with their ancestry, teach them the way to prosperity and success, and provide them with a social order for longhouse life.

The Iban place great emphasis on ancestry. *Tusut* (family trees) enable them to unravel their genealogy, the origin of which is usually a mythical spirit. Tusut provide a cultural map for the Iban, validating their status and position in society, and are used to link different people within a community. They are recited, often in a poetic manner, as the names mentioned lend themselves to rhyme. The concept of space is also expressed in myths, such as those

featuring the Iban warrior, Keling. As is usual with oral traditions, the myth has several local versions.

Other traditions are recited or chanted on particular occasions, such as *pengap* (incantations) at festivals, and *sampi* (ritual incantations and prayers). The *pelian* (a healing rite) is recited by the *manang* (specialist curer) during healing rituals, and the *sabak* (dirge) is recited at wakes. More frequently heard are those performed for entertainment, such as *renong*, songs of merriment sung in ceremonies to honour guests. Moral stories are also included in the corpus of Iban oral literature, especially in *apoi suloi*, which make use of comedo-tragic characters.

Bidayuh tradition

The Bidayuh comprise a number of distinct local groups, and are the southerly neighbours of the Iban (see 'Bidayuh, Melanau and Kajang sub-families'). The Bidayuh oral tradition is distinct from that of the Iban, notwithstanding their similar cultural bases; both occupy similar terrain, form longhouse communities with a focus on agriculture, believe in the spirit world, and in the past engaged in head-taking.

Bidayuh ceremonies, rituals and dances all have their basis in the oral tradition. For example, the planting season is marked by a ritual during which souls of paddy are invoked through the spirits, Sikara and Sigura, who will ensure that the coming planting season is bountiful. Even the dances performed at celebrations have legends and folk tales as their themes. 'Jangen' tells the melancholy story of an orphaned girl, while the legend of the duel between Sawan Madu and Tangkilang Remang for the hand of Dayang Madu is enacted in a dance imitating the movements of the eagle. 'Tulak Bala', which is

Iban elder Meramat anak Embon swings whilst singing the epic 'Sugi'.

In the absence of a traditional written form, Iban oral literary elements were often incorporated as designs in *pua kumbu* (literally 'blanket wrap'), the example of which below makes overt homage to the god of war and his attendants. Pictographic wooden tablets (*papan turai*) (bottom right) served as memory aids for recitation by shamans (*lemambang*).

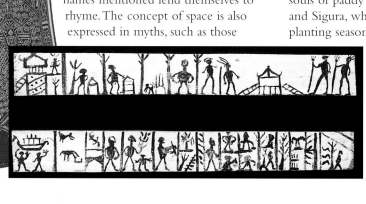

performed to rid the village of an epidemic, tells of a man who died in such an epidemic and serves to teach the community the ritual with which to combat such pestilence.

Tales from northern Sarawak

The many ethnic groups found in the upper and innermost regions of Sarawak include the Kenyah, Kayan, Kelabit and Lun Bawang (see 'Northern Sarawak languages'). The diversity of these groups is reflected in their varied oral traditions, although many commonalities are to be found among them.

Epics, rather than myths, predominate these oral traditions, highlighting the preoccupation of these groups with their migration from their respective places of origin, such as the Kayan *Apo Kayan* and the Kenyah *Usun Apau* (or *Apau Julau*). Heroic epics are additionally appealing to the northern Sarawak groups as a result of their distinctive stratified social structures, in which leadership is in the hands of an upper class. Among the Kayan and Kenyah, this group is called the *Maren* and the *Keta'u*, respectively. The heroes depicted in the epics reinforce the special position and qualities of these upper class groups.

The recitation of epics is in a poetic language, proficiency in which is much honoured by the Kayan in particular. It is not an ordinary language, but one which is cultivated by both the singer and the audience over long periods of socialization. Audience participation in reciting the chorus line (*nyabei*) at the end of each stanza is a unique feature of Kayan epic-telling. Well-known Kayan epics include *Aban Balan*, *Usung Bayung*, *Litung Aren* and '*Taqna Lawe*, each of which has a distinctive tune to accompany it.

A specialized poetic language or register is also used in Kenyah epics, which include *Balan Nyanding* and *Oyau Abing*. *Buring Bangaw* is a heroic tale alluding to the Usun Apau, the place of origin of the Kenyah. The Kelabit sing their epics, such as the *Sedadai*, *Adih* and *Sedarir*, in a specialized

Rabung (spirit images carved from sago pith) are used to capture spirits by Melanau shamans.

manner. Among the Lun Bawang, a genre similar to the epics of the other groups is the *buek*, which comprises a combination of history and mythology. Other Lun Bawang story forms include the *laba* (short, humorous tales about ordinary life); *nawar adaÌ* or *nawar mangai* (chants seeking good omens) and songs such as *benging* (for courtship), *tulu* (wedding songs) and *tidum* (lullabies).

The Malay and Melanau traditions

As with the Peninsular Malays, the conversion to Islam of the coastal Malays and Melanaus has not rid them of their pre-Islamic heritage (see 'Malay oral traditions'). Rituals and celebrations are often associated with planting and harvest times by these communities, which continue to be predominantly involved in farming and fishing.

Malay fishermen near Kuching enact the harvesting of a type of shellfish known as *ambal* (unique to this location) in a workplay called *mencari ambal*. 'Doh Beladoh Lanang' is the title of a song sung by residents along Sungai Batang Samarahan who go out in groups of between 40 and 60 people to collect the ambal, usually during the northeast monsoon period. When they spot the shellfish, participants are required to abstain from smiling, carrying an umbrella, wearing shoes and speaking foul language.

Healing ceremonies similar to those of the Peninsular Malaysia Orang Asli are held by the Melanau (see 'Orang Asli oral traditions'). The *dukun* (traditional healer) orders a spirit image to be carved from sago pith. To the accompaniment of gongs, drums and singing, the spirit of the illness is then transferred to this carving, known as a *rabung*, which is subsequently set adrift in the river.

Another oral tradition of the Melanau associated with illness (or rather, the prevention of it) is the *kaul beliseng*, an annual ceremony to appease the spirits that cause disease and death.

The Borneo Literature Bureau recorded and published a number of Sarawakian folk tales.

Performance styles

1. Following mourning, an Iban shaman chants as he prepares to sever the deceased's plant counterpart (*beserara' bungai*).
2. A Saribas Iban genealogist (*tukang tusut*) laying out cigarette wrappers while reciting the genealogy of a couple during a marriage ceremony. The wrappers signify the descending generations of the couple's families from a common ancestor.
3. Bidayuh priestess-shamans (*dayung boris*) swinging together as they sing the *boris*, or ritual invocation.
4. Kenyah sung poetry makes use of a distinct linguistic register.
5. The Kejaman woman on the right is seen here singing with a typical shrieking refrain.

Oral traditions of Sabah

Shared influences have led to similarities between Sabah oral traditions and those elsewhere in the region. This is apparent from the numerous folk tales and legends, such as creation myths, preserved by the various Sabah ethnic groups. This oral literature is recited on numerous occasions, including ceremonies conducted by priestesses, who combine the roles of ritual specialist, faith healer and spirit medium.

Regional similarities

Similarities between Sabah folk tales—such as that of Teruna Luntit and Puteri Dumpurak, the attribution of the origin of plants to the dissected remains of a deity, and tales of the mouse deer, or Pelanduk, tales of the Bajau and Kadazandusun—and those of other parts of the region attest to common influences. Agricultural rites, such as the belief in the rice soul and its preservation to ensure a bountiful crop, are also embedded in the common cultural roots of the region as a whole. Similarities in the oral traditions of the Malays and Bajaus may be a result of the adherence of both of these groups to the Muslim faith, although links between the non-Muslim Kadazandusun and the Malays hint at even older ties. Nevertheless, despite their similarities, striking differences remain.

A Bonggi storyteller keeps a small audience enthralled in Kampung Sabur, Banggi.

Priestesses: repositories of oral literature

Priestesses traditionally played a central role in Sabah society, and are still revered today. They have the triple role of ritual specialist, faith healer and spirit medium. Reciting *rinait* (lengthy sacred texts) accompanied by rituals, they act as mediators between the living and spirit worlds, and thus dictate traditional customs and practices. Their services are essential at a variety of ceremonies including festivals, the blessing of a new longhouse, burials, and ritual healing of the sick. Their skills take many years of apprenticeship to master.

Traditional themes

A wide variety of stories exist within Sabah's oral literature, although some themes are more common than others. The traditional belief system of the Kadazandusun, the largest of Sabah's ethnic group (see 'Language groups of Sabah'), infiltrates much of their oral literature, notwithstanding that most of them have now converted to Christianity.

Many Kadazandusun tales revolve around a spirit world inhabited by a pantheon of both good and bad spirits—whose home is Mount Kinabalu—ruled over by two powerful deities known by different names by the different Kadazandusun groups. Penampang Coastal Kadazan speakers name them Kinoingan and Suminundu his wife. These deities are perceived as benevolent, as opposed to certain minor spirits (*rogon*) seen as destroyers of things valuable to man, such as crops and water. Some of these spirits, for example Komakadong, Balan-Balan and Tandahan, are even believed to snatch dead bodies being prepared for burial. To appease these spirits, ceremonies are held, presided over by a *bobohizan* (priestess or ritual specialist).

Creation is a particularly well represented theme in the oral tradition. Creation myths explain the origin of things, for example the Kadazandusun tale of the origin of land and water leeches, and the legends that tell of the origin of the Bajau and monkeys. Such myths also explain the origin of beliefs and practices, for example the reason that the Kadazandusun of Tempasuk do not eat snakes.

Oral performance styles

The oral traditions of Sabah are displayed in recitation, including stylized forms of vocalization such as crying and ritual chanting, the latter by priestesses. These ritual specialists recite lengthy

Kaamatan: focal point of Kadazandusun oral tradition

Kaamatan commemorates a common theme in Sabah's oral literature, the sacrifice of the beautiful and obedient daughter of Kinoingan (the Creator god), which took place during a time of famine. Following her death, her various body parts grew into various species of edible plants, and her blood turned into rice. Animals and human beings also arose from parts of the girl. Her miraculous effort preserved the Kadazandusun race.

The sacrifice of Kinoingan's daughter is honoured in the annual beauty contest, Unduk Ngadau.

The festival also honours the rice spirits (known as *bambaazon* by Coastal Kadazan speakers and *bambarayon* by Central Dusun speakers). Celebrations, with some local variations, usually commence with the homecoming of the bambaazon, starting with the selection of the most promising stalks of rice just before harvesting begins. This is followed just after sunset at the end of harvesting by a ceremonial thanksgiving with chanted ancient prayers that continue far into the night, overlapping with preparations for the feeding of the bambaazon. The festival ends with a feast.

The rice souls are enshrined in the seven ears of rice taken by the *bobohizan* (priestess) at the beginning of the harvest. The bambaazon is first hung in a hut in or near the rice field before it is taken for a ceremony (*sumalud*) at the owner's house at the end of the harvest, after which it is finally hung in the rice store.

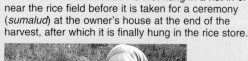

LEFT: Offerings made to the rice spirit include chicken, eggs, rice and bananas.

FAR LEFT: Priestesses performing rice fertility rites in Papar.

LEFT: Papar *bobohizan* chanting *rinait* overnight during *balai* (fertility) ceremonies.

RIGHT: Ranau Kadazandusun *bobolian* performing rice spirit rituals.

BELOW: Certain rituals extend over several days, including large-scale rain-making rituals, such as the *Monumbuidoh Mahanton*.

BELOW LEFT: Penampang Kadazan priestesses and assistants led by a *bobohizan* during the annual Magavau procession.

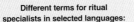

Different terms for ritual specialists in selected languages:

bobohizan	Coastal Kadazan
bobolizan	Rungus Kadazandusun
bobolian	Tambunan Kadazandusun
tantagas	Tuaran Kadazandusun
penyupi	Tatana Kadazandusun
bolijan	Labuk-Kinabatangan Kadazan
babalian	Timogun Murut
bolian	Tambanuo

sacred texts (*rinait*) which contain formulas for the correct form of behaviour and action in religious and daily social life, as well as the creation myths of their respective ethnic groups. Rinait are vivid narratives comprising many hundreds of stanza couplets, one in the normal language and one in an ancient ritual language. They describe the spirit world and their ideal equivalents in the secular world, highlighting belief in the concept of *doppelgänger* (whereby spirit world figures have a parallel among humans). Much of the recitation is designed to propitiate the spirits, either to keep away the rogon, or to invoke the return of good spirits.

Among the smaller ethnic groups of Sabah, the coastal Iranun have an oral tradition centred on stylized recitation. Their *edsair* (long stories in poetic form), which describe historical or mythical events, serve both as entertainment and as a form of instruction. Another style, *tinubau*, is used to tell stories from the epic poem *Darangen*, possibly the longest Southeast Asian poem. Yet another form, the *tarsila* (genealogies), is recited melodiously by experienced genealogists, and is similar to the recitation of the myth of *rang dungo* by the Lundayeh, used to illustrate their ancestry.

Community elders perform a medley presentation of traditional Kadazandusun oral arts, organized by the Kadazandusun Language Foundation.

Mount Kinabalu in legend

Mount Kinabalu, the highest peak in Borneo, features in many Sabah legends as it is believed to be the dwelling place of the spirits. The name Kinabalu is thought to be derived from the Kadazandusun words *aki nabalu* ('the revered home of the dead'). Traditionally, those climbing the mountain conducted ceremonies to appease the spirits. This practice has now been replaced by an annual commemorative ceremony conducted by the guides of Kinabalu Park.

A 19th-century print showing Mount Kinabalu's jagged peak as seen from Gaya Island.

Home of the gods

Among the Coastal Kadazandusun, a legend is told of the deity Kinoingan who watches over the world from the top of Mount Kinabalu. When a baby is born, he ties a number of knots in a piece of string, each representing a year in the baby's life. He then unties one knot each year until the last knot is untied, and the person represented by the string dies. Occasionally, Kinoingan falls asleep while tying the knots. If this occurs before he has tied the first knot, the baby will die before it is one year old. Should he sleep later, he may be forgetful when he awakes, take another piece of string and tie yet more knots. The person whose life this represents will then have a long life.

It is also told that the souls of the dead ascend Mount Kinabalu, crossing on their way the Tempasuk River near the house of Kinoingan's daughter. She looks to see if the last knot of each soul has been untied. If it has not, she sends the soul back home, causing a person who appears to be dead to come back to life.

Guides offer an annual sacrifice to appease spirits residing on Mount Kinabalu.

Malay myths and legends

Malay culture is rich in myths and legends. Many predate the conversion of the Malays to Islam, no later than the 15th century, and some pre-existing cultural elements have been retained. Myths and legends continue to pervade Malay folklore and day-to-day life through the practice of folk traditions, such as the propitiation of evil spirits and curing rituals. They also serve to justify elements of Malay culture and society, such as the right of the Malay sultans to rule.

Langkawi: island of legends

The island of Langkawi, in fact an archipelago of some 99 islands, is the source of a disproportionately large number of legends in comparison to its relatively small size. Today the island is a popular international tourist destination.

1. It is told that fairies used to come down to the Telaga Tujuh (Seven Wells) waterfall to bathe and frolic.

Myths

Myths are accounts that validate beliefs and rituals. Regardless of each myth's origin, they today comprise a fusion of animist, Hindu and Islamic elements. Elements of each of these are incorporated in the incantations (*jampi serapah* or *mantera*), of the *pawang* and the *bomoh* (practitioners in magic and curative rituals), and may include, for example, the qualities of the guardian of the midstream (*mambang tali arus*), the dualistic quality of the Hindu deity Shiva, the creator and the destroyer, and the special ability of King Solomon (Nabi Sulaiman) to understand animal languages.

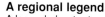

A model of the Spectre, or Wild, Huntsman of Malay legend as pictured in the book *Malay Magic* by W. W. Skeat, published in 1900.

Animistic influences are particularly apparent in the myths that endorse beliefs relating to the natural cycle. Traditionally, Malay fishermen held rituals to propitiate the mythical guardians of the sea and midstream for a bountiful catch, and for protection from mishaps. Belief in the *penunggu* (local protective spirits) spawned *bela kampung* (village defence) rituals which were enacted to bless the village and its inhabitants, and ward off evil influences and diseases. Agricultural rituals continue to be held in relation to the rice cycle, linked to the myth of the rice soul (*semangat padi*). The practices of the pawang and the bomoh can be traced to the mythical archetypal magician (*pawang yang tua*), present at the first creation of the world. Islamic elements in this myth reflect the evolution of Malay culture.

Royal myths

Malay social hierarchy, especially the rationalization of political institutions, including the legitimization of the status of the sultans, is shrouded in myth. An

A regional legend

A legend about a traveller known by various names, including Si Tanggang, Nakhoda Manis, Nakhoda Muda and Malim Kundang, is found all over the Malay World. There is evidence to suggest that it originated among the Orang Asli. The story illustrates the importance of filial piety, a highly esteemed value in Malay culture.

The legend is of an ungrateful son who, after becoming rich and marrying a princess, refused to recognize his poor mother for fear of revealing his humble past to his royal wife. During the long period Si Tanggang was away from home, his mother cooked his favourite foods and waited at the harbour every day for his return. When he finally arrived, Si Tanggang spurned his mother's greetings, and denied that he even knew her. As he did so, the sky began to darken, the wind howled, and huge waves broke on the shore, and Si Tanggang, his royal wife, his crew and his ship were turned to stone.

In many places throughout the Malay World, people still point out rocks resembling the shape of petrified boats or ships as evidence that the events in the legend really did take place. The best-known such formation in Malaysia is the Batu Caves near Kuala Lumpur, the interior of which is believed to be the fossilized hold of Si Tanggang's ship.

Top: The Batu Caves are said to be the fossilized remains of Si Tanggang's ship.

Above: Si Tanggang's exploits were depicted in the 1961 Malay film of the same name.

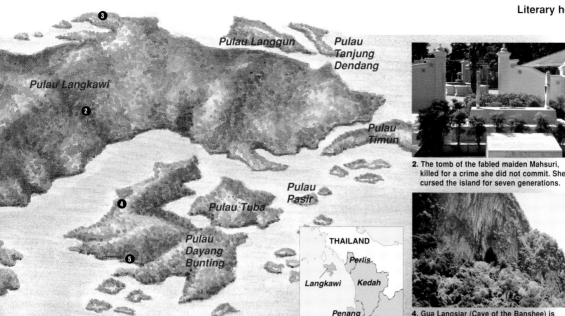

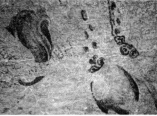

2. The tomb of the fabled maiden Mahsuri, killed for a crime she did not commit. She cursed the island for seven generations.

3. Ancient paintings outside Gua Cerita (Cave of Legends), where the legendary Prince of Rum and Princess of China took refuge.

4. Gua Langsiar (Cave of the Banshee) is popularly believed to be haunted by female spirit that lives on human blood.

5. Legend has it that childless women who bathe in the Tasik Dayang Bunting (Pool of the Pregnant Maiden) will become fertile.

animistic legacy persists, having survived the conversion of the Malays to Islam, and serves to explain the elevated position of rulers through tales of miraculous births or divine choice. The Malay rulers are said to have emanated from a clump of bamboo, or from the froth at the crest of waves. From Hindu mythology, the Malays derived the idea of Mount Seguntang Mahameru in Palembang, Sumatra—the seat of the 7–11th century Srivijaya empire—as the abode of the *dewa* (gods), the forebears of their royal rulers.

The *Sejarah Melayu* ('Malay Annals') records the dynastic myth of the old Melaka line, connecting it to the Srivijaya kingdom and thus legitimizing its royal heritage and right to rule the people, albeit within the bounds of social justice (see '*Sejarah Melayu*'). Pre-Islamic and Islamic elements are juxtaposed in the work: the heavenly princes who descended from Mount Seguntang Mahameru are said to have been descended from Iskandar Zulkarnain (Alexander the Great), the 'two-horned king' mentioned in the Qur'an, and the just Muslim king, Nushirwan Adil. One of the descending princes entered into a social contract with the local chief, whereby the chief's Malay followers would be loyal to the prince, while the prince, as ruler, could punish—even execute—them for committing various misdemeanours. Under no circumstances, however, could he shame them.

Legends and epics

Legends are tales of extraordinary people of more recent origin than those portrayed in myths, and deal with deeds which are spectacular by ordinary human standards. The distinction between legend and history is often blurred in Malay culture as a result of the lack of an ancient written tradition. However, the historicity of oral legends—such as that of Si Tanggang—is often at least purportedly supported by unusual landmarks or artefacts. Epics, in contrast to legends, are derived from well-known

literary works such as the Hindu-derived sagas of the *Ramayana* and *Mahabharata* (see 'The *Ramayana*' and 'The *Mahabharata*').

One legendary figure, Badang, was a hero of immense strength in old Singapore (Temasik). He not only defeated adversaries from other countries, but hurled a large stone that could, from that time, be seen at the mouth of the Singapore River.

In Kelantan, Puteri Sadong, a historical figure, is associated with Bukit Marak, a hillock in Pasir Putih which contains traces of past human habitation. Many ancient kingdoms were located in the northeast of the Malay Peninsula. Their purported remains—be it earth fortifications, graves or even the present-day names of locations—are claimed to prove their historical existence, although tales about them are told as legends.

Other Malay historical figures live on—and have their exploits embellished—in legends. The famous Melakan warrior, Hang Tuah, is a national hero precisely because he is such a wondrous legendary character. As his exploits in the historical *Sejarah Melayu* are not that spectacular, the legends surrounding him probably derived from the masterly epic *Hikayat Hang Tuah* (see '*Hikayat Hang Tuah*').

There are numerous other heroes in Malay epics and legends. From Kedah there is Panglima Hitam, a Robin Hood-like character, and Panglima Nayan, an anti-hero whose name has become an idiom for a person who behaves recklessly. Si Bongkok, the hunchback warrior, hailed from Tanjung Puteri in Johor. His exploits have in more recent times been turned into a stage drama, as have those of other legendary characters (see 'Modern Malay drama'). In addition to Puteri Sadong, two other royal ladies feature in well-known legends: Mahsuri, who cast a seven-generation curse on the island of Langkawi because she was wrongfully accused of infidelity, and Cik Siti Wan Kembang, an early female ruler of Kelantan.

P. Ramlee (left) in the title role of the 1956 Malay film *Hang Tuah*, with Ahmad Mahmud. Set during the Melaka sultanate (c.1401–1511), the tale combines historical and mythical elements.

Much of the content of the Malay-language magazine *Fantasi*, published in the 1980s and 1990s, was drawn from Malay folklore.

Traditional Malay poetic forms

Traditional Malay poetic forms were used for a number of purposes in addition to entertainment, including prosaic matters such as the recording of history and laws. Only three of the numerous forms have proved to be of enduring importance: the mantera, *the* pantun *and the* syair. *Of these, the* pantun *is the most versatile and continues to be widely used in a number of entertainment genres, including popular songs.*

Berbalas pantun (verse capping) competitions, traditionally a village activity, are now held at national level with schools and universities competing against one another.

Pantun caught the imagination of Victor Hugo and other European poets, and were re-created as the 'pantoum' that spread to Germany, the Netherlands, and Britain, the latter with somewhat less success.

Mantera and other free verse forms

The oldest Malay poetic form, *mantera*, comprises the rhythmic incantations—otherwise lacking formal structural rules—created by and for a society that lived at close quarters with forests, rivers, hills, lakes and seas, each of which were at times both awesome and life-threatening. Mantera were composed and used for protection from wild animals and super-natural powers, as well as to enhance beauty, voice or strength.

Many unwritten Malay customary laws and social rules (*adat*), whether in the form of *perbilangan* (proverbs), *perumpamaan* (maxims), or regular verses, are also essentially poetic in conception and product. An example is the famous dictum, *di mana bumi dipijak, di situ langit dijunjung* (wherever one stands, there the sky is upheld) which plays with symmetry and alliteration. Such forms are also built on word images which assist their memorization.

Pantun

The most favoured Malay poetic form is the famous *pantun*, a four-line verse complete in itself. It is often considered the highest form of Malay verse, and variations are found throughout the Malay Archipelago among numerous dialect groups—from Patani in southern Thailand down the Malay Peninsula to Singapore, throughout the Indonesian Archipelago from Aceh (north Sumatra) in the west to Bali in the east, as well as in Borneo. The Malaysian-Sumatran branch is regarded as the most ancient and richest, with a treasury of thousands of collected quatrains that have survived in the *mantera*

Poetry garden

Plants, including spices, feature prominently in traditional Malay poetry, especially in the foreshadower (*pembayang maksud*) section of a *pantun*.

> *Buah berangan masaknya merah,*
> **Lada cili** *dalam perahu;*
> *Luka di tangan nampak berdarah,*
> *Luka di hati siapa yang tahu.*

> *Labu putik di Tanjung Jati,*
> *Pucuk* **lengkuas** *dalam dulang;*
> *Baru bertemu kehendak hati,*
> *Belum puas ditinggal pulang.*

> **Halia** *ini tanam-tanaman,*
> *Ke barat juga akan condongnya;*
> *Dunia ini pinjam-pinjaman,*
> *Akhirat juga akan sudahnya.*

chilli (*lada*)

galangal (*lengkuas*)

> Red is the ripe chestnut,
> Chillies are loaded in a boat;
> A cut in the hand oozes out blood,
> But who can see a wounded heart.

> Unripe pumpkins in Tanjung Jati,
> Shoots of galangal in a platter;
> My sweetheart have I just seen,
> Alas, she left soon after.

> The ginger is but a plant,
> To the west does it incline;
> This world is but borrowed property,
> The promised land is one of eternity.

ginger (*halia*)

(incantations), proverbs, songs, Hikayat (histories), narratives and rituals. *Pantun berkait* (linked pantun), a development in form and idea in a series of related quatrains, was the core of the narrative Sumatran Minangkabau *kaba* (tales of court life sung to the accompaniment of a three-stringed lute) as well as the descriptive lyrics of Malay narrative Hikayat.

The first two lines of the pantun are called *pembayang maksud* (foreshadower) and the second *maksud* (purpose). The former teases the listener with its images, symbols and echoes of the latter, in a world initially divided between the image and reality, the shadow and the truth, the external and the internal, and finally of nature and the human being. The **a-b-a-b** rhyme enhances the tight, self-

Dondang Sayang

Pantuns form the lyric element of the Dondang Sayang love songs of the Straits Chinese community, known colloquially as Babas and Nyonyas (see 'Creoles'), whose traditional customs incorporate elements of both Malay and Chinese culture. Folk singers, often exchanging melodious witty repartees with one another, perform to the music of an ensemble comprising violin, harmonium, drum and gong, and take advantage of the richness of the Baba Malay creole.

In the heyday of the genre in the early 20th century, Dondang Sayang practitioners had amateur clubs located in Penang and Melaka, the main population centres of the relatively small Baba community.

Singing troupes still stage performances, but these are now confined mainly to weddings and Chap Goh Meh, a festival which falls annually on the 15th or final day of the Chinese lunar new year celebrations. In years gone by, when young Nyonya girls were only allowed to appear in public during Chap Goh Meh, love-lorn Baba balladeers would serenade the targets of their affection, betrothing themselves in song and verse to the delight and amusement of listeners.

Before World War II, Dondang Sayang singers and musicians rode gaily decked bullock carts and trishaws.

sufficient structure, finally wrapping up a profound, witty or emotionally true conclusion. The following traditional pantun reveals the intricate network of sounds and images, as well as the verse's division into symmetrical parts and the rhyming format:

Air yang dalam bertambah dalam   **a** foreshadower
Hujan di hulu belumlah teduh   **b** image, nature
Hati yang dendam bertambah dendam   **a** meaning/reality
Dendam dahulu belumlah sembuh.   **b** world of man

Heavier and heavier falls the rain
The rains of the hills are yet to cease
The longing heart yearns and yearns
The old longing is yet to be appeased.

Although it may be composed in six, eight or ten lines, and even linked (as in pantun berkait), the four-line form is the most popular. This short form lends itself to a popular mode of verbal charade, on the one hand, and a sophisticated mould for ideas and fine emotions, on the other.

Jikalau tidak kerana bintang
Masakan bulan terbit tinggi?
Jikalau tidak kerana abang
Masakan datang adik ke mari?

Were it not for the stars above
Why does the moon rise up on high?
Were it not for you, my love
Should I ever venture nigh?

The most exquisite romantic emotions and the most ironic of situations can be aptly expressed in the memorable and musically terse quatrains of the pantun. As a result, lullabies, love songs, Dondang Sayang (literally, 'song of love'), and even rock songs are often based on pantun. They also comprise the format for teasing question and answer repartee between males and females, including *berbalas pantun* (verse capping), a light-hearted poetic contest between two groups, and in previous times, Dikir Barat (a verse contest between two chorus groups each led by a singer).

Syair

The *syair* is a narrative form almost as versatile as the pantun. Indeed, there are in all nine ways of rendering the syair. The term itself derives from the Arabic *syi'r*, although the form is an entirely indigenous creation. Each line generally comprises four words,

Romantic *syair* written in scroll form which recounts a bird's love for a butterfly, believed to be an allusion to real life events.

Syair Siti Zubaidah
Also known as *Syair Siti Zubaidah Perang Cina*, this long *syair* is one of several that has features and functions identical to the prose Hikayat form. It tells of Siti Zubaidah's marriage to prince Zainal Abidin, his imprisonment by the Chinese following their attack on his father's kingdom, and his subsequent rescue. It ends with her coronation as queen.

ABOVE: Artist's impression of a scene from *Syair Siti Zubaidah Perang Cina* in which Siti Zubaidah (disguised as a man) attacked the Chinese navy by way of revenge for capturing her husband.

LEFT: Final two pages of a manuscript of *Syair Siti Zubaidah Perang Cina* dated 1874 in the collection of the National Library of Malaysia.

and in its simplest and most common form, verses are of four lines, each of which rhyme; a relatively simple task in Malay as many words end in vowels, partly due to the use of suffixes.

Malay syair have been written on a variety of subjects, including both fiction and real life matters, such as religious stories and advice on ways to behave. Romantic, allegorical syair have much in common with the Hikayat form (see 'The Hikayat'). The best-known syair narratives are those relating the tales of Siti Zubaidah, who fought to save her husband from his enemies, and Dandan Setia, a young heroine who endured much suffering looking for her lost love.

Showing versatile narrative possibilities, the syair form was also employed during the mid-17th century by the famous Sufi poet Hamzah Fansuri—credited by some as creating the form—in the theological poem entitled *Syair Perahu*.

Wahai muda, kenal dirimu,
Ialah perahu tamsil tubuhmu
Tiadalah berapa lama hidupmu
Ke akhirat juga kekal diammu.

Know thyself, your heart's doors
The temporal body is but a barque insecure
Your life is merely a measure
It is in the hereafter that you linger.

In the mid-18th century, the syair began to be used in new ways, including journalistic reports, religious advice to youths, the weather, and short anecdotes. The form was especially flexible and adaptable, capable of humour, moral anger and irony, and served as the forerunner of early modern Malay and Indonesian poetry (see 'Poetry in Malay').

Traditional poetry in the modern world

Cindai
Cindailah mana tidak berkias
Jalinnya lalu rentah beribu
Bagailah mana hendak berhias
Cerminku retak seribu

Which cindai does not
   harbour a past
   Its thousand threads
   coming apart
How can I ever beautify
   my visage
   Into a thousand pieces in
   the mirror shattered

The lyrics of the title song of singer Siti Nurhaliza's album *Cindai* (patterned silk cloth) are formed of *pantun*.

BELOW: *Pantun* are now sent by SMS. A *pembayang* (foreshadower) forms part of Hari Raya greetings to be completed by the recipient.

Beduk berbunyi di pagi hari Tanda raya sudah kembali...

Rarer forms of traditional Malay poetry

In addition to the mantera, pantun *and* syair, *there are several less well known traditional Malay poetic forms. These include the* seloka, talibun, gurindam, teromba *and* nazam. *With the exception of* teromba, *which is still used by at least one dialect group, these forms have to some extent fallen out of favour. All of the forms are primarily oral, apart from* nazam, *and are composed for different purposes, ranging from entertainment to recording of law.*

Dato' Khalid Bonget (seated centre), one of Negeri Sembilan's most proficient *teromba* exponents, testing students' teromba recitation skills at the Negeri Sembilan Cultural Museum.

Seloka

A loose poetic form, *seloka* have many structural features similar to those of the *mantera* (incantations), though different in content and function. Both forms were of Indian origin. Malay seloka was perhaps inspired by or evolved from the Indian prosody *shloka*, the verse-form used in the rendition of the *Ramayana* and *Mahabharata* epics. However, unlike its predecessor, seloka is normally short (seldom exceeding 10-15 lines) and is steeped in sarcasm and irony. In common with most Malay poetic forms, seloka reflects a penchant for a playful, witty and indirect means of criticizing moral wrongs and indiscreet actions. It also exemplifies the crafty idiomatic use of words to snub individuals or situations. Nevertheless, seloka is a seldom used verse-form, perhaps as a result of the form's lack of versatility. Few traditional seloka survive.

Gurindam

The term *gurindam* was traditionally used interchangeably with *bidalan* (parables) or *kiasan* (metaphors), the more common Malay oral literary forms. It was much later that the term came to denote verses used as parables. This more specific definition was given by the 19th-century Malay literary laureate, Raja Ali Haji, through his work *Gurindam Dua Belas* ('The Twelve-couplet Gurindam' or 'The Twelve Aphorisms'). Gurindam then came to be popularized as a Malay poetic form of indefinite length comprising two-line rhyming verses. Each verse is complete in itself, although the ideas within it can run on to subsequent verses. Gurindam verses differ from those of other Malay poetic forms, as the first line appears to pose a question to which the second line is a response.

Gurindam Dua Belas

RIGHT: Gurindam Dua Belas ('The Twelve-couplet Gurindam' or 'The Twelve Aphorisms'), written by Raja Ali Haji in Jawi in 1847.

BELOW RIGHT: The best-known gurindam, it has subsequently been published in Romanized Malay, with English translations.

BELOW: An extract that shows how Raja Ali used the gurindam form to convey moral instruction based upon Islamic principles.

Apabila terpelihara mata
Sedikitlah cita-cita.

Apabila terpelihara kuping
Khabar yang jahat tiadalah damping.

If one's eyes stop roaming
then one's need stops mounting.

If one controls one's ears
Bad news will not come near.

The content of gurindam is usually tendentious, with a directly stated moral. As with syair and pantun, the composition of gurindam has been largely superseded by modern free verse (*sajak*). However, the form continues to appear, albeit infrequently, in the works of contemporary poets.

Talibun

The metrical verse-form found in oral prose narratives, specifically in the more elaborate folk tale genre known as the folk romance, is known as *talibun*. It is also commonly known as 'rhythmic prose', in contrast to the other more prosaic style of recounting these narratives. Talibun is used to describe scenes, rituals and themes in the narratives. It is a highly stylized form consisting of set phrases or formulas which are used repeatedly in particular scenes within the narratives. For example, there are set formulas for the 'having an audience scene', the 'departure scene', and the 'courting scene'. There are also set phrases to depict themes such as loyalty, feasting and royal births.

Talibun are normally very short, comprising beautifully selected words and images—metaphors and similes, arranged metrically and rhythmically, though not necessarily rhymed. In certain court scenes especially, the language becomes very refined, stylized and ostentatious, almost ceremonial. Indeed, the talibun illustrates the ideal values of the courtly culture as imagined by the composer.

The formulaic and rhythmic character of talibun serves as an aid to recollection by the performer, while the sound and beauty of the images created intoxicate listeners, causing a sense of forgetfulness that might be said to soothe the soul.

Teromba

The *teromba* form is found among the ethnic Minangkabau in Sumatra and Negeri Sembilan. The term is itself Minangkabau for 'genealogy'; applied to poetry it refers to the verse form that enumerates the Minangkabau community's *adat* (customary) laws. It is thus also known as *perbilangan* (enumeration).

In primarily oral societies, literary or artistic forms became the most effective means of preserving tribal knowledge, ethics, beliefs and even laws and regulations. The teromba is one such form. Its loose structure makes it possible for teromba to adjust its form to accommodate the different dictates of the adat laws which encompassed almost every aspect of communal life in the Minangkabau matrilineal society.

In their structure and poetic form, teromba resemble talibun, and indeed may be considered a variant form. However the verses of teromba vary in length, from very few to twenty or thirty lines depending on the article of law being enumerated.

Although its content is rather technical, the teromba form does not lack aesthetic merit. In particular, the form makes interesting use of idioms to express the contents of proverbs and maxims, and is a versatile and living verse-form. It continues to be used on almost all important occasions in Minangkabau life, from the solicitation of a marriage partner to the division of wealth and property.

Nazam

Nazam is an Arabic word meaning poetry, poem or an arrangement. Like *syair*, another Arabic loan word for poetry or poem, the nazam form itself does not, however, originate or derive from any Arabic prosody. Rather, nazam is likely to be a variant of the syair quatrain; indeed, their structural similarity has often caused confusion between the two. Both nazam and syair are written poetic forms, and thus can be quite long: nazam can be up to 1000 lines, while syair can be even longer and more elaborate (see 'Traditional Malay poetic forms').

Differences do, however, exist. Nazam has a more flexible number of words per line, and of lines per verse; and it has a varied rhyming pattern. It may assume a four-line verse, ending with an **a-a-a-a** rhyme, or an **a-a-b-b** rhyme; or, perhaps most popularly, it may consist of two-line verses with an **a-a**, **b-a**, **c-a**, **d-a** rhyme. Also, unlike the syair form, nazam is solely a religious form of poetry.

Dikir Nazam, normally sung by a group of women, was traditionally performed on Prophet Muhammad's birthday and other important occasions.

Male (right) and female (left) students learning nazam at a workshop organized by the Institut Seni Malaysia Melaka (Malaysian Institute of Arts, Melaka).

Examples of the different forms

The rarer traditional poetic forms display a variety of styles and content, as shown in the examples given below. Some of the examples are complete, while others are drawn from larger prose works of the Hikayat genre. The identities of the poets of these traditional works are no longer known.

Seloka
Wit, humour and sarcasm are all apparent in these lines from a famous seloka:

Baik budi emak si Randang	Such is the kindness of Mother Randang
Dagang lalu ditanakkan	She prepares food for any passing stranger
Tidak berkayu rumah diruntuh	Pulls down her house if there is no firewood
Anak pulang kelaparan	Her children return she lets them starve
Anak di pangku diletakkan	She puts aside the baby on her lap
Kera di hutan disusui	To suckle the monkey from the jungle
Dagang lalu awak terhutang	The stranger leaves, she is left with debts
Beras habis, padi tak jadi!	The rice runs out, her padi crop fails!

Talibun
This example describes the arrival of royal subjects:

Yang beranak mendukung anak
Yang capik datang bertongkat
Yang buta datang berpimpin
Yang tuli bertanya-tanya
Yang kurap datang mengekor angin

The one with child, carried the child
The limp came on crutches
The blind came led by the hand
The deaf kept asking questions
The one with scabies kept far behind

An extract drawn from the epic
Hikayat Seri Rama:

Dari jauh menjunjung duli
Sudah dekat langsung menyembah
Terangkat kadam jari sepuluh
Kuncup bagai sulur bakung
Jari seperti susun sirih.

From a distance he bowed in obeisance
As he came near he went on his knees
His ten fingers raised above his forehead
Clasped together like the twine of the
  bakung plant
Fingers held like arranged betel leaves.

Teromba

Usang-usang diperbaharui
Lapuk-lapuk dikajangi
Yang elok dipakai
Yang buruk dibuang
Kalau singkat minta disambung
Kalau panjang minta dikerat
Kalau koyak minta ditampal

What is worn-out to be made new
What is mouldy to be repaired
That which is good to be used
That which is old to be thrown away
If it is short, lengthen it
If it is long, shorten it
If it is torn, patch it

Gurindam
From the *Hikayat Malim Dewa*:

Seperti gurindam orang dahulu kala
Awak tua Bandar terbuka
Emas habis dagangan murah...

As the proverbial sayings
  of the man of yore
The town flourished
  but you were too old
The goods were cheap
  but you had no gold...

Nazam
Part of the *Kanz al-'Ula*, a biography of Prophet Muhammad:

Maka sangat segera besar Rasul yang mulia	Thus the reverent messenger grew up quickly
Pada malam dan siang serta sentosa	While living peacefully day and night
Maka besarlah ia dalam harinya itu	And became bigger with each passing day
Banding budak yang lain pada sebulan ia	Faster than a child of the same age
Maka pada bulan yang lima dari bulannya itu	When he was in his fifth month
Maka berjalan lambat dan perlahan ia	He began to walk slowly
Maka gagahlah ia serta fasih berkata	He became strong and able to speak well
Pada sembilan bulan dengan nyata dan mulia.	At nine months old, undoubtedly.

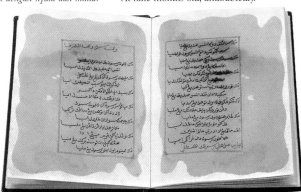

Nazam Nabi Muhammad (Nazam of Prophet Muhammad) recounts the life of the Prophet and is written in an attractive style.

The Malay written tradition

Other than stone inscriptions, Malay written works only appeared in the Peninsula after the adoption of Islam and Arabic script. At the Malay royal courts, Islamic scholars then began to produce religious works and scribes to document genealogies and current events. Letters were written for diplomatic purposes, laws were codified, and myths and legends were written in both verse and prose. Many original manuscripts still survive in collections around the world.

Misa Melayu ('Malay Story'), by Raja Chulan, tells of the 18th-century rulers of Perak, focusing in particular on Sultan Iskandar Zulkarnain Shah, who ruled from 1752 to 1765.

Religious works

Following their conversion to Islam, from the 13th century onwards, the various Malay Sultans promoted religious learning. The best-known centres for religious studies included Melaka, Aceh in Sumatra, Brunei, Patani in southern Thailand and Banten in Java. The Aceh court was the most developed and other sultanates tried to imitate it. The rulers of these states often attracted scholars, including foreigners, to their court, patronized them together with writers, and even established bureaucratic posts for religious administration. Various Malay sultanates enhanced their reputations through the activities of these *ulama* (Muslim scholars). Both literary output and intellectual activities, such as discussion on religious philosophy and Sufism (the doctrines of various Muslim mystical orders which emphasize the direct experience of God), were

Artist's impression of a scene from the palace of the Sultan of Melaka during the 15th century, when the royal court was the centre of Malay literary activity.

encouraged. The establishment in the Malay Peninsula of centres of religious learning—later known as *pondok*—began in the royal courts.

Emanating from the royal courts during the 16th–18th centuries were the works of scholars such as Hamzah Fansuri whose Sufi poems (*syair*) remain unmatched to this day (see 'Traditional Malay poetic forms'); Shamsuddin Pasai and Abdul Rauf Singkel who wrote on theology; and Nur-al-Din al-Raniri who wrote a number of significant religious works (see 'Religious literature'). Numerous religious works, based on well-known *kitab* (holy books) of the Western Asian Muslim world and translations of works by leading scholars such as al-Ghazaly, were produced during this period and are known as *kitab Jawi* or *kitab kuning* in the Malay Archipelago. The treatise *Taj al-Salatin*, too, was written during this period and may be classed alternatively as a theological text or as a work on statecraft.

A popular religious literature by lower-ranking religious teachers flourished outside the royal courts. Tales of Prophet Muhammad and his companions, simple teachings of religious tenets, and religious chants known as *zikir* or *ratib*, flourished among the common folk. Often read aloud by a religious teacher to his followers, they helped to spread Islam in the Malay Archipelago.

Other historical genres

The written tradition of classical Malay literature flourished in the Malay port cities, patronized by the ruler's court. The influence of Islam was felt in all genres. Even those tales that pre-dated the arrival of Islam, such as the epic *Ramayana*, were altered to give them a more Islamic appearance. Malay letters, too, opened with Islamic prayers and salutations.

History and contemporary events were recorded by scribes. Some of these records, known as *silsilah* or *salasilah* (genealogies), glorified the particular ruler or dynasty with which they were concerned, and were heavily influenced by mythology wherein the dynastic genealogy was usually founded. The most famous such text is the *Sejarah Melayu* ('Malay Annals'), originally known as *Sulalatus-Salatin* ('Genealogy of Kings'), concerning the rulers of Melaka and Johor (see '*Sejarah Melayu*'); another, *Silsilah Raja-Raja Riau* ('Genealogy of the Riau Kings') traces the history of the Malay kings of

The Arabic origin of Jawi

The Islamization of the Malay population, by the 15th century CE, was accompanied by the adoption of the Jawi script. Based on that of Arabic, it is similarly a syllabary (a writing system in which each character represents a syllable). However, as Arabic did not reflect all the phonemes present in the Malay language, the creation of a number of new characters was necessary, as had been the case with the Persians beforehand.

The additional phonemes are represented in the Rumi script as 'p', 'g', 'ch' and 'ny'. The new characters that were developed to represent these were based on the characters for those Arabic phonemes which were most similar to the Malay phonemes. Early forms of these new characters appear in Jawi texts dating from as early as the 16th century, for example the *Aqa'id Al-Nasafi* (see 'Literary heritage'). Here, the dot used for the character for 'g' was placed below the character, rather than above it, and the character representing the phoneme 'ny' was written with the three dots in its 'bowl' when appearing by itself or at the end of a word, but with the dots below the 'bowl' when at the beginning or in the middle of a word.

A new Jawi character was created by Dewan Bahasa dan Pustaka (Institute of Language and Literature) in the 1990s to represent the sound of the letter 'v', that had previously been represented by the character for 'w'.

Jawi is now only used for Islamic education, and most Malays born after Independence are unable to read and write it. However, they remain able to read the Qur'an as diacritic marks are used to denote vowel sounds, and Arabic has only three vowel sounds of 'a', 'i', 'u'.

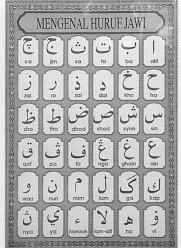

MENGENAL HURUF JAWI

All but five of the 36 letters of the Jawi alphabet are the same as the Arabic alphabet.

Malay grapheme	Jawi character	Developed from Arabic character
p	ڤ	(f) ف
g	ݢ	(k) ک
ch	چ	(j) ج
ny	ڽ	(n) ن
v	ۏ	(w) و

Johor-Riau. The fortunes of other sultanates are recorded in the Malay story form known as Hikayat (see 'The Hikayat'). These include *Misa Melayu* ('Malay Story'), *Hikayat Pahang* ('Story of Pahang'), *Hikayat Seri Kelantan* ('Story of Kelantan') and *Hikayat Johor* ('Story of Johor'). However, the Hikayat form also extended to include romances. Many were influenced by stories from other countries, including Islamic moral guidance tales from the Middle East, Javanese tales from the Panji cycle (see 'Panji romances'), and Indian romances.

Similar to the Hikayat are legal digests which provided laws for land ownership, customary practices, the sea, and harbour regulations (see 'Malay legal digests'). The most celebrated of these is *Hukum Kanun Melaka* ('Melaka Code of Laws'), which combines Islamic injunctions and Malay customary laws first established during the reign of Sultan Muhammad Shah (1424–1444), and which later formed the basis of laws of other Malay kingdoms, such as Pahang and Johor. Melaka also had a code governing its maritime law, the *Undang-Undang Laut Melaka* ('Melaka Maritime Laws'), which reflected maritime activities undertaken at the time.

Another written Malay literary form is the syair, a long narrative poem (see 'Traditional Malay poetic forms'). Examples include *Syair Ken Tambuhan* from the Panji cycle, *Syair Siti Zubaidah Perang Cina, Syair Bidasari*, and philosophical discourses such as those of Hamzah Fansuri. In the 18th and 19th centuries, the genre was popular for recording historical events, examples being *Syair Perang Banjar Masin, Syair Musuh Kelantan, Syair Sultan Maulana* (Kedah), *Syair Sultan Zainal-Abidin III* (Terengganu) and *Syair Sultan Abu Bakar* (Johor). Until the mid-19th century, the syair was also a favourite medium for conveying religious teachings. For instance, Raja Ali Haji wrote a collection of didactic syair specifically for the young Muslims. This tradition continued well into the first half of the 20th century when Malay newspapers often featured syair to mark auspicious events.

The work of literary pioneers

Traditionally, authors of historical texts did not record their names; hence, the identities of only a few are known.

Bukhari al-Jauhari
Little is known of this literary figure. There is even academic dispute over his origin—it has been suggested that he may have come from Bokhara in Persia—but most scholars now agree he came from Johor. He either wrote or translated into Malay *Taj al-Salatin* ('The Crown of Kings') in Aceh in 1603. His work continued to influence Malay culture significantly until the 19th century.

Manuscript of *Taj al-Salatin*, preceded by a three-page passage taken from the tales from the Prophets.

Munshi Abdullah bin Abdul Kadir (1796–1854)
A third-generation Melakan of Yemeni and Indian origin, Munshi Abdullah (artist's impression, right) served as translator, letter writer and teacher for Raffles and visiting merchants. His works include an autobiography, *Hikayat Abdullah*; two travel journals of his journeys to Kelantan (*Kisah Pelayaran Abdullah dari Singapura ke Kelantan*) and Jeddah (*Kisah Pelayaran Abdullah ke Jeddah*); and four *syair* (narrative poems), the most important of which was *Syair Singapura* (or *Kampong Gelam*) *Terbakar* recounting his experience in a Singapore fire. He edited the *Sejarah Melayu* and translated *Hikayat Galilah dan Daminah* from a Tamil work, *Panchatanderan*. His approach reflected the start of modern realism in Malay writing including the rise of a personal, critical perspective rather than the traditional community view.

Frontispiece of the first edition of *Hikayat Abdullah bin Abdul Kadir Munshi* (1849).

Raja Ali Haji (c. 1809–1873)
A member of the Bugis royal family of Riau, Raja Ali Haji collaborated with his father to compile the *Tuhfat al-Nafis* (also known as *Sejarah Raja-Raja Melayu dan Bugis),* a wide-ranging history of Malay and Bugis interaction over almost two centuries. Raja Ali Haji also composed manuals for correct government practice in a kingdom; verses of moral guidance, *Gurindam Duabelas* (1847); a grammar of Malay for children (1851); and an incomplete two-volume encyclopedia of Malay language and customs, *Kitab Pengetahuan Bahasa*, begun in 1858.

Illuminated version of the *Tuhfat al-Nafis* in Romanized Malay published by Dewan Bahasa dan Pustaka in 1998.

Preserving and restoring Malay manuscripts
Ancient manuscripts deteriorate due to a combination of factors including acidic paper and ink (particularly those from the 19th century onwards), fungi, and environmental pollution. They must therefore be treated with extreme care; optimum storage conditions require manuscripts to be kept in acid-free containers at a constant temperature of between 20 and 25 °C, and a humidity level of between 55 and 65 per cent.

Important repositories for Malay manuscripts, such as the National Library of Malaysia in Kuala Lumpur, have departments staffed by technicians skilled in the processes required to restore manuscripts that have

deteriorated. There are several steps involved in the restoration of each page. First, the pages are cleaned (1) by either by dry-brushing with a special grit-free powder or, with solvents such as water, ethanol or chloroform, depending on the material on which the manuscript is written, and the type of ink used. Next, they are de-acidified with a mixture of methanol and barium hydroxide (2). They are then restored either traditionally, by sticking them to tissue paper (3), or with paper pulp in a 'Leaf Casting' machine (4). Finally, the restored pages are trimmed (5).

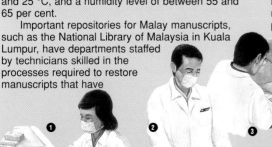

Example of a manuscript before (top), and after restoration (above).

The art of the Malay letter

From the earliest 16th-century examples to those of the late 19th century, Malay letters encapsulate the finest features of Malay language and culture. Serving a primarily diplomatic function, they were subject to elaborate rules of form, composition and appearance, dependent upon the relative rank of the correspondents. These important historical documents provide a glimpse into the complex structure of Malay society.

The earliest known Malay Peninsula letter, dated 1719, is from the Sultan of Johor to Louis XV of France.

In this 1811 letter to Lord Minto, the Governor-General of Bengal, the Sultan of Kedah requested help against the Siamese. Assistance was not however forthcoming and the state fell to the invaders in 1821.

This 1856 letter, from Sultan Muhammad of Selangor to E. A. Blundell, Governor of the Straits Settlements, merely acknowledges receipt of a letter. However, a scribbled note on the back shows it was a response to Blundell's announcement of the outbreak of the Crimean War. The seal at the bottom of the letter is from an unrelated document.

RIGHT: Magnificent ceremonies accompanied the despatch and receipt of royal letters. This artist's impression is based on a description in the *Sejarah Melayu* ('Malay Annals').

A record of diplomacy

Whilst there is evidence that Malay letters were being sent much earlier, the earliest surviving letter written in Malay is that sent by Sultan Abu Hayat of Ternate (in present-day Indonesia) to the King of Portugal in 1521. This, like the majority of Malay letters, is an exercise in the art of diplomacy.

The earliest known letter from the Malay Peninsula, written by Sultan Abdul Jalil Riayat Shah of Johor to Louis XV, King of France and Navarre, dates back to 1719. This letter was written in response to a request from the French for trading facilities in Terengganu (which was then a vassal of Johor-Pahang), and informs that permission was granted by the Sultan in return for guns and bullets.

In the course of the 18th and 19th centuries numerous other letters were exchanged between the Malay Sultans and various British captains and governors, providing an important and fascinating insight into the socio-political status of the Malay World at that time. In one such, a particularly long letter from Sultan Mansur of Terengganu to Francis Light in February 1792, the Sultan requested a closer relationship between Terengganu and Penang, and informed Francis Light of Siam's intention to invade Kelantan and Terengganu within the year. It also refers to trade between Terengganu and Penang, and between Terengganu and China. Not long after this the Sultan of Kedah wrote to Francis Light in a letter dated 24 May 1792. In this, the Sultan reconfirmed the receipt of five years' revenue from Francis Light, for the lease of Penang to the East India Company.

Form and elements of the Malay letter

The writing of Malay letters was a serious business. Laboriously written from right to left in Arabic or Jawi script, they were elaborately sealed and sometimes heavily decorated. Such was their complexity that several guides, known as *kitab terasul*, were produced for the professional scribes who crafted them. The manuscript *Taj al-Salatin* ('The Crown of Kings'), written in 1603, included two such chapters, stating that '*the work of the sword can be carried out by the pen but not vice versa*'.

Each letter opens with a phrase or heading in Arabic, often in intricate calligraphy; the

Envelopes

The choice of material for the envelopes in which Malay letters were to be conveyed was important, and was—as with the contents of the letters themselves—linked to the relative status of the correspondents. Generally, it appears that letters from one chief to another were wrapped in yellow or white cloth, sometimes silk. If to a prince, the wrapping would usually be royal yellow silk, or if the occasion seemed to demand it, cloth of gold. From inferiors to superiors, the envelope was invariably yellow. Commoners used paper envelopes. The manner in which the envelopes were sealed also varied depending on the status of the correspondents.

TOP: Silk envelope and paper wrapper addressed to Raffles, c. 1811.

RIGHT: Cotton envelopes such as this, containing a letter from Datuk Temenggung Abdul Rahman of Johor to Raffles in Bengkulu (dated 23 August 1824), were also used in the 19th century.

most common phrase being *Qawluh al-haqq* (His Word is the Truth). Another common heading is *Al-mustahaqq* (The Deserving). The language employed throughout the letters is long-winded, in keeping with the Malay trait of taking great lengths to avoid giving offence. Following the heading, the letters continue with a passage highly praising the recipient. For example the Sultan of Johor and Pahang's 1787 letter takes an entire paragraph to express the Sultan's esteem for the intended recipient, 'Senyur Gurnadur' Francis Light, describing his unblemished character and efficiency as governor. The central contents of the letter are then couched in the usual circuitous terms. By way of contrast, letters from European officials to the Malay Sultans did not exhibit such humility and restrained use of language; rather the subject matter of the letter was tackled directly following a brief salutation.

Most of the letters were written on single sheets. For longer letters, sheets were pasted or sewn together to form a long scroll.

Golden letters

Royal Malay letters were occasionally illuminated in gold. However, little is known of the theory or practice of this illumination. It is not mentioned in the any of the *kitab terasul* or other Malay texts, and, despite some fine examples there is no discernible stylistic tradition, although it is likely that Malay artists and illuminators were influenced by letters received by the Malay Sultans from the west Asian states and Europe.

Several of the Peninsular Malay sultanates produced surviving examples, including those of Johor-Pahang-Riau and Terengganu. Others, however, such as Kedah and Perak, are not known to have produced any. From the available evidence it appears that such lavish illumination was determined by the relevant rank of recipient and sender and the purpose of the letter.

The largest known Malay seal is that of Sultan al-Jaafar Muazam Syah of Perak, dating from 1859.

Seals

The most important formal element of the Malay letter, seals (*cap*, *meterai*, *tera* or *mohor* in Malay) have been in use in the Malay World for over 1,000 years. As elsewhere in the world, they functioned as a symbol of authority, and were used instead of a signature. The seals were often the only part of a letter to give details of the sender. The actual seal matrices (or stamps) that made the seal impressions were made of silver.

The wording on the seals, usually in Arabic, or Malay written in the Jawi script, commonly included the sender's name, title, date and location, as well as an Islamic expression such as '*al-wathiq bi'llah*'.

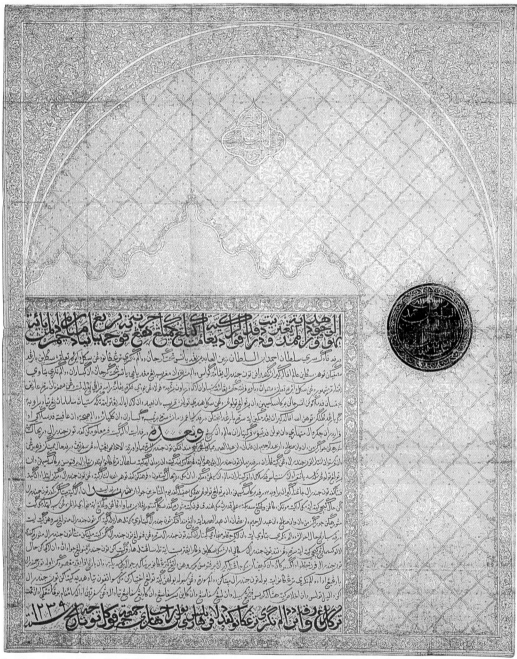

The seal of the Bendahara of Pahang (1806) reads '*Al-wakil al-Sultan Mahmud Syah Datu' Bendahara Sewa Raja ibn Bendahara Paduka Raja sanat 1221*'.

An erroneously carved seal of the Laksamana of Perak with its imprint the 'wrong' way around.

Red wax seal from 1810 belonging to Tunku al-Sayid al-Syarif Husain bin Abdul Rahman Aidid from Penang.

A golden letter from the Sultan of Terengganu

This letter from Sultan Ahmad of Terengganu to the Dutch Governor-General in Batavia (Jakarta), Baron van der Capellan, is dated 18 Rejab 1239 (19 March 1824). Now in the collection of the Museum für Völkerkunde, Berlin, it is written in ink and gold on paper, with a lampblack seal, and measures 498 by 383 millimetres.

The final paragraphs of the letter are illustrative of the colourful and diplomatic language used by correspondents in such royal letters:

> '*And as for you, General, if it be within your pleasure and willingness, please do not discontinue asking your people to come to Terengganu to trade, buying and selling a little, and if there is anything in this country of Terengganu that you wish to have, you may say so in your letter. We will assist to the best of our ability.*
>
> *There is nothing that we can offer you as a gift as proof of our sincerity but a long kris, a pair of spears, a pair of cloths of considerable width, and a pair of ivories, all of which are of no great value. You can equate them to a flower on its stalk. The End.*
>
> *This epistle was written in the state of Terengganu on the eighteenth day of the month of Rejab, Friday, seven o'clock in the year 1239.*'

Malay legal digests

Following an ancient tradition of both oral and inscribed laws, legal digests in manuscript form were first devised during the Melaka Sultanate (1401–1511). These were later used as a model by other Malay sultanates for the compilation of their own legal digests. A number of these digests have survived to the present day, each codifying oral customary laws, and designed to assist Malay rulers to administer and keep law and order in their respective states.

The *Hukum Kanun Melaka* ('Melaka Code of Laws') as copied by Sayid al-Sharif Jamaluddin ibni Sayid al-Sharif Abdullah in Java in 1762.

Ancient origins

Historians surmise that oral customary laws have existed since the very first Malay kingdoms. This oral tradition continues in Negeri Sembilan, with the administration of customary law known as *teromba* still practised by adherents of *adat perpatih* (matrilineal law). In Sabah and Sarawak, the various ethnic groups accept their local hereditary customs as law (*adat*) and it is only recently that these traditional laws have been committed to writing.

The most ancient example of written Malay, a stone inscription of Telaga Batu found in south Sumatra, has been dated to the 7th century CE. It gives details of the ancient government of Srivijaya, and briefly explains the statecraft employed by the government. The contents of the inscription may be considered law, indicating that written law existed in Malay society from this early date.

Following the oral tradition of customary law, Malay written law from the Islamic period displays the influence of Hinduism, as is evident from the incorporation of the Manu law (Hindu traditional law). This may be attributed to the pre-Islamic historical role of the Hindu-Buddhist tradition in the Malay World, which later led to a merger of Hindu-Buddhist thought with Islamic practices. Nevertheless, the laws contained in the legal digests that have survived are all locally focused.

Undang-Undang Melaka and its influence

The earliest written law of this nature was produced during the Melaka Sultanate of the 15th century. Written in the Jawi script, it is known as the *Undang-Undang Melaka* ('Laws of Melaka') or *Hukum Kanun Melaka* ('Melaka Code of Laws'). Among the varied contents of the 44 articles of the *Undang-Undang Melaka* are statements of the special rights accorded to the ruler and his family, the duties of dignitaries, government protocol, local taboos, penalties for crimes such as theft and murder, and guidelines for performing Islamic rituals.

The *Undang-Undang Melaka* also contains land law and maritime law, the latter in articles 23 and 24, the inclusion of which was in consonance with Melaka's role as a key entrepôt. This maritime law was later considered an entity in itself, and became known as the *Undang-Undang Laut Melaka* ('Melaka Maritime Laws'). It includes the duties of the captain and his sailors, and states the punishment for those who committed adultery, possessed or profited from runaway slaves, or committed other crimes on board ship. It also lays down the rights of those who rented space in a ship, and of the captain to trade when he arrived at his destination.

The *Undang-Undang Melaka* had a great impact and influence on the subsequently drafted laws of other states. Of these, the *Undang-Undang Johor* ('Laws of Johor') was written in the early 16th century, when Sultan Mahmud Shah of Melaka established the new government of Johor-Riau after fleeing the invasion of Melaka by the Portuguese in 1511. The *Undang-Undang Pahang* ('Laws of Pahang') was composed in 1596 for Sultan Abdul Ghaffur, a descendant of the Melaka sultans.

The Kedah chronicles

A number of Kedah legal texts are influenced by the *Undang-Undang Melaka*. The earliest of these, the *Tarikhi-Tahiri*, dates from 1650. It records that Kedah, as a port city, used the same law as that of the Mogul government in India. Among the provisions that it contains are those relating to the imposition of taxes:

An account of the Malay laws, customs and ceremonies of Johor, dating from 1808.

Adat perpatih

The socio-legal code surrounding the matrilineal system of descent in Negeri Sembilan is known as *adat perpatih*. A comprehensive code of customary law, it prescribes such things as customs, constitutional law, criminal law, and a code of ethics, and is derived from a synthesis of Jakun Orang Asli customary law (also matrilineal) and that of the Sumatran migrants who constitute the majority of the population of the state.

Adat perpatih is part of the oral tradition known as *perbilangan* (enumeration), and is supported by two documents written in Jawi, *Tromba Sungai Ujung* and *Tromba Perut Tebat Rembau*.

TOP RIGHT: The *istiadat kerjan Penghulu Luak Ulu Muar* (headman of Luak Ulu Muar government-building ceremony) is compulsory for a new headman under *adat perpatih*.

RIGHT: One of the many stages of the *istiadat nikah kahwin* (marriage ceremony) prescribed by *adat perpatih*.

Inscribed with laws, the Terengganu stone is dated 1303 CE. It is the oldest example of Malay written in the Arabic (Jawi) script, as well as being the earliest confirmation of Islam in the Malay Peninsula.

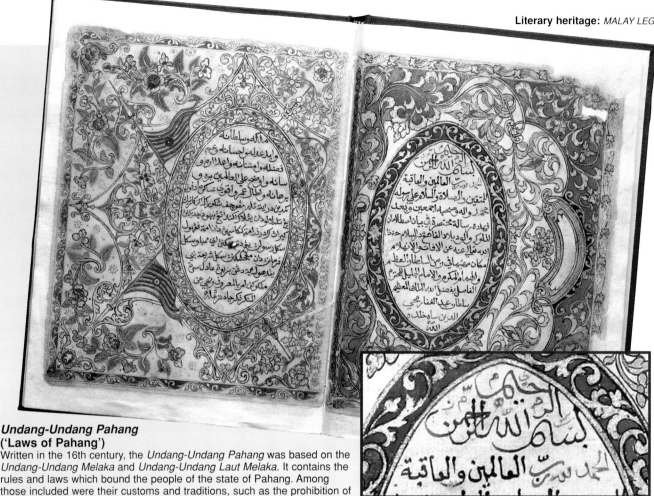

Undang-Undang Pahang
('Laws of Pahang')

Written in the 16th century, the *Undang-Undang Pahang* was based on the *Undang-Undang Melaka* and *Undang-Undang Laut Melaka*. It contains the rules and laws which bound the people of the state of Pahang. Among those included were their customs and traditions, such as the prohibition of the use of the colour yellow by commoners (it was reserved for royal use), and the correct use of court language when in the presence of royalty. Other, less unusual, laws related to maritime trading, crime (both on land and at sea), slavery, adultery, and the question of children born out of wedlock, as well as matters relating to diplomacy.

The exquisite illumination of the *Undang-Undang Pahang* is unusual in a manuscript from the Malay Peninsula in that it makes use of numerous colours, including gold. The manuscript commences with the universal Muslim opening phrase '*Bismillahir Rahmanir Rahim*' ('In the name of Allah, most Gracious, most Merciful').

on foreigners, on sailing from Kalingga and Gujerat, on ship captains, on slaves, and on tin products. Other provisions regulate the use of port facilities, the safeguarding of port premises, the calibration of scales and measures, and the manner of receiving foreign missions and diplomats.

Another set of Kedah laws, the *Tembera Kedah*, dates from 1667. This text contains regulations prohibiting stealing, gambling, cockfights, alcohol and opium smuggling, the worship of trees and stones, and imposes penalties on Muslims who fail to attend the mosque or avoid paying tithe (*zakat*). All purchases and sales are stated as having to be agreed to by the headman, and tax was levied on the slaughter of buffaloes. One chapter on agriculture deals with the owner of a buffalo that destroys or trespasses on another's property.

A further two texts are still in existence: the *Hukum Kanun Dato' Kota Setar*, which deals with marriage customs, funeral ceremonies and palace customs, and another dated 1784—simply referred to as *Undang-Undang* ('Laws')—which prescribes the intricacies of Kedah palace etiquette.

The Perak chronicles

Perak used a different legal text, the 'Ninety-Nine Laws of Perak' (*Undang-Undang Sembilan Puluh Sembilan Perak*), which was brought in from

Hadhramaut, in the south Arabian Peninsula, during the 17th century by one Sayyid Hussein Al-Faradz. It was used by his descendants, who became ministers in Perak in the mid-18th century. The document is written in the form of questions and answers between one Raja Nusyirwan Adil and his minister, Buzurmihr. Its contents reflect a Persian influence, particularly the references to desert animals which were not found in Perak.

The work deals with a wide range of matters including evidence of murder and bad behaviour, punishment for murderers not sentenced to death, divorce and the rights of divorced men. Agricultural matters are also discussed, such as the ownership of rice fields, taxes on goats, buffaloes and elephants and the wages due to farm workers. Payment for the cleaning of mosques is also addressed.

Other works, the *Undang-Undang Dua Belas* ('The Twelve Laws') and *Undang-Undang Kerajaan* ('Government Laws'), deal with slavery and property rights, and try to accommodate the customs of the Buginese with whom Perak often fought during the 18th century.

Hukum Maksiat di Kelantan ('Vice laws of Kelantan'), written on paper with 18th-century watermarks, is likely to have been written in the late 19th or early 20th centuries. The manuscript prohibits conduct such as charging interest, gambling, and free association between men and women. Punishments such as mutilation of the hand for theft were carried out in Kelantan as late as the end of the 19th century.

The Hikayat

The word 'hikayat' is a loan word from Arabic which means 'all kinds of histories'. The meaning in Malay, however, has changed through time so that in the title of a work, the word simply means 'story' or 'the story of'. Most of the numerous traditional works in the narrative form—including epics, stories of heroic and religious characters, and histories—use the word in their titles. The term encompasses the oral, handwritten and printed forms.

Structure of the Hikayat

The stories in the Hikayat genre have a structure of their own, developing from that of the quest-myth. They present authentic life experiences imbued with a great deal of idealism through the use of myths, imagination and exaggeration. While the real world does feature in the stories, so does the unreal world of the heavens (*kayangan*), filled with gods and goddesses. Hikayat characters move between earth and the heavens by using a flying cloak, riding on a large bird, or travelling in a special coach.

The Hikayat have no central theme other than that of a love story with a happy ending. There is, however, a pervasive moral element; that the good will be well rewarded while the bad will be punished. As such, the hero always succeeds in his quest and overcomes impossible tasks, usually assisted by magical beings.

Hindu and Islamic influences

Although it is said that the Hikayat form entered Malay literature after the coming of Islam, the tradition of oral storytelling had existed in Malay society much earlier. Malay folklore abounds with stories such as *Hikayat Malim Deman* ('The Story of Malim Deman') which share structures similar to, although somewhat simpler than, those of the written Hikayat.

Indeed, prior to the influence of Islam, the corpus of Malay tales had already been enriched by elements from the Indian epics, the *Ramayana* and the *Mahabharata*. This is apparent in works such as *Hikayat Seri Rama*, based on the *Ramayana*, in which the characters use Malay and Indian names (see 'The *Ramayana*'). Similarly, the Malays created the Pandawa stories from the *Mahabharata*, including *Hikayat Pandawa Jaya* (see 'The *Mahabharata*'). These Indian-influenced Hikayat include Hindu elements consisting of reincarnation, rebirth, and the role of the Dewata Mulia Raya, Vishnu and other gods. Punishment in the form of curses from the gods often forms part of the story.

With the coming of Islam came stories of the prophets and Islamic warriors, Muslim princes, and other historical figures. Islamic epics such as *Hikayat Muhammad Hanafiah* ('The Story of Muhammad Hanafiah', a contemporary of Prophet Muhammad) and *Hikayat Amir Hamzah* ('The Story of Amir Hamzah', a paternal uncle of Prophet Muhammad) can also be categorized as religious literature (see 'Religious literature'). Romances such as *Hikayat Saiful Yazan* and *Hikayat Shah Mardan* were also brought by Muslims from the Middle East and India. These stories entered Malay literature through a process of direct translation, adaptation and re-telling; in the same way as the romances containing Hindu elements. These included *Hikayat Marakarma* ('The Story of Mr. Extreme Poverty'—*marakarma* is Sanskrit for 'very poor'), which was renamed *Hikayat Si Miskin* ('The Story of Mr. Poor') as a result of the influence of Islam, and *Hikayat Inderajaya* ('The Story of Inderajaya', the hero), which was renamed *Hikayat Shah Mardan,* giving the hero an Islamic sounding name.

Hikayat Merong Mahawangsa

Among the Hikayat of the northern Malay Peninsula is the epic story of *Hikayat Merong Mahawangsa*, in which a proposed marriage between the children of the emperors of Rome and China, the two most powerful kingdoms in the world, was opposed by the mythical bird of Langkawi, which feared smaller kingdoms would be wiped out by such a union. The bird abducted the Chinese princess, and attacked the Roman fleet to prevent the marriage.

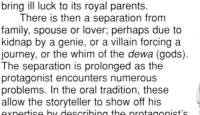

The mythical *helang* (eagle) is depicted in a prominent statue on the island of Langkawi, which derived its name from the bird.

A typical Hikayat storyline

The story, set in a prosperous country, begins with the emergence of a royal problem: perhaps an heirless king, an unmarried prince or princess, or a prediction that a newborn child will bring ill luck to its royal parents.

There is then a separation from family, spouse or lover; perhaps due to kidnap by a genie, or a villain forcing a journey, or the whim of the *dewa* (gods). The separation is prolonged as the protagonist encounters numerous problems. In the oral tradition, these allow the storyteller to show off his expertise by describing the protagonist's experiences and making him or her appear both hopeless and helpless, in prose and in song.

Each Hikayat ends in a joyful reunion between the hero or heroine and his or her family and the confirmation of the moral of the story—that good will triumph.

Hikayat Malim Deman begins with Malim Deman asking permission from his royal parents to embark on a journey after dreaming of meeting Nenek Kebayan (Wise Old Woman).

After retrieving a golden shell with a diamond ring and a strand of hair floating in a river, Malim Deman's hunting dog is washed downriver by undercurrents.

Puteri Bongsu, the fairy princess who had placed the shell in the river, comes looking for her lost flying cloak and stumbles upon Malim Deman disguised as an old fisherman.

Another group of stories in the Hikayat genre combines both Hindu and Islamic elements, created either during the transition period when Hindu influences were giving way to those of Islam, or perhaps created purposely to retain the fantastic and romantic Hindu elements. Both the Hindu and Islamic elements enhance the aesthetic value of the Hikayat. Each such story begins with the initial holy sentence of the Qur'an and, throughout, the language uses many Arabic words and phrases, and even sentences. The stories themselves compare the love that bonds the hero and heroine throughout their separation with the experiences of Nabi Allah Yusof (Joseph) and Siti Zulaikha (Asenath) or Nabi Allah Sulaiman (Solomon) and Princess Balqis (Sheba). In each story, Allah is responsible for the hero's success.

Hikayat Binatang, published in 1846, was reputedly translated into Malay from English by Munshi Abdullah bin Abdul Kadir.

Written and printed Hikayat

Written Hikayat (used in the wider sense to include the *syair* verse form as well as the usual prose) make use of the highest form of literary Malay (see 'Traditional Malay poetic forms'). Interestingly, most are set outside the Malay World—in India, Persia or the Middle East, or in imaginary locations.

Evidence suggests that Hikayat production peaked between the 15th and 16th centuries. Prior to the early 19th century many Hikayat were undoubtedly handwritten in Jawi, but with only a limited circulation. However, from then on, the arrival of the printing press in Penang, Melaka and Singapore enabled Hikayat to be distributed to a wider readership until their popularity declined with the appearance of the Malay novel in the 1920s (see 'Early Malay novels').

Nenek Kebayan intervenes between the princess and Malim Deman, who then returns her cloak. They fall in love and get married. Nenek Kebayan blesses the couple, who live happily ever after.

Illuminated Hikayat manuscripts

Malay Hikayat exist in both verse and prose forms. They were initially passed on orally from one generation to the next. When first committed to writing at the latest in the 16th century, they were produced as beautifully decorated manuscripts, painstakingly copied until the advent of printing in the 19th century.

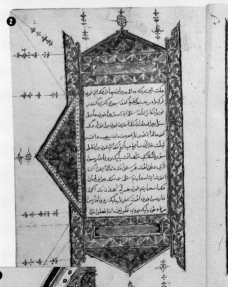

1. *Hikayat Raja Iskandar Zulkarnain* (1817).
2. Frontispiece of *Hikayat Isma Yatim*, late 18th to early 19th century.
3. Detail from frontispiece of *Hikayat Isma Yatim*.
4. Illuminated beginning of *Hikayat Pancatanderan* (*Hikayat Galilah dan Daminah*).

Hikayat Hang Tuah

One of the foremost epics of the Malay World, Hikayat Hang Tuah *is believed to have been first written down in the 17th century, recording earlier oral stories. It relates the personal history of the ideal Malay hero: from his early beginnings, through a number of courageous exploits, to his mysterious end. It also traces the parallel growth of the feudal Melakan empire which contributed to Hang Tuah's greatness.*

Versions of Hikayat Hang Tuah

Two versions of the *Hikayat Hang Tuah* in the collections of the National Library of Malaysia in Kuala Lumpur.

The double illuminated frontispiece of an undated *Hikayat Hang Tuah* manuscript comprising 445 pages.

A blend of fact and fiction

Hang Tuah—around whom *Hikayat Hang Tuah* revolves—was a historical figure during the reign of Sultan Mansur Shah in 15th-century Melaka. As the story was not produced in written form until much later, the historical facts of Hang Tuah's life have become mixed with events from other periods, both pre- and post-dating the 15th century. The work also contains material from legends. This has led some to believe that Hang Tuah may be a purely legendary figure; however, there is historical evidence to the contrary. Hang Tuah is a Malay cultural hero, and indeed icon, recognized and admired by the Malay community not only in Malaysia, but also in Indonesia, Brunei and Singapore.

Destined for greatness

The story begins by relating the ancestry of Sultan Mansur Shah, and describing his realm, Melaka, home to Hang Mahmud and his son, Hang Tuah. As is common in many epics, the signs of Hang Tuah's greatness are clearly delineated from the very beginning: Hang Tuah's father was so alerted by a dream in which a ray of moonlight shone on the boy's head. The family later moved from Lingga to Bintan (in the Riau Archipelago, now part of Indonesia), a kingdom offering better prospects.

In Bintan, Hang Tuah—together with his friends Hang Jebat, Hang Kasturi, Hang Lekir and Hang

Modern images of Hang Tuah

1. The 1956 movie *Hang Tuah* starred P. Ramlee in the title role, and was one of the first Malay movies in colour.
2. Artist Waveney Jenkins' relief of Hang Tuah, displayed at the National History Museum in Kuala Lumpur.
3. An illustrated children's book based on tales in *Hikayat Hang Tuah*.

Lekiu—proved his prowess, loyalty and singular personality. At the age of about ten, they defeated pirates in the waters of Singapura (Singapore), and upon their return to Bintan they rescued the *bendahara* (chief minister) from an attack by an inhabitant who ran amok, in the true sense of this Malay-derived word. As a result of this courageous act, Hang Tuah and his friends were all adopted by the bendahara, and became royal pages in the court. After the Portuguese attacked Bintan, the ruler of Bintan—later to be known as Sultan Mansur Shah—moved to Melaka. As loyal subjects, Hang Tuah and his friends moved with him to become knights of the empire.

Heroic deeds

Taught the arts of war, religion, and statehood by special teachers, Hang Tuah and his friends emerged as exemplary officers, with Hang Tuah excelling more than the others. Hang Jebat, his closest friend who subsequently became his adversary, is described as having a strong voice and views, while it is told that Hang Tuah was gentle in both voice and manners, as well as possessing precocious wisdom and maturity.

Hang Tuah went on to attain the total trust of the Sultan of Melaka—he moved as though the palace had no doors (*tiada berpintu lagi*)—and followed the latter's every word. The story then moves on to the conflicts that arose within the palace. Hang Tuah was accused by Patih Kerma Wijaya, the ruler's old and trusted Javanese confidant whom Hang Tuah had replaced, as having an affair with the ruler's *gundik* (concubine). In the Malay court, there was only one punishment for this crime of treason, and Hang Tuah, although beloved by the ruler, was duly sentenced

Evidence of the legend

A number of historical sites in Melaka testify to the existence of Hang Tuah and other characters in the Hikayat. They are now popular tourist attractions.

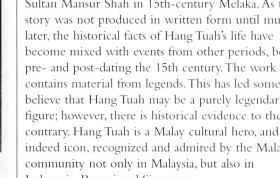

1. The Hang Li Po well, named after the Chinese bride of Sultan Mansur Shah, referred to in the story.
2. Hang Jebat's Mausoleum.
3. The burial place of Hang Kasturi.
4. Hang Tuah's tomb, located at Kampung Duyong.

to death. Fortunately, he was saved by the wise bendahara, who understood human passions and court intrigues.

Hang Tuah atoned for his alleged crime by stealing the glamorous princess of Pahang, Tun Teja, as a bride for the Sultan and returned to regain his former position in the court. A second accusation of an affair with a concubine resulted in Hang Tuah being sentenced to death for a second time. This accusation led to a duel between Hang Tuah and Hang Jebat, resulting in the death of the latter.

In the course of the epic tale, Hang Tuah, with his magical and superhuman qualities, was able to defeat a number of enemies of Melaka, as well as to enhance the name and renown of his country and ruler. The tasks that he undertook for ruler and country were truly Herculean: from arresting thieves to retrieving a favourite horse of the ruler's son, and from defeating groups of Javanese warriors to mediating between local chiefs.

Hang Tuah later progressed to become a wise ambassador, bringing word of the great Melakan empire to China, India and the Holy Roman Empire. Following a pilgrimage to Mecca, Hang Tuah ended his life almost as a mystic.

Interpretations

The story of Hang Tuah illustrates a number of themes, the key one being the importance of loyalty and the rewards that it brings. Hang Tuah is generally understood to epitomize the commoner rising through the ranks and serving his country, and the story illustrates the importance of this to the state. Indeed, the implication is that Melaka would not

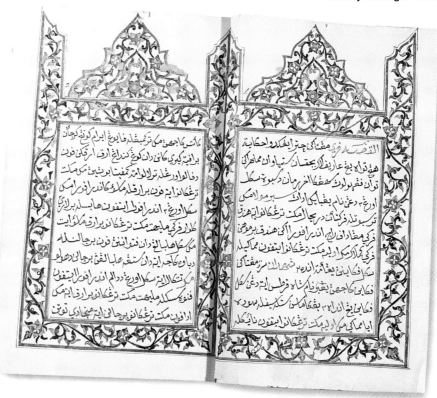

have achieved such greatness without Hang Tuah. Also significant, although perhaps of somewhat less importance, *Hikayat Hang Tuah* portrays the archetypical rebel against the feudal state, in the guise of Hang Jebat.

Some scholars consider the bendahara to be the true hero of the story, in that he saved Melaka with his wisdom. The importance of this trait can therefore also be seen as a theme of the story. In the 1960s and 1970s, Hang Jebat was reinterpreted in modern Malaysia as the real hero of the work: a forerunner of a new age of democracy, who stood up to the feudal social structure. This view resonated with certain post-colonial Malay aspirations during those decades. Nevertheless, it is Hang Tuah who remains the archetypical Malay hero.

Pages from a beautifully decorated manuscript of *Hikayat Hang Tuah* dated 1882 held by the School of Oriental and African Studies, London.

Russian translation of *Hikayat Hang Tuah*. The Malay original has also been translated into English, French, and German.

The duel between Hang Tuah and Hang Jebat

The best-known episode in the story of Hang Tuah is his duel to the death with his friend Hang Jebat. Hang Tuah was sentenced to death for a second time, due to another false accusation that he had had an affair with the Sultan's concubine, and went into hiding.

Hang Jebat was appointed to replace Hang Tuah in the royal court. However, as a result of the injustice done to his friend, Hang Jebat rebelled against the Sultan, usurped the palace and had an affair with the Sultan's concubine. This so enraged the Sultan that he had Hang Tuah fetched from his hiding place to fight Hang Jebat. Hang Tuah, faced with a difficult choice, chose his ruler over his good friend who, as a traitor, had committed the greatest of crimes.

A duel ensued between Hang Tuah and Hang Jebat, during which other Melakans stood beneath the palace floorboards and jabbed spears at Hang Jebat. Ultimately, Hang Tuah stabbed Hang Jebat, who then ran amok killing those who had taunted him, and finally died in Hang Tuah's arms.

Sejarah Melayu

The Sejarah Melayu ('Malay Annals'), is a major historical Malay text based on an older work, the Hikayat Melayu ('Malay story'). It tells the story of the rise and fall of the Melaka empire, including the origins of the sultans, the prevalent beliefs and customs, the coming of Islam, and the empire's relationships with other powers. The work follows the traditional Malay concept of history which combines myths, legends and folklore with factual records of historic events, and both Hindu and Islamic influences are identifiable. A number of versions have subsequently appeared.

At its peak during the reign of Sultan Mahmud Shah (1488–1530), prior to the Portuguese conquest in 1511, the Melaka empire extended across large areas of the Malay Peninsula and modern Indonesia.

An important historical document

In 1612, Sultan Alauddin Riayat Shah III, the ruler of Johor, assigned his *bendahara* (chief minister), Tun Seri Lanang, to rewrite and update the *Hikayat Melayu* which had came to Johor from Goa earlier that year. Unfortunately, it is not known for certain which Goa it came from. It may have been Goa in Sulawesi, Indonesia, or perhaps the Portuguese colony of Goa in India. Yet another possibility is Gua (Guha), north of Kuala Lipis in Pahang.

What emerged was a historical narrative renamed *Sulalatus-Salatin* ('Genealogy of Kings'), although it has since at least 1938 been better known as *Sejarah Melayu*. The book describes the colourful, cosmopolitan life of the Melaka sultanate with wit and humour. Written in the finest literary language of the time, with a liberal sprinkling of Sanskrit, Persian, Javanese, Arabic and Portuguese words, the text records the cultural history, philosophy and values of the Malays. An important historical reference and the best known of all Malay literary works, it has long been essential reading for an understanding of Malay historiography, political culture and language.

Tracing the lineage

The *Sejarah Melayu* recounts that Raja Suran, a descendant of Raja Iskandar Zulkarnain (Alexander the Great)—named as the ancestor of the Malay rulers—sired three sons. They left Dika, an undersea kingdom, on a white bull and landed at Mount Seguntang Mahameru in Sumatra. Demang Lebar Daun, the chief of Palembang, welcomed them and assigned each prince to a state. The youngest of the three princes ruled Palembang with the title of Sri Tri Buana (also known as Sang Nila Utama). He defined the bond and relationship that should exist

The illuminated beginning of the so-called 'longer' version of the *Sejarah Melayu*, completed by Muhammad Hasan ibn al-Haji Abdul Aziz in Batavia (Jakarta) on 8 October 1834.

between the Malay ruler and his subjects. He believed that the people would remain loyal subjects as long as they were treated justly; and even if they became disloyal or behaved offensively, their rulers should judge them fairly.

Sri Tri Buana later settled in Bintan island in the Riau archipelago before moving to Temasik, which he renamed Singapura (Singapore). Three generations of rulers in Singapura fought off attacks from the Javanese Majapahit Empire. The next ruler, Parameswara (later known as Sultan Sri Iskandar Shah), lost Singapura to Majapahit after punishing his concubine without investigating her alleged misdeed. The girl's father, Sang Rajuna Tapa, one of the ruler's ministers, avenged his family's shame by siding with the Javanese. Parameswara fled north and founded Melaka where both he and his son converted to Islam. His son, who assumed the title of Sultan Muhammad Shah, introduced court ceremonies, laws and regulations into the Melaka administration.

The height of empire

The *Sejarah Melayu* portrays the development of Melaka into a prosperous and powerful state, ruled by a number of able Islamic rulers with enlightened ministers. Sultan Muzaffar Shah, Sultan Mansur Shah and Sultan Alauddin Riayat Shah, together with their officials, brought both renown and power to Melaka. Sultan Muzaffar Shah achieved peace with Siam through battles and diplomacy, while Sultan Mansur Shah gained the friendship of Majapahit and China by marrying princesses from both countries.

This model of the palace of Sultan Mansur Shah in about 1460 is displayed at the Melaka Museum. It is based on the description given in the *Sejarah Melayu*.

his leadership, developed Melaka into a peaceful and prosperous trading centre and further extended the empire to Kampar in Sumatra. His son, the unjust Sultan Mahmud Shah, succeeded him.

Sultan Mahmud Shah is portrayed negatively. He put to death an official who expressed doubt about his rightful ascension to the throne, and ordered a rival suitor executed. He overlooked the misbehaviour of his favourites even if they broke the law; and, while behaving similarly himself, refused to tolerate his brother's affairs with women, and had him killed. Further, his marriage to the fiancée of the Pahang ruler created ill feeling between Melaka and Pahang.

Yet, despite the sultan's misdeeds, Melaka prospered—to a large extent due to the leadership of the wise bendahara—and attracted foreign traders, including the Portuguese. However, the bendahara made a grave mistake by failing to introduce his daughter, Tun Fatimah, to the ruler before betrothing her to Tun Ali. For this oversight and an alleged plan to overthrow him, Sultan Mahmud Shah executed the bendahara and his family, and married Tun Fatimah. When the accusation against the bendahara proved false, he abdicated in favour of his eldest son, Sultan Ahmad Shah, and became a recluse.

Among the many tales related in the *Sejarah Melayu* is that of a swordfish attack on Singapura (Singapore). The inhabitants initially suffered many casualties, until a boy suggested that they build a defensive wall of banana stems. This they did, and survived the attack as a result. It has been suggested that the attack is an allusion to the invasion of the Majapahit fleet.

The work focuses in particular detail on the reign of Sultan Mansur Shah, documenting the many historic incidents of the period, including the exploits of Hang Tuah and his compatriots who visited Majapahit. The annals reach their apogee in the duel between Hang Tuah and Hang Jebat, each upholding his own interpretation of loyalty to the ruler and to each other (see '*Hikayat Hang Tuah*').

The Melaka empire is recorded as having expanded with the acquisition of Inderagiri and Siantan in Sumatra, as part of a dowry obtained by Sultan Mansur Shah. Melaka also defeated the Sumatran kingdom of Siak, and installed a Melakan prince as ruler of Pahang. At the same time, Melaka competed with the Sumatran sultanate of Pasai to be the centre of Islamic scholarship, and intervened in Pasai's internal affairs. Melaka's greatness was further enhanced when an envoy of the Chinese emperor arrived to fetch a cure for his ruler's illness. Sultan Mansur Shah's heir, Alauddin Riayat Shah, noted for

Decline of the empire

In 1511, Alfonso d'Albuquerque, the Portuguese viceroy of India, captured Melaka. Sultan Mahmud Shah and Sultan Ahmad Shah and their court fled to Johor. However, Sultan Mahmud Shah secretly ordered Sultan Ahmad Shah to be killed as he was creating factions among court officials. Further Portuguese attacks, this time on Johor, forced Sultan Mahmud Shah to flee to Bintan island, and eventually to Kampar, Sumatra, where he was succeeded upon his death by his son with Tun Fatimah, Sultan Alauddin Riayat Shah II.

The *Sejarah Melayu* concludes by tracing the Melaka lineage to the next ruler, Sultan Alauddin Riayat Shah III, who commissioned the chronicles.

Variant editions

Manuscripts
At least 32 manuscripts of the *Sejarah Melayu* exist, written in Malay in the Jawi script. Copied by hand, each differs to a greater or lesser extent in terms of words and sentences, and even characters and events.

ABOVE RIGHT: Opening pages of a version copied in Melaka by Muhammad Tajuddin Tambi Hilam bin Zainal Abidin, dated 17 February 1873.

RIGHT: A copy of the *Sejarah Melayu* acquired by Russian volunteer, and future Admiral, I. F. Kruzenstern on a visit to the Malay Peninsula in 1798. It is now kept in the Library of the Institute of Oriental Studies, at the Russian Academy of Science (St. Petersburg branch).

Printed editions

1. Title page of the 1821 edition of the first complete English version of the *Sejarah Melayu*, translated by Dr John C. Leyden; 2. Cover of a subsequent reprint displaying Leyden's portrait; 3. The Jawi edition of the *Sejarah Melayu* published by the Methodist Publishing House in 1924, edited by W. G. Shellabear; 4. The Romanized Malay (*Rumi*) version of Shellabear's text is perhaps the best known version of the *Sejarah Melayu*.

The *Mahabharata*

The Mahabharata, an epic of Indian origin, is considered a holy book by Hindus. It was probably first brought to the Malay World by Hindu missionaries in the early centuries of the Common Era, either through oral narration or in the form of shadow play and drama. Written versions of the epic tales only appeared from the 16th century, as evidenced by the Early Modern Malay in which they were written.

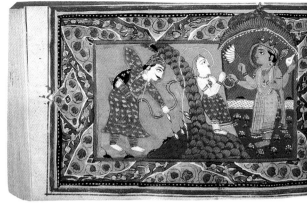

An undated edition of the *Mahabharata* kept at the International Institute of Islamic Thought and Civilization (ISTAC) in Kuala Lumpur. It comprises 248 pages and includes 7 miniatures.

Tapestry in the Batu Caves, Kuala Lumpur, depicting the warrior Rajuna (Arjuna) in a chariot engaged in battle with the Korawa.

Composition

The *Mahabharata* ('The Great Bharata Family'), began as a short ballad in prose and verse. It was later expanded from many sources, to reach its final form in about 400 BCE. Composed of some 100,000 couplets, divided into 18 parts or books, it was compiled in this form in Sanskrit by the Indian Rsi Vyasa. There is also a supplement, the *Harivamsa*.

The main story, which is of war, occupies only about a quarter of the epic; the remainder is episodic and covers a wide variety of subjects, including cosmology, ethics, history and philosophic interludes. The best-known part of the work—albeit a relatively short one—is the *Bhagavad Gita*, Rajuna's (Arjuna's) dialogue with his mentor, Krishna.

Story outline

Although most elements of the story remain unchanged, there are a number of differences between the Malay, Javanese and Indian versions of the story. One such difference is the name of the characters. Here, the Malay form is used followed in parentheses by the Indian form.

The main story of the *Mahabharata* tells of the fight for control of the kingdom of Astinapura (Hastinapura) between two branches of the Bharata clan, the Korawa and the Pandawa. It culminates in the huge 18-day battle of Kurukshetra, also known as the Bharatayuddha (the war of the Bharata), that historically occurred between 850 and 650 BCE.

The Korawa and the Pandawa were two sets of cousins who originated from a common ancestor, Vichitravirya, the King of Astinapura. He had two sons, Dastarastra (Dhritarashtra) and Pandu. As Dastarastra, the elder of the two, was blind, it was Pandu who succeeded to the throne after

Vichitravirya's death. However, Pandu died at a young age, and Dastarastra then became king. He took good care of Pandu's five sons (the Pandawa), treating his nephews in the same way as his own 100 sons (the Korawa).

The Korawa grew jealous of the Pandawa, and enmity arose between the two sets of cousins over the succession to the throne of Astinapura. This led to the Pandawa twice being exiled from the country, each time as a result of losing a game of dice. During the first period of exile, the Pandawa were involved in a number of adventures and met the princess Draupadi, who in the Indian version married all five brothers at the same time, but in the Malay and Javanese versions married only the eldest brother, Dharmawangsa (Yudhisthira). Upon their return from exile, the kingdom was divided between the Pandawa and the Korawa by Dastarastra. The second period of exile followed a game of dice between Dharmawangsa and Sakuni, the adviser of the Korawa, resulting in the loss of the Pandawa's portion of the kingdom. The Pandawa then spent 13 years in exile, and encountered many misfortunes.

The Pandawa finally returned to Astinapura to fight the Korawa, resulting in the great 18-day battle, which was won by the Pandawa.

Malay *Mahabharata* tales

Malay versions of the *Mahabharata* stories are believed to have originated from Javanese translations of the original epic. Translation or adaptation from Javanese to Malay probably took

The appearance of Vishnu

Vaishnuvistic Hindus, who revere the deity Vishnu, make up a small percentage of the Hindus in Malaysia. They also revere the *Mahabharata* as a holy text. Vishnu appears in the story in 10 different forms, intended to establish righteousness on earth. Each of these forms is depicted in statuettes located in the Batu Caves Hindu temple near Kuala Lumpur: (from left) Parasurama Avataram, Rama Avataram, Balarama Avataram, Krishna Avataram, Kalki Avataram, Narasimma Avataram, Vamana Avataram, Macca Avataram, Kurma Avataram, and Varana Avataram.

place around 1200 to 1300 CE when Javanese influence on the Malay World was at its height. Scenes from the *Mahabharata* are also depicted in Wayang Kulit (shadow play).

Several versions of the epic, written in Jawi, are preserved in Hikayat (see 'The Hikayat') under various titles. Throughout these versions, the core of the story—the war between the Pandawa and the Korawa, symbolizing the fight between good and evil—remains the same. However, overt features of the Hindu religion are played down, with the focus being on universal values instead. The Malay versions of the epic were publicized to scholars in 1875 by van der Tuuk (see 'Language stocks and families') in an article in a Batavian journal on Malay manuscripts in the possession of the Royal Asiatic Society.

The most 'complete' version of the story is found in *Hikayat Pandawa Lima,* which covers almost all the important parts or books of the original Indian *Mahabharata,* and is similar in style to a Wayang Kulit script. This became incorporated into the Malay literary corpus relatively late compared to other local versions. Other Hikayat containing stories from the *Mahabharata* concentrate only on selected tales. The *Hikayat Pandawa Jaya,* for example, concentrates on the 18-day battle of Kurukshetra.

Underlying themes

Underlying the story of conflict and war is the message that evil can never win. Evil, embodied in the Korawa, is manifested in greed, envy and lust. On the other hand, virtue, personified by the Pandawa, is reflected in filial and fraternal loyalty as well as in humility and generosity. Virtue is especially reflected in the character of King Dharmawangsa, the eldest of the five Pandawa, notwithstanding its inevitable triumph, virtue may suffer setbacks.

The Malay tales taken from the *Mahabharata* also depict the evil of warfare, and the emotions that arise from having to fight (and even kill) one's own kinsmen. Although the Pandawa won the war, both they and the Korawa suffered terribly, including losing members of their own families. The war is also a reflection of heroic human qualities such as valour, loyalty, justice and maturity.

The *Mahabharata* tales also bear the message that no one is perfect. A person who may appear 'good' may at times exhibit failings. A clear illustration of

In Malay literature
Tales from the *Mahabharata*, written in prose as Hikayat (see 'The Hikayat'), appear under various titles, the most comprehensive of which is *Hikayat Pandawa Lima*. Other titles include *Hikayat Pandawa, Hikayat Pandawa Jaya, Cerita-cerita Pandawa Lima,* and *Hikayat Sang Boma.*

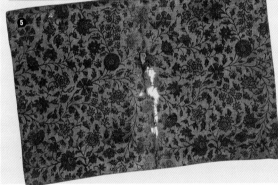

1. *Hikayat Pandawa Lima,* the original of which is at the National Library of Indonesia, Jakarta.
2. Two printed Romanized versions of tales derived from the *Mahabharata,* the *Hikayat Pandawa Lima* and the *Hikayat Purasara.*
3 and 4. Detail and page from an illuminated manuscript of *Hikayat Maharaja Boma* in the collection of the National Library of Malaysia.
5. The outer cloth binding of a manuscript of *Hikayat Perang Pandawa Jaya* dated 1804, with a locally designed pattern of carnations and foliage. It was collected by John Leyden, probably in Kedah.

this appears in the *Hikayat Pandawa Lima*. Rajuna, besides having the Pandawa's good qualities, was also extraordinarily handsome, a trait which he used to seduce beautiful women, mostly other men's wives, much to the disapproval of his eldest brother, Dharmawangsa. Vanity and lust went hand in hand and this caused Rajuna much misery.

In Wayang Kulit
Tales from the *Mahabharata* were traditionally performed as Wayang Kulit (shadow play), particularly in Johor, and formed much of the extensive repertoire of the Wayang Kulit Purwa, probably the oldest shadow play form, which originated in Java where the original *Mahabharata* stories were added to, and altered. Once established in the Malay Peninsula, the Malay language over time replaced the Javanese.

Early 20th-century Javanese illustration of the Pandawa clan, taken from Wayang Kulit. Malay shadow play versions of the *Mahabharata* were derived from Javanese renderings.

Different stories were performed for various rites of passage, such as birth or circumcision, and other significant occasions including recovery from a serious illness. Through Wayang Kulit performances, stories from the *Mahabharata* became well known to rural Malays. Though primarily entertainment, the tales also had a didactic value, especially in teaching the young about the good and the evil in life.

The *Ramayana*

The Indian epic of the Ramayana *was brought to the Malay Peninsula over a thousand years ago. Originally written in Sanskrit, the tale was translated into Malay and enjoyed through both oral storytelling and shadow play performances. There are now two leading versions of the story in Malay, the* Hikayat Seri Rama *being the literary version, and the* Hikayat Maharaja Wana *used in shadow play.*

Heritage

Valmiki, an Indian sage and poet, is believed to be the author (and narrator) of the Sanskrit epic, the *Ramayana* ('The Romance of Rama'), composed about 300 BCE. In its present form, the epic contains 24,000 couplets, divided into seven books; however it is thought that the first and last of these books were later additions to the original story.

The epic spread to many lands including Indonesia, where it was translated into vernacular languages and became well known, both through oral storytelling and theatrical performances (and, in more recent times, movies and television); a written version was also produced in Java in the 10th century. In the Malay Peninsula, the stories of the epic were passed down from generation to generation by oral storytellers and shadow play puppeteers who adopted the *Ramayana* into their repertoire, in the course of which it was localized.

Balinese woodcarving depicting Rama handing his ring to Hanuman to deliver to Sita who was held captive by Rawana in Lanka.

Themes

The *Ramayana* serves not only to entertain, but also to educate. Its themes focus on wisdom, love, justice, beauty, courage, self-control, and skill in warfare. Indeed, the story serves as a lesson in statecraft.

A key theme is the benefit of leading a virtuous and good life. Rama and Sita symbolize the good and virtuous, Rawana represents the bad and evil. It

Outline of the story

The *Ramayana* is the tale of Rama, the son of the king of Ayuthia, and his wife Sita Devi. After Rama is deprived of his rightful accession to the throne, he goes into voluntary exile with Sita and his brother Laksamana. Rawana, a demon, lures Sita away by adopting the guise of a golden deer, and takes her to his island kingdom of Lanka. To search for his wife, Rama enlists the aid of a monkey nation led by a general,

Hanuman, who discovers Sita in Lanka. Rama wins a monumental battle against Rawana, regains his wife, and ascends the throne of Ayuthia. Nevertheless, all is not well. The people accuse Sita of adultery during her period in Lanka. As a result, Rama sends his wife to a hermitage, where she gives birth to their twin sons. Only much later are Rama and Sita reunited.

A depiction of the story of Rawana disguising himself as a golden deer in order to lure Sita away from Rama and his brother Laksamana.

is not only the characters of Rama and Sita that are admired; it is also their physical appearance. Rama represents the ideal of princely heroism, a very handsome man with all the desirable manly qualities, while Sita is representative of incomparable feminine beauty and wifely devotion. Thus, virtue and beauty always go together. The story also advocates harmony between husband and wife, where an intruder should be looked upon with suspicion, and loyalty between brothers. Evil and ugliness, too, are inevitably linked together, as illustrated in the person and character of Rawana. Other positive traits are represented by the characters Laksamana (brotherly love) and Hanuman (loyal service).

Written forms

The *Hikayat Seri Rama*, the story of the *Ramayana* written in Malay in the Hikayat form, is considered one of the great Malay literary works (see 'The Hikayat'). It was probably first written down in the 15th century, although the oldest extant copy was acquired by Archbishop Laud in 1633. The *Hikayat Seri Rama* has variations from the original Hindu epic, resulting from the localization of the story as it was passed down orally over the centuries. Islamic elements were added after the introduction of Islam to the Malay Peninsula. For example, the heroine of the Ramayana, Sita Devi, is known as Siti Dewi in the Malay Hikayat; Siti is a Muslim Arabic name.

Many collections of *Ramayana* stories have been published in Malaysia, for both adults and children. Among those published in Malay for adults were Maxwell's *Cerita Seri Rama* ('The story of Sri Rama') (1886) and the text entitled *Hikayat Seri Rama* (1915) edited and published by Shellabear. Before Independence, when books written in Malay were scarce, simplified versions of the *Ramayana* tales were popular as school texts.

Ramayana tales in Malay folk theatre

Until the 1950s, shadow play performances and oral renditions by storytellers (see 'Malay oral traditions') of tales from

the *Ramayana* were regular events in Malay villages. This tradition is now only continued in certain parts of Kelantan and Kedah, especially during weddings and after the harvest. The epic is performed in Wayang Kulit Siam, a modern form of the classic Wayang Kulit Purwa (which itself uses stories from the *Mahabharata*). The version used is based on the *Hikayat Maharaja Wana* and the *Cerita Kusi Serawi*, versions that differ from the classical *Hikayat Seri Rama*. In particular, they introduce changes and adaptations which incorporate Islamic and Malay elements to replace the Hindu components of the original stories. Each puppeteer, too, lends his own style to the stories, according to his local background. Furthermore, it is the minor, later adventures of Rama, his followers and their descendants, that are more frequently performed.

Although the original epic has no comic characters, Wayang Kulit performances of stories from the *Ramayana* always include two such characters, Pak Dogol and Wak Long. They entered Rama's service after the death of Rawana and are Rama's trusted companions, often assisting him in his heroic adventures. Pak Dogol, unmistakable because of his distended navel, has both heavenly and earthly roles.

The names of the main characters vary from story to story, and are often given localized Malay names rather than the Indian originals. However, as the same puppet is always used to depict a character, by whatever name called, there is no confusion in the minds of the audience. To further avoid confusion, the puppets of the main characters are always painted the same colour: Rama is always dark green, while Laksamana is red, Siti Dewi yellow, Hanuman white, and Rawana black.

Two versions of *Ramayana* tales printed in romanized Malay.

Following early work by W. Maxwell, Professor Amin Sweeney published a compilation of oral versions of the story of Rama in his book, *Ramayana and the Malay Shadow Play*.

Illuminated initial folio of a copy of the *Hikayat Sri Rama* completed on 21 February 1835.

Ramayana characters in Wayang Kulit

These Wayang Kulit puppets represent, from left, Hanuman, the monkey king; Seri Rama's virtuous wife, known as Siti Dewi in Malay; the hero, Seri Rama; and Rawana, the evil king of Lanka.

Panji romances

The Panji romances are an extensive cycle of stories about a prince (Panji) and his elusive fiancée (Chandra Kirana). They originated in Java, where they were used in Wayang Topeng (Javanese masked theatre). In the Malay Peninsula, they were held in particularly high regard, having been passed down through the generations in a number of ways, including oral storytelling, shadow play, and written form (both prose and verse). With localization, the names of some of the characters have changed from the Hindu-influenced original.

Written in the early 19th century, the Panji-based *Hikayat Pendawa Lebur* has 145 pages, the first two of which are illuminated with floral designs.

Origin and spread

The old Javanese word *panji* or *apanji* means 'prince'. Later, it came to be a royal title awarded to members of the Javanese court. During the height of the Majapahit empire in the 14th and 15th centuries, the term 'panji' was accepted as a title of 'princes of the blood'. Hence, the heroes depicted in the stories are called 'Panji' in place of their own names, which were often very long.

Although the romances are purely literary creations, they are set in the Javanese historical past, with their own sets of myths and links to historical events. Various Hindu elements are contained in the Panji stories, suggesting that they belong to the Hindu period of Southeast Asian civilization. However, given the content and language of the Malay versions of the Panji stories, it is likely that these stories entered the Malay literary scene only after the arrival of Islam in the Peninsula.

The Panji romances entered historical Malay literature from Java through literal translation, adaptation and the process of retelling. The term 'translation' is however used loosely here, because it merely involved transferring the story from Javanese into Malay. Although the stories retain most of their Javanese or panji elements, Malay storytellers, like their counterparts in other Southeast Asian countries including Thailand, Myanmar and Laos, also include numerous local elements in their stories. The subsequent transcription and translation of these stories into the Malay Jawi script naturally became a literary activity of Malay copyists.

Structure

The Panji romances are stories about Raden Inu Kertapati, a Javanese prince, and his fiancée, the princess Raden Galuh Chandra Kirana. Raden Inu is the Crown Prince of the fictional Kuripan, while Raden Galuh is the daughter of the King of Daha. Princes and princesses from other states, such as Gegelang and Singosari, are also featured in the romances in various supporting roles. The princes and princesses, who are cousins, are encouraged to marry within their group in order to retain the combined power of the four states, and to maintain the purity of their royal blood.

The romances are classic love stories about Raden Inu (Panji) and Raden Galuh who have been betrothed since young. They grow up into adulthood feeling secure in the knowledge that they are meant for each other, and slowly developing feelings of love, faithfulness and respect for one another, even without ever having met.

However, things change when either the hero (or occasionally, the heroine) is forced to leave the palace, usually as a result of some supernatural intervention. This separation

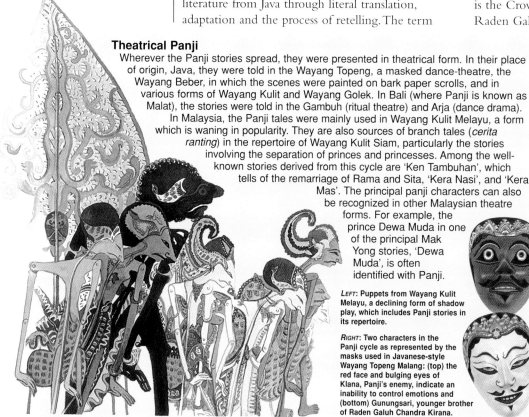

Theatrical Panji

Wherever the Panji stories spread, they were presented in theatrical form. In their place of origin, Java, they were told in the Wayang Topeng, a masked dance-theatre, the Wayang Beber, in which the scenes were painted on bark paper scrolls, and in various forms of Wayang Kulit and Wayang Golek. In Bali (where Panji is known as Malat), the stories were told in the Gambuh (ritual theatre) and Arja (dance drama). In Malaysia, the Panji tales were mainly used in Wayang Kulit Melayu, a form which is waning in popularity. They are also sources of branch tales (*cerita ranting*) in the repertoire of Wayang Kulit Siam, particularly the stories involving the separation of princes and princesses. Among the well-known stories derived from this cycle are 'Ken Tambuhan', which tells of the remarriage of Rama and Sita, 'Kera Nasi', and 'Kera Mas'. The principal panji characters can also be recognized in other Malaysian theatre forms. For example, the prince Dewa Muda in one of the principal Mak Yong stories, 'Dewa Muda', is often identified with Panji.

LEFT: Puppets from Wayang Kulit Melayu, a declining form of shadow play, which includes Panji stories in its repertoire.

RIGHT: Two characters in the Panji cycle as represented by the masks used in Javanese-style Wayang Topeng Malang: (top) the red face and bulging eyes of Klana, Panji's enemy, indicate an inability to control emotions and (bottom) Gunungsari, younger brother of Raden Galuh Chandra Kirana.

period is devised to enable the hero (or heroine) to start on a journey in search of his or her betrothed, and to experience life beyond sheltered palace existence. The paths of Panji and Raden Galuh cross many times (not recognizing each other because they have never met, and because of disguises), but they are not allowed to meet until the gods allow. Finally, they are united to live in eternal bliss.

Hindu elements

Hindu characters in the Panji stories introduce supernatural elements and make impossible feats possible. From the very beginning of a story, the position of Betara Kala and other Hindu gods such as Arjuna and Samba is established. It is because of their wrath that the episodes in each story begin to take place. They are always there to perform impossible feats, such as bringing the dead back to life, and creating storms and hurricanes in order to cause chaos, as well as to decide when to end a separation, or to orchestrate a meeting.

Other elements typical of the Hindu literary and religious tradition include characters retreating into isolation for meditation, reincarnation, sprinkling holy water to resurrect the dead, the hero or heroine setting off on a journey and the characters disguising themselves.

These Javanese–Hindu elements did not seem to disturb Malay copyists or translators. Indeed, after the coming of Islam to the Malay Peninsula, Hindu influence lost its religious significance, and became recognized purely as part of the Malay cultural

One of several Panji tales printed as Hikayat in Romanized Malay.

heritage. It is likely, however, that it was the exotic, magical and mythical Hindu elements that initially attracted Malay readers and listeners to the stories.

Popularity

The simple storyline of the Panji stories has contributed to their popularity. With their episodic structure, the length of each tale can be adjusted by a storyteller to suit his audience, and new episodes can be added at any point in the story.

The stories were particularly popular among the 19th-century Malay courts, especially those of Kedah and Johor; particularly among female members of the courts. The large number of Panji stories that survive in original manuscripts, printed Hikayat, and the performing arts such as shadow play, attests to the high regard in which the stories were and, indeed, continue to be held, in Malay and Javanese society.

The Panji stories are popular throughout Southeast Asia. Besides being circulated in the two dominant languages, Javanese and Malay, versions of the stories appear in the Balinese, Cambodian, Thai, Laotian, Tagalog and Myanmar languages. In Bali, they are known as the *Malat* stories, while in Palembang (Sumatra) they are called the *Panji Angreni* tales. The Panji tales of Cambodia present the hero as Eyano, a variation of the Old Javanese Hino and Ino alias Inu. In Thai literature, the stories appear in two versions, the *Dalang* (shadow play) version and the *Inau* (Malay/Javanese Inu) stories.

TOP: Wayang Kulit puppets of Panji (right) and one of his servants.

ABOVE: The hero and heroine of the Panji stories, Panji and his fiancée, Raden Galuh Chandra Kirana.

Hikayat Misa Taman Jaya Jayeng Kusuma

One of the longest Malay Panji stories, *Hikayat Misa Taman Jaya Jayeng Kusuma* is representative of the Panji genre and its themes of love, wandering, war and disguise.

The fat clown, Semar, attempting to draw a picture of the beautiful princess Raden Galuh, unwittingly draws the fierce goddess, Durga.

Prince Raden Inu (Panji), is to be engaged to Raden Galuh, whom he has never seen. He decides not to marry her when he sees the portrait by Semar.

Panji later meets Raden Galuh for the first time, and is captivated by her incredible beauty.

That night he tries to enter her room, but finds her gone, kidnapped by the god Betara Kala.

Betara Kala leaves Raden Galuh in the forest; she then travels to various kingdoms. Meanwhile, Panji sets out to find her.

Panji and Raden Galuh adopt many disguises and fight many battles. On one occasion, when Raden Galuh is disguised as a man, they fight one another.

In one of the seven major battles in the story, Panji is disguised as an ascetic when the hermitage he is staying in is attacked.

Finally, after countless adventures, trials and tribulations, Panji and Raden Galuh are reunited.

Religious literature

The teachings of the Qur'an and Hadith were supplemented by tales of Prophet Muhammad and the other Islamic prophets, both orally and written, in the Hikayat, and less romantic kitab (holy book), formats. These works have been instrumental in advancing the understanding of Islam in the region. The Qur'an itself is not considered mere religious literature by Muslims, but rather as the direct word of God (kalimah).

Shaykh Nur-al-Din al-Raniri (d. 1658)

This Muslim theologian and author originally from Rander in India arrived in Aceh in 1637, where he was in the service of the Sultan of Aceh. He left in 1644, by which time he had mastered the Malay language and written a number of significant religious works, as well as the famous *Bustan al-Salatin* ('Garden of Kings') on statecraft. He was particularly vocal in his condemnation of the Hindu epics on the grounds that they were opposed to the Islamic concept of *tauhid*, belief in the One God or Allah.

So impressive was Shaykh Nur-al-Din's use of Malay in works such as *Hidayat al-Iman bi Fadl al-Mannan* (above) that it has been suggested that he may have known the language prior to his arrival in Aceh.

Early Islamic texts in the Malay World

Many stories were brought to the Malay World with the arrival of Islam to supplement the teaching of religious tenets and to help followers better understand the religion. They were also often told for entertainment. They entered Malay life as oral traditions and were entrenched in the community before they were recorded in written Malay using the Jawi script. No records exist as to when the tales were first committed to writing, however it is likely to have occurred during the 17th century.

Basic Islamic teachings were, and continue to be, contained in the bodies of knowledge known as *Tauhid* and *Fikah*. The former teaches monotheism while the latter prescribes the rules of Muslim life. Concise manuals on these were written following the Islamization of the peninsular Malay kingdoms between the 13th to 15th centuries, and subsequently expanded into works known as *Ilmu Kalam*.

Early Muslim writers, both Malay and non-Malay, began to compose and adapt Islamic stories into Malay. They rejected the polytheism and anthropomorphism of the Hindu epic tradition that dominated the Malay World prior to the arrival of Islam. Narratives elaborated on those in the Qur'an and showed how the prophets fought against idolatry to establish Islam as the religion of God. In contrast to the Hindu epics, characters were primarily historical figures such as Prophet Muhammad, other prophets, and famous Muslim personalities, later including pious Malay Muslims.

While Islamic stories were translated into the Malay language, the Qur'an remained in the original Arabic. The version above, held in the collection of the Institute of Islamic Thought and Civilization (ISTAC) in Kuala Lumpur, is a facsimile copy of the Holy Qur'an written and illuminated in Baghdad in 1000–1 CE.

Hikayat Nabi Muhammad

As with most stories of the prophets, *Hikayat Nabi Muhammad* ('Story of Prophet Muhammad') has a historical basis to which imaginary elements have been added to enrich the narrative. The story pitches Prophet Muhammad against a powerful enemy, Raja Khaibar. This fictitious king was immensely wealthy, and was protected by a great city and a cunning magician, Hawan, who further strengthened the city with elements of the Zoroastrian religion.

The fight against these two adversaries was led by the historical figure Ali bin Abu Talib, Prophet Muhammad's uncle, who, it is told, wielded the magical sword, Zulkafar, with which he could kill thousands of enemies in a single blow. The story assures its Muslim readers that God will fight with them in defence of their faith, thus assuring them of victory.

English translation of frontispiece

In the name of Allah, most Gracious, most Merciful, <u>And unto Him do we seek help</u> [in red ink]. This is the story told by Fatimah (may Allah's grace be upon her), of all the events relating to Allah's Apostle (may Allah's grace be upon him) when he stayed in the house of Ali (may Allah's grace be upon him), teaching his daughter, Fatimah. And thus says Allah's Apostle (may peace and Allah's blessings be upon him), 'O my daughter, Fatimah, whosoever is the woman...'

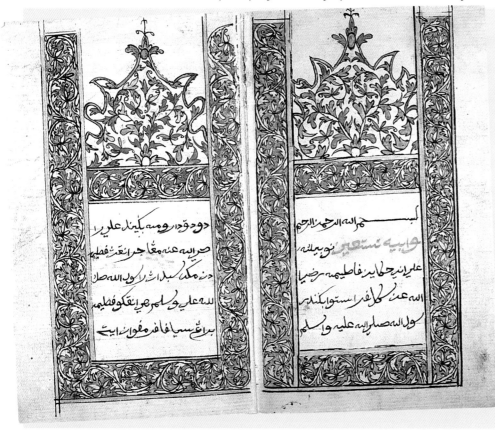

The first two pages of *Hikayat Nabi Muhammad mengajar anaknya Fatimah*, illuminated in blue, red and ochre ink.

Tales of Prophet Muhammad

Many more stories focus on Prophet Muhammad than on the other prophets. The *Hikayat Nur Muhammad* ('Story of the Light of Muhammad') recounts that his being began before the creation of Adam, existing in the form of a light, and his birth is related in a number of tales including *Cerita Nabi Lahir* ('Story of the Prophet's Birth'). Other (better known) stories concern his receiving the revelation of Allah through the angel Jibrail (Gabriel) while meditating—the event known as the *Hijrah*—which marked the start of the Muslim calendar.

The *Sirah* stories, concerning his character and life, were narrated by Muslim *qussas* (professional storytellers) who often enlivened the tales for illiterate audiences by adding fictitious episodes. These gave rise to the development of numerous legends regarding the Prophet's personality. The narratives of Prophet Muhammad's life inspired writers of Malay romances to write a number of such stories including *Hikayat Peri Menyatakan Mu'jizat Nabi* ('Story of the Prophet's Miracles') and *Hikayat Bulan Berbelah Dua* ('Story of the Splitting Moon'). One such tale, called *Hikayat Nabi Bercukur* ('Story of the Prophet's Shaving'), is considered heretical by some

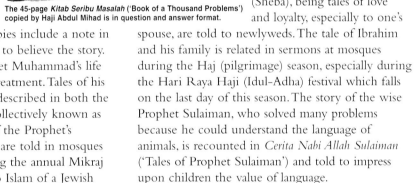

The 45-page *Kitab Seribu Masalah* ('Book of a Thousand Problems') copied by Haji Abdul Mihad is in question and answer format.

Muslim experts, and some copies include a note in the margin telling readers not to believe the story.

Certain episodes of Prophet Muhammad's life have received more detailed treatment. Tales of his ascension to heaven (*Mikraj*), described in both the Qur'an and the Hadith, are collectively known as *Hikayat Nabi Mikraj* ('Story of the Prophet's Ascension to Heaven'). These are told in mosques and religious gatherings during the annual Mikraj celebration. The conversion to Islam of a Jewish rabbi named Abdullah ibn Salam by Prophet Muhammad, while teaching in Persia, was developed into a Hikayat, *Kitab Seribu Masalah* ('Book of a Thousand Problems'). Several classical Malay romances concern the Prophet's war exploits. Known as *maghazi*, these include *Hikayat Nabi Muhammad* ('Story of Prophet Muhammad'), *Hikayat Raja Khaybar* ('Story of Raja Khaybar'), *Hikayat Raja Rahib* ('Story of Raja Rahib'), and *Hikayat Raja Handaq* ('Story of Raja Handaq').

Prophet Muhammad's death is related in *Hikayat Tatkala Nabi Pulang ke Rahmatullah* ('Story of the Time when Prophet Muhammad Died'). There are several Malay versions of this story, originally written in Arabic under the title *Qissah Wafat Rasulillah*.

Tales of other prophets

The *Qisasul Anbiya'* ('Stories of the Prophets') is a collection of stories translated into Malay from the Arabic original bearing the same title by Al-Haji Azhari Al-Khalidi, with stories taken from the Qur'an, the Hadith and the *Tafsir* ('Interpretation of the Qur'an'). Published in Penang in the early 20th century, it focuses on the 25 great prophets of Islam, starting with Adam and ending with Muhammad. It has become a major source of tales written on the individual prophets.

The history of Islam, as told in the Qur'an, began with Adam, who instructed his children in the religion of Allah. This same teaching was revealed to various prophets who came after Adam, including Ibrahim (Abraham) and Musa (Moses), until Muhammad. Accounts of their lives were written by Muslim authors in the Near East, and adapted into Malay in narratives such as *Hikayat Nabi Yusuf* ('Story of Prophet Yusuf' (Joseph)) and *Hikayat Nabi Musa* ('Story of Prophet Musa').

The telling of some of the tales is reserved for special occasions. For example, the stories of Adam and Hawa (Eve), Yusuf and Siti Zaleha (Asenath), and Sulaiman (Solomon) and Balkish (Sheba), being tales of love and loyalty, especially to one's spouse, are told to newlyweds. The tale of Ibrahim and his family is related in sermons at mosques during the Haj (pilgrimage) season, especially during the Hari Raya Haji (Idul-Adha) festival which falls on the last day of this season. The story of the wise Prophet Sulaiman, who solved many problems because he could understand the language of animals, is recounted in *Cerita Nabi Allah Sulaiman* ('Tales of Prophet Sulaiman') and told to impress upon children the value of language.

Colophon of a version of the *Hikayat Nabi Yusuf* written on hide.

Four versions of *Hikayat Nabi Bercukur*

1. Manuscript copied in Kandi, Sri Lanka, in 1905.
2. Manuscript with cloth binding.
3. Pocket-sized illuminated manuscript.
4. Undated manuscript in the National Library of Malaysia.

97

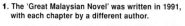

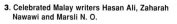
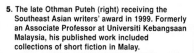

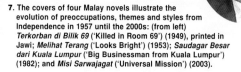

1. The 'Great Malaysian Novel' was written in 1991, with each chapter by a different author.

2. Launch of *Yin You Er Ge* ('Nursery Rhymes') by Teo Huat (right), published by Pelangi Press in 2003. The launch was officiated by the President of the MCA (Malaysian Chinese Association) Datuk Seri Ong Kah Ting (centre).

3. Celebrated Malay writers Hasan Ali, Zaharah Nawawi and Marsli N. O.

4. Professor Muhammad Haji Salleh (left) receiving the Anugerah Sastera Negara (National Literary Award) from His Majesty the Yang di-Pertuan Agong Sultan Azlan Shah in 1990.

5. The late Othman Puteh (right) receiving the Southeast Asian writers' award in 1999. Formerly an Associate Professor at Universiti Kebangsaan Malaysia, his published work included collections of short fiction in Malay.

6. Poet and critic Chen Xue Feng wrote *The Past 15 Years of Malayan Chinese Poems* (1962).

7. The covers of four Malay novels illustrate the evolution of preoccupations, themes and styles from Independence in 1957 until the 2000s: (from left) *Terkorban di Bilik 69* ('Killed in Room 69') (1949), printed in Jawi; *Melihat Terang* ('Looks Bright') (1953); *Saudagar Besar dari Kuala Lumpur* ('Big Businessman from Kuala Lumpur') (1982); and *Misi Sarwajagat* ('Universal Mission') (2003).

8. Malay novels on display at the Kinokuniya bookshop in Kuala Lumpur City Centre (KLCC).

9. Karim Raslan, a Cambridge-educated lawyer, has had short stories published in the leading British literary journals *Granta* and *Wasafiri* and anthologized by the publisher Penguin.

10. Writer and poet Dr Murasu Nedumaran compiled the landmark work *Malaysia Thamil Kavithai Kalanjiam* ('Collection of Malaysian Tamil Poems').

11. *Tuntut* ('Demand'), by Akiya (the pen name of Semai Orang Asli radio presenter and author, Mahat anak China) is a collection of Orang Asli short stories written in Malay.

12. *Flashman's Lady*, set in 19th-century Sarawak, written by British writer G. M. Fraser, scriptwriter of the Bond movie, *Octopussy*.

13. N. A. Senguttuvan's Tamil compilation *Ari Noorraandu Malaysia Siru Kadaigal* ('Half Century of Malaysian Short Stories 1950–2000').

14. The anthology *Xin Mahua Wen Wenxue Daxi* ('Singapore-Malaysia Chinese Literature Series'), published in 1965, contains a selection of novels, short stories, poetry, drama.

MODERN LITERATURE

As early as the 19th century, Munshi Abdullah bin Abdul Kadir veered away from the classical Malay prose form, the Hikayat, by inserting into his two main works, *Hikayat Abdullah* and *Kisah Pelayaran Abdullah*, descriptions of significant events that he observed during his lifetime. However, it was not until the 20th century that new forms of Malay literary expression truly

Majallah Guru magazine's first edition in 1924 created an important outlet for aspiring Malay literary talent.

emerged. The first new forms to emerge, in the 1920s, were the novel and the short story (*cerpen*). These were followed in the 1930s by the modern Malay free verse form known as *sajak*, which contrasted with the formulaic *pantun* and *syair*.

While these genres developed through the tumultuous years of World War II and anti-colonial sentiment, deliberate efforts to develop modern forms of literary expression only gained momentum following Independence in 1957. These efforts bore fruit: Malay literature reached maturity in the 1990s, with many established authors, poets and playwrights leading the way, several of whom have been awarded the Anugerah Sastera Negara (National Literary Award).

The large numbers of Chinese and Indian immigrants who arrived in Malaya in the 19th and early 20th centuries brought with them long-standing literary traditions. It was, however, only after several years that members of these communities in Malaya began to produce their own literature. Even then, writers were initially preoccupied with their respective homelands. A distinctive Malaysian voice and the use of local themes were discernible only after World War II. Writers in these languages continue to produce a significant amount of quality work, even without the centralized support afforded the Malay literary fraternity.

Works by foreign writers in English appeared with the establishment of British settlements in the Malay Peninsula. However, locally produced English literature developed only much later—no more than a handful of works were written before Independence—and the volume of work appearing has continued to be small. This may be attributed to some continuing resentment felt towards the language of colonialism, and to the fact that English is a first language to only a very small minority of Malaysians.

While there is an ancient tradition of Malay theatre, scriptwriting in the Western mould is a relatively recent development. Local dramas have nonetheless evolved substantially, often in line with international trends. Domestically written English plays appeared even later and, like local English literature, have a relatively limited appeal to the Malaysian public.

Built in 2003 from over 2,000 books, this 20-metre structure was credited as the tallest book-tower in Malaysia.

Early Malay novels

The transition from the traditional Hikayat narratives, in lyrical and free prose, to the modern 'novel' form was influenced by Malay interaction with the Middle East, and facilitated by the increasing availability of printing technology and the introduction of secular education. Early authors were often teachers and journalists, who wrote and were initially published in the Jawi script. Themes were driven by political and economic developments, but also focused on social issues.

Syed Sheikh Al-Hadi (1867–1934) (above), was the pioneer of the modern Malay novel with *Hikayat Faridah Hanum* (a later Jawi version is shown, right). He was also a co-founder of the ground-breaking Malay magazine *Al-Imam* (top right).

Defining elements
Structurally, early Malay novels in many ways resembled traditional Hikayat. Both genres used coincidences to initiate and move the story forward, Malay *pantun* (quatrains) and *syair* (narrative poems), and black-and-white characterization; and both had happy endings. However the novels also featured elements of realism, journalistic language, common speech, and dealt with topical issues.

Ahmad Kotot's *Hikayat Percintaan Kasih Kemudaan* ('Story of Love and Youth'), published in 1927–8.

The first novels
With the bestselling *Hikayat Faridah Hanum* ('Story of Faridah Hanum') (1925–6), Syed Sheikh Al-Hadi pioneered the novel genre in Malay literature. Set in Egypt, its social reform messages were nevertheless relevant to Malay society. Its success enabled him to start his own printing firm, Jelutong Press, in Penang.

Other novels of the same period also had foreign characters and backgrounds. Abdul Hamid bin Haji Ahmad's novel *Perjodohan Yang Setia* ('Faithful Marriage') was based in Sulawesi, Indonesia; and Zulkarnain Yaakub's *Hikayat Khalik dan Malik* ('Story of Khalik and Malik') and *Hikayat Perempuan Asyik* ('Story of a Preoccupied Woman') was set in the Middle East. The influence of *Hikayat Faridah Hanum* was also apparent in the themes of several novels that followed at the end of the 1920s, namely romantic love in the modern age, for example in Ahmad Kotot's *Hikayat Percintaan Kasih Kemudaan* ('Story of Love and Youth') and Zainun Aruf's *Rahsia Kemudaan* ('Secret of Youth').

The first novel with a local setting and characters was Ahmad Rashid Talu's *Kawan Benar* ('True Friend') (1927). He followed up with *Iakah Salmah?* ('Is That Salmah?') (1928), the longest novel of the period (648 pages). Rooted in daily life, it depicted Malay society undergoing changes and dealt with women's emancipation through Salmah, a young English-educated woman who opposed what she saw as the customs and mores that impeded the progress of Malay women.

Abdullah Sidek's 1939 novel, *Iblis Rumah Tangga* ('Devil in a Marriage') tells of a neglected wife resorting to prostitution.

The Malay novel developed rapidly in the 1930s due to a heightened awareness of the importance of education, the marked growth in the student population that resulted, and the related increased demand for reading materials. Publishing facilities became more widely available with the rise of publishing houses such as the Muhammadiah Press, Jauhariah Press, Trio Company, Ipoh Malay Press, Klang New Press, Persama Press, Sungai Ujung Press, and Teruna Press located in the urban areas of Penang, Ipoh, Muar, Seremban, Kuala Pilah, and Klang (see 'Language and the print media').

Pre-war influences and themes
The influx of Chinese and Indian immigrants that peaked in the 1920s and 1930s created hostility and unease among the Malays, who saw the newcomers and their customs as alien to their own cherished values, mores and way of life. Political changes fanned anti-British sentiment among Malay writers, who recorded the troubled times with unabashed candour. Perceptive to their surroundings, writers also described various social circumstances to educate readers about their plight.

During the pre-war period, two groups of writers came to the fore: teachers, including Abdullah Sidek, Harun Aminurrashid, Muhammad Yassin Makmur and Ahmad Bakhtiar; and journalists, who included Ishak Haji Muhammad, Shamsuddin Salleh and Raja Mansur bin Raja Abdul Kadir.

Timeline	1920s	1930s
Political and social environment	The British began an open-door migration policy for Chinese and Indians that angered Malays.	British Malaya was hard hit by the global economic depression as rubber and tin prices hit rock bottom. Malays outnumbered by non-Malay immigrants.
Prominent themes	Longing for independence from Britain and seeds of nationalism sown by early political writings.	Social mores and ills exposed, e.g. traditions of forced marriage and other strict conventions.
Selected novels	Political allegories in *Pengasuh* ('Educator'), a Kelantan newspaper; *Hikayat Faridah Hanum* ('Story of Faridah Hanum'); *Iakah Salmah?* ('Is that Salmah?').	*Putera Gunung Tahan* ('Prince of Gunung Tahan'); *Senyuman Pemuda* ('Smile of Youth') (above); *Duri Perkahwinan* ('Thorn of Marriage').

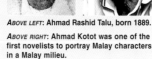

ABOVE LEFT: Ahmad Rashid Talu, born 1889.

ABOVE RIGHT: Ahmad Kotot was one of the first novelists to portray Malay characters in a Malay milieu.

Ahmad Bakhtiar wrote mainly historical novels

One major topic that was addressed in novels from this period was the issue of forced marriages. Novels advocating freedom in choosing marriage partners included *Senyuman Pemuda* ('Smile of Youth')(1934) and *Bidadari Tanah Melayu* ('Angel of Malaya'), *Kasih Membawa Maut* ('Love that Brings about Death'), *Pengaruh Cemburu* ('The Influence of Jealousy'), and *Selamat Tinggal Malaya* ('Farewell Malaya'). Other social issues addressed were economic backwardness and family break-ups, moral decadence among Malay youths, and marital discord—the latter two problems believed to be influenced by colonialists and immigrants. Novels on these social ills included *Duri Perkahwinan* ('Thorn of Marriage') (1937), *Melarat Isteri Kerana Suami* ('Wife Made Destitute by Husband') (1937), *Kisah Sumbang* ('Story of Improper Behaviour') (1938) and *Iblis Rumah Tangga* ('Devil in a Marriage') (1939).

The eponymous war novel *Zain Zawiyah*, by Haji Ahmad Murad Nasaruddin, was published in both the Roman (left) and Jawi (right) scripts.

Nationalistic sentiments were also commonly expressed. Ishak Haji Muhammad's *Putera Gunung Tahan* ('Prince of Gunung Tahan') (1937) and *Anak Mat Lela Gila* ('Child of Mat Lela Gila') (1941), were particularly coloured by colonialism, and fanned the spirit of nationalism. The former novel highlighted how the British wrested political and economic control of Malaya through deceitful means. The latter novel criticized religious groups that abused their status for their own ends, and focused on Malay backwardness, which according to the author was due to divisions among the Malays as well as their lack of ambition.

In a somewhat different vein, the novel *Mari Kita Berjuang* ('Let's Fight') (1941), by Abdullah Sidek, advocated self-reliance and cooperative labour as a means of improving the economic plight of the Malays. *Perang Cita-Cita* ('War of Ambition') (1941) demonstrated the prudence of saving as a means of amassing capital for economic activities.

A pioneer female novelist also emerged: Rafiah bt. Yusuf, who wrote of true love in *Cinta Budiman* ('Virtuous Love') (1941).

Postwar novels

Novels published during the period from 1946 to Malayan Independence in 1957 dwelt on themes such as the hardship experienced during and after World War II, and the nationalistic fight against the proposed Malayan Union, which would have given the British a stronger hold over the Malay sultanates, and reduced the rights of the Malays.

The most notable war novels were Ahmad Murad Nasaruddin's *Nyawa di Hujung Pedang* ('Life at the Tip of the Sword') (1946) and *Zain Zawiyah* (1948). The former tells of a young Malay man's betrayal by his best friend, and how he escaped Japanese execution when the war ended abruptly. Harun Aminurrashid's *Siapakah Yang Bersalah* ('Who Is Wrong?') (1949) and *Sebelum Ajal* ('Before Death') (1949), and *Pahlawan Rimba Malaya* ('Warrior of the Malayan Jungle') (1946) by Keris Mas, depict the aspirations of their protagonists to free themselves from the Japanese.

Other subjects were, however, still tackled, in works such as Ahmad Lutfi's novels *Pelayan* ('Waitress') (1948) and *Bilik 69* ('Room 69') (1949). These survive as social critiques indicting husbands' attitudes and irresponsibility towards wives: as a result of abject poverty and ill-treatment, desperate women were led into prostitution.

Ishak Haji Muhammad (1909–1991)

Anak Mat Lela Gila ('Child of Mat Lela Gila') (below left) and *Putera Gunung Tahan* ('Prince of Mount Tahan') (below right) by Ishak Haji Muhammad (also known as 'Pak Sako') set the pace for criticizing Malay feudal leadership and British colonialism in the 1930s and 1940s.

Angkaran Sasterawan 50 (1950 Generation of Writers)
Better known as 'ASAS 50', this literary organization was founded by 19 young Malay poets and fiction writers influenced by their Indonesian counterparts on 6 August 1950 in the house of Mohd Ariff Ahmad (Mas) in Singapore. ASAS 50's ideology was 'art for society'. The literary works produced during the 1950s echoed the fight for independence, although the organization had no political links. It continues as a literary body, and many new writers have joined since its formation.

ASAS 50's founder members pictured in 1950, including renowned poet Masuri S. N., seated second from left.

1940s

As nations became embroiled in World War II, the country fell under Japanese Occupation. With the defeat of the Japanese in 1945, calls for independence from the British increased.

Colonial deception, wartime experiences, Malay self-reliance, social criticism: male domination, and the plight of Malay women.

Malays demonstrating against the proposed Malayan Union in 1946.

Mari Kita Berjuang ('Let's Fight')(far left); *Pelayan* ('Waitress'); *Nyawa di Hujung Pedang* ('Life at the Tip of the Sword') (left); *Cinta Budiman* ('Virtuous Love').

1950s

The nationalist fight for freedom led to Malaya's bloodless Independence in 1957. The communist Emergency continued throughout the decade.

Postwar economic hardship, protest against the British and calls for independence, historical novels.

Cinta Gadis Rimba ('The Love of a Jungle Girl') (above left); *Muda Tak Sudah* ('Forever Young') (left).

Abdullah Sidek, a Malay school teacher in Johor, was a popular writer before and after World War II.

Post-Independence Malay novels

Independence served as a catalyst for important changes in the Malay novel. The widening of the literary horizon, promotion of novel writing through competitions, the increased economic viability of novel publication, and a marked increase in the number of novelists, served to entrench the position of the novel in the Malay literary world. Recording the spirit of the age with a range of thematic preoccupations and varied perspectives, modern Malay novels make up a respected genre, and give an insight into a Malay tradition of storytelling.

First historical novel
A notable exception to the preoccupation of early post-Independence Malay novels with poverty and colonialism was Harun Aminurrashid's *Anak Panglima Awang* (Son of Panglima Awang), published in 1958. Set in 16th-century Melaka, it portrays Awang, a Malay captive on a Portuguese ship, who became the first man to circumnavigate the world. This pioneering work established the historical novel as part of the Malay form of storytelling. The novel was a compulsory text for Malay literature students in national schools during the 1960s.

Harun Aminurrashid
(1907–1986)

A. Samad Said's landmark novel *Salina* tells of a backstreet prostitute in Singapore who befriends and supports a young man. Some critics hailed it as the greatest novel of the 1960s, while others disagreed.

Growth from seeds of disillusionment

The persistence of poverty among the Malays after Independence in 1957 led to novels that castigated the new Malay leaders, such as *Kail Panjang Sejengkal* ('When a Span is the Length of a Fishing Rod') by A. Samad Ismail. Village heads and religious leaders, too, were portrayed in a negative light, as in *Krisis* ('Crisis') by Alias Ali and *Angin Hitam* ('Black Wind') by A. Wahab Ali. The triumphs of peoples translocated as a result of new rural development projects were recorded in Atan Long's *Subuh* ('The Dawn'), Ibrahim Omar's *Desa Pingitan* ('The Secluded Village'), and Abdul Talib Mohd. Hassan's *Saga* ('Saga').

A novel-writing competition held in 1958 by Dewan Bahasa dan Pustaka (Institute of Language and Literature) brought to the fore Hasan Ali's *Musafir* ('The Sojourner') and A. Samad Said's *Salina*, the latter establishing realism as a dominant feature of the Malay novel in the 1960s. Most novels from this decade continued the preoccupation with colonialism and Malay poverty. Novels such as *Lingkaran* ('Coil') by Arena Wati, *Yang Miskin dan Yang Mewah* ('The Poor and the Wealthy') by Ishak Haji Muhammad, and *Angin Timur Laut* ('The Sea's East Wind') by S. Othman Kelantan documented this turbulent period in stark detail.

Hasan Ali's *Musafir* was first published in 1959, and reprinted numerous times. In 2001 it was re-issued as part of Dewan Bahasa's series of selected 20th-century novels.

Cities and villages were the favoured narrative backdrops. Novels such as Shahnon Ahmad's *Ranjau Sepanjang Jalan* ('No Harvest but a Thorn') contrasted the valiant struggles of the rural poor with their ruthless exploitation by middlemen. Works that centred on the city, such as A. Talib Mohd Hassan's *Pelarian* ('The Fugitive') and Baharuddin C. D.'s *Arca Berdiri Senja* ('Statue Against the Sunset'), often portrayed it as a place of moral decadence and materialism, where dreams were often dashed.

Post-Independence, the publication of novels became a viable business enterprise and several new publishing houses were established. Kuala Lumpur quickly replaced Singapore as the Malay literary centre, and several novel-writing competitions were held by both government and non-government bodies. Writers' associations, too, mushroomed throughout Malaysia.

Modern Malay values

The Islamic resurgence of the 1970s and 1980s compelled Malay novelists to adopt a more explicit and deliberate stance vis-à-vis Islam. Novels appeared that stressed the all-embracing nature of the religion, such as Harun Haji Salleh's *Hidayah* ('God's Guidance'), and Siti Hawa Mohd Hassan's *Ku Ingin Kasih Mu* ('I Beseech Your Love').

Other Malay novels of the period addressed the new urban ethos of individual comfort and interest. *Seribu Musim Kering* ('A Thousand Dry Seasons') by

Timeline	1957 to 1969	1970s
National development	Malaysia formed in 1963. Singapore later seceded in 1965, during an era of uncertainty. Racial tensions overflowed on 13 May 1969.	In the aftermath of the 1969 riots, the New Economic Policy granted special privileges and rights to native (*bumiputera*) Malaysians, primarily the Malays.
Prominent themes	Struggle of the poor, effects of poverty; colonialism, demand for social justice.	Existentialism and philosophical meaning of life; human bondage; socio-economic concerns.
Selected novels and novelists	A. Samad Said's *Salina*, *Lingkaran* ('Coil') (right) by Arena Wati; Atan Long's *Subuh* ('The Dawn'); Ibrahim Omar's *Desa Pingitan* ('The Secluded Village').	*Interlok* ('Interlocked') (above) and *Buih di atas Air* ('Bubbles on Water') by Abdullah Hussain; *Seribu Musim Kering* ('A Thousand Dry Seasons') by Nora.

Baharuddin C. D., born in 1946.

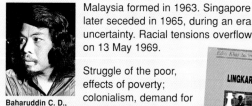

LINGKARAN

ARENA WATI

Anwar Ridhwan's novels are written in measured language, in a romantic style.

INTERLOK
ABDULLAH HUSSAIN

National Literary Award recipients

On 5 July 1979, Prime Minister Tun Hussein Onn announced the establishment of the Anugerah Sastera Negara (National Literary Award) for works by Malaysians in the national language. The award is made annually, but may be withheld if no suitable candidate is found. Recipients are selected by the Minister of Education and a panel of 10 judges appointed by the Prime Minister. The award carries a letter of recognition, a cash prize, the provision of writing and publishing facilities, and the purchase by the government of a print run of 50,000 copies of the winner's selected texts for distribution to schools. As of 2004, there have been nine recipients.

1981: Keris Mas, pen name of Haji Kamaluddin bin Muhammad (1922–1992)
In addition to having written five novels, several essays and numerous criticisms, Keris Mas is noted for the wit, critical mind and firm grasp of Malay displayed in various collections of short stories.

1982: Haji Shahnon bin Ahmad (b.1933)
A pioneer in the use of dialect and regional language in creative writing in Malay (see 'Regional varieties of Malay'). Later in his career he achieved notoriety with the publication of the highly controversial Malay novel, *Shit* ('Shit').

1983: Usman bin Awang (1929–2001)

A distinguished man of letters in the Malay literary world, particularly in the fields of Malay poetry (*sajak*) and drama writing.

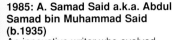

1985: A. Samad Said a.k.a. Abdul Samad bin Muhammad Said (b.1935)
An innovative writer who evolved from poetry and short stories to novels, drama and literary criticism. He is best known for his novel *Salina* which introduced a stark realism into the Malay literary tradition.

1988: Arena Wati, pen name of Muhammad bin Abdul Biang @ Andi Muhammad Dahlan bin Andi Buyung (b.1925)

The author of several novels such as *Lingkaran* ('Coil'), *Royan* ('Post-natal Depression'), and *Sandera* ('Debt-slave'), as well as short stories, poems, and non-fiction.

1990: Muhammad bin Haji Salleh (b.1942)
A professor and creative writer, Muhammad writes in English and Malay (see 'Short stories and poetry in English' and 'Poetry in Malay'). He has won various international and local awards for his poetry, and is an active verse translator.

1993: Noordin bin Hassan (b.1929)

An outstanding dramatist, his works include the landmark play *Bukan Lalang Ditiup Angin* ("Tis Not the Grass That's Blown by the Wind'), said to reflect and refract the 13 May 1969 racial riots, and other well-known theatrical works (see 'Modern Malay drama').

1995: Haji Abdullah bin Hussain (b.1920)

His magnum opus, *Imam* ('Islamic Religious Leader'), stands out among the novels written following the Islamic resurgence in Malay literature.

2003: S. Othman Kelantan (b.1938)
A retired Kelantanese teacher and lecturer, this writer's novels create and sustain stories that largely revolve around the poor, and include a message.

The writer (right) being presented with his award by the Yang di-Pertuan Agong (left).

Nora and *Bila Lagi Kompang Berbunyi* ('When Will the Drums Beat') by Marwilis Haji Yusof, *Hujan Pagi* ('Morning Rain') by A. Samad Said, *Bila dan di Mana* ('Whence and Where') by Khadijah Hashim, and *Buih di atas Air* ('Bubbles on Water') by Abdullah Hussain, all underscored this ethos as a poor substitute for traditional Malay values and norms.

Many of the novels of the 1980s and 1990s focused on the corporate world. With Keris Mas's *Saudagar Besar dari Kuala Lumpur* ('Big Businessman from Kuala Lumpur') setting the pace, they explored high-level corruption, corporate struggles and economic success. Many of them, such as *Wee dan William* ('Wee and William') by Azizi Haji Abdullah, *Merentas Sungai Sejarah* ('Cutting across the River of History') by Mohd Nazmi Yaakub, and *Arca* ('Statue') by Muhd Nasruddin Dasuki, portrayed Malays as corporate players, unlike earlier works which usually featured only ethnic Chinese business-

men. Information technology was the theme in well researched novels such as Azmah Nordin's *Syumul* ('Sacred') and Aminah Mokhtar's *Dominasi Tebrau* ('The Tebrau Domination'). Islamic concerns, too, persisted in novels such as Hasan Ali's *Nurul Hidayah* ('Nurul Hidayah Corporation'), Abdullah Hussain's *Imam* ('Islamic Religious Leader') and Aziz Jahpin's *Biar Buang Anak* ('Abandon a Child if Needs Be').

A further development in the 1990s, initiated by Mohd Affandi Hassan, was the use of Malay literature as a forum for intellectual discourse. In *Pujangga Melayu* ('Malay Philosopher'), for example, he addressed the issue of polygamy, giving insights often ignored in other works, which tended to dwell on the more salacious aspects of having multiple wives. Elsewhere, he argued that 'Genuine Literature' such as his was essential as a legacy for future generations, and in the process cast a radical light on the modern Malay literary heritage.

Warta GAPENA, a monthly journal published by Gabungan Persatuan Penulis Nasional Malaysia (GAPENA) (Federation of National Union of Writers of Malaysia), the umbrella organization for state-based Malaysian writers' associations.

1980s

Creation of a Malay bourgeoisie and mercantile class as part of the nation's continuing socio-economic progress. Islamic resurgence.

Increased social awareness, economic hardship; struggle against injustice. Relevance of Islam in contemporary life.

Sesudah Fajar sebelum Senja ('After Dawn before Dusk') (top left); *Langit Petang* ('Evening Sky') (left); *Saudagar Besar dari Kuala Lumpur* ('Big Businessman from Kuala Lumpur').

Penulis Sayembara (Competition Novelist) Azizi Haji Abdullah.

1990 to present

Malaysia's economic success meant a growing educated Malay consumer society with high aspirations. Infrastructure development and technological advancement.

Bourgeois dreams; acquisition of wealth and issues related to the nouveau riche; the good life; drug abuse.

Mohd Affandi Hassan's *Pujangga Melayu* ('The Malay Philosopher'); Aminah Mokhtar's *Dominasi Tebrau* ('The Tebrau Domination').

Anugerah ('Award'), by Zaharah Nawawi (above left): at 1351 pages it is the longest Malay novel. Provocative author, Mohd Affandi Hassan (above right).

Short stories in Malay

The legacy of the oral tradition of short folklore tales was continued in written form with the modern short story, which first appeared in the 1920s with the rise of Malay newspapers. After the deprivations of World War II, new socio-political themes emerged. In the 1960s and 1970s yet more styles emerged, influenced by Western literary trends, although these distanced some readers. The genre revived in the 1980s and has subsequently continued to thrive.

Father of the Malay short story
Many names were associated with the short story in the 1920s and 1930s, but one in particular stands out. Abdul Rahim Kajai was the foremost journalist of the 1930s and was at the helm of a number of newspapers at different times, including *Utusan Melayu* from 1939 to 1941. His short stories have been enshrined in the collection *Pusaka Kajai* ('Kajai's Legacy'), published posthumously after World War II. They exemplify the spirit and style of the 1930s, when writers had yet to throw off the literary shackles of the past, such as the legacy of the formal Hikayat genre.

Several short story anthologies have been published, principally by Dewan Bahasa dan Pustaka.

Early development
The first *cerita pendek* (short story) or *cerpen* appeared in *Pengasuh*, the first newspaper published on the east coast of the Malay Peninsula in the early 1920s. As its publisher, the Council of Islamic Affairs and Malay Customs of Kelantan, was not in fact confined to merely religious matters and state affairs, the stories were anecdotal and similar to traditional short oral narratives in that they were both entertaining and didactic. Two educational journals, *Panduan Guru* and *Majallah Guru*, were popular literary forums later in the decade. Other publications and newspapers such as *Masa*, *Dunia Melayu* and *Penyuluh* also carried short stories by writers including Nor bin Ibrahim, Muhammad Yusuf Ahmad and Ismail Sulaiman.

The genre became more definitive in 1930s publications such as *Warta Ahad*, *Majlis* and *Warta Jenaka*. These and other shorter-lived Malay newspapers became a favourite medium of communication for Malay journalists and editors including Syed Sheikh Al-Hadi, his son Syed Alwi, Abdul Rahim Kajai, Abdul Wahab bin Abdullah, Onn bin Ja'afar, Syed Hussein bin Ali Alsagaf, Othman Kalam, Ibrahim Haji Yaakob and Ishak Haji Muhammad. The pre-war short stories by these writers entertained readers with their sheer romanticism—characters had paired names such as 'Jamil-Jamilah' and 'Amin-Aminah'—and sermonized with moral teaching and guidance.

During the Japanese Occupation (1941–5), works by Ishak Haji Muhammad, Abdul Samad Ismail and Abdullah Sidek appeared in the propagandist Japanese media such as *Semangat Asia*, *Fajar Asia* and *Berita Malai* (see 'Language in the print media'). Themes were calculated to rally the readers behind the Japanese war effort. Due to strict censorship, writers had to utilize all sorts of subterfuge to hide their resentment of the Japanese.

Local publishing companies were quickly re-established after World War II, particularly in Singapore; more than 40 magazines and newspapers appeared, many including short stories in their issues.

New young writers
The socialist writers belonging to Angkatan Sasterawan 50 (1950 Generation of Writers; better known by the abbreviation 'ASAS 50') transformed the short story (see 'Early Malay novels'). Although romanticism and didacticism lingered among older writers until the early 1950s, the new generation tempered them with a more realistic choice and treatment of themes such as the struggle for independence, poverty, and the pursuit of social justice for urban industrial workers. The collection *Mekar dan Segar* ('Fresh and Blooming') presents a useful survey of stories from that period, with works by writers such as Kamaluddin Muhammad (Keris Mas), Abu Yazid Abidin (Wijaya Mala) and Abdul Samad Ismail (Asmal), the last of whom questioned the inflated pretensions of the new breed of young writers in *Ingin Jadi Pujangga* ('Want to Become a Great Writer').

More young writers emerged in the early 1960s, including A. Samad Said, Shahnon Ahmad, Arena Wati, and three female writers: Salmi Manja, Anis Sabirin, and Adibah Amin. By this time, the obsession of ASAS 50 writers with addressing socio-political issues had caused a reaction, turning literary attention to the individual. Writers began to approach broad social issues from a more subtle, human angle. The predicament of the traditional healer in the face of modern medicine, young upstart civil servants, the pomposity of rising politicians, the

Onn bin Ja'afar had several pieces of short fiction published in *Lembaga Malaya*, the weekly magazine that he started in 1934.

Short stories written by Wijaya Mala (Abu Yazid Abidin) are collected in the posthumously published *Di Kota dan Desa* (1980) ('In the Town and Countryside').

pretensions of the nouveau riche, and the ironies of life, all provided fodder for fictional themes. Rural socio-economic development as a result of government projects also proved a rich source of inspiration. Simpler stories told of the obvious benefits accruing from the projects, while more insightful and polemical stories examined the unintended outcome of ill-planned ventures.

During the 1960s, the number of short story writers who were journalists began to decline. New writers emerged from other professions and various levels of education; for the first time, many practitioners were undergraduates, including Anis Sabirin, Awang Had Salleh, Anwar Ridhwan and Mohd Affandi Hassan. The period also saw the emergence of non-Malay writers writing in Malay, such as Akbar Goh and Amir Tan.

It was during the 1960s that Dewan Bahasa dan Pustaka (Institute of Language and Literature) began actively to support the short story genre, organizing competitions and writing courses, and publishing a journal dedicated to literary affairs, *Dewan Sastera* (see 'National language policy'). While the short story remained the literature of the newspapers, magazines and journals, published collections of works by single and multiple authors began to provide permanence to the short story's otherwise transient existence.

Short stories are frequently published in the literary journal *Dewan Sastera* published by Dewan Bahasa dan Pustaka, whose office appears on the cover of this 1977 edition.

Contemporary short stories

The 1970s heralded the arrival of more young local graduate writers such as Ahmad Mahmud, Zahari Affandi and Wahab Awangtih who were influenced by foreign literary styles such as 'anti-hero', 'stream of consciousness', and 'interior monologue'. This trend is particularly apparent in Anwar Ridhwan's collection *Parasit* ('Parasite'). Fatimah Busu, on the other hand, took inspiration from classical Malay literature. Other young writers who moved away from the traditional style included Othman Puteh, Mana Sikana, and Zakaria Ali. Even those writers who addressed religious themes, such as Azizi Haji Abdullah, Othman Rasul, and Abdullah Tahir, treated their stories in a more sophisticated style than the overt approach of the 1930s to 1950s.

The decade was also marked by a surge in the number of non-Malay,

predominately Chinese, writers such as Lim Swee Tin, Cheng Poh Hock, Teo Huat, Siow Siew Sing, Oh Ah Guan, Lai Chong and Peter Augustine Goh. They were joined in the 1980s by Lee Cheng Beng, Lawrence Quek, Chai Loon Guan, Lee Kok Chih, Selina S. F. Lee and John Chiah Lai. These writers brought new non-Malay themes and perspectives to the genre.

Experimentation with foreign styles and contemporary philosophies during the 1970s in some cases only served to alienate the reading public, as it did with audiences of Malay drama (see 'Modern Malay drama'). This was particularly so with the absurdist trend and the treatment of the short story as an art form rather than a mere story. One leading young writer in particular, Marsli N. O., deviated from the conventional format to such an extent that his work often appears incomprehensible to the ordinary reader.

During the 1980s and 1990s, cerpen, together with modern poetry, underwent a period of remarkable growth (see 'Poetry in Malay'). In 1996–7 alone, the Annual Literary Award Panel evaluated 1559 short stories and 52 anthologies. The range of themes and their treatment increased in sophistication during the course of these two decades as well. Ideological conflict was no longer addressed directly in terms of the contrast between conservatism and modernity, or pragmatism and idealism, for example, but rather was explored through tales of the professional world, business manipulation, the share market and politics. The impact of globalization, too, was a popular issue in works as the 20th century drew to a close.

Non-Malay writers

Many of Chinese writer Amir Tan's (1) short stories have been collected in the anthology *Suara dari Langit* ('Voice from the Sky') (2). Lee Kok Chih (3) and Selina S. F. Lee (4) have also been widely published.

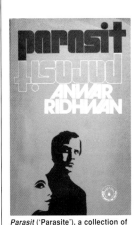

Parasit ('Parasite'), a collection of short stories by Anwar Ridhwan, was first published by Dewan Bahasa dan Pustaka in 1976.

Sultan Idris Training College and the Malay Literature Bureau

The Institution which had the greatest impact on the pre-war Malay literary scene was the Sultan Idris Training College, subsequently elevated and renamed Universiti Pendidikan Sultan Idris in 1997. Located in Tanjung Malim, Perak, it was established by the British in 1922 to train local teachers for Malay villages, from where it drew its students. Although the curriculum was aimed at providing villagers with practical skills, Malay language and literature were also included. Indeed, great emphasis was placed on these by O. T. Dussek, the college's first principal who retained the post for 17 years.

Both students and staff were involved in numerous literary activities, such as debates, writing and cultural performances. Literary works, including short stories, were published in a fortnightly newspaper, *Cenderamata*, published by the Malay Literature Bureau, which was moved to the college in 1923, with Zainal Abidin Ahmad (Za'ba) as its chief translator (see 'History of Malay'). At first producing Malay school textbooks, it later published Malay classics and translations of simplified English classics.

The training and literary exposure gained at the college led to its graduates being at the forefront of the new breed of Malay writer. Among these were Ahmad Murad, Ishak Haji Muhammad, Hasan Ali, Masuri S. N., and Othman Puteh (see 'Early Malay novels').

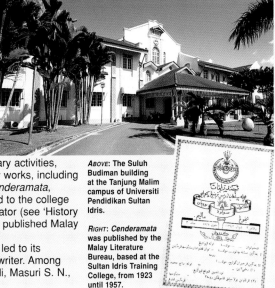

ABOVE: The Suluh Budiman building at the Tanjung Malim campus of Universiti Pendidikan Sultan Idris.

RIGHT: Cenderamata was published by the Malay Literature Bureau, based at the Sultan Idris Training College, from 1923 until 1957.

Poetry in Malay

From the 1930s, traditional, more regular, Malay poetic forms were gradually superseded by free verse ('sajak'), better suited to 20th-century demands of social protest, particularly independence from colonial rule and Japanese Occupation. Like short stories, poetry proved both a popular and effective medium in the widely read local newspapers and magazines. Since Independence, a wider range of works has emerged.

The late Usman Awang's elegant poetry is marked by the gentle lyricism of Malay classical literature.

A new term for a new style

Sajak, derived from the root word *sanjak* (rhyme), was initially coined by Za'ba (see 'History of Malay') for a style of Malayan poetry directly influenced by the European free verse form. This marked a radical change from traditional and regular Malay poetic forms, such as *pantun* and *syair* (see 'Traditional Malay poetic forms'). Nevertheless, syair remained influential, and provided the foundation for the themes of the new poems.

The free verse form first appeared in Malaya in the poems of Indonesian writers published in the journal *Poedjangga Baru* during the early 1930s. Educated in Dutch schools, where they were themselves introduced to this new form, they found it well suited to their situation and personalities. Takdir Alisjahbana, Amir Hamzah and Sanusi Pane, in particular, experimented with free verse and adapted it to form part of the Indonesian literary tradition. The first Malayan free verse poet was Harun Aminurrashid, who was published in *Poedjangga Baru* (see 'Post-Independence Malay novels'). It was only years later that his colleagues

An Indonesian cultural journal, *Poedjangga Baru* inspired many Malaysian poets to try their hand at the free verse form of poetry in the 1930s.

from the Sultan Idris Training College in Tanjung Malim (see 'Short stories in Malay') followed his example with other formal and linguistic experiments.

These early experiments with the form were marked by the continued use of the rhythm of pantun and syair beside the more robust and truncated sajak form. However, short lines and verses became popular, perceived as marks of rebellion against the older regular forms. Favoured themes were patriotism, stressing the need for Malays to forge ahead like the other newly arrived races in Malaya, and the self, a theme previously very much suppressed in Malay society. Few of the curious young poets and teachers during this early period successfully mastered the genre, however, with the exception perhaps of Ngumba and Muhammad Yassin Makmur.

During the Japanese Occupation of the Malay Peninsula (1941–5) creativity was stifled by rigid censorship. 'Asia for Asians' was promoted as a theme while freedom from colonial rule and Japanese brutality was strictly forbidden. Only poems passed by the censors were published in newspapers, particularly *Berita Malai*, established by the Japanese and staffed by local journalists. Malay nationalism slowly developed and poems that called for Malay unity were published, as well as some religious poetry.

Early Masters

Masuri S. N.

Masuri, together with Usman Awang, was one of the first poets to truly master the *sajak* (free verse) form;

together they improved the form to a malleable Malay vehicle, Masuri choosing to keep it regular and line-based. Masuri belonged to Angkatan Sasterawan 50 (1950 Generation of Writers, better known as 'ASAS 50') (see 'Early Malay novels'), whose members used poetry to promote nationalism and freedom for the oppressed.

Usman Awang

An early master of the *sajak* form, Usman initially gave it a pantun rhythm, and later developed it as poetry 'for the sake of society'. His poems are characterized by the gentle lyricism of classical literature, giving them an elegant and graceful movement, and themes that progressed with the times: from social issues concerning sidewalk hawkers to questions relating to the environment and political freedom. His tone likewise became sharpened. Although not a founder member, Usman later joined Angkatan Sasterawan 50.

'Tanahair'

Engkau Tanahair pemilik perut yang berbudi
Penampang hujan, penyedut sinar matari
Lahirlah anak-anakmu dari semaian-semaian petani

O native land with soil so rewarding
catching rain inhaling sunshine
let your children be born of the pleasant seedlings

Female poets

The Malay literary scene has been enriched by female poets such as Salmi Manja, the pen name for Saleha bt. Abdul Rashid, a member of ASAS 50, who was prolific in the 1950s and 1960s. Her poems, such as 'Antara Puspa-Puspa' ('Among Flowers') and 'Keluhan' ('Sigh'), portray the world of women. She was followed by one of the early female university graduates, Anis Sabirin, who depicted the rebellious tone of the new Malay woman in her poem 'Kubunuh Cinta' ('I Murder Love') (1960), although her later poem, 'Segelas Susu dan Roti Segenggam' ('A Glass of Milk and a Small Loaf of Bread') (1963) talks about the value of love in the family.

Salmi Manja exhibited concern for the plight of the Malay woman.

Zurinah Hassan was awarded the National Literary Prize in 1971 and received it each year until 1976, the last year in which it was awarded. Her socially critical poetry voices her experiences and feelings as a woman in a troubled motherland and talks about fishermen, farmers and labourers. Another poet, Zaihasra, successfully experimented with the long poem and the tragic dilemma of historical figure Tun Fatimah of Melaka.

ABOVE: Zurinah Hassan produced two collections in the 1970s.
RIGHT: Zaihasra passed away in 1989, aged forty-two.

Siti Zainon Ismail

This prolific poet and author, first published in 1967, integrates art and poetry, sketches situations and

emotions with gentle and melodious brush strokes (as in the sample right). She has been productive in a range of literary genres, writing poetry, short stories and cultural criticism.

Selected leading poets

A. Samad Said
Primarily a fiction writer, A. Samad Said has nevertheless remained at the forefront of Malay poetry since the 1950s. His works include *Benih Harapan* ('Seeds of Hope') (1973), *Daun Semalu Pucuk Paku* ('Touch-me-nots and Fern Shoots') (1975) *Balada Hilang Peta* ('The Ballad of the Lost Map') (1991), and *Al-amin* (2000).

Baharuddin Zain
Better known as Baha Zain, this poet started as a writer of protest poetry in the 1960s. His tone later mellowed following a period of several years spent in Indonesia during the 1970s. Urban and self-conscious, Baha is a modern poet who continues to craft poetry in which he engages in self-examination.

Muhammad Haji Salleh
Often linked with Latiff Mohidin and Baha Zain as a poet of the 1970s, National Laureate Muhammad first wrote poetry while studying in England in 1963. His works such as *Sajak-sajak Pendatang* ('Immigrant Poems') (1974) reflect a blend of intellect and emotion. He won the Asean Literary Award in 1978.

Kassim Ahmad
Important, although by no means prolific, Kassim Ahmad was active from 1958 to 1968. Often critical in his contents, he was an early exponent of Malay intellectual poetry, and drew much of his imagery from classical Malay literature such as *Sejarah Melayu* ('Malay Annals').

A. Ghafar Ibrahim
One of foremost proponents of personal expression, artist and lecturer A. Ghafar Ibrahim tries to shock his audience out of the melodious lines of gentle poetry with strong contemporary images, in the process creating a new melody. His *sajak* collection, *Tan Sri Bulan*, was published in 1973.

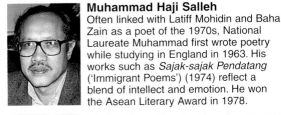

T. Alias Taib
A consistently productive poet, T. Alias Taib sees his poetry as the opening of doors to real life, a life lived by an individual himself, and shared with others. Relatively quiet in style, and perhaps coming from a desire to communicate in a less public way, his poetry is both subtle and rich.

Moechtar Awang
The 1980s were witness to the 'back to roots' movement in Malaysian literature as a whole, perhaps as a reaction to the more cosmopolitan path taken by poets such as Baha Zain and Latiff Mohidin. Moechtar Awang was among the more successful poets of this attempt to reuse the literary traditions of the past.

Lim Swee Tin
A landmark of the 1980s and 1990s was the growing stature of ethnic Chinese poet Lim Swee Tin. Beginning with the romantic strains of 'Eva', he emerged as one of the leading non-ethnic Malay poets. In *A Child and other Poems* (1993), he dreams that '*poems can soften the hard nature of humans*'.

A. Latiff Mohidin
This renowned artist brings a graphic element to his poetry. First published in the early 1960s, and particularly prolific in the 1970s, Latiff Mohidin has five books of poetry to his credit. He has strong contacts with world literature and has continued to craft poetry into the 21st century, with an often surrealist style.

Extract from 'Sungai Mekong' ('Mekong River') (1966)

sungai mekong	mekong river
kupilih namamu	i choose your name
kerana aku begitu sepi	for i am desolate
kan kubenamkan dadaku	i shall plunge my breast
ke dasarmu	down to your bed
kaki kananku ke bulan	my right leg to the moon
kaki kiriku ke matari	my left leg to the sun
kan kuhanyutkan hatiku	I shall allow my heart to drift
ke kalimu	with your waters
namaku ke muara	my name to the sea
suaraku ke gunung	my voice to the mountains
sungai mekong	mekong river
nafasmu begitu tenang	how tranquil your breath
lenggangmu begitu lapang	how untroubled your gait
di tebingmu	on your bank
ada ibu bersuara sayu	a mother's voice calls forlorn
mencari suara puteranya yang hilang	for the voice of a lost son
waktu ia merebahkan wajahnya	when she lowers her face
ke wajahmu	against your face
kau masih bisa senyum senang	you can still smile with ease

Kemala
In the 1960s, Kemala at first wrote on rural life and social problems. Then, after winning the 1972 Literary Prize with *Meditasi* ('Meditation'), his poems, in a variety of styles, focused more strongly on Islamic mysticism, resulting in the influential collection *Kaktus-Kaktus* ('Cactuses') in 1976.

Shafie Abu Bakar
With a deep religious interest, this poet has a heavier and somewhat more considered style than Moechtar Awang. His poems explore Islamic philosophy, a choice influenced by his academic study of the Malay Sufi poets, and also record his personal spiritual journey.

Rahman Shaari
Although he started to write poetry much earlier, Rahman came to the fore as an intellectual poet in the 1980s. He presents rumination, insight and discussion rather than emotions. Writing in clear language, he avoids the use of the archaisms sometimes employed by his contemporaries.

Zaen Kasturi
This contemporary poet has emerged as a spokesman for modern Malaysian life, making use of contemporary Malay language patterns. In the modernist *Katarsis* ('Catharsis') (1993), he depicts a splintered mosaic of modern Malaysia where the traditional harmony is shattered by the din of the city.

Fiction in Chinese

Mainland China has a long literary history, with novels such as The Water Margin *published as early as the Ming Dynasty (1368–1644). In Malaysia, locally written Chinese literature, known as* mahua wenxue, *or* mahua *literature, only started to appear in the early 20th century. Relatively few novels have been written, and short story writers have been somewhat more prolific, and perhaps influential, than novelists. The Chinese language newspapers are particularly active in nurturing and promoting locally produced writing.*

The cover of *A Selection of Novels by Wei Yun* (left) is adorned with a portrait of the author. *Qian Tan* ('Shallow Waters') (right) is one of Wei Yun's best-known novels, and was one of only nine *mahua* novels published prior to 1965.

Mahua writing

Malaysian Chinese-language literature is commonly known as *mahua wenxue. Mahua* is a contraction of the word 'Malaya' and the Mandarin term for 'Chinese'. *Wenxue* means 'literature' in Mandarin. Mahua literature first appeared in 1919, spurred on by the Wusi Movement (May Fourth Movement) in China, the cultural, intellectual and literary revolution, the latter in the form of *baihua* (modern writing). The 'early period' continued until 1965 when Singapore, where many mahua writers resided, separated from Malaysia. Subsequently, these writers were no longer categorized as being mahua.

Novels

Prior to World War II, only one mahua novel was written, entitled *Nong Yan* ('Dense Smoke'), by Malayan-born Lin Cantian; and only 16 further novels had been published by 1965. Some of these, such as *Zai Maliujia Haixia* ('By the Strait of Melaka') by Zhao Rong, were Malayan-orientated. Others focused instead on countries including Vietnam, Indonesia, and especially mainland China.

Novels published in the 1970s included Hong Xu's *Xingfu Zhi Ge* ('In Praise of Happiness'), which appeared in serial form in the newspaper *China Press* and Zi Xi's *Shengdan Hua Kai* ('When Christmas

Zheng Yan's *Shengqi Shan Xia* ('At the foot of Penang Hill') is representative of the shift towards local themes.

Yu Chuan's novel *Zhuozhuang* ('Luxuriance'), published in 1980, is the tale of a bus conductor.

The *Hua Zong* awards
First organized by Chinese-language newspaper, *Sin Chew Jit Poh*, now known as *Sin Chew Daily*, in 1991, the prestigious international *Hua Zong* (Floral Trail) literary awards have since been held biennially. They have gained the distinction of becoming known as the 'Oscars' of the international Chinese literary community.

The awards afford writers the opportunity to gain both financial rewards and prestige, and aim to both promote and develop Chinese writing in Malaysia. Awards are offered for several categories of writing, including

Sin Chew Daily Chairman Tan Sri Tiong Hiew King (left) presenting the 2nd *Hua Zon* World Chinese Literature Award (2004) to Taiwanese writer Chen Yingzhen (right), witnessed by 2003 winner Wang Anyi (centre).

Flowers Bloom'). The latter has a simple plot imbued with moral values. It revolves around the love of Shiwei, the youngest daughter of a millionaire, for a gardener's son; her father, however, wants her to marry a playboy. Following a series of climaxes, the story ends on a happy note.

From the late 1970s onwards, even fewer novels were published. Nearly all focused on local themes. Among them were Fang Beifang's *Toujia Men Xia* ('Under the Boss's Roof'), Fang E'zhen's *Hua Tian Ya* ('Paint the Wide, Wide World'), Wen Rui'an's *Tun Huo Qinghuai* ('Feelings of Anger'), and *Zhuozhuang* ('Luxuriance') by Yu Chuan. Perhaps the best known was Li Yongping's *Ji Ling Chunqiu* ('The Chronicle of Ji Ling'). The 1990s saw the publication of the masterful works *Sailian Zhi Ge* ('In Praise of Sailian') and *Qun Xiang* ('A Herd of Elephants'), both by Zhang Guixing.

Mahua novels

1930s	1950s	1960s	1970s	1980s	1990s

Nong Yan ('Dense Smoke') by Lin Cantian (1935) was the first *Mahua* novel.	*Chi Liang De Zaocheng* ('As Morning Approaches') by Fang Beifang (1959).	*Zai Maliujia Haixia* ('By the Strait of Melaka') by Zhao Rong (1961).	Zi Xi's *Shengdan Hua Kai* ('When Christmas Flowers Bloom') (1975).	Fang Beifang's *Toujia Men Xia* ('Under the Boss's Roof') (1980).	*Sailian Zhi Ge* ('In Praise of Sailian'), by Zhang Guixing (1992).

reporting, literature, novels, prose, poems, and children's literature. Awards are also offered for novice writers (below 20 years old), and special recommended awards.

At the 6th Hua Zong Awards in 2001 the International Chinese Literary Lifetime Achievement Award, comparable to the Nobel Prize for Literature, was awarded for the first time. The recipient of the award is chosen by a panel of judges comprising 18 reputable writers and literary critics.

Lectures and workshops complement the award ceremonies. To date over 500 such events have been organized which have attracted a combined audience in excess of 300,000. Over 100 renowned international Chinese writers have participated as guest speakers.

Leading Chinese-language writers are awarded the Hua Zong statue.

Prize-winning author
In 1999, Li Zishu (right) won the First Prize for Literature awarded by *Sin Chew Daily* for her short story 'Liu Nian' ('A Given Year'). Other stories by her include 'Tianguo Zhi Men' ('Door to Heaven') and 'Weixing Li Zishu' ('A Mini-short Story of Li Zishu').

The first mahua short stories

The very first short story to be published was 'Dongfang de Xin Ganxiang' ('Reflections on a Wedding Feast'), written by Shuang Shuang, and published at the end of 1919. The story concerned arranged marriages and their disastrous consequences, usually resulting in divorce.

Shuang Shuang's story started a trend of mahua 'problem stories' which focused on Malaysian Chinese socio-cultural issues. Subsequent writers on these themes included Su Zhengyi, Jing Jin and, most successfully, Lin Dubu. He wrote four of the most influential short stories of the period: 'Zhen Gege Xiang Shenme' ('What is Elder Brother Zhen Thinking?'), 'Xiaoyixiao' ('Please Smile'), 'Liang Qingnian' ('Two Young Men') and 'Tongchuang Hui' ('A Get-together of Classmates').

In the so-called 'developmental period' from 1925 to 1931, writers such as Tuo Ge, with 'Ganmao' ('Having a Cold'), and Zhou Zimeng, with 'Shizhang' ('Division Commander'), created short realist stories, often critical of materialism. However, the chosen setting for these stories was China. Short stories set in Nanyang (Malaya) first appeared with the economic downturn of 1927–8. Writers dealt with themes such as unemployment and the nascent Independence movement. Short stories—such as 'Ku' ('Bitterness') and 'Renjian Diyu' ('Hell on Earth') by Chen Guifang, and 'Yi Ge Chefu de Meng' ('Dream of a Rickshaw Puller') by Li Cuigong—dealt with life under colonial rule within conservative Chinese society. Very few short stories were written during the 1930s. Leading works included 'Baba yu Niangre' ('Baba and

Nyonya') by Qiu Shizhen, 'Xue Ying' ('Shadow of Snow') by Cai Zenjian, 'Qiu Long' ('Lock-up') by Rao Chuyu, and 'Ta de Meimeng Xing le' ('His Dream was Shattered') by Zhen Ge. Those dating from the late 1930s to the early 1950s were influenced by war, particularly China's resistance against Japan. Notable stories included 'Weiqu' ('Dissatisfaction') by Ding Qian, 'Zai Xuepo Zhong de Weixiao' ('A Smile in the Flow of Blood') by Liu Bing, 'Shui Shuo Women Nianji Xiao' ('Who Thinks We Are Not Mature?') by Jin Ding, 'Taonan Tu Zhong' ('During an Escape Journey') and 'Xin Yifu' ('New Clothes') by Ru Ying.

Post-war short stories

After 1950, there was a revival in the fortunes of the mahua short story, which began to attract a large number of readers. Well-known, and prolific, writers during the period included Fang Beifang, Wei Yun, Wen Zichuan, Yao Tuo, and Yuan Shang Cao. They pioneered a new generation of short story writers, writing on a variety of subjects coloured by events under British colonial rule, and mirroring the people's wish for Independence. 'Huanxiang Yuan' ('Hope of Returning Home') by Wei Yun tells of the hardship and bitterness felt by the migrating Chinese. Wen Zichuan's 'Taiwushi He Pan' ('On the Banks of the River Thames'), on the other hand, describes the emotions and thoughts of Malaysians living in the United Kingdom.

Until relatively recently mahua writers were inclined towards the idealism brought about by the social revolution in China. Certainly, this continued to be the case in the 1970s and 1980s, as is evident in the works of writers such as Pan Yutong, Yun Li Feng, Wen Zheng, Meng Ping, Ding Yun, Shang Wanyun and Yuan Shang Cao, all of whom had short story collections published. Even in the 1990s and early 2000s, this trend remained apparent in short stories written by Xiao Hei, Liang Fang, Nian Hong, Li Zishu, Zhang Yuping, Li Tianbao, Song Ziheng, Duan Muhong, and Huang Jinshu.

Recent short story volume in the Malaysian Chinese Writers' Association's comprehensive anthology of mahua wenxue.

Yao Tuo

Yao Tuo (originally called Yao Tian Ping) was born in China and migrated to Malaya in 1957. He subsequently became editor of two magazines, *Xuesheng Zhoubao* ('The Student Weekly Magazine'), and *Chao Foon* or *Jiao Feng* ('Wind of Nanyang').

Not only a writer and editor, Yao Tuo was also a successful publisher.

He also wrote a number of novels and many short stories. His short stories generally focused on the daily life of the Malaysian Chinese, including love, marital problems, and social practices (particularly those of his own family), as well as depicting life during World War II. His works were collected in a number of anthologies published between 1958 and 1981: *Wanwan de Anbi* ('Winding Coastlines'), *Si Ge Jiehun de Gushi* ('Four Stories of Marriage'), *Wuli'ao Zhi Hua* ('Flowers of Wu Li Ao') and *Yao Tuo Xiaoshuo Xuan* ('Collection of Yao Tuo's Short Stories').

A 1966 edition of literary magazine Chao Foon ('Wind of Nanyang') edited by Yao Tuo. Printed from 1957 to 1999, the magazine was relaunched in 2002.

Malaysian Chinese writer Pan Yutong (better known by his pen name, Ling Zi) won literary awards in Taiwan in 1981 and 1982.

Teo Huat (Nian Hong)

Teo Huat's writing includes over 60 children's stories.

Writing under the pen name Nian Hong, prize-winning author Teo Huat has been a prolific writer of short stories and children's books. His first short story was published in the *Nanyang Siang Pau* newspaper in 1959, and his first collection was published as a book in 1961. He has since had another four collections published: two in Malaysia, one in Singapore and one in Hong Kong. His stories have also been published in Taiwan.

In 1971 he was the first Chinese writer to receive the Tun Razak Literature Award, for the Malay translation of one of his Chinese short stories.

Poetry in Chinese

As with mahua *(Malaysian Chinese) fiction, mahua poetry was directly influenced by the May Fourth Movement in China. Early mahua poets imitated the style of China's famous poets; their content too reflected social life in China. In the 1950s and 1960s, poets from Hong Kong and China emigrated to Malaysia and contributed to mahua poetry. Contemporary Malaysian-born poets remain prolific.*

Pioneer poet

Mi Jun (above) was born in Malaya, but studied in China. His poems, such as 'Yindu Laoren' ('An Old Indian man') and 'Tiao Longling' ('Dance Longling' (a Malay dance)), were published in local Chinese magazines *Chen Xing* and *Dushu Shenghuo*. In 1949 he returned to China, and the following year produced a book of poems, *Redai Shi Chao* ('Collected Poems of The Tropics'). His verse made use of strong and vivid words and images, and was rich in local flavour.

Early mahua poetry

The first mahua poem of the *xin shi* (new poems) form was entitled 'Yuanlai Xuesheng' ('Oh! He's a School Student'), written by Xiao Ya in 1920. His contemporary, Lin Dubu, was, however, more prolific. Lin Dubu's poems, such as 'Huodong Jiushi Kuale' ('Activities are the Source of Happiness'), published in 1921, encouraged Chinese youths to be hard-working and independent, a theme shared by other poets including Hu Jianmin, Zi Chun, Shi Qiao and Tian Duo.

These pioneer poets were followed by others, such as Tuo Ge, Zhou Zimeng and Tan Yunshan, writing on more romantic subjects, in poems such as 'Ting Qian Moli' ('Jasmine in the Front Yard'), 'Huimie yu Chenlun' ('Destruction and Weakness'), and 'Xian Shi' ('Poems Contribute'), respectively.

In the 1930s, poetry became more popular, and was of generally better quality than the prose of the period. Poems focused on the life and thoughts of the Chinese youths who migrated to Nanyang (literally, South Seas, but also used to refer more specifically to Malaya). Works included 'Deyi Renmen de Ge' ('The Song of the Lucky') by Hai Ruo, 'Ping Ying Ji Xu Shi' ('A narrative poem in the Ping Ying collection') by Leng Xiao and 'Hongmao Lu Shang Zagan' ('Feelings while on a Journey') by Hua Cai. Another group of poets in the 1930s—including Ding Lang, Zhang Fang, Qin Hanzeng, Lin Gechen and Zeng Huading—focused on the aesthetics of diction, rhythm and style.

青云亭

三百多年了，还语重心长地
屹立在风雨飘摇里
无非是要向我的子孙诠释
我象徵的意义
我精神的真谛

The first verse of 'Qing Yun Ting' (the name of a Chinese Temple in Melaka), by You Chuan.

As with short stories of the period, 1930s Malaysian Chinese poetry was predominantly set in the milieu of China, and focused particularly on China's resistance to Japan. The collective emotions of the Chinese in Nanyang, and of peoples throughout the world fighting colonialism, were well expressed in Luo Nongfu's poem, 'Yuanshi Yimin' ('The Abandoned Native'). A related theme was the effect of the economic depression, well illustrated by Si Hu's 'Diqiu Yi Jiao de Youchou' ('Anxiety in a Corner of the World'), and the fear of unemployment in 'Zoulang Li de Yi Qun' ('People Along the Five-Foot Way') by Wen Lang.

From the end of the 1930s until the 1950s, as result of World War II and the accompanying Japanese invasion, mahua poetry focused on a relatively narrow range of themes. These included the importance of Independence, condemnation of terrorism and the patriotism spirit of national defence. An excellent example of these combined themes is Ke Meng's 'Maiguozei Toulao' ('Traitor'). Other poets during this period dwelt on anti-Japanese sentiments, hardships endured in Malaya, and the salvation of both China and Malaya. Of particular note are the highly descriptive poems

The Malaysian Chinese Writers' Association

The Malaysian Chinese Writers' Association has been an influential force in the local literary scene since its founding in 1978. Starting with approximately 100 members, it now has a membership of some 350. It promotes and encourages creative writing and literary research with the aim of developing Malaysian Chinese Literature, and also co-ordinates with contemporary Chinese writers in the country. In addition it looks further afield, exchanging writing skills and experiences with writers of other languages both in Malaysia and overseas to keep abreast of international literary developments.

The Association has published many literary works written by its members, and organized numerous literary seminars, symposia, and writing-skill camps in various parts of the country.

ABOVE: *Nanyang Siang Pau* newspaper's Group Editor-in-Chief Dato' Hoong Soon Kean (left) presenting a lifetime achievement award from the Association to poet Yu Tian (right) in 2003, witnessed by the President of the Association, Dai Xiaohua (centre).

LEFT: Members of the Association's first executive committee in 1978.

The North Peninsular Teaching and Learning Monthly Magazine

The North Peninsular Teaching and Learning Monthly Magazine (*Jiao Yu Xue Yuekan*), first issued in December 1960, accepted poems for publication and, starting with its eighth issue, had a special column for new poetry 'Xin Shi Zhi Ye' ('A Page for New Poetry') which often contained as many as eight poems. When the magazine reached its 80th issue, the name of the column was changed to 'Shi Ye' ('Poetry Page'), and then again to 'Shi Zhi Ye' ('Page of Poetry') from the 89th issue. In the magazine's first ten years, some 800 poems were published. Perhaps the most outstanding contributors were Mo Shang Sang and Lin Qiong. In September 1964, the magazine published an anthology *Shiluo Le De Xiao* ('The Lost Smile') for young poets, and another, *Women Zhe Yi Dai* ('Our Generation'), in 1965.

Originally intended for teachers and students, the North Peninsular Teaching and Learning Monthly Magazine was ultimately known as a literary journal.

Wen Renping

Also known as Bernard Woon Swee-tin, Wen Renping played a major role in the development of *mahua* poetry between the 1960s and the 1980s. His poems are full of symbolism, and deep emotions towards Chinese society.

He was chief editor of *Dama Shixuan* ('Anthology of Mahua Poems'), published in 1974, and published three further anthologies entitled *Wu Xuan Qin* ('Musical Instrument without Strings'), *Liufang Shi Yi Zhong Shang* ('Exile is Hurting') and *Zhongsheng de Shen* ('The God of All Living Creatures') in 1970, 1978 and 1979 respectively. Wen also compiled a selection of his literary observations into a book, *Wenxue Guancha* ('Literary Observation'), roughly half of which focused on poetry, published in 1980.

Born in 1944, Wen Renping was once a school teacher. One of his major works was *Liufang Shi Yi Zhong Shang* ('Exile is hurting').

Tian Lang Xing Poetry Society

One of Wen Renping's most important contributions to *mahua* poetry was the founding of the influential Tian Lang Xing ('Sirius' or 'Dog Star') Poetry Society. He was later succeeded by university lecturer Xie Chuancheng (also known as Chiah Seng), who focused on interpretations of modern poetry.

One of several anthologies published by the Tian Lang Xing society.

of Dongfang Bingding, such as 'Yibai Wushi Ge' ('A Hundred and Fifty'), 'Dianche Lai Le' ('The Bus has Arrived') and 'Liu Sanjie Guo Xinnian' ('The Third Miss Liu Ushering in the New Year') in which he described life among the Chinese of different social strata, with particular focus on the lower class. A number of poets from China migrated to Nanyang during the Sino-Japanese War (1937–45) such as Yang Jiguang, Yi Jin and Yi Teng.

Following World War II, Liu Si's poetry focused on humanitarian aspects of life, particularly in poems such as 'Zhenyi de Biaoxian' ('The Spirit of Justice'), depicting the bravery of the Chinese people against their enemies and colonialism. Tao Mu's poetry, on the other hand, dwelt on moral values and education, as in 'Bu Heli Yao Fankang' ('If Its Not Fair, Let's Voice It').

New groups: the 1950s

In the early 1950s a new group of poets, preoccupied with issues in China, rose to the fore. They included Huang Jixu, with poems such as 'Huansong Chen Jiageng Xiansheng Hui Guo' ('Sending Mr Cheng Jiageng Home with Great Joy'). Also during this period, Zhou Can wrote a poetic analogy with the title 'Haizi de Meng' ('A Child's Dream') in which he discussed, among other things, his ideals and the colours of nature. In the middle of the decade several new young poets became popular, as they reflected the aspirations of the new breed of young intellectual. Among them were Du Hong, best known for his poetry collection *Wu Yue* ('The Month of May'), and Zhong Qi, whose most notable poem was 'Modika' (i.e. *Merdeka*, the Malay term for Independence).

Magazines from the three leading literary groups of the 1960s, each covering a different area of the peninsula: (1) *Xin Chao* ('The New Tide'), southern states; (2) *Huang Yuan* ('The Waste Land'), central states; (3) *Hai Tian* ('Sea and Sky') Monthly, northern states.

At the end of the 1950s, a number of Chinese writers emigrated from China to Malaysia. Among them was Li Kuang, from Hong Kong, who was frequently published in the newspapers *Sin Chew Jit Poh* and *Nanyang Siang Pau*. He developed a new style of poetry known as *Dou Gan* (dried beancurd) due to the square shape of the blocks of verse.

Post-Independence poetry

New local poets emerged following Independence in 1957. They were aided by the formation of the Hai Tian (Sea and Sky) poetry society in the early 1960s by Yao Tuo (see 'Chinese fiction') and his friends Hui Shi, Chen Huihua, Xiao Ai and You Cao. The society focused on the northern Peninsula states, and attracted young poets such as You Mu, Xiao Meng, Dan Ying, Liang Yuan, and Bing Gu whose poems of love and youthful idealism were widely acclaimed. Other regional groups were also active during the period.

Leading poet and novelist Diao Wenmei's first collection of poems *Haojiao* ('The Bugle') came out in 1960, and in 1962 Chen Xuefeng's critique, *The Past 15 Years of Malayan Chinese Poems* was published. From the 1960s until the 1980s, Wen Renping was a particularly active mahua poet. Other influential poets during these decades such as Lin Wucong, Fu Chengde, and Bi Chen focused on the status of the Chinese in Malaysia and other topical issues.

More recently, Wu Tiancai's four poetry collections, published between 1989 and 1994, were particularly well received. Younger poets, too, such as Long Chuan, have contributed poems to the mahua genre since the 1990s, on different aspects of society, philosophy, and culture.

Cichang Jie, the title of Jiang Zhengxuan's poetry collection, refers to Kuala Lumpur's Petaling Street by its vernacular Chinese name. Its literal translation is 'Tapioca Factory Street': there were once many such factories along the street.

Mahua Qi Jia Shi Xuan ('Poems of Seven Poets'), published by the Malaysian Chinese Writers' Association in 1994, contains selected poems by poets from various parts of the country: (clockwise from top right) Wen Renping, Tian Si, Fu Chengde, You Chuan, Fang Ang, He Naijian, and Wu An.

Tamil fiction

Until 1945, local Tamil literature was mainly oral, comprising folk songs sung on the rubber estates where the majority of Tamils worked. Some written literature began to appear towards the end of the 19th century, although, until Independence, themes were generally drawn from the immigrant Tamils' homeland in India. Nevertheless, a truly Malaysian voice did emerge, and with strong support from the Tamil media, a thriving literary scene has developed.

Roll call for labourers on a rubber estate. The collective Tamil experience as estate labour continues to be a source of inspiration for local Tamil writers.

Tamil novel, *Nesamalar or The Dream of the Educated*, by S. Sivamaniam, published in 1936, appeared with an English title page. It was fashionable at the time for Tamil novels to have two titles.

Novels: from serializations to books

Rathina Malai Alladhu Kaanamal Pona Kumarathi ('A Garland of Gems or A Lost Young Woman') by S. L. Madhava Rao, was the first Tamil novel, published in serial form in 1912 in the journal *Ngyana Sooriyan*. In the 1930s, newspapers *Tamil Nesan* and *Tamil Murasu* also began to publish novels in this form.

The first Tamil novel to be published in book form was *Karunakaran Alladhu Kaadhalin Matchi* ('Karunakaran or The Greatness of Love') by K. Venkatarathinam, in 1917. This was followed by Puloli K. Subramaniam's novels *Balasundaram Alladhu Sanmaarkka Jeyam* ('Balasundaram or the Victory of Virtuous Behaviour') in 1918, and *Ariya Malar* ('Rare Flower') in 1923. Later pre-war novels mostly focused on the Tamil homelands of Tamil Nadu and Ceylon (Sri Lanka). However, M. Srinivasagam Selvathurai used a local setting, and localized dialogue in his novel *Korakaanthan Aalladhu Thenmalaya Giriyil Vada Ilangai Thuppali* ('Horrible Kanthan or Northern Ceylon Detective in South Malaya Hill').

Semmannum Neela Malargalum ('Red Sand and Blue Flowers'), winning entry in the Malaysian Tamil Writers Association's first novel writing competition, 1969.

Following an eight-year period of inactivity as a result of World War II, five novels were published between 1949 and Independence in 1957, with themes that focused on solutions to the social problems of estate workers, such as alcoholism, and the caste and *kangany* (estate supervisor) systems.

Post-Independence novels

A number of new writers emerged after Independence. They began to view Malaya (from 1963, Malaysia) as their homeland and were driven by the idea of an independent, indigenous Tamil literature devoid of foreign influence. Novels such as *Thuyarapaathai* ('The Path of Sorrow'), *Malaraatha Malar* ('Unblossomed Flower'), and *Kaanal Neer* ('Mirage') continued to portray the life and problems of immigrant plantation workers. The 14 novels published during the 1960s included *Vadaatha Malar* ('Undried Flower'), *Ithaya Vasaal* ('Entrance of Heart') and *Pokkiri Raja* ('Mischievous Raja'), and were mainly romances or thrillers set in Malaysia.

Estate life also featured prominently in the novels of the 1970s. These addressed topical, contemporary social problems such as drug abuse among youngsters; *Pasithirukkum Ilam Kosukkal* ('Hungry Mosquitoes') by Ilanchelvan is a particularly good example. The high-handedness of estate management was well portrayed in *Ilatchiya Payanam* ('Ideal Journey') by I. Ilavalagu.

The 1980s were equally productive. Novels focused on personal relationships, friendship and love. Historical novels set in Malaysia appeared for the first time, including two set in the 15th-century Melaka Sultanate: *Aadum Manjal Oonjal* ('A Swaying Yellow Swing') by B. Chandrakantham and *Thee Malar* ('Fire Flower') by S. Kamala. In the 1990s, middle-class Indian professionals began to show an interest in writing Tamil novels. The period was also marked with the social and economic problems faced by Indians migrating from the shrinking plantation sector to the burgeoning cities. Of particular note were *Suvar* ('Wall') by medical doctor S. Sockalingam which focused on drug addicts, and *Thediyirukkum Tharunangal* ('Awaited Moments') by R. Karthigesu, a university professor, which touched on urban family life.

Major post-Independence novels

1960s	1970s	1980s	1990s

1960s

Vadaatha Malar ('Undried Flower') by Kurusamy

1970s

Pasithirukkum Ilam Kosukkal ('Hungry Mosquitoes') (left) by Ilanchelvan and *Ilatchiya Payanam* ('Ideal Journey') (right) by I. Ilavalagu.

1980s

Thee Malar ('Fire flower') by Su. Kamala won the 1987 Anbanandan Literature Award.

1990s

Thediyurukkum Tharunangal ('Awaited Moments') by R. Karthigesu.

Short stories

Tamil short stories appeared in Singapore as early as 1888, written by Cikgu Magadhum Saybu, editor of the weekly *Singai Nesan* ('Singapore Admirer'), entitled 'Vinodhana Sambashanai' ('Fascinating Conversations'). However, the first truly Malayan Tamil short stories only appeared in 1930 when V. Sinniah Pillai published a book of five stories entitled *Navarasa Kathaa Manjari: Ivai Iniya Karpithak Kathaigal* ('Collection of Multi-tasted Stories: These are Sweet Imaginary Stories').

With the advent of numerous journals and magazines in the 1930s, short stories increased in popularity. Editors realized the potential of the form in educating readers without being overtly didactic. Short stories were even used by religious bodies (Hindu, Muslim and Christian) as a medium to spread their respective faiths.

Towards the end of the 1930s, stories focused on the emancipation of the depressed local working class, the kangany system of labour recruitment, and the evils of drinking. Prominent writers such as S. Halasyarathan, S. Vedambal, N. Palanivel, K. N. Annamali and Murusamy Pillai dealt with a variety of related themes, including life in the rubber estates, cruel and ruthless employers, and the reformative trend in the Indian community. The particular plight of urban Muslim shop assistants was dealt with in the stories 'Tholilaalar Kathai' by N. P. A. Almin and 'Kadait Theru' by K. A. Karim.

During the Japanese Occupation (1941–5) although no novels were written, about 100 short stories addressing a potpourri of themes were published in local Tamil-language newspapers and magazines.

Three-volume short story collection, *Verum Vazhvum* ('Roots and Life'), compiled by writer Syd Peer Mohamed.

Post-war development of the short story

The genre expanded still further during the post-war period until Independence, with active support from the two major daily newspapers, *Tamil Nesan* and *Tamil Murasu*. Particularly influential was the literary

Female short story writers at the launch of the collection *Kayalvizhi* ('Fish-like eyes') in 2003.

Support from *Tamil Murasu* and the Tamil Bell Club

G. Sarangapany, a social leader and founder of the *Tamil Murasu* newspaper, encouraged students to write short stories, poems and essays in his newspaper, for which he allotted a full page each week. Participating students became members of a club, known as the *Manavar Manimanram* (Students' Bell Club), organized by the newspaper. The number of members swelled to the extent that an association—*Manimanram* (Bell Club)—was formed, under G. Sarangapany's guidance. Prominent members and leaders of the Club were proficient orators and writers. Starting in 1952, *Manimanram* and *Tamil Murasu* held *Tamilar Thirunal* (Tamil People's Day) celebrations all over Malaysia, with events in fact spread over several months rather than focused on a particular day. Speakers from Tamil Nadu were invited and several competitions were held to promote Tamil culture to youths.

RIGHT: G. Sarangapany, editor of the *Tamil Murasu* newspaper from 1935, was also a Tamil social leader who contributed to the development of the Tamil language and its literature in Malaysia.

LEFT: S. A. Anbanandan was the first leader of *Manimanram*, the Tamil Bell club. He was also a renowned singer, poet, actor and director.

column, *Kadhai Vaguppu* ('Story-writing Class'), by Suba Narayananan and Biroji Narayanan, which ran in *Tamil Nesan* from 1950 to 1951.

From Independence until 1969, short stories emphasized inter-lingual and inter-ethnic relationships. Patriotic themes, too, were popular as a result of the Indonesian Confrontation, the Philippines' claim over Sabah, the birth of Malaysia, and Singapore's entry into and exit from Malaysia. Some 20 short story collections were published, and although themes were local, style was influenced by Dravida Munnetra Kalagam, a political movement in Tamil Nadu.

More than 35 short story collections appeared in the 1970s, and a third newspaper, *Tamil Malar*, began to promote short stories. Writers tackled issues such as poverty, citizenship, work permits, unemployment, housing and the general decadence of society. Several writers from the 1960s and 1970s, such as M. Jeevanandham, quit the field in the early 1980s to take up more lucrative occupations, leaving a vacuum that was filled by inexperienced young writers. As a result, quality deteriorated somewhat. Sponsorship from the press also ceased, although short stories continued to be published, especially in Sunday issues. As many of the young writers were attracted to the cinema, large numbers of short stories had themes, plot, characters and dialogues heavily influenced by Tamil cinema.

The 1990s saw the continuing urban migration of Malaysian Indian plantation workers, a theme reflected by short story writers such as Pushpa Leelavathi (better known by her pen name, Pavai). A number of important collections have been published since the 1990s, including *Verum Vazhvum* ('Roots and Life'), Syd Peer Mohamed's three-volume anthology of Malaysian short stories published between 2000 and 2002, and N. A. Senguttuvan's *Arai Nootraandu Malaysian Sirukadhaigal 1950–2000* ('Half a Century of Malaysian Short Stories 1950–2000').

Tamil literature appears in nearly every issue of the Malaysian Tamil press, including daily newspapers *Tamil Nesan* (top left) and *Malaysia Nanban* (top right), and weekly publications, *Wanabady* (bottom left) and *Nayanam* (bottom right).

The title to this collection of short stories by N. Patchaibalan, *Mauram Kalaikirathu* ('Ending My Silence'), is drawn from one of the stories contained within it.

Tamil poetry

Local Tamil poetry began to develop in the late 19th century, building on the ancient tradition of the subcontinent. It was only much later that local poets broke away from the more rigid traditional forms, a move which, at least at first, generated a certain amount of friction within the Tamil literary community. Over the years, a large corpus of work has been produced in both the traditional and new (free verse) forms, a result of the foresight and dedication of certain key individuals and organizations.

Participants at one of the many poetry-writing workshops organized by the Malaysian Tamil Writers Association.

Although he never visited Malaya, Subramaniam (better known as *Barathiar*), a pre-World War II poet from Tamil Nadu, remains highly revered by Malaysian Tamil poets, who have been profoundly influenced by his work.

The poetic tradition

Tamil has an impressive poetic history, incorporating ancient epics such as the *Ramayana* and *Mahabharata*, *Silappathigaram*, and *Manimaegalai* (see 'The Ramayana' and 'The Mahabharata'). Malaysian Tamil poetry, however, developed much later, the first published collection being the 10-song anthology *Arumukap Pathigam* ('Devotional Songs on Lord Murugan') in 1887. This was followed by a compilation of Hindu songs by C. N. Sathasiva Pandithar.

Some 30 anthologies were published prior to 1946, consisting of praise to the deities worshipped by plantation workers, life in the estates and the suffering of the workers. A new style of poetry—with a simplified formal style, and reformist content—known as *Marumalrchi Kavithaigal* (Renaissance Poetry) was introduced in Tamil Nadu during this period, led by the poet known as Barathiar, and was subsequently imitated by Malaysian Tamil poets. This led to the establishment in 1943 of the *Kavitha Mandalam* (Poetry Zone) organization, which published its first anthology in 1947.

N. A. Senguttuvan's 'Collection of Thirukkural' (*Thirukkural Paathiral*), explains ancient Tamil poems in poetic form.

Support and development of Tamil poetry

However, after 1948—which coincided with Indian independence—the *Marumalrchi Kavithaigal* form declined, although other forms prospered. Several organizations assisted in the development of local poetry, such as the Melaka-based *Thamil Pannai* (Tamil Farm) which operated from 1950 to 1956, the *Madurai Thamizh Sangam Pandidhar* (Tamil Nadu Madurai Tamil Association), and the *Tamil Murasu* newspaper, which held *Rasanai Vaguppu* (Poetry appreciation sessions) and arranged the *Tamilar Thirunal* (Tamil People's Day) festival, first held in 1952. The *Kolalampoor Tamil Pannai* (Kuala Lumpur Tamil Farm) and religious leader Swamy Ramathasar of Penang provided further assistance to local poets.

The years after Independence saw increasing support from the Tamil daily newspapers, and many other (often short-lived) publications including the National Plantation Workers' Association weekly *Sangamani*, as well as *Navarasam* (1958) and the monthly *Madhavi* (1959–63).

The poetry competition organized by daily newspaper *Tamil Murasu* in 1960 and the *Kavi Arangam* (Poetry Hall) sponsored by its rival, *Tamil Nesan,* later in that decade, were particularly useful in unearthing new talent. Towards the end of the 1960s the youth-based Tamil Bell Club, the National Land Finance Cooperative Society, and the Malaysian Tamil Writers Association were also active in promoting Tamil poetry.

A number of collections were published during that decade, starting with *Kavithai Thirattu* ('Poetry

The Malaysian Tamil Writers Association

The Malaysian Tamil Writers Association has played a major role in promoting and developing Tamil literature, particularly poetry. It has organized numerous poetry forums led by established poets, starting with *Onbaan Suvai Kaviyarangam* (Nine taste poetry forum) in 1964. Poems written for these forums were published as a collection, *Arangeriya Kavithaigal* ('Proclaimed Poems'), in 1977. In recent years, the Association has created a strong platform for the development of Tamil poetry; the quarterly *Puthukavithai* (free verse) conferences gives inspiration and guidance to new poets.

LEFT: Programme for the Association's 1988 Silver Jubilee.

RIGHT: Writers at a short story forum organized by the Association held in Slim River in 1976. Association President Murugu Subramaniam is seated fourth from the left.

Comparison between formal poetry and free verse

The formal style of Tamil *Marabuk Kavdhaigal* (traditional poetry) in fact encompasses a number of traditional Tamil poetic forms, each with their own relatively strict rules of rhyme, rhythm and metre. A wide range of themes have been addressed by Malaysian Tamil poets in this style, which has a long history in the Tamil homeland of Tamil Nadu, India. These include nature, religion, love, the Malaysian nation and society, royalty, leaders and other dignitaries, the Tamil language, life and work on the estates, betrayal by the *kangany* (estate supervisors), and romance. Songs have also been written in this style for both radio and theatre, as well as for children.

The modern free verse style, *Pudhukavithaigal*, first used by Malaysian poets in the 1960s, is not bound by the rules and conventions of traditional Tamil poetry. Generally shorter in length too, reliance is instead placed on the multi-layered meanings of the carefully chosen words employed by the poet.

Dr Murasu Nedumaran's *Malaysia Thamizh Kavithai Kalanjium* ('An Anthology of Malaysian Tamil Poetry') covers traditional poetic works from 1887 to 1987.

An example of *Marabuk Kavdhaigal* (traditional poetry)

The first of two verses of the poem, 'Rubbarum Thamilarum' ('Rubber tree and Tamils') by S. A. Anbanandnan, the first Tamil Bell Club president:

> *Engirundho Thamilanai pol ingu ezh(l)undhu*
> *Nilam parthu thannai oonri*
> *Thanga magan oliyalum Gangai aval*
> *Arulalum Semmai oori*
> *Mangalamai Ilai virithu malarndhaalaam*
> *Rubber enum mangai pearthu*
> *Thangamudi Mani vaithal pol nirayil*
> *Vaithittaar selvam petraar!*

> *Sangu nira paal pozh(l)iyum thanga mara*
> *Selvangal sotta eendhu*
> *Than kadamai mudithuvitu thanai azh(l)ikka*
> *Koduthu vittu saaaidhal pola*
> *Sengurudhi neerakki sembudalai*
> *uramakki saindhu poga*
> *Angirundhu vandhaano avanukkum*
> *Rabbarukkum matram kaanean!*

Rubber came from somewhere like Tamils
Planted in good land
Grown with golden rays and gifted water
Blossomed like a girl
They replanted it as placing a ruby in a crown
and it earned money for them!

It gives its white milk until the last drop
And its duty done allows itself to be destroyed.
In the same way,
He also gave his blood as water, his body as fertilizer
Was it for this he came from there (India)
I could not see any difference between him (Tamil) and rubber.

Examples of *Pudhukavithaigal* (free verse)

'Ivan natta' ('He planted')
by K. Punniyavaan

> *Rubber marangal ellaam*
> *Nimirndhu*
> *Nindru vittana.*
> *Ivan*
> *Nadumbodhu kunindhavan.*
> *Innum*
> *Nimirave illai.*

The rubber trees
Planted by him were
Grown straight up.
He bent down
To plant them.
But he never stood up
Still bent down.

'Ottodu sella vaendia' ('Rain should run off the roof')
by V. Rajeswary

> *Ovvoru mazh(l)aithuliyum*
> *Ullae ettip paarppadhu*
> *Koorai nee*
> *Kooda illaadhadhaal dhanae.*

The rain drops
Which were supposed to go by
The roof tiles,
Try to see inside (the house)
Because you,
The roof of my life,
Are not with me.

Collection') by M. V. Thillai and Sangu Shanmugam. The Malaysia-Indonesia confrontation in 1963 led to the publication of a number of *Porparani* (War Song) poems. On the tenth anniversary of Tun Sambanthan's National Land Finance Cooperative Society (1968), poetry forums were held all over the country, and at the anniversary celebrations a national level poetry forum was organized.

Contemporary works

Dozens more poetry books were published during the 1970s and 1980s. Of these, the most remarkable was the exhaustive *Malaysia Thamizh Kavithai Kalanjium* ('An Anthology of Malaysian Tamil Poetry'), compiled and published by Dr. Murasu Nedumaran. Towards the end of this period, traditional, formal poetry saw a marked decline as a result of the appearance of a new form, *Pudhukavithaigal* (free verse), adopted from the subcontinent, with a style similar to English blank verse and French *vers libre*. The first such poem to be published in Malaysia, in 1964, was *Kallappartugal* ('Villains in Folk Dramas') by C. Kamalanathan.

This new poetic form immediately drew criticism from poets writing in the traditional, formal, style. It was nevertheless promoted from the outset by Athi Kumaran in the *Tamil Malar* newspaper, and later in the weekly magazine, *Vanampadi*. Further support for Pudhukavithaigal

came from the daily newspaper *Tamil Osai*, which ran from 1981 to 1988. Three figures in particular promoted and developed the form: Akkini, who wrote one of the most inspirational works, *Kana Magudangal* ('Crowns of Dreams'); Rajahkumaran who wrote the column *Sasanam*; and Ilvachelvan, who organized poetry forums. Towards the end of the 20th century, poets such as Pachai Balan even experimented with the Japanese Haiku form.

The influence of Tamil radio broadcasting

Following Independence in 1957, Kuala Lumpur took over from Singapore as the headquarters of government radio transmission. This proved a huge boost to Tamil-language broadcasting, such that the 1960s have come to be acclaimed as the 'golden era' of Tamil broadcasting. This in turn served as a spur to the literary scene.

During that decade, in addition to the standard radio fare of news, sports, music, and drama, many new formats were introduced. Among them were musical dramas, and perhaps more unconventionally, musical reenactments of current affairs. A literary magazine programme was also regularly broadcast, educating the Tamil-speaking population on their rich literary heritage and developments in local Tamil poetry and other literary forms. An annual '*Vaanoli Vizha*' ('Radio Festival') was organized which brought together writers and performers for live shows.

RIGHT: R. Balakrishnan, head of the Radio Television Malaysia (RTM) Indian service during its 'golden era', speaking in 1966.

LEFT: RTM's Radio Six continues to broadcast in Tamil.

Novels in English

Starting in the 1930s, Malayan, and subsequently Malaysian, authors began to write in the English language, previously solely the domain of expatriate authors. Themes were initially linked to ancestral homelands and matters related to domestic tensions. Truly local themes only appeared after World War II, focusing on the Japanese Occupation, the Emergency and embryonic nationalism. The literary tradition became established in the 1970s and has continued to grow since.

A former government information officer, Chin Kee Onn captured the trauma of the post-war period in these novels published in Britain.

From early ventures to post-war melodrama

Even before World War II, local writers began to utilize their expertise in the English language to record contemporary struggles and the changing lives of Malayans. Gregory de Silva wrote a series of novels such as *Sulaiman Goes to London* (1938), *The Princess of Malacca* (1939), *Only a Taxi Driver* (1939) and *Lupa* (1939).

Following the war, Chin Kee Onn produced novels about the Japanese Occupation and the ensuing communist insurgency (Emergency). *Ma-rai-ee* (1952), also known as *Silent Army*, gave a first-hand account of life under the Japanese, while *The Grand Illusion* (1961) records the disillusionment with the tyrannical and inhumane strictures of the Malayan Communist Party. Han Suyin's *And the Rain My Drink* (1953) traces the conflicts arising from the confused loyalties and ties afflicting different classes and factions in the country.

The 1960s were characterized by melodrama in the works of John M. Chin and Johnny Ong. Chin's first book, *The Nyonya* (1962), tells of a young man who discovers from his aunt's diary that she is actually his mother. He followed this with *The Santubong Affair* (1964). Ong wrote *Sugar and Salt* (1964), which records the economic rise of the Wong family and the difficulties of intermarriage, and *Run Tiger Run* (1965).

Emergence of the Malaysian novel

In the late 1970s, a literary tradition for the Malaysian novel in English began to emerge. The novels of Lee Kok Liang, Lloyd Fernando and K. S. Maniam strove for an authentic Malaysian expression, searching for answers to life in a materialistic, multiracial, multicultural Malaysia.

Scorpion Orchid (1976) by Fernando takes on the sensitive issue of race, while *Flowers in the Sky* (1981) by Lee probes some of the country's cultural and religious traditions; and Maniam's *The Return* (1981)

Novellas

1. *The Santubong Affair* (1964), by John M. Chin, tells of a man who murders a tycoon who seduced his mother and is, in fact, his father.
2. Continuing his focus on the family, Johnny Ong's second book, *Run Tiger Run* (1965), examines family conflicts.
3. Ong's third book, *The Long White Sands* (1977), reveals a cultural vacuousness reflected in its indifference towards discovering a Malaysian ethos.

is an Indian Malaysian's search for a place in the land his forefathers settled in. The themes addressed are in stark contrast to the romantic literature produced on Malaya and Malaysia by European authors.

Women writers only appeared in 1994, when Chuah Guat Eng and Marie Gerrina Louis became the first Malaysian women novelists in English. Chuah uses the detective thriller *Echoes of Silence* to reassess the colonial heritage and postcolonial adjustments of her protagonist. Louis's *The Road to Chandibole* speaks out for the oppressed Indian woman who has to survive class and gender discrimination in a plantation estate. Her subsequent novel, *Junos* (1995), charts the progress of a group of Indian immigrants from poverty to prosperity.

Diasporic writers

Notwithstanding the solid body of work produced, opportunities in literary publishing are limited, with socio-political conditions unfavourable to English-language writing. This has led several Malaysians to look outwards to realize their literary ambitions.

Beth Yahp, born in 1964, went to study in Australia at the age of 20. While still at university, she wrote and published short stories. After graduating, she stayed on and eventually wrote the novel *The Crocodile Fury*, which went on to win the Victorian Premier's Prize for First Fiction in 1993. Set in a convent school on a jungle-covered hill in Kuala Lumpur, Yahp weaves myth and magic, ghosts and dragons into an engaging story about family secrets and lives entwined with tales of a crocodile that stalks the surrounding jungle.

Another diasporic writer, Shirley Geok-lin Lim, long established as a poet and short story writer and now settled in the United States, brought out her first novel in 2001 (see 'Short stories and poetry in English'). Entitled *Joss and Gold*, set in the political turmoil and social change of 1969 and beyond, it chronicles the struggles of a Malaysian woman caught between two worlds.

The theme of Indian immigrant struggle is once more taken up by Rani Manicka in *The Rice Mother* (2002). Published in Britain, this traces three generations of a family from Sri Lanka, starting with the grandmother who was forced to follow her husband to Malaya and raise five children in poverty.

Leading novelists and their work

Lloyd Fernando

Lloyd Fernando was born in 1926 and attended school in Singapore prior to World War II. During the 1950s he read English and Philosophy at the University of Malaya in Singapore, then the only local university, working part-time as a radio broadcaster and newsreader to pay his way. He then

went on to lecture in English, subsequently becoming Professor of English at Universiti Malaya in Kuala Lumpur from 1967 to 1978. Upon retirement he studied law, qualified as a barrister and practised as an Advocate and Solicitor in Kuala Lumpur. Before writing his first novel, *Scorpion Orchid*, he wrote a number of short stories and radio plays.

As with *Scorpion Orchid*, his second novel, *Green Is the Colour* (1993), is concerned with the need to find an identity in a multicultural context and within the pressures of a monolithic nationalistic ethos. Through the main characters, Fernando presented his hope that binaric thinking will yield to a more humane awareness of heterogeneity, for any single set of imposed values can only be short-sighted. Differences embraced, acknowledged and respected will pave the way to a meaningful pluralistic unity.

In recognition of Lloyd Fernando's contribution to Malaysian literature, an award named after him was given to the best student in the English Department of Universiti Malaya, Kuala Lumpur, in 1998.

Scorpion Orchid

The first Malaysian novel to take a forthright look at the country's racial dilemma, *Scorpion Orchid* was first published in 1976. It has subsequently been used as a text in a number of tertiary institutions offering courses on Malaysian literature in English. A Tagalog version of the book is also available. The novel was rewritten by Fernando as a play, which made its debut in 1994.

Taking as its historical setting the racial riots in Singapore on the eve of Independence, Fernando explores the unease of four friends representing the Malay, Indian, Chinese and Eurasian communities, who realize that after decades of living together they still remain strangers. Through the enigmatic figure of Tok Said, a character who is racially indeterminate, and Sally, whose race changes according to the perception of the beholder, the novel challenges chauvinism and suggests a national consciousness that transcends race. Fernando makes free use of extracts from the historical *Sejarah Melayu* ('Malay Annals'), *Hikayat Pelayaran Abdullah* ('Story of the Voyage of Abdullah') and other local classics in the novel, serving as a link between contemporary Malaysian English literature and the classical traditions of the region.

'He loved the orchid whose stems flower, curving free away from the supporting posts, but feared the scorpion which lurked among the roots in the rich soil: the character Sabran in Scorpion Orchid (above).

Programme cover from a performance of the play *Scorpion Orchid*, in Singapore in 1995.

K. S. Maniam

A former Associate Professor of English at Universiti Malaya, K. S. Maniam had his first novel, the autobiographical *The Return*, published in 1981. In it, he traces the search for order and identity of a third-generation Indian immigrant, whose mastery of the English language both liberates him from his own communal traditions and sets him adrift between cultures, and the triumphs and defeats of his family

In A Far Country (1993), Maniam's second novel, sees the protagonist, Rajan, traverse not only racial boundaries but also the perimeters of time and space. Maniam suggests that, although for sanity and pragmatic purposes one may have to assent to identity boundaries, these are of no final importance. With this knowledge, Rajan is able to divest himself of some of his social masks and adopt a more humane approach to others.

Maniam's 2003 novel, *Between Lives*, is more accessible than the somewhat dense *In A Far Country*. A haunting narrative set in contemporary Malaysia, it revolves around protagonist-narrator Sumitra, who works at the Orwellian-Kafkaesque Department of Social Reconstruction, and her involvement with the memory-laden old woman, Sellamma.

Extract from *In a Far Country*

Following the description of his son's mental collapse, the central Malay character, Zulkifli (Zul), speaks directly to the story's narrator.

'He is living and not living,' Zul said. 'We can accept the results but we still have to look for the cause. You ran away that time. From the tiger. I've become old and wiser, when I look back I see you and others like you as the cause. We lived well, maybe too peacefully, before you all came with your ideas and energies. Ideas that can even destroy the tiger, the oldest symbol of our civilisation. You gave up everything to come to this land. We offered you what we had. But you all became greedy and wouldn't share. Saw no other world but the world of progress and money. And we had to make the sacrifices. This time I want you to experience what my son went through.'

'I can try, Zul,' I said.

'He saw the tiger,' Zul said. 'I made him see the tiger. Yet, when he went to the city, everything was destroyed.'

Lee Kok Liang

Flowers in the Sky (1981) brought together a Chinese Malaysian monk, a lapsed Christian, a Hindu priest, a member of a mystical and erotic Tantric sect, a Muslim and a mute devotee of a temple, who struggle to find a balance between the physical and the spiritual. The novel presents the cultural and religious barriers that exist in the multicultural, polyglot society of its setting.

In the posthumously published *London Does Not Belong to Me* (2003), set in London and Paris in the early 1950s, Lee portrays the disillusion and isolation of a diverse group of expatriates hailing from the far corners of the crumbling British empire.

Chuah Guat Eng

In the elegantly crafted *Echoes of Silence* (1994), Chuah Guat Eng looks at the colonial heritage of Malaysia and postcolonial adjustments. The detective story serves as prop to the first-person narrator's odyssey of self-discovery: a reassessment of her linkages to the land, its history and legacies and the roles played by women in the nation's past. Metaphors of orphanhood and parentage are central to the novel's themes, not merely incidental as in John M. Chin's novellas of the 1960s.

Short stories and poetry in English

Short stories in English by local writers did not appear until after Independence in 1957, somewhat later than poetry, the first collection of which appeared in 1950. The literary roots of both genres traverse a broad expanse of people, time and space. This is apparent from the sense of cultural heterogeneity in the works produced, with writers and poets, a number of whom are diasporic, drawn from all three of the larger Malaysian ethnic groups.

The panel of the 1991 NST-Shell Short Story Competition comprised (from left) Muhammad Haji Salleh, Lee Kok Liang, Krishnen Jit, and A. Samad Said. Winning entries from the 1989–90 competition were published in the acclaimed collection, *Haunting the Tiger and Other Stories*.

A leading collection

'A New Sensation' is among the priceless items in the anthology *Twenty-two Malaysian Stories* (1968) edited by Lloyd Fernando. It has been reprinted numerous times and highlights short fiction of the 1950s and 1960s. Fernando followed it up with *Malaysian Short Stories* in 1981, but this was a far less successful volume. Through both, he introduced the literary potential of home-grown talents to a Malaysian reading public more exposed to imported literature from the West, and gave space to emerging writers such as K. S. Maniam, Shirley Geok-lin Lim, M. Shanmughalingam, Siew-Yue Killingley, Maureen Ten and Stella Kon. Their stories foreground the rich textures and cross-cultural tensions of Malaysian life, not simply for exotic local colour but to convey the inner experience of its people.

The seventh reprint of the popular short story collection, published in 1992.

In the 2000s, new authors' works have been collated In the Silverfish New Writing anthology series, as well as a collection of Malaysian women's writing, published by Silverfish Books.

Pioneer short story writers

A seminal figure in the development of short story writing is Lee Kok Liang. His semi-autobiographical first story, 'Return to Malaya' was published in August 1954, and his debut collection, *The Mutes in the Sun and Other Stories*, was published in 1964. A strong sense of place and character emerges in his work with themes such as alienation, unfulfilled desires, change in society, and the limitations of human behaviour. His prose is vivid without being overly descriptive, yet it can be sensuous and powerful. Another, later, collection of his short stories, *Death Is a Ceremony* (1992), includes two notable stories, 'Dumb, Dumb, by a Bee Stung' and 'It's All in a Dream', that deal with the abuse of political power.

In terms of pioneerhood status and technical accomplishment, Lee is perhaps matched only by Wang Gungwu, who wrote 'A New Sensation' under the pseudonym Awang Kedua. This story about a Chinese Malaysian on the threshold of adulthood is an outstanding story of the 1950s. Wang did not however sustain his literary pursuit, and went on to distinguish himself as a historian.

Lee Kok Liang's short story collection, *The Mutes in the Sun*, demonstrates his mastery of the genre.

Decline, revival and the future

Malaysian writing in English was sparse for over a decade from the late 1970s in the context of the renewed emphasis on the national language, although Shirley Geok-lin Lim had begun to write before this period. A short fiction revival took place in the late 1980s and early 1990s with a series of

competitions organized by writer-actor Kee Thuan Chye, beginning with The New Straits Times-McDonalds Short Story Competition in 1987 and followed by four more sponsored by The New Straits Times and a new partner, Shell. The competitions provided much needed encouragement, and managed to unearth new talents including Syed Adam Aljafri, who eventually published *Reminiscences: A Collection of Short Stories* (1996). One of the better known writers to meet with success in these competitions was K. S. Maniam, who wrote 'The Loved Flaw' (which won the New Straits Times-McDonalds Short Story Competition in 1987), and 'Haunting the Tiger' (which won the first NST-Shell Short Story Competition in 1989–90) among others.

Among the more contemporary writers, Che Husna's 'Melor' tales and her delightful evocation of rural scenes in *The Rambutan Orchard* (1993) are filled with intense nostalgia. This would appear to be in marked contrast with the exuberant note struck by lawyer Karim Raslan who, with an ironic yet impish delight, exposes the fake and the hypocritical wherever he finds it in Malaysian life. His confidence in the eclecticism of local lifestyles runs through his *Heroes and Other Stories* (1996).

The first English-language poets

At the forefront of a search for a Malayan English-language poetic tradition were Beda Lim and Wang Gungwu, both undergraduates at the University of Malaya in Singapore in the late 1940s. Wang produced the first local English-language collection *Pulse* (1950), and one which set an example by using Malayan images and subjects. Its diction and poetics, however, remained rooted in English literature.

Ee Tiang Hong, a Melaka-born Baba and another alumnus of the University of Malaya in Singapore, successfully found a Malaysian voice for his poetry in his first volume, *I of the Many Faces* (1960). This and subsequent volumes—

Wong Phui Nam's poems

In the preface to his first collection of poetry, *How the Hills Are Distant*, Wong registers an important statement, which to some extent summarizes the condition of Malaysian English-language poets:

'[T]hese poems ... need to be written. They are of a time, of a place, of a people who find themselves having to live by institutions and folkways which are not of their heritage, having to absorb the manners of languages not their own. Such little knowledge as comes to them of the human predicament is no less knowledge than what comes to other peoples in other times and places.... On looking back I realise I have written these poems for those who truly understand what it means to have to make one's language as one goes along'.

The poems in *How the Hills Are Distant* explore his cultural and spiritual place in the world

except for his second volume, *Lines Written in Hawaii* (1973), which is more personal and private—dealt with public themes relevant to Malaysia's plural society. His disenchantment with government policy in the 1970s is best expressed in his third volume, *Myths for a Wilderness* (1976). In 1975, he emigrated to Australia, although his poetry continued to be heavily influenced by his homeland. Indeed in his 1985 volume, *Tranquerah*, he still wrote with a Malaysian accent, as he tried to come to terms with his exile. He died in 1990. His last volume, *Nearing a Horizon*, was published posthumously in 1994.

Wong Phui Nam, a contemporary of Ee's at the University of Malaya in Singapore, was more pragmatic and less politically committed, writing linguistically rich and sophisticated poetry. Following his first effort, *How the Hills Are Distant*, a collection of poems he wrote during the 1960s, Wong didn't publish anything for some 20 years. He then return-ed with several collections including *Remembering Grandma and Other Rumours* (1989), *Ways of Exile* (1993) and *Against the Wilderness* (2000).

Other early English-language poets include Omar Mohd Noor, a contemporary of Wong Phui Nam, who wrote in a direct, spare style reminiscent of Philip Larkin and e.e. cummings, and Lee Geok Lan, whose poems dealing with identity and human relationships have been published in the press.

Poets in English and Malay

Salleh Ben Joned was born in 1941, studied in Tasmania, and taught for a while at the English Department of Universiti Malaya. In his bilingual poetry collection, *Sajak Sajak Saleh: Poems Sacred and Profane* (1987), he reflects Muhammad Haji Salleh's practice of combining the writing of poetry in both Malay and English.

Anugerah Sastera Malaysia (National Literary Award) recipient Muhammad Haji Salleh began writing poetry in English and Malay as a trainee teacher in England during the 1960s. He published a collection of English poetry in 1978 entitled *Time and Its People*. It highlights the human condition and its relation to time, and articulates the search for identity in the midst of social change.

Diasporic and more recent poets

In addition to Shirley Geok-lin Lim, now resident in the United States, there are several other diasporic Malaysian poets. Although Ooi Boo Eng, who taught at Universiti Malaya's English Department until his emigration to Australia in the early 1980s, has no published volume of poetry, he has developed a coterie following as a magazine and academic journal poet. Hilary Tham, who emigrated to the United States in 1971, has published six volumes of poetry, including *Bad Names for Women, Lane with No Name: Memoirs & Poems of a Malaysian-Chinese Girlhood*, and her latest, *The Tao of Mrs Wei*.

Other contemporary poets include Kee Thuan Chye, of a generation that came after the first wave of Malaysian Anglophone poets and was unaffected by the poetics of English literature, who has made interesting use of myth and symbolism to explore profound themes. Cecil Rajendra, a lawyer, has been writing social protest poems that approximate sloganeering rather than art, and has thus had a mixed critical reception at home and abroad. His collections of poetry include *Bones and Feathers* (1978) and *Hour of the Assassins and Other Poems* (1983). Dina Zaman, one of the most promising of the current generation of poets, deals with what it means to be a woman in multicultural Malaysia.

Written in English, *Sajak Sajak Saleh: Poems Sacred and Profane*, by bilingual poet Salleh Ben Joned, met with controversy due to the language used which was considered vulgar by some.

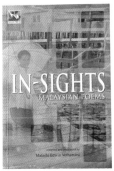

In-sights, published in 2003, is an anthology of Malaysian poetry written in English and translated into English from Malay, by several local poets.

Shirley Geok-lin Lim

Shirley Geok-lin Lim's first published work was the short story 'Journey', which she wrote in 1967 while an undergraduate at Universiti Malaya. The feminist perspective of this story has remained central to her later writing. Her subsequent story, 'Mr Tang's Girls', won second prize in the 1982 *Asiaweek* Short Story Competition. Also in 1982, her collection *Another Country and Other Stories* was published, containing stories reflecting her Melaka *peranakan* (Malay for 'locally-born Chinese', or Straits Chinese) background and cosmopolitan outlook.

Now Professor of English and Women's Studies at the University of California in Santa Barbara, the United States, this talented writer is also a successful poet. She is the only Malaysian poet to win a major international literary prize, the Commonwealth Poetry Prize, for best first poetry book in 1980 with her collection, *Crossing the Peninsula and Other Poems* (1980). A strong feeling of exile comes through her subsequent volumes of poetry. *No Man's Grove* (1985), *Modern Secrets* (1989) and *Monsoon History* (1994) traverse her Malaysian past and American present as she searches for a sense of belonging, and in *What the Fortune Teller Didn't Say* (1998), she revisits her painful childhood and dreams of her home country even as she tries to adjust to her adopted land.

Among the works written by Lim (left) are the award-winning collection of early poems, *Crossing the Peninsula & Other Poems* (right), and the later collection *Monsoon History* (above right).

'Imagine'
by Shirley Geok-lin Lim

Imagine—
a sheet of glass
reflecting nothing
but itself.

No image—
all surface
a pure depth.

Still—
words are significations
of things other than.

All poetry
necessarily
begins with a lie.

Malaysia in foreign literature

From as early as the 3rd century CE, and especially under British rule, the land that is now called Malaysia attracted considerable interest among explorers, literary travellers, colonial administrators, anthropologists and botanists, some of whom came, saw and wrote. As a result, there now exists a large corpus of writings comprising novels, short stories, reports, memoirs, autobiographies, travellers' tales, historical accounts, anthropological and botanical descriptions. These works present a vivid record from the perspective of the outsider.

European literary figures including Somerset Maugham, Rudyard Kipling, Noel Coward, and Herman Hesse, stayed at the Eastern and Oriental Hotel in Penang during the inter-war years.

Writings under the Portuguese and Dutch

Ancient perspectives on what is now Malaysia came from a variety of sources. To the early European consciousness, it was just a set of confusing images and incredible tales brought back by those returning from the East such as Alexander the Great in the 3rd century and Marco Polo in the 13th century. It was regarded as part of the Malay World referred to as Chryse (Greek for 'golden'), situated vaguely beyond India

The earliest known descriptions of Melaka by a European were compiled by Tome Pires who visited in 1512, a year after it fell to his Portuguese countrymen. He recorded Malay court intrigues, customs, laws and commerce. In 1518, another Portuguese visitor, Duarte Barbossa, completed his account of, among other things, the lifestyle of the Malay ruling class. A third Portuguese, Emanuel Godhino de Eredia, wrote on the decadent preoccupation of the nobility with cock-fighting and music. In 1522, Antonio Pigafetta, an Italian, presented his Emperor with an account of his travels to Borneo with the expedition led by Ferdinand Magellan.

The Dutch occupation of Melaka started in 1641. Balthasar Bort, Dutch Governor of Melaka from 1665 to 1677, gave an account of the occupied city under his stewardship. Thirty years later, as a result of their rebellion against the occupying force, the Malays earned themselves a notorious place in

Portuguese map of the Malay Peninsula (upside down) dating from 1542. The illustrations provide an insight as to how early European travellers perceived the region and its inhabitants.

the travel book *A Voyage Round the World* by Italian traveller and doctor of law John Francis Gemilli. In 1726, another Dutch scholar, Francois Valentyn, completed his own version of the history of Melaka, and Portuguese Captain de Vellez Guirreiro wrote an account of Johor in which he waxed lyrical over the Sultan while calling his subjects barbarians.

Travel writing under the British

By the mid-19th century, more explorers and some botanists visited and started writing. Alfred Russel Wallace's *The Malay Archipelago* (1858) remains a useful resource, and Isabella Bird's *The Golden Chersonese and the Way Thither* (1883), with its insightful accounts of Anglo-Malay and Anglo-Chinese relations, is an eyewitness record of life under British rule. Other observations of the leisurely lifestyle of bygone days can be found in A. B. Rathborne's *Camping and Tramping in Malaya* (1898), Rounsevelle Wildman's *Tales of the Malayan Coast* (1899), Hunter S. Banner's *A Tropical Tapestry* (1929) and John Cameron's geographically misplaced title *Our Tropical Possessions in Malayan India* (1865).

Although these books were written in the form of description and reportage, they were, like fiction, structured within a framework of anecdotes and personal narratives. Books of this period shared the notion of the East as an exotic and mysterious land, a notion that was already in circulation at the time among orientalists and armchair travellers. A perfect example of exotica is the story of piracy and adventure in the Strait of Melaka in G. A. Henty's *In the Hands of the Malays* (1905).

Works of colonial administrators

By the end of the 19th century, colonial civil servants and other expatriates who had spent long years in villages and settlements took time off from the pressures of administration to reminisce over their exotic immersions. Frank Swettenham, British Resident of the Federated Malay States, wrote *Malay Sketches* (1895) which included such sundry topics as a tiger hunt and a fishing picnic. The Resident of Pahang from 1896 to 1905, Hugh Clifford, turned part-time fiction-writer, dishing out slices of life in the outpost he knew so well. *Since the Beginning*

Different views of the Chersonese

Isabella Bird's *The Golden Chersonese* (1883) and Emily Innes' *The Chersonese with the Gilding Off* (1885) present markedly different views of 19th-century British Malaya. This was a result of the authors' contrasting status, and social circles: Bird mixed with the colonial elite, while Innes endured petty officialdom and the Malay kampong.

Isabella Bird (above) wrote *The Golden Chersonese* (far left), published just two years before Emily Innes' somewhat gloomier, although no less endearing, work, *The Chersonese with the Gilding Off* (left).

(1898), *A Free Lance of Today* (1903) and *A Prince of Malaya* (1926) display Clifford's understanding and intimate knowledge of the Malay World.

Works by fiction writers

While neither Swettenham nor Clifford was a literary trumpet-major, there were at least three heavyweight writers who wrote on Malaya: Joseph Conrad, Somerset Maugham, and Anthony Burgess.

Joseph Conrad wrote four novels and two short stories that are specifically Malaya-based: *Almayer's Folly* (1895), *An Outcast of the Islands* (1896), 'Karain' and 'The Lagoon' in *Tales of Unrest* (1898), *Lord Jim* (1900) and *The Rescue* (1920). His novels revolve around white protagonists, often portrayed as disillusioned creatures trapped in alien circumstances beyond their control. At the same time, they also represent many characteristics of the early colonial man—the obsession with the greatness of an idea, the need to have little 'empires' of their own, the warring impulses, the divided loyalties. Unlike the novels, the short stories revolve around the personal tragedies of romanticized Malay characters with manners and values that appear curiously European.

Somerset Maugham's Malayan short stories are about administrators and planters engaged in their own private struggles, living under codes and manners of a seemingly calm and ordered public life under British rule. The stories provide an insight into the pretentious social milieu of colonial society.

The most comprehensive and absorbing study of colonialism at the wrong end of colonial history, however, is Anthony Burgess' *The Malayan Trilogy* (1956–9).

Post-Independence writing

In the immediate years after Independence in 1957 there was a spate of literary works by mostly British writers on the Japanese Occupation (1941–5). Ronald Hastain's *White Coolie* (1959) records this painful period as well as the changing relationship between the

Joseph Conrad

Several of the works of Polish-born Joseph Conrad—the anglification of his original name, Konrad Korzeniowski—concerned Malaya, a result of the time that he spent in the region during his early career as a merchant seaman. He first visited Singapore in 1882, at the age of 25, and stayed for six weeks on that occasion. It was time well spent, as it provided one of the main themes of *Lord Jim*, considered by some to be his finest work. The fate of the ship S.S. *Jeddah* was then a major topic of debate; the ship—together with nearly one thousand Malay passengers bound for Saudi Arabia to perform the Haj—had been abandoned by its master and three British officers when it broke down and began to take in water. Fortunately the ship and its passengers were in the end rescued, just off the African coast. Conrad used the ship's chief officer, A. P. Williams, as one of the models for the composite character, Lord Jim.

Much of Conrad's work was thinly disguised autobiography.

British and the disenchanted natives. Accounts of internment suffered by British soldiers are found in J. Clavell's *King Rat* (1962) and William Allister's *A Handful of Rice* (1961).

Similarly, the jungle warfare of the Emergency (1948–1960) feature in novels such as Harry Miller's *Menace in Malaya* (1954), John Slimming's *In Fear of Silence* (1959), Michael Keon's *The Durian Tree* (1960), Alan Silitoe's *Key to the Door* (1961), and Leslie Thomas' *Virgin Soldiers* (1967).

William Allister's *A Handful of Rice* recalls the horrors endured by British prisoners of war in Malaya during World War II.

More directly concerning Independence, Donald Moore's *Far Eastern Journal* (1960) represents the typical expatriate sentiment that the country was ill-prepared to contain the communist onslaught. On the other hand, expatriate academics such as Patrick Anderson in *Snake Wine* (1955) and James Kirkup in *Tropical Temper* (1963) were not inspired by the new political and social order, dwelling instead on university life and dull cultural visits. Neither was Graham Greene impressed with the political drama of the Emergency; in fact, in his literary memoir *Ways of Escape* (1980) he described the country he visited as 'dull as a beautiful woman'.

After Independence, the rainforests of Sabah and Sarawak have remained destinations for travel writers. Although they still dwell on the strange and the exotic, they show little of the condescension of their colonial predecessors. Books of fiction have also been engendered by similar adventures in Sarawak, such as G. M. Fraser's *Flashman's Lady* (1988). Recent foreign writing on Malaysia, however, has been more academic than creative.

The Malayan Trilogy

Anthony Burgess' *The Malayan Trilogy* (1956–9) is a collection of three novels: *Time For a Tiger* (1958), *The Enemy in the Blanket* (1958), and *Beds in the East* (1959), held together by the common story of Victor Crabbe, an education officer in British Malaya during the twilight of colonial rule. Thematically, the trilogy constitutes a single continuum of the unfolding problems of a plural society trying desperately to achieve a sense of unity before Independence, and portrays the attitudes of the British community in Malaya slowly coming to terms with its progressive marginalization in an era when colonialism had finally become redundant.

The Malayan Trilogy by British author Anthony Burgess, who later wrote *A Clockwork Orange* (1962).

Fauconnier's Malaya

Malaisie (literally 'Malaysia', but published in English under the title *The Soul of Malaya*), by the successful French planter Henri Fauconnier, is set in colonial Malaya. It won the *Prix Goncourt*, France's highest literary award, in 1931.

Henri Fauconnier with his younger brother, Charles, in Henri's House of Palms in 1922 (left). An illustration from a later edition of the novel, drawn by his brother, Charles (right). An early French edition of Fauconnier's *Malaisie* (centre).

Contemporary foreign writers, fascinated by the states of Sabah and Sarawak, have written works ranging from fictionalized histories (left) to modern travel reportage (above).

Modern Malay drama

Modern Malay drama developed only after World War II. Drawing from indigenous Malay theatre and Bangsawan, it differed in that it followed written scripts. Also influenced by Western theatre, modern Malay drama has progressed through a number of distinct phases: the Sandiwara, the realistic, the generally unsuccessful experimental period, the reaction to this in the 1980s, and eventually to a resurgence in the 1990s as a result of government funding.

Traditional Malay theatre, such as Mak Yong in Kelantan and elsewhere, continues to be performed, despite the rise of 'modern' Malay drama.

A departure from traditional theatre

The traditional Malay theatrical forms, including Mak Yong, Mek Mulung, Jikey, Kuda Kepang and Wayang Kulit, have several features in common: an episodic plot structure, an amalgamation of songs dance, music, dialogue, stylized movements, improvisation and curing rituals involving the world of spirits. Their myriad forms satisfied a variety of communal needs, and were performed on *bangsal*, makeshift stages or performance areas.

Bangsawan marked the transition from traditional theatre to the modern form. It was popular in the 1930s and 1940s, and presented tales of kings and nobility in a proscenium theatre.

The modern Malay dramatic forms have been influenced by both the traditional and Bangsawan forms; the main difference is the emergence of written, rather than oral, scripts.

Early modern drama: Sandiwara

Sandiwara simply means 'drama' in Malay. It began as a dramatic genre in the 1950s, with historical and legendary themes, known as *drama sejarah* (historical plays) and *purbawara* (old style plays). The genre was a reaction against the improvisation and stylization of Bangsawan, and a response to the political and educational conditions of the time. Playwrights sought to stimulate Malay nationalism, besides educating the audience about the rich traditions and heritage of their colonized land. Characters tended to be everyday people with common flaws and traits, and plots were simple and developed in a linear, chronological manner.

Sandiwara play *Si Bongkok Tanjong Puteri* ('The Hunchback of Tanjong Puteri') by Shaharom Husain is based on a traditional Malay folktale, and remains popular.

RIGHT: Kala Dewata's play *Atap Genting Atap Rembia* (Tiled Roof, Thatched Roof). A comedy satire, it explores the issue of class difference as it tells of the love between a wealthy urban girl and a poor village boy.

The Realistic period

Realistic plays, also known as 'sitting room' plays, as the entire play often took place in the sitting room, became popular in the 1960s, although this did not lead to the demise of either Bangsawan or Sandiwara. Playwrights attempted to realistically portray social dilemmas encountered by ordinary people. They propagated notions of national development, emphasizing rural

Istana Budaya's 2003 production of *Alang Rentak Seribu* (Alang and his Myriad Ways). Written as a comedy by Syed Alwi in 1973, it is nevertheless a thought-provoking play.

development and the enhancement of education of the poor. Plays addressed life in a fast changing modern society. In addition to the rural-urban dichotomy, prominent themes included romantic relationships, the need for people to change, and the significance of good education. A common element was the kampong, an idealized village which must be changed to keep abreast of the times.

Atap Genting Atap Rembia ('Tiled Roof, Thatched Roof'), by Kala Dewata, the pen name of Mustapha Kamil Yassin, is the epitome of 1960s realistic plays. Other notable playwrights from the period include the late Usman Awang, and Awang Had Salleh, whose works include *Serunai Malam* ('Flute of the Night') and *Buat Menyapu Si Air Mata* ('To Wipe Away the Tears') respectively.

Leading Sandiwara playwright Kalam Hamidy's 1961 collection, *Seruling Gembala* ('Herdsman's Flute'), contains Sandiwara, drama, and pantomime scripts.

Experimental plays

The 1970s began in the aftermath of the devastating racial riots of 13 May 1969: a dramatically altered political scenario and major new government policies. In this uncertain and confused era,

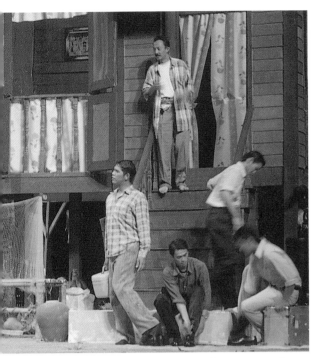

playwrights such as pioneer Noordin Hassan, who first broke the fetters of realism, and young educated playwrights such as Dinsman, Hatta Azad Khan, and Johan Jaaffar became interested in asking deeper social and political questions.

The resulting dramas lacked the neatly arranged linear plots of the realist plays, with playwrights heavily influenced by the Western theatre of the absurd. Stories were set in undefined places at unspecified times, with undeveloped, amorphous characters (with names such as *peladang* (farmer)), and uncertain plots. Some even targeted previously untapped theatrical audiences, such as Bidin Subari's *Tingginya Menyapu Awan* ('Sweeping the Clouds') which targeted the Malay squatter community.

Despite some early success, the experimental plays ultimately failed to attract new audiences, and indeed pushed away existing audiences comfortable with the old, familiar, easily understood themes.

Rejuvenation of Malay drama

During the 1980s attempts were made to address the malaise of Malay theatre, and overcome the negative effects of the 'absurd' experimental plays. New plays emerged that relied heavily on the Bangsawan form, but generally only met with limited success.

In 1991 the Ministry of Culture, Arts and Tourism met with theatre activists and scholars to discuss this issue of popularizing Malay drama. The result was a series of one act comedic dramas. Syed Alwi returned with *Di Kampung Di Kota* ('In the Village, In the City'), and director-turned-playwright Rahim Razali made his debut with *Malam Gelap di Bukit Damansara* ('A Dark Night in Damansara Heights'). Both of these plays bore a deep resemblance to the realistic plays of the 1960s, particularly Kala Dewata's *Atap Genting Atap Rembia* and Usman Awang's *Visitors to Kenny Hill*.

Government support led to a Malay theatrical renaissance: the National Arts Academy (Akademi Seni Kebangsaan) began to train a new generation of actors, producers and directors in 1994, and the National Theatre (originally known as Panggung Negara, now renamed Istana Budaya (Palace of Culture)) opened in 1999.

New talent has also emerged in the form of Roseminah Tahir, Siti Rohaya Atan, Erma Fatima, Zaifri Husin and Samoza, all involved in writing, producing and directing plays.

The plays of Noordin Hassan

Bukan Lalang Ditiup Angin
First produced in the early 1970s, the landmark play *Bukan Lalang Ditiup Angin* ("Tis Not the Grass That's Blown by the Wind') changed the direction of Malay drama. It pioneered the anti-realistic, absurd, abstract, surrealistic trend of the experimental period of modern Malay theatre, and continues to exemplify the 'Noordinian' dramatic technique of a play within a play within a play.

Dewan Bahasa dan Pustaka published the script of *Bukan Lalang Ditiup Angin* in 1979.

The play deals with a group of deprived and hard-working farmers—led by the character Ihsan assisted by Kintan—who are forced to confront the likes of the rich and oppressive Chulan. The play is framed by the story of Pak Leman who lost all in a cock-fight.

Peran

The 1991 play *Peran* (literally 'Clown') concerns psychiatrist Dr Akli, known as Dr Shrinker, not only as he is a shrink, but because he uses a shrunken head in his therapy sessions.

The influence of Bangsawan
Several plays written and produced in the 1980s and 1990s were heavily influenced by elements of the Bangsawan genre that had been popular before World War II, primarily as a reaction to the excesses of the 'absurd' period of Malay drama during the 1970s.

BELOW LEFT: Legendary Malay hero Laksamana Bentan is the main character of a typical Bangsawan production. Traditional music accompanies the performance, set in an ancient Malay kingdom.

BELOW: In *Raja Lawak* ('King of Comedians'), by Zakaria Ariffin, the central character is a well-known Bangsawan comic actor.

RIGHT: Poster from the 1989 production of *Pentas Opera* ('Opera House'), another play oy Zakaria Ariffin with Bangsawan actors as the main characters.

Drama in English

From the appearance of the first Malaysian drama in English in the 1960s, the genre has developed enormously, growing in both range and confidence. It has outgrown the traditional link between the language and British colonialism; playwrights writing in English are drawn from each of the major Malaysian ethnic groups. Since the 1980s, comedic plays have proved particularly popular with writers and audiences alike. Occasionally the use of political satire has led to government restriction.

Early original work

The first English-language play written by a Malaysian to be staged was *Arise O Youth* in 1966, written by school teacher Edward Dorall, who had in 1965 won the Arts Council Playwriting Competition with *The Young Must Be Strong. Arise O Youth* featured a Malaysian setting and characters and dialogue in idiosyncratic English. Dorall was more successful in rendering Malaysian speech in *A Tiger is Loose in Our Community* (1967), a musical about teenage love and gang rivalries which conveyed the economic and social tension between racial groups.

It was also in 1967 that nationalistic Malaysians gained control of the Malayan Arts Theatre Group (MATG), the bastion of expatriate theatre culture, which had until then staged productions consisting of mainly Shakespeare, Shaw and Wilde.

Patrick Yeoh was a particularly prodigious playwright during this period. His most significant work was *The Need to Be*, which departed from conventional middle-class concerns to focus on the hopes and delusions of a squatter family.

1969 setback

Dramatic activity in English suffered a setback as a consequence of national policies that marginalized writers who did not use the national language following the 13 May 1969 racial riots. Nevertheless, further works were written and produced, one of the earliest being *The Happening in the Bungalow* (1970) by Lee Joo For, a teacher and abstract-expressionist painter who churned out plays virtually at will. Lee emigrated to Australia in 1973, reportedly because he saw no future for English-language writing in Malaysia. Other playwrights such as Syed Alwi switched to writing in Malay. Edward Dorall, after completing a trilogy of plays, stopped writing. One of the three, *The Hour of the Dog* (1970), is arguably his best play, and the first to address the tensions arising from political detention.

Beginning of a revival

A revival of sorts began in the early 1980s with the formation of theatre groups such as KAMI and Five

ABOVE: Edward Dorall was for several years a lecturer at Universiti Malaya.

BELOW: The Kuantan Arts Theatre Group's production of *The Young Must Be Strong* in 1967. The lead role was played by M. Manivasan, standing on the left. He was also the president of the group.

RIGHT: Playwright Kee Thuan Chye (centre, red shirt) and friends reading from the script of one of his plays at a Kuala Lumpur bookshop. Several of his plays were published in 2004.

The Malaysian Arts Theatre Group (MATG)

Malaysians, led by playwright-director Syed Alwi, gained control of this previously expatriate organization in 1967, changing the group's name from 'Malayan' to 'Malaysian'. The first all-Malaysian production was *Lela Mayang*, written by K. Das, in Kuala Lumpur in 1968. MATG followed up with several more English-language productions, including *The More We Are Together* and the politically sensitive *Going North*, both by Syed Alwi, *The Need to Be* by Patrick Yeoh, and *All the Perfumes*, another work by K. Das.

The 1968 production of *Lela Mayang*. Although the play itself is in English, the title is obviously Malay: the name of the main character.

Arts Centre. Novelist K. S. Maniam's first play, *The Cord* (1984), became the maiden project of Five Arts Centre. His later plays, *The Sandpit* and *The Skin Trilogy*, portray the Indian community's search for the Malaysian Dream, capturing Tamil rhythms within their fluent English.

Kee Thuan Chye wrote the controversial *1984 Here and Now* (1985), which was only passed by government censors due to an oversight. In 1987, reacting to Operation Lallang in which more than 100 Malaysians were arrested and detained without trial under the Internal Security Act, he wrote *The Big Purge*, which was staged in the United Kingdom, but not Malaysia. Censorship kept Chin San Sooi's *Refugee: Images* waiting in the wings for six years. The play dealt with the issue of the Vietnamese boat people and Malaysia's treatment of them. Submitted for approval in 1980, it was only granted a permit in 1986, when the issue had blown over. Government censorship thereafter relaxed in certain subject areas, although since 2003 the situation has regressed somewhat under Kuala Lumpur's City Hall.

Also notable during the 1980s was Leow Puay Tin's first play, *Tikam-Tikam: And The Grandmother Said* (1983), fine-tuned in 1988 to become *Two*

Grandmothers, and presented as a doublebill with her *Three Children* (1987), in which Melaka Chinese working-class protagonists search for their 'true identities'. Thor Kah Hoong's *Caught in the Middle* (1987) spawned two sequels, and started a trend towards comedy that was to develop further in the 1990s. It also brought together the key players of what is now Malaysia's foremost group of political satirists: The Instant Café Theatre Company (ICT).

Comedy and contemporary drama

Malaysian drama in English resurged in the 1990s with official recognition of the language's importance. Even Syed Alwi returned to writing in English, with *I Remember—The Rest House* (1993) and *Member of the Club* (1995), both set during World War II and invoking the clash between indigenous Malayans and the colonial administration.

It was also the decade of comedy, led by ICT, founded by a small group of actor-friends. Among them was Jo Kukathas, daughter of playwright K. Das. ICT spin-offs include Dramalab, created to facilitate the writing of original plays, and Comedy Court, which uses racial stereotypes as its comic fodder. Among those who have come out of the latter's workshops are Yasmin Yaacob, whose hit comedy *Flight Delayed* was invited to arts festivals in Singapore and Cairo, and Jit Murad, whose first play was *Gold Rain and Hailstones* (1993). In 2002, Dramalab produced Jit's ambitious *Spilt Gravy on Rice*, which won the inaugural Cameronian Arts Awards for Best Script, with themes of succession and legacy that echoed Malay politics. Another major force in Malaysian dramatic comedy is Huzir Sulaiman, whose plays mock overzealous attitudes and provoke Malaysians to laugh at themselves.

Important 1980s plays

Two plays in particular during the 1980s caught the attention of both audiences and the press. Kee Thuan Chye's *1984 Here and Now* was loosely based on Orwell's *1984* and was highly critical of the socio-political situation and government policies. Thor Kah Hoong's comedy *Caught in the Middle*, on the other hand, comprised a series of skits and short scenes, centred around the inhabitants of a housing estate in suburban Petaling Jaya, and made extensive use of improvisation. It presented the foibles of terribly ordinary Malaysians and gave them voices in all the major languages of Malaysia.

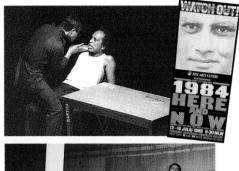

ABOVE RIGHT: 'You are a threat to the nation's security!' the interrogator (Kee Thuan Chye) accuses Wiran (Salleh Ben Joned) in a scene from the controversial *1984 Here and Now*.

RIGHT: One of the innovative sets used in the hit comedy *Caught in the Middle* featured a giant television screen.

Kuali Works, set up in 1994 to empower and train women for theatre, also produces original plays such as Ann Lee's *KL Knock Out* (1996), about a female boxer, and *Hang Li Po* (1998), about a historical Chinese princess. Kuali Works co-founder Karen Quah's independent play *Light Bulbs* (1996) was invited to the New York Fringe Festival, as was Shahimah Idris's *From Table Mountain to Teluk Intan* (2000), a mostly autobiographical play concerning racism and violence in South Africa and Malaysia.

Other notable works include Kee Thuan Chye's satire *We Could ★★★★ You, Mr Birch* (1994), and Lloyd Fernando's prizewinning *Scorpion Orchid* (1995), based on his 1976 novel (see 'Novels in English'). A noteworthy young playwright is Mark Teh, a founder member of radical youth group Akshen, which promotes the role of youth in national life.

Programme for Singaporean production of Leow Puay Tin's *Ang Tau Mui* (1994) which has as its central character a single shopping centre janitor who speaks highly lyrical Malaysian English.

Contemporary comedy

Instant Café Theatre

The Instant Café Theatre Company (ICT), comprising actors, musicians, directors and writers, was formed in December 1989. Initially intended merely as a source of alternative entertainment, it developed into a new and distinctive voice in contemporary Malaysian writing and theatre, creating wickedly funny satirical revues which lampooned everything from Malaysian social mores to political skulduggery.

The company has served as a breeding ground for many contemporary Malaysian performers and comedians. Since its inception it has performed hundreds of revue shows for the Malaysian public and for both private and corporate functions in most of the major Malaysian towns and cities, as well as in Hong Kong and Singapore.

ABOVE: Founder-member Jo Kukathas performing as a deputy minister.

BELOW: Promotional postcard for ICT's popular *Bolehwood Awards*.

Huzir Sulaiman

Renowned for his hard-hitting satirical comedy, Huzir Sulaiman, who once did a short acting stint with ICT, is perhaps best known for the popular *Atomic Jaya* (1998), the tale of Malaysia's fictional attempt to build its own nuclear weapon.

Poster for the 2003 production of *Atomic Jaya*.

Jit Murad

Comedian Jit Murad was a founding member of ICT.

Comedy Court

Comedy duo Indi Nadarajah and Allan Perera performed all of the many roles in 2002's *The Usual Suspects*.

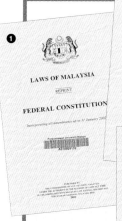

LAWS OF MALAYSIA

REPRINT

Act 32

NATIONAL LANGUAGE
ACTS 1963/67

Incorporating all amendments up to 31 August 1999

LAWS OF MALAYSIA

REPRINT

FEDERAL CONSTITUTION

Incorporating all amendments up to 31 January 2002

FEDERATION OF MALAYA

Act of Parliament

No. 26 OF 1963

MALAYSIA ACT

National language

152. (1) The national language shall be the Malay language and shall be in such script as Parliament may by law provide:

Provided that—

(a) no person shall be prohibited or prevented from using (otherwise than for official purposes), or from teaching or learning, any other language; and

(b) nothing in this Clause shall prejudice the right of the Federal Government or of any State Government to preserve and sustain the use and study of the language of any other community in the Federation.

1. Key provisions of government language policy are to be found in the Federal Constitution, the National Language Act, and, for Sabah and Sarawak in particular, the Malaysia Act. Article 152 of the Federal Constitution underlies all Malaysian language policy.

2. The first meeting of the committee to consider the existing education policy in 1955, chaired by Education Minister, Dato' Abdul Razak (seated under the Federal Crest). The resulting Razak Report led to the introduction of Malay as the medium of instruction in most state-funded primary schools.

3. A multi-ethnic choir promoting the national language at the launch of the 'Love Our Language' movement.

4. English-language newspaper *Malai Sinpo* was published by the Japanese administration from 1943 to 1945 during the Japanese Occupation (1941–5).

5. *Fajar Asia* was one of several Malay magazines published during the Japanese Occupation. Malay publications were encouraged during this troubled period, although they were subject to heavy censorship.

6. A poster from *Cintailah Bahasa Kita* (Love Our Language), one of several national language campaigns.

7. The International Islamic University, which has its main campus in Kuala Lumpur, uses English and Arabic as its mediums of instruction.

PELANCARAN

GERAKAN CINTAILAH BAHASA KITA

OLEH
Y.A.B. DATO' SERI DR MAHATHIR BIN MOHAMAD
PERDANA MENTERI MALAYSIA

Malai Sinpo

10 CENTS. KUALA LUMPUR, WEDNESDAY, JULY 19, 2604 (1944), SYOWA 19. VOL. 7, NO. 489.

SORI DAIJIN TOJO'S CLARION CALL TO THE NATION

NEW CHIEF OF ARMY GENERAL STAFF APPOINTED

Commander-In-Chief Of The Kwantung Army

Tokyo, July 19.
THE War Office last evening announced that General Yoshijiro Umezu, Commander-in-Chief of the Kwantung army, has been appointed Chief of the Army General Staff.

It simultaneously announced that General Otozo Yamada, Inspector-General of Military Training, has been appointed Commander-in-Chief of the Kwantung army, in succession to General Yoshijiro Umezu.

Field-Marshal Gen Sugiyama has been appointed Inspector-General of Military Training.

Lieut.-General Michio Sugawara has been appointed Inspector-General of Army Aviation and concurrently Chief of the Army Aviation Headquarters. General

Empire Faces Most Vital Situation

Tokyo, July 18.
SIMULTANEOUSLY with the announcement by Dai Honyei on the Saipan situation Sori Daijin (Premier) Hideki Tojo this afternoon issued a statement which reads as follows:

'In the Marianas since June 11 officers and men of our Imperial forces have by their vigorous fighting dealt severe blows to the enemy, but the island of Saipan finally has fallen into enemy hands. I am moved with great trepidation, by the thought that deep anxiety has been caused to Tenno Heika. To the spirit of the brave officers and men and our other countrymen who have died heroic deaths in the southern waters in performance of their high duty of defending the Empire I wish to tender an expression of my most profound and sincere feelings.

'Two and a half years have elapsed since the Imperial Rescript declaring war was graciously granted. During this time officers and our Imperial forces have waged military operations on a grand scale everywhere. The one hundred million of our countrymen to overcome hardships of every kind and all of them, in their several fields of endeavour, have made their utmost efforts for the successful prosecution of the War in Greater East Asia. However, enemy, especially the United States has since gradually increased the intensity of his counter-attacks and has at last advanced to the Marianas.

'The Empire has now been confronted with a situation which in history is the most important. It affords us at the same time one opportunity to crush the enemy. For the sake of our Empire there is at present only one road upon which we must advance. It is to crush the enemy and win the war, and only that, without least illusion and without least thought of life or death, devoting our total energy to the task and by effecting the lessons of war with the blood of our men in arms and our other countrymen. Only by doing this shall we be able to answer the many men who have become

Sori Daijin Hideki Tojo

guardian deities of our Empire in the War of Greater East Asia.

'The aim of the War of Greater East Asia is clear from the Imperial Rescript declaring war. To us this war is a war to decide the rise or fall of our Empire and also a war for the liberation of Asia. But to the enemy this is a war to enslave Greater East Asia and to dominate the world. It is a fight between the defence of existence and evil ambitions, between liberty and aggression.

'The time for decisive fighting is now at hand. Now is the time completely to crush the Anglo-American counter-offensive by collaborating with the various peoples of Greater East Asia and our European allies. The real war is to be fought from now on. Let us, all of our one hundred million people together, renew our pledge and our determination to make the supreme sacrifice and concentrate the traditional fighting spirit of our country, handed down through three thousand years, on the attainment of the ultimate victory, thereby setting the mind of Tenno Heika at rest.'

Bangkok, July 14.—Italo Misuno, Director of the Southern Affairs Bureau of the Ministry of Greater East Asia Affairs, arrived here by air to-day on an extensive inspection trip of the Southern Regions.

FAJAR ASIA

2

15 Ngasto 2603
25 sen

PENGAWAL ASIA TIMUR RAYA

Cintailah
BAHASA
KITA

LANGUAGE PLANNING AND USE

National-level language planning is necessary in a multilingual society such as Malaysia for various reasons: to enhance efficiency in communication between government and the people, to ensure a common language for education; and to maximize economic opportunity.

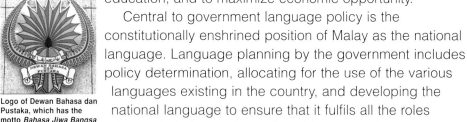

Logo of Dewan Bahasa dan Pustaka, which has the motto *Bahasa Jiwa Bangsa* ('Language, Spirit of Nation')

Central to government language policy is the constitutionally enshrined position of Malay as the national language. Language planning by the government includes policy determination, allocating for the use of the various languages existing in the country, and developing the national language to ensure that it fulfils all the roles demanded of a modern, vibrant language. Language policy is implemented by ministries, especially the Ministry of Education, and by the Dewan Bahasa dan Pustaka (Institute of Language and Literature). Schools, colleges and universities are also agents of policy implementation.

It is vital that a national language is accepted by the people of a nation. This is done by making it the main medium of instruction in schools and universities, and requiring a pass in the national language to be obtained to receive certain qualifications, and to secure scholarships and jobs. These are just some of the strategies employed by the Malaysian government.

Language planning also affects the media. In the allocation of language use, television and the radio programmes may be measured in terms of the amount of time given to the various languages spoken. This is an important consideration, especially for government-run channels. The length of time allocated to a particular language to some extent reflects the relative position of that language in the country's policy.

The position and size of words in a particular language on a signpost or a billboard also reflects the deemed importance of that language. Hence, in most states of Malaysia, the Malay text in these media is positioned above, and sized larger than, that of other languages. In public places and government buildings only Malay and English usually appear. Private enterprises, however, often add one or two other languages: Chinese and Tamil, in Peninsular Malaysia, or sometimes Thai, in the north, and Iban or Kadazandusun in Sarawak and Sabah, respectively.

Language policy and its implementation have been effective in changing Malaysia's linguistic landscape, and will continue to be so in the future.

Tamil comedians at a live performance organized by Radio Malaysia's Indian Service during the 1960s. Malaysian broadcasters have always presented multilingual programming schedules.

National language policy

Malaysia is one of several nations—including Norway, Israel, Tanzania and Indonesia—that has designated a specific national language, in this case Malay. Similar to these other nations, Malaysia has explicit policies relating both to its national language and the to the other languages spoken in the nation. These policies have focused on maintaining and enhancing the status of Malay, as well as its development into a language able to meet the demands of the diverse roles that it fulfils as a result of its official status.

Petition writer outside the Kuala Lumpur Magistrates' Court helping people to fill in official documents. During the colonial period these were written in English, but are now in Malay.

Announcement in 1972 of the introduction of the new standardized Malay spelling system, devised in cooperation with Indonesia.

The choice of national language

With so many first languages spoken in the country, the designation of the national language was a key concern prior to Independence in 1957. Despite the fact that many nations have more than one national language, and despite the absence of any sociological surveys or language preference studies, only one language was chosen as the national language: Malay.

Malay was the most widely used language in the nation (spoken as a first language by 49 per cent, and as a language of wider communication by over 70 per cent, of the population), far exceeding not only any other indigenous language, but also the colonial language, English, and the major immigrant languages such as Hokkien and Cantonese Chinese, and Tamil. Furthermore, Malay was strongly identified with the dominant political party then negotiating Independence, the United Malays National Organisation (UMNO). The language's political role was also linked to the broader regional expression of Malay nationalism, which at that time was reverberating throughout Indonesia, Thailand, Singapore and Brunei. The use of Malay in government administration (although limited at that time) and in the colonial educational system (at least in primary schools), and its possession of a standardized spelling system and a print-media tradition further contributed to Malay's being chosen as the national language.

The Federal Constitution stipulates that Malay is the national language, although English was designated as a second official language until 1967. The latter was to allow for the smooth transition of administration and education into the national language. Although it no longer has an official role, English has continued to maintain an important, if unofficial, role in many fields, including business, the legal system and high-level government discourse.

With the formation of Malaysia in 1963, resulting from the combination of Singapore (until 1965), Sabah, and Sarawak with the Federation of Malaya, the status of Malay as the national language was reiterated, with a further 10-year period for English as second official language in Sabah and Sarawak. Although no official status was

Dewan Bahasa dan Pustaka

Objectives

1. To develop and enrich the national language.

2. To develop literary talent, particularly in Malay.

3. To print, publish or to promote publication in Malay and other languages.

4. To standardize spelling and pronunciation and devise appropriate technical terms in Malay.

Dewan Bahasa dan Pustaka's building in Kuala Lumpur.

Dewan Bahasa dan Pustaka (Institute of Language and Literature) was established in 1956 in Johor Bahru, and moved to Kuala Lumpur in 1957. Originally a government department, it was made a statutory body in 1959.

The organization attempts to fulfil its objectives by organizing conferences, seminars, dramas, and poetry readings, as well as through its many publications. These include dictionaries, both general (monolingual and bilingual) and on specialized subjects, original Malay literary works, and Malay translations of foreign literature. It also publishes several magazines and journals.

allocated to any other languages, the Constitution recognizes the rights of ethnic groups to maintain their own languages.

Managing language development

Once Malay was chosen as the national language, steps were taken to expand its role and to standardize it. A national language agency, Dewan Bahasa dan Pustaka (Institute of Language and Literature) ('DBP'), was established in 1956. Although its initial emphasis was on encouraging the use of Malay through national language competitions, its most important contributions have been the expansion of Malay vocabulary, especially in technical fields, and the establishment of a new international standard spelling system. Even before Independence, attempts

The early days

ABOVE: Ungku Aziz Abdul Hamid (seated, centre), seen here with his staff in 1956, was the first Director of Dewan Bahasa dan Pustaka, when it was located in Johor Bahru.

LEFT: Tun Syed Nasir was the second Director, seen here at his desk in the DBP. The sign on his desk reads 'Use our national language'.

Promoting the national language

Dewan Bahasa dan Pustaka (DBP) has implemented a number of measures to promote the use of the national language. Campaigns have included national language 'weeks' and 'months' held in the 1960s. More recently the *Cintailah Bahasa Kita* ('Love Our Language') campaign commenced in 1998.

Brochures (right) from DBP campaigns to promote the use of Malay, such as the *Bulan Bahasa Kebangsaan* (National Language Month) campaign (below right). Other promotional methods include the translation into Malay of foreign literature, such as *The Prince and the Pauper* (below).

Changing technical terms

One of the first tasks of the DBP was to build a corpus of technical terms. Committees were established, and new terms coined based on direct translation, pronunciation and spelling, or the creation of acronyms. Many of these terms were changed in 1975 when new rules for formulating technical terms were implemented.

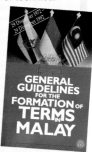

English version of the guidelines for forming Malay terms.

English	Malay (pre-1975)	Malay (post-1975)
biology	kajihayat	biologi
analysis	cerakin	analisis
anthropology	kajimanusia	antropologi
oxygen	oksijan	oksigen
carnivore	maging	karnivor
erosion	hakis	erosi

Artist's impression of a national language rally at Merdeka Stadium in 1962. The late Tun Syed Nasir is seen addressing the rally, flanked by Prime Minister Tunku Abdul Rahman, and deputy Prime Minister Tun Abdul Razak.

had been made to develop Malay vocabulary, and DBP built on this, introducing hundreds of thousands of technical terms into the language. Moreover, it has published several Malay dictionaries, including the prestigious monolingual *Kamus Dewan*, first published in 1970 and now in its third edition (see 'History of Malay').

As well as DBP, both the Ministry of Education and the Prime Minister's Department have been active participants in the development of Malay. This has enabled the language to be used by a greater number of Malaysians in a variety of roles.

Regional policy development

The development of Malay as a national language cannot be separated from the region-wide use of Malay. Since Independence in 1957, the spelling system based on the Latin alphabet (known as *Rumi*) has increased its dominance, as it has in all Malay-speaking countries (including Indonesia, Brunei, Thailand and Singapore), although the Jawi script has retained an honorary position.

Regional efforts to standardize the spelling system have been a success. Negotiations to this end began between Indonesia and Malaysia in 1966, although other efforts at standardization have not been so well received. For example, efforts to change the pronunciation of Malay to a system based on spelling have proved unsuccessful. Even television news broadcasts are inconsistent, with the pronunciation on government channels differing from the major private channel, TV3.

Standardization of the Malay language on a regional basis is entrusted to the Majlis Bahasa Brunei Darussalam-Indonesia-Malaysia (Brunei Darussalam-Indonesia-Malaysia Language Council) (MABBIM).

Language policy in action

The national language policy has resulted in government administration being conducted almost entirely in Malay. In the education system, on the other hand, while Malay instruction is compulsory, it is not the medium of instruction in all schools, and there is a policy to promote the learning of other languages. English remains the de facto language of commerce, but has largely been replaced by Malay in the courtroom.

Parliamentary business has since 1967 been conducted in Malay, although during debates Members of Parliament may request permission from the Speaker to use other languages.

Language in government administration

Prior to 1957, English was the language of government administration in the states that formed Malaysia, gradually being replaced by Malay after Independence. In 1967, Malay became the sole language for official written business. In meetings, however, the rule remains relaxed, with participants allowed to switch to English for clarification, although minutes are kept in Malay.

Rules, regulations, statutes and reports are all published in two versions, Malay and English. Previously the English version prevailed, now it is Malay. Statutory bodies follow a similar pattern. Parliamentary business was conducted in English until 1967, with simultaneous interpretation into Malay. In 1967, Parliament switched to Malay, although members not proficient in Malay could speak in English with simultaneous interpretation into Malay; however, by the 1980s all Members of Parliament were proficient in Malay and interpreters were no longer required. The State legislative councils in Peninsular Malaysia have always used Malay. In Sabah, however, English continued to be used as the official language of state-level administration until 1973, 10 years after Malaysia's formation. In Sarawak, the administration only switched to Malay in 1985.

Language in education

Before Independence, schools existed for each of the majority languages: English, Malay, Chinese (Mandarin), and Tamil; the last three known as vernacular schools. There were both primary and secondary English schools, enabling students to enter universities in Singapore and English-speaking countries, at which Malay or other languages were elective subjects at secondary level. Apart from a few Chinese schools in larger towns, vernacular schools generally only offered primary education.

Following Independence, the 1957 National Educational Policy allowed for the use of Malay, English, Mandarin, and Tamil (and, to a smaller degree, other languages) as mediums of instruction.

The language of money

The changing RM10 banknote offers an insight into the prevailing language policies and their implementation since Independence.

1. English is the main language on this 10 dollar note first issued in 1961.
2. The first series RM10 note issued by Bank Negara in 1961 spelt the number 10 as *Sa-Puloh* in Malay.
3. By 1983 the modern Malay spelling *Sepuluh* was used.
4. The same spelling is used on the right-hand margin of the note that was circulated from 2003.
5. *Sepuluh Ringgit* also appears in Jawi on the rear of the 2003 note.

Later, under the Education Act 1970, English was removed as a language of instruction, with schools that used it gradually converting to Malay. These schools became known as national schools. The role of Malay also expanded in Chinese- and Tamil-medium (national-type) schools. Students from all schools must achieve a pass in Malay to be awarded a certificate in examinations, while a pass is not necessary in English, although it is a compulsory subject.

Three languages are thus learned in national-type schools, as opposed to two in national schools. However, a third language is sometimes taught in national schools, as a result of the Pupils' Own Language (POL) policy. Other schools, partially government-funded, emphasize the teaching of Islam; Arabic is thus the main medium of instruction, while Malay and English remain compulsory.

Pupils' Own Language (POL)

The POL policy compelled national schools to provide POL classes where requested by pupils who could form a class of at least 15. Intended to enable mother tongue or native language education, originally only Mandarin and Tamil were commenced in this way. However, in the 1980s, Iban POL classes commenced in Sarawak, and in the 1990s, Kadazandusun classes were introduced in some Sabah schools, and Semai for Orang Asli in a small number of schools in Perak and Pahang.

The term 'POL' has now officially been replaced with 'other languages', ostensibly to encourage pupils to acquire a language other than the national language and English, and not necessarily their mother tongue. This 'other language' may also be a foreign language. Three such languages are currently taught: Arabic, French and Japanese.

Pupils at St. Anthony's Primary School in Dontozidon, Penampang, Sabah, studying Kadazandusun.

School language policy

Two Education Review Committee reports, chaired by Dato' (later Tun) Razak in 1956 (relating to primary education) and Rahman Talib in 1960 (extending the policy to secondary schools) were instrumental in shaping the languages used and taught in Malaysian schools.

Languages taught in government schools

School type	Level	Mediums of instruction	Compulsory language(s)	Additional languages
National	Primary and Secondary	Malay, English (for Maths and Science)	English	POL
National-type (Chinese)	Primary	Chinese (Mandarin), English (for Maths and Science)	Malay, English	n/a
National-type (Tamil)	Primary	Tamil, English (for Maths and Science)	Malay, English	n/a

The 1960 Education Planning Committee chaired by the Education Minister Abdul Rahman bin Talib (seated second from left). As a result of the committee's report, Malay was extended as the medium of instruction to national secondary schools. It followed the 1956 Razak Report which created the division between national and national-type schools.

Marketing leaflets from banks feature English as the most prominent language, although Malay and Chinese are also used to appeal to a wider range of potential customers.

From the late 1990s, concerns arose that the standard of English among Malaysians had deteriorated (see 'English'). Acting on this, the government re-introduced English as the medium of instruction for mathematics and science in 2003.

Government-funded tertiary institutions have to use Malay as the main medium of instruction, although another language is permitted where more effective. In many cases, the language used is English, particularly for courses in medicine, dentistry, engineering and the sciences. The International Islamic University, partially funded by the government, uses English and Arabic as mediums of instruction, although Malay is taught as an additional subject.

English is the medium of teaching in the many private colleges that have been established since the 1980s, mostly located in the Klang Valley. These colleges organize courses for entrance into foreign universities, especially in the United Kingdom, United States, Canada, Australia and New Zealand, and administer twinning programmes with them. Nevertheless, all of these institutions are encouraged to teach Malay as a compulsory language.

Private college brochures are largely printed in English, which is also the usual medium of instruction.

Arabic, Chinese, and Tamil are also used as languages of instruction at local universities to a limited extent: Arabic in faculties specializing in the teaching of Islam, and Mandarin and Tamil in the Departments of Chinese and Indian Studies respectively. Malaysian universities also offer many other foreign languages as additional or elective subjects, including classical languages such as Sanskrit.

The professions, business and industry

The National Language Act 1967 acknowledged the need for English in the professions, and as a means of communication with the outside world. It allowed the continued use of English for certain professional purposes including legal advice, opinion and related correspondence, medical reports, instructions and prescriptions, all work associated with the assessment and collection of taxes and the investigation of tax cases, and all dealings with foreign governments, international bodies and consultants and experts from abroad.

Communication among professionals is invariably conducted in English, and multinational corporations based in Malaysia have helped English to emerge as the main medium of business communication too. English is also the de facto language of information technology. The technological vocabulary used in these fields is known as English for Specific Purposes (ESP); there are often no equivalent terms in Malay. Indeed, there is a dearth not only of terms, but also of manuals, books, and journals in Malay in fields such as science and technology, and banking and finance.

Malay is used more extensively in the lower ranks of business organizational structures, and is the dominant language on the factory floor. Code-switching between English and Malay is widespread.

The language of the law

Prior to 1967, all written law was in English, although sometimes a Malay translation was provided. It was also the de facto language of the courts until 1981, when the lower courts in the Peninsula started to use Malay.

The situation changed further in Peninsular Malaysia with the amendment of the National Language Act in 1989, to state that all court proceedings 'shall be in the national language'. Nevertheless, English, or a mix of Malay and English, may still be used at the discretion of the court, and there are no restrictions on the language of witness testimony. Multilingual court interpreters are provided free of charge to assist those testifying in other languages. Pleadings in all courts and all court records, formerly only in English, are now entirely in Malay in the lower courts. The use of Malay has also increased in the High Court, Court of Appeal, and Federal Court, although the continued entry into the legal profession of English law graduates, and the continued use of English in legal publishing, has led to some English usage being retained.

In Sabah and Sarawak, the use of English in court continues. English may also be used for appeals to the Federal Court from the courts of those two states. Additionally, any native language in use in Sabah and Sarawak may be used in their respective native courts or for any code of native law and custom (*adat*).

ABOVE: Lawyer in discussion outside a courtroom in Kuala Lumpur. English still plays an important role in the legal profession.

BELOW: Other vernacular languages are used in the Native Courts of Sabah and Sarawak, in proceedings such as this in Nabawan, Sabah.

Language in the print media

From a single English-language paper in the early 19th century, the local print media industry has expanded to include widely circulated newspapers in all four of the most commonly used languages: Malay, English, Chinese and Tamil. Sections in other local languages also appear within some of their pages. An even larger range of magazines and books are produced, providing a variety of outlets for writers in several languages and styles. Content is largely controlled by self-censorship as a result of government licensing and strict sedition laws.

Malaysians have a choice of daily newspapers, both broadsheet and tabloid, in each of the four most widely spoken languages.

The early press

The first, English-language, newspaper was *The Prince of Wales Island Gazette* which entered circulation in 1806. Initiated by A. B. Bone, a British printer in Penang, it served British interests. Its contents were mainly governmental and religious notices, trade information and promotions, and news of contemporary developments in England and India.

More English-language newspapers followed, based predominately in the Straits Settlements of Penang, Singapore and Melaka. In Kuala Lumpur, *The Malay Mail* was particularly successful. *The Straits Times* is the only other early English paper that survives, albeit in Singapore, although Malaysia's the *New Straits Times* is a direct offshoot, having been locally incorporated in 1972 following Singapore's withdrawal from Malaysia in 1965. Notably, it was only as late as the 1950s that an English-language daily, *Singapore Standard*, first employed local editorial staff.

The first Chinese-language newspaper, notwithstanding its description as a magazine, was the *Chinese Monthly Magazine*, published in 1815 in Melaka by missionary William Milne. The paper aimed to propagate Christian activity in mainland China. Other Chinese newspapers were subsequently established in Singapore during the late 19th century. Malay and Indian newspapers appeared relatively late. The first local Tamil newspaper was *Tangai Sinegan*, published in 1876. *Bintang Timor*, the earliest Malay language newspaper, only commenced publication in Singapore in 1884; although several other papers, including another *Bintang Timor* (1900) published in Penang, appeared before the end of the 19th century. The *Straits Chinese Herald* (1894), in Chinese and Malay, was the first bilingual newspaper.

Also during this period, Malay magazines appeared and began to grow in importance. The first Malay magazine was *Bustan Ariffin,* which also appeared in English as *Malay Magazine*, edited with the assistance of Munshi Abdullah. The early Malay newspapers and magazines were, however, written by and for the local Arab communities. It was only in the mid-1930s that *Utusan Melayu* emerged as the first newspaper owned and staffed by Malays.

Language usage by the early newspapers in all four languages (English, Malay, Chinese and Tamil) reflected the linguistic standards and styles of the day. Most local words were spelt according to English vocalization. For instance *Sungai Ujung* (Ujung River) was spelt *Soongye Oojong,* '*Raja Ali*' appeared as *Rajah Alli*, *penghulu* (headman) was spelt *panghooloo*, and *Gunung Pasir* (Mount Pasir) was spelt *Goonong Passier.*

Jajahan Malayu, published in Taiping from 1896–7, was among the first Malay newspapers to be printed in the Malay States.

Changing faces and policies

Significant changes in Malayan journalism took place during the 1920s and 1930s. Coinciding with the gradual move of the Malay press from Singapore to Kuala Lumpur, Malay consciousness grew, and editorials began to cover controversies on subjects such as language, custom and religion.

Further changes resulted from the Japanese Occupation during World War II. Almost all English

The Malay Mail

The Malay Mail.

FAR LEFT: First edition, 14 December 1896.

LEFT: J. H. Robson, founder of *The Malay Mail*, initially served as reporter, editor, business manager, and production manager.

BELOW: The offices of *The Malay Mail* in Kuala Lumpur's Market Square, c. 1910.

Newspaper circulation and readership (Average net sales 1 July 2002 to 30 June 2003)

English		Chinese		Sabah	
Star people's paper	307,019	星洲日報 SIN CHEW JIT POH	319,071	**Daily Express** INDEPENDENT NATIONAL NEWSPAPER OF EAST MALAYSIA	27,249
NEW STRAITS TIMES INCORPORATING BUSINESS TIMES	135,040	南洋商報 NANYANG SIANG PAU	146,902	詩華日報 See Hua Daily News	20,799
Malay		**Tamil**		**Sarawak**	
Utusan MALAYSIA	246,006	தமிழ் நேசன் Tamil Nesan	41,570 (unaudited)	詩華日報 See Hua Daily News	52,742
Berita Harian	228,462	நண்பன் Malaysia Nanban	71,700 (unaudited)	THE BORNEO POST	47,321

Source: Audit Bureau of Circulations, Malaysia

newspapers closed, their expatriate staff being for the most part interned. Some, however, continued, such as *The Malay Mail* and *The Straits Times*, renamed *Shonan Times*. The Japanese also published their own papers in English (*Malai Sinpo*, *Penang Daily News*, and *Shonan Shimbun*), Malay (*Penang Shimbun*, *Semangat Asia*, *Berita Perak*, and *Berita Malai*), Chinese (*Shonan Shimbun* and *Melaka New Newspaper*) and Tamil (*Sutandira India*, *Sutandirotayam* and *Yuvabharatham*).

The structure of the local print media industry, and the policies and regulations that continue to affect it, developed after the war, during a period marked by particularly dramatic events. These included the Emergency (1948–60), when Malaya faced a serious communist threat. Various laws of continuing importance were passed during this time to control publications and subversive acts. Amongst

these laws was the Printing Press Act 1948, subsequently amended in 1984 to become the Printing Presses and Publications Act. The far-reaching amendments to the Sedition Act 1948 that were introduced after the 13 May 1969 riots prohibit discussion in the media of four sensitive issues, namely the Malay language policy, the special rights of the Malays, the special roles of the sultans and other Malaysian royals, and the citizenship policy towards non-Malays.

Answering critics of its purported stranglehold on the press, the government has argued that a 'guided' press is important for national security and nation building in multi-ethnic Malaysia.

Contemporary press

Notwithstanding the restrictions imposed on the press, a vibrant local industry has developed, displaying the diversity of Malaysian languages, ethnic groups, cultures, and religions. Malay, English, Chinese, and Tamil newspapers circulate widely throughout the nation. The leading Malay-language newspapers are *Utusan Malaysia* (started in 1967) and *Berita Harian* (started in 1957), while the English press is dominated by the *New Straits Times* and *The Star* (started in 1971). The leading Chinese dailies are *Sin Chew Jit Poh* (started in 1929) and *Nanyang Siang Pau* (started in 1923). *Tamil Nesan* (established in 1924) and *Malaysia Nanban* (established in 1980) are the only Tamil language newspapers.

In addition, regional newspapers also flourish in the East Malaysian states of Sabah and Sarawak, some of which contain sections or articles in languages indigenous to those states (Kadazandusun in Sabah, Iban in Sarawak). Furthermore, over 250 different magazines are published throughout the country, mainly by smaller enterprises.

Book publishing

Malaya's first publishing house, MPH, was established in 1815. Although MPH no longer publishes, there are a number of publishers in the country, including the Oxford University Press, since 1969 known as Penerbit Fajar Bakti (mainly educational books, in both Malay and English), Pelanduk Books (mainly Malay and English non-fiction), and Dewan Bahasa dan Pustaka (Malay books).

The MPH story

In 1815, Christian missionary William Milne decided to choose Melaka to establish a permanent mission press. This eventually led to the establishment in Singapore of Methodist Publishing House (MPH), Malaya's first publishing house, by Captain William G. Shellabear in 1890. MPH subsequently changed hands and names over the years. By 1963 when the sovereign state of Malaysia was proclaimed, MPH had become 'Malaysia Publishing House' and began a shift away from publishing to the operation of bookstores, at first in Selangor and Penang. In 2002, MPH was bought over by Jalinan Inspirasi Sdn Bhd, part of a large Malaysian conglomerate controlled by local businessman Tan Sri Syed Mokhtar Al-Bukhary. Today, MPH, now known as MPH Bookstores Sdn Bhd, is purely a retail operation, with 25 branches in Malaysia, as well as outlets in Singapore and Indonesia.

The Malaysia Message, an early Christian newspaper published by MPH.

MPH's, and Malaysia's, largest bookstore, located at the One Utama shopping centre near Kuala Lumpur.

Gila-gila, first published in 1978 by Creative Enterprise Sdn Bhd, started a trend which has resulted in a large number of humorous cartoon magazines, particularly in Malay.

Former Prime Minister Tun Dr Mahathir Mohamad often gave press conferences in both Malay and English.

Language
in the broadcast media

The multiethnic nature of the Malaysian population has posed a challenge to broadcasters since the early 20th century. Broadcast language policy and practice have evolved from amateur radio transmissions during the colonial British era, through the wartime propaganda of the Japanese Occupation, and the national language policies of Independence and the Formation of Malaysia, to the less stringent contemporary policies. Language use continues to evolve in the face of new technology and an ever widening range of audience choices.

Wisma Angkasapuri, in Kuala Lumpur, is the headquarters for government television and radio broadcasting.

Radio ownership by ethnic group in 1937	
European	1,796
Chinese	1,351
Indian	144
Malay	116
Others	104
Total	**3,471**

Early multilingual broadcasting

In 1921, a British engineer working with the Johor Government, A. L. Birch, performed the first successful (Morse code) radio transmission in the Malay Peninsula. and in 1922 British engineers in Singapore successfully tested the performance of radio telephony. Birch later set up the Johore Wireless Society, which was at the forefront of radio development in Malaya.

Subsequently, many other wireless societies were formed in the larger Malayan towns. The Singapore Radio Society (SRC) was more multiracial than most, with wealthy Chinese merchants in Kuala Lumpur being particularly active. Within its first year, however, it closed and several of its members formed the Malayan Amateur Radio Society (MARC) in March 1925. The MARC broadcast a variety of programmes, mostly in English, including a 'children's concert'.

Indian programme operator at Radio Malaya, 1961.

Transmissions in Malay, from an unknown source, were first reported in 1926. The Amateur Radio Society of Kuala Lumpur, which transmitted under the code ZGE, and the Amateur Radio Society of Pinang (ZHJ), both formed in the late 1920s, broadcast in English, Malay, Thai and Chinese.

The privately operated British Malaya Broadcasting Cooperation (BMBC) was officially established in 1937. It operated two channels, ZHL and ZHP. In 1940 the government of Malaya took over BMBC and changed its name to Malayan Broadcasting Corporation (MBC) which broadcast multilingual programmes. On an average day there were 12 hours in English, three hours in Malay, five hours in Chinese (Cantonese, Mandarin, Hokkien and Teochew), and four hours in Indian languages (Tamil and Hindustan), as well as programmes in Arabic, French, and Dutch. This multilingual broadcasting enabled the British colonial authorities to reach the majority of the population.

Wartime broadcasting and beyond

Broadcasting language policy changed during the Japanese Occupation, the most striking feature of which was that Malay became the dominant language. Nevertheless, the other languages still remained on air. In 1942, the distribution of broadcast hours was shared almost evenly between Malay, Chinese, Indian, English and the Japanese, with slightly more airtime given to the Chinese dialects and Indian languages. However, in 1943 and 1944 the number of broadcast hours in Malay comprised almost 70 per

With the establishment of Radio Television Malaysia's Orang Asli radio station, Radio 7, in 1959, Ading Kerah, a Temiar, became the first Orang Asli radio presenter.

cent of the total, although this decreased to less than 50 per cent in 1945. Following the surrender of the Japanese, the British authorities resumed control of the radio service, which adopted the name Radio Malaya in 1946. English programmes dominated, with Malay, Chinese and Indian also broadcast.

Language usage in radio broadcasts in Sabah and Sarawak generally mirrored that of the Peninsula. The first Sarawakian radio service began to transmit from Kuching in 1954, while in Sabah radio broadcasting began in 1952, and was officially launched in 1955. English broadcasts dominated, with substantial time devoted to programmes in Chinese, Malay and, unlike the Peninsula, other ethnic dialects such as Iban, Bidayuh, Kadazandusun.

Voice of Malaysia

Radio Television Malaysia's overseas radio service, Voice of Malaysia (VOM), first broadcast on 15 February 1963 in three languages: English, Mandarin and Indonesian. Other languages were subsequently added: Arabic (1972), Thai (1972), Tagalog (1973), Chinese (Mandarin) (1978) and Myanmar (1978).

Its various language services are transmitted to Indonesia, Australia, New Zealand, China, Japan, Hong Kong, Taiwan, Philippines, Thailand, Myanmar, North Africa and the Middle East, with a target audience of foreign listeners and Malaysian students overseas. Programmes broadcast include news and commentary, current affairs, music and drama, sports, and live coverage of national events, and are aimed to project a good international image of Malaysia. In 1995, the Voice of Islam started broadcasting in English and Malay to the Asean region.

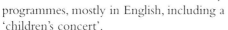

VOICE OF MALAYSIA

FREQUENCIES

B.MALAYSIA	6175	Khz	49	M
ENGLISH	15295	Khz	19	M
MANDARIN	11885	Khz	25	M
INDONESIA	6175	Khz	48	M
INDONESIA	9750	Khz	31	M
INDONESIA	6100	Khz	49	M
ARABIC	15295	Khz	19	M
THAI	6100	Khz	49	M
TAGALOG	1475	Khz	203.4	M
MYANMAR	6100	Khz	49	M

The Voice of Malaysia
P.O.Box 11272, 50740 Kuala Lumpur
Tel: 603-282 5333, 282 4976 Fax: 603-284 7594

VOM is modelled on the United States' Voice of America, which broadcasts in 45 languages.

Post-Independence broadcasting

Upon Independence in 1957, the multilingual broadcast language policy remained unchanged. However, the proportion of broadcasts in Malay increased significantly after the formation of Malaysia in 1963. The change took place in all radio stations throughout Malaysia. In Sabah, for instance, more than 50 per cent of radio airtime was given to programmes in Malay, followed by English, Chinese, Kadazan, Indonesian and other local dialects. By the mid-1980s the amount of time dedicated to English-language programming was less than half that of 1963; indeed, more airtime was given to broadcasts in the Dusunic, Murutic and Sama-Bajau languages.

The dominance of Malay broadcasting declined, however, with the introduction of private radio stations in the early 1980s. Most of the privately owned stations that have subsequently been established broadcast in English and Chinese, which are more popular languages with urban audiences.

One interesting development is that the government operates several radio stations broadcasting in the languages of Malaysia's smaller ethnic groups, including the Orang Asli in the Peninsula, the Iban in Sarawak and the Kadazan in Sabah.

Language and television

Television was introduced in Malaysia in 1963. At first, primarily for reasons of availability and affordability, English-language programmes dominated. However, due to strong audience pressure, more locally originated content began to be broadcast, particularly in the 1970s.

Radio Television Malaysia (RTM), owned and operated by the Ministry of Information, has from its establishment in 1963 operated two television stations, TV1, which originally broadcast entirely in Malay, and TV2 which broadcast in English, Chinese, Tamil, and other languages. However, the policy regarding the assignment of broadcast language to these two channels has often shifted, such that the former has broadcast non-Malay-language programmes, and the latter has aired Malay programmes. Under the now-defunct Broadcasting Act 1988, 70 per cent of airtime had to be devoted to local programmes, whether in Malay, Chinese, English or Tamil. In 1998, the Multimedia

Commission, part of the Ministry of Energy, Communication and Multimedia, took over the responsibility of governing private radio and television broadcasting from the Ministry of Information. Both Ministries have an open policy regarding the usage of languages for broadcasting.

Choice of broadcast language by the private terrestrial television channels is determined by ratings. Two of these channels, TV3 (established in 1984) and NTV7 (established in 1998), use Malay as the major language of broadcast, especially in the news and other public service programmes, although other forms of programmes, such as entertainment and dramas, are often in English and Chinese. Channel 8 and Channel 9 (both of which started in 2003) use English and Chinese more than Malay, and Indian languages garner little airtime.

Each television and radio station has its own internal guidelines as to news broadcast languages. RTM fulfils its social responsibility by ensuring that news is broadcast in the four main languages, Malay, English, Chinese and Tamil.

1. Thirty Selangor schools competed in TV1's 1973 'Malay Kuiz Sekolah-sekolah' ('Schools Quiz'). Malay language programmes have for many years dominated television viewer ratings.
2. Mandarin animated series broadcast on Channel 8. The channel's target audience is urban Chinese.
3. TV2 is the only terrestrial channel to broadcast daily news bulletins in Tamil.
4. Channel 9's 'Makansutra', presented by K. C. Seetoh, is a food travelogue produced in English.

Programme transmission duration by language (2003)

Programme language	Duration (hours)	Hours viewed per person
Malay	13,245	371
Chinese	3,824	140
English	8,863	153
Tamil/Hindi	1,410	43

Source: Nielsen Media

Channel share 2003

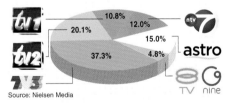

10.8%
12.0%
20.1%
15.0%
37.3%
4.8%

Source: Nielsen Media

ASTRO

Satellite media operator ASTRO, a major shareholder of which is government-investment holding company Khazanah Nasional Berhad, began transmission in 1996. It broadcasts over 44 television and 16 radio channels in different languages: 27 of the television channels are in English, 10 in Chinese, and one each in Malay (sometimes mixed with Indonesian and English programmes), Arabic and Indian. The four other channels provide programmes in a mix of languages including Arabic, Malay, Tamil, Hindi, Japanese, and other international languages. Although most of the channels are international franchises, ASTRO operates nine channels itself, airing content in each of the four dominant languages of Malaysia.

Of ASTRO's radio channels, seven out of the 16 broadcast in English (Opus, Hitz.FM, Mix.FM, Light & Easy, Classic Rock, Golden Oldies, Nostalgia and Jazz), three are in Malay (Era.FM, Malaysia's most popular radio station, with over 4 million listeners; Wirama Melayu; Sinar; and Varia), two are aired in Chinese (Melody and My.FM), two in the Indian languages, Tamil and Hindi (Osai and India Beat), and there is a single Arabic channel (Musiq'a).

Monthly guides to ASTRO's broadcasts.

Min, a Malay-language film by Ho Yuhang, tells of a Chinese girl adopted by a Malay family in search of her identity. It was awarded the special jury prize at the Festival of Three Continents in Nantes, France, in 2003.

Glossary

A

Acrolect: Highest level of speech in terms of phonological, grammatical and lexical correctness; equated to the speech of a good native speaker.

Acronym: A pronounceable name made up of a series of initial letters or parts of words.

Adat: Customary law.

Affix: A linguistic element added to a word or root to produce a derived or inflectional form.

Afro-Asiatic: Another name for Semitic, used to label the group of languages known by this name, which includes Arabic and Hebrew.

Agglutinative: The type of word formation which makes use of affixes attached to root-forms.

Anugerah Sastera Negara: National Literary Award, for Malay-language writing.

Aspectual affixes: Affixes that indicate the stage in the process of an action (i.e. waiting to be done, in the process of being done, or already completed).

Austroasiatic: Language stock that includes the Mon-Khmer and Tai-Kadai language families, spoken on mainland Southeast Asia.

Austronesian: Language stock, previously known as Malayo-Polynesian, comprising languages distributed from Taiwan to New Zealand, and Madagascar to Easter Island.

Autonym: Refers to the term used by an ethnolinguistic group to refer to themselves.

B

Bahasa bahasan: Colloquial Malay.

Bahasa baku: Standard, or formal, Malay.

Baihua: Modern Chinese writing style used as a result of the May Fourth Movement.

Basilect: Lowest level of speech in terms of phonological, grammatical and lexical correctness.

Bes: Type of Orang Asli illness-causing spirit.

Bidalan: Malay parables. An oral literary form, traditionally the term *gurindam* was used interchangeably.

Bobohizan: Ritual specialists or priestesses in Coastal Kadazandusun. Known by different names in other Sabah languages.

Bomoh: A Malay shaman. Also known as a *pawang*.

Bumiputera: Malay term meaning 'sons of the soil'. It refers to specific officially designated ethnic groups: the Malays, the Orang Asli, the Melaka Portuguese, the Siamese of the northern Malaysia and the indigenous ethnic groups of Sabah and Sarawak.

C

Cerpen: Colloquial expression for Malay short stories. A contraction of the Malay words 'cerita' (story) and 'pendek' (short).

Code-switching: The ability of speakers to switch from one language or register to another, depending on place, topic and participants.

Colophon: An inscription at the end of a book or manuscript that shows the title, copyist, date, etc.

Contact language: A speech form used by a group of speakers of different languages or dialects.

Creole: A language that has its origin in extended contact between two language communities.

D

Dialect: A variation in any particular language, which identifies a particular group of speakers through linguistic features.

Diglossic: A situation in which certain varieties of a language are considered 'high' and 'low'; alternatively, a language the written and spoken forms of which differ, e.g. Tamil.

Dravidian: Family of languages spoken in south and central India and Sri Lanka. Includes Tamil, Malayalam and Telegu.

E

Elliptical sentences: Type of sentence which has undergone some ellision, but still makes sense as a full utterance, e.g. the Malay *Ke mana?* (Where are you going?), a shortened version of *Encik hendak pergi ke mana?*

ESP (English for Specific Purposes): Variety of English that is used for a specified purpose, e.g. that used by the legal profession.

Ethnonym: The name of a people or ethnic group.

Etymology: The study of the sources and development of words and morphemes.

Expressive: A word or phrase used in expressing emotions, for example the exclamation, 'Ah!'

F

Fossilized: A linguistic term denoting a consonant permanently attached to its root.

Frontispiece: Illustration facing the title page of a book.

G

Gawai Batu: The Iban whetstone festival.

Gawai Hantu: An Iban festival, given roughly every generation (per longhouse) to honour the dead.

Gawai Pangah: The traditional Bidayuh head-taking festival celebrated once in four or five years, which now focuses on the old skulls in their possession. The 'Pangah' is the round wooden building in which these are stored.

Ghazal: Songs comprising religious and romantic verses.

Glottal stop: A speech sound produced by tightly closing the glottis, preventing the explosion of the sound.

Grapheme: The complete class of letter or combination of letters that represent one speech sound. For example, the 'f' in foot, the 'gh' in tough and the 'ph' in phase are different graphemes of the same speech sound.

H

Head-modifier: The usual sequence of Malay phrases. The head is the word with the central meaning to the speaker; the modifier is the word that tells more about the head; e.g. *rumah besar* (literally 'house big').

Hikayat: A traditional Malay literary genre containing elements of both the real and spiritual worlds.

Home language: Language or dialect used by family members among themselves.

I

Ideogram: A sign or symbol used in writing systems such as that of the Chinese languages that represents a concept or thing rather than a word for it.

Incopyfixation: Partial reduplication where the final consonant of a root is copied to an earlier position as an infix. The main inflectional device in the Temiar Aslian language.

Indo-Aryan: A language grouping

under which are subsumed Sanskrit and the North Indian languages, Persian and the Indo-European languages.

Indo-European: A language family comprising languages of Europe and North India.

Inflectional affixes: Affixes that indicate that grammatical functions, e.g. the suffixes '-ed' and '-es' in verbs in English.

J

Jawi: Malay script adapted from that of Arabic.

K

Kiasan: Malay figures of speech including metaphors and similes.

Kitab: Any book teaching aspects of Islam.

Kitab terasul: Guides produced for the professional scribes who created the elaborate Malay letters.

Kristang: The language of the Portuguese-descended Eurasians of Melaka.

L

Language community: Group of people speaking the same language who permanently occupy a geographical area.

Language family: A grouping of languages which share similar features in terms of speech sounds, word and sentence formation, and lexical items.

Language group: Same as language community.

Language phylum: Group of languages which are related to one another and whose time-depth is more than 5000 years.

Language stock: A language grouping with a time-depth of 2,500–5,000 years.

Loan word: A word in a particular language which has its origin in another language.

M

Maghazi: Classical Malay romances concerning Prophet Muhammad's war exploits.

Mahua wengxue: Locally written Chinese literature.

Maksud: Malay word meaning 'purpose'; the third line of a *pantun*.

Malay World: The geolinguistic world which uses Malay as a first or second language, or as a contact language.

Marabuk Kavdhaigal: Traditional form of Tamil poetry, characterized by rigid rules of rhyme and metre.

May Fourth Movement: Intellectual upsurge in China in 1919, sparked off by passionate opposition to the terms of the Versailles Peace Conference.

Mesolect: Speech level between the acrolect and basilect. People speaking a language other than their own and speaking it rather well are considered at the mesolect level.

Morpheme: A speech element having a meaning or grammatical function that cannot be subdivided into further such elements.

Morphology: Word formation.

Morphophonological: A linguistic feature which depicts the functioning together of the rules of morphology and phonology.

N

Nasal preplosion: Phonological feature in which a plosive sound precedes a nasal sound.

P

Panji: Javanese prince whose name is given to a series of romances in Malay literature.

Pantun: A traditional Malay poetic form comprising four line verses with an **a-b-a-b** rhyme.

Particle: A grammatical element equivalent to a word but which cannot stand on its own to function as a full word.

Pawang: see *Bomoh.*

Pelanduk tales: Mousedeer tales.

Phoneme: One of the set of speech sounds in any given language that serves to distinguish one word from another.

Phonology: The study of the sound system of a language or languages in general.

Pidgin: A language made up of elements of two or more other languages and used in contact situations especially by speakers of other languages.

Pinyin: The modern Romanized Chinese script, based on phonetics rather than ideograms.

POL (Pupils' Own Language): Any Malaysian language, other than Malay and English, which is taught as an elective subject.

Pudhukavithaigal: The Tamil free verse form.

R

Ratib: Religious (Islamic) chant.

Reduplication: the doubling of a whole word or any part of a word, e.g. *rumah-rumah* (houses) in Malay.

Register: A language variety used in specific social-cum-professional situations; e.g. academic register, legal register, royal register.

Root: Alternative term for 'root-word'; also refers to the historical origin of words.

Root-word: A word that forms the base in the formation of derived words, usually in agglutinative languages such as Malay.

Rumi: Malay term for the Romanized script.

S

Sajak: Modern Malay poetry.

Salasilah (or *silsilah*): Written Malay genealogies concerning rulers or dynasties, such as the *Sejarah Melayu* ('Malay Annals').

Sang Kancil tales: Refer to Pelanduk tales.

Sanskrit: An ancient language of India. The oldest recorded member of the Indic branch of the Indo-European family. Although used only for religious purposes, it is an official language of India.

Sebutan baku: Form of standard Malay pronunciation wherein pronunciation of the word is determined by its spelling.

Semantics: The study of meaning, and the relationship between words or sentences and their meanings.

Sentence inversion: Permutation of sentence structure.

Sino-Tibetan: A family of languages that includes most of the languages of China, as well as Tibetan and Burmese.

Social dialect: A variety of language used in social interaction. Its form is determined by situation and context, ranging from formal to informal, intimate to distant, and high to low, etc.

Sound system: System of sounds (not just confined to phonemes) in a particular language.

SOV (Subject-Object-Verb): The abbreviation, commonly used by linguists, of the order of elements in a sentence structure where they so appear.

Speech community: Another term for language community.

Speech system: System occurring in a particular language, at the pronunciational, grammatical, or lexical level.

Speech variant: Dialect, at the regional (geographical) as well as social levels.

Syair: Traditional Malay verse form, of Arabic origin, usually comprising four-line verses and an **a-a-a-a** rhyming pattern.

Syllabary: A writing system in which each character represents a syllable, e.g. Arabic and Jawi.

Syntax: The grammatical arrangement of words and morphemes in a language.

T

Tai-Kadai: A language family belonging to the Austroasiatic stock, of which the Thai language is a member.

V

Verb stem: The basic element in the formation of a word to which affixes are added.

Vowel harmony: The compatibility of different vowels occurring in different syllables.

W

Wusi Movement: Alternative name for the May Fourth Movement.

Bibliography

Abdul Rahman Napiah (1987), *Drama Moden Malaysia: Perkembangan dan Perubahan*, Kuala Lumpur: Dewan Bahasa dan Pustaka.

Adelaar, K. A. (1995), 'Borneo as a crossroad for comparative Austronesian linguistics', in P. Bellwood, J. J. Fox and D. Tryon (eds.), *The Austronesians*, 75–95, Canberra: Australian National University.

Ahmad Kamal Abdullah, Hashim Awang, Ramli Isnin, Sahlan Mohd Saman, Zakaria Ariffin (1992), *History of Modern Malay Literature Vol. II*, Kuala Lumpur: Dewan Bahasa dan Pustaka.

Arif Karkhi Abukhudair (1995), 'A Phonetic, Morphological and Semantic Analysis of Arabic Words in Malay', *Jurnal Bahasa Moden*, 9: 95–103.

Asmah Haji Omar (1979), *Language Planning for Unity and Efficiency: A Study of the Language Status and Corpus Planning of Malaysia*, Kuala Lumpur: Universiti Malaya.

—— (1982), *Language and Society in Malaysia*, Kuala Lumpur: Dewan Bahasa dan Pustaka.

—— (1983), *The Malay Peoples of Malaysia and Their Languages*, Kuala Lumpur: Dewan Bahasa dan Pustaka.

—— (1992), *The Linguistic Scenery in Malaysia*, Kuala Lumpur: Dewan Bahasa dan Pustaka.

—— (2003), *Language and Language Situation in Southeast Asia*, Kuala Lumpur: Universiti Malaya.

Bellwood, Peter (1997), *Prehistory of the Indo-Malaysian Archipelago*, Honolulu: University of Hawai'i Press.

Benadict, P. K. (1942), 'Thai, Kadai and Indonesian: A new alignment in Southeastern Asia', *American Anthropologist*, 44 (5), 76–161.

Benjamin, G. (1976), 'Austroasiatic Subgroupings and Prehistory in the Malay Peninsula', in P. J. Jenner, L. C. Thompson and S. Starosta (eds.), *Austroasiatic Studies*, 37–128, Honolulu: Univesity of Hawai'i Press.

—— (1983), 'Peninsular Malaysia' and part of 'Southern Mainland Southeast Asia', in: S. A. Wurm and S. Hattôri (eds.), *Language Atlas of the Pacific Area, Volume 2*, Canberra: Australian Academy of the Humanities and Tokyo: The Japan Academy.

Blust, R. A. 'The Austronesian settlement of mainland Southeast Asia', in K. L. Adams and T. Hendak (eds.), *Papers from the 2nd Annual Meeting of the Southeast Asian Linguistic Society*, 25–83, Phoenix: Arizona State University.

Collins, James T. (1980), *Ambonese Malay and Creolization Theory*, Kuala Lumpur: Dewan Bahasa dan Pustaka.

—— (1998), *Malay, World Language: A Short History*, Kuala Lumpur: Dewan Bahasa dan Pustaka.

Crawford, John (1952), *Malay Language: Grammar Dictionary with a Preliminary Dissertation, Volume 1: Dissertation and Grammar*, London: Smith, Elder and Co.

Cuisinier, Jeanne (1957), *Le Theatre d'Ombres a Kelantan*, Paris: Gallimard.

Dyen, Isidore (1965), 'A Lexicostatistical Classification of the Austronesian Languages', *International Journal of American Linguistics*, Memoir 19.

Farid Mohd Onn (ed.) (1965), *Cheritera Seri Rama*, Kuala Lumpur: Dewan Bahasa dan Pustaka.

Gallop, Annabel Teh (1994), *The Legacy of the Malay Letter*, London: The British Library Board.

Halimah Mohd Said and Ng Keat Said (eds.) (1997), *English is an Asian Language: The Malaysian Context*, Kuala Lumpur: Persatuan Bahasa Moden Malaysia and The Macquarie Library Pty Ltd.

Harun Mat Piah (1989). *Puisi Melayu Tradisional: Satu Pembicaraan Genre dan Fungsi*, Kuala Lumpur: Dewan Bahasa dan Pustaka.

Harun Mat Piah, Ismail Hamid, Siti Hawa, Abu Hassan Sham, Abdul Rahman Kaeh and Jamilah Haji Ahmad (2002), *Traditional Malay Literature*, Kuala Lumpur: Dewan Bahasa dan Pustaka.

Heah Lee Hsia, Carmel (1989), *The Influence of English on the Lexical Expansion of Bahasa Malaysia*, Kuala Lumpur: Dewan Bahasa dan Pustaka.

Hendon, Rufus S. (1966), *The Phonology and Morphology of Ulu Muar Malay*, Yale University Publications in Anthropology, Number 70.

Hood Musa (1964), *Rampaian Pandawa Lima*, Kuala Lumpur: Dewan Bahasa dan Pustaka.

Johan Jaaffar, Mohd Thani Ahmad and Safian Hussain (1992), *History of Modern Malay Literature, Vol. 1*, Kuala Lumpur: Dewan Bahasa dan Pustaka.

Khalid M. Hussein (1964), *Cheritera Pandawa Lima*, Kuala Lumpur: Dewan Bahasa dan Pustaka.

King, Julie K. and King, John Wayne (1984), *Languages of Sabah: A Survey Report*, Canberra: Australian National University.

Koster, G. L. (1997), *Roaming through Seductive Gardens: Readings in Malay Narrative*, Leiden: KITLV Press.

Kua Kia Soong (1999), *A Protean Saga: The Chinese Schools of Malaysia*: Dong Jiao Zong

Higher Learning Centre.

Malachi, Edwin Vethamani (2001), *A Bibliography of Malaysian Literature in English*, Kuala Lumpur: Sasbadi Sdn Bhd.

Mohd Taib Osman (ed.) (1975), *Tradisi Lisan di Malaysia*, Kuala Lumpur: Kementarian Kebudayaan, Belia dan Sukan Malaysia.

Mohd Yusof Hasan (1989), *Novels of the Troubled Years*, Kuala Lumpur: Dewan Bahasa dan Pustaka.

Nordin Selat (1976), *Sistem Sosial Adat Perpatih*, Kuala Lumpur: Utusan Melayu Sdn Bhd.

Roolvink, R. (1967), 'The Variant Versions of The Malay Annals', *Bijdragen tot de Taal, Land- en Volkenkunde*, 123 (3): 301–24.

Safar, H. M., Asiah Sarji and Gunaratne, S. A. (2000), 'Malaysia', in Shelton A. Gunaratne (ed.), *Handbook of the Media in Asia*, New Delhi: Sage.

Solehah Ishak (1987), *Histrionics of Development: A Study of Three Contemporary Malay Playwrights*, Kuala Lumpur: Dewan Bahasa dan Pustaka.

Wilkinson, R. J. (1907). *Papers on Malay Subjects I. Malay Literature*. Kuala Lumpur.

—— (1961), *Malay- English Dictionary* (reprint). New York: Macmillan and Co. Ltd.

Winstedt, R. O. and Sturrock, A. J. (eds). (1957), *Hikayat Awang Sulung Merah Muda*. Singapore: Malay Publishing House.

—— (eds.) (1957), *Hikayat Malim Deman*. Singapore: Malay Publishing House.

Zainal Abidin Ahmad (1962), *Ilmu Mengarang Melayu* (reprint) Kuala Lumpur: Dewan Bahasa dan Pustaka.

Index

S

Sabah: languages, 38–45; oral traditions, 70–1
Sabah Malay, see Kedayan Malay
Sabah Museum, 39, 41, 43
Sajak, 76, 99, 106
Salasilah, *see* Silsilah
Saleha bt. Abdul Rashid, *see* Salmi Manja
Salleh Ben Joned, 119
Salleh Dollah, 65
Salmi Manja, 104, 106
Sama Bajau languages, 38, 42
Samad Said, A., 102, 103, 104, 107
Sandiwara, 122
Sang Kancil tales, 65
Sangu Shanmugam, 115
Sanskrit, 10, 12, 13, 18, 2, 57; inscriptions, 56
Sarangapany, G., 113
Sarawak: languages, 30–7; oral traditions, 68–9
Sarawak Literary Society, 30
Sarawak Malay, 26–7, 33
Schmidt, Wilhelm, 46
Schools, 130; Chinese, 51, 55; English, 60; Malay, 60; Punjabi, 57; Tamil, 57, 59; Telugu, 57
Sea Dayak, see Iban
Seals, 81
Sejarah Melayu, 63, 73, 78, 88–9
Selakau, 12, 13, 30, 31, 32, 33, 34, 45
Selako, *see* Selakau
Seloka, 76
Semai: language, 11, 46, 47, 48, 49; oral tradition, 66, 67
Semangat Asia, 104, 133
Semelai, 47, 67
Sengoi, 47
Senguttuvan, N. A., 98, 113, 114
Senoi, 47
Serudung, 43
Shafie Abu Bakar, 107
Shaharom Husain, 123
Shahimah Idris, 125
Shahnon Ahmad, 26, 102, 103, 104
Shamsuddin Pasai, 78
Shamsuddin Salleh, 100
Shaykh Nur-al-Din al-Raniri, 96
Shellabear, W. G., 89, 133
Shi Qiao, 110
Shuang Shuang, 109
Si Hu, 110
Si Tanggang legend, 72, 73
Silakau, *see* Selakau
Silitoe, Alan, 121
Silsilah, 78
Silva, Gregory de, 116
Sindhi, 57
Sinhalese, 57

Sinniah Pillai, V., 113
Sino-Tibetan, 11, 13
Siow Siew Sing, 105
Siti Hawa Mohd Hassan, 102
Siti Nurhaliza, 75
Siti Zainon Ismail, 106
Sivamaniam, S., 112
Slimming, John, 121
Sockalingam, S., 112
Solheim, William, 12
Southwell, C. H., 36
Srinivasagam Selvathurai, M., 112
Sru people, 35
Stone inscriptions, 82
Storytellers: Malay, 65; Orang Asli, 66
Straits Chinese, 16, 17, 50; creoles, 17
Straits-born Indians, 17
Strassman, Sipol, 33
Su Zhengyi, 109
Suba Narayananan, 113
Sugan Panchatcharam, 57
Sulalat al-Salatin, 63, 88
Sultan Idris Training College, 105
Suluk, 38, 42, 45
Summer Institute of Linguistics (SIL), 39, 41, 43, 44
Sung poetry: Kenyah, 37
Sweeney, Amin, 64, 93
Swettenham, Frank, 120
Syair, 75, 79, 106; *Bidasari*, 79; *Ken Tambuhan*, 62, 79; *Siti Zubaidah*, 75, 79
Syed Adam Aljafri, 118
Syed Alwi, 104, 123, 124, 125
Syed Hussein bin Ali Alsagaf, 104
Syed Sheikh Al-Hadi, 23, 100, 104

T

Tagal, 38, 42
Tai-Kadai, 11, 13
Taj al-Salatin, 78, 79, 80
Talib Mohd. Hassan, A., 102
Talibun, 76
Tambanuo, 44
Tamil language, 6, 11, 13, 18, 21, 56, 57, 58–9
Tamil literature, 7, 57; fiction, 112–13; poetry, 114–15
Tan Yunshan, 110
Tao Mu, 111
Tari Endang, 64
Tatana, 40
Teh, Mark, 125
Teknonyms, 36
Telaga Batu, 82
Television programmes, 135: Chinese, 55; Indian, 57
Telugu, 11, 13, 57
Temiar, 46–7, 48, 67
Temuan, 27, 47

Tengara, 43
Teo Huat, 98, 105, 109
Teochew, 51, 52
Teochew Association, 51
Terengganu Stone, 22, 82
Teromba, 76–7, 82
Thai, 10, 13, 18
Tham, Hilary, 119
Thamil Pannai, 114
Thillai, M.V., 115
Thomas, Leslie, 121
Thor Kah Hoong, 125
Tian Duo, 110
Tian Lang Xing Poetry Society, 111
Tidong, 43, 45
Timugon, 43
Tioman Island, 26, 27
Tok Selampit, 65
Tolkappiyam, 58
Topping, 34
Tromba: Perut Tebat Rembau, 82; *Sungai Ujung*, 82
Tukang Cerita, 65
Tun Jugah Foundation, 30, 32
Tun Seri Lanang, 88
Tuo Ge, 109, 110
Tusut, 68
Tuuk, Herman N. van der, 10, 91

U

Ukit, 35
Undang-Undang: Johor, 82; *Laut Melaka*, 79; *Melaka*, 82; *Pahang*, 82
Universities, 39, 55, 59, 60, 131
Upper Kinabatangan, 44
Usman Awang, 103, 106, 122, 123
Utsat community, 19
Utusan Melayu, 8, 104, 132

V

Valentyn, Francois, 120
Valmiki, 92
Vedambal, S., 113
Venkatarathinam, K., 11

W

Wahab Ali, A., 102
Wahab Awangtih, 105
Wallace, Alfred Russel, 120
Wang Gungwu, 118
Warta Ahad, 104
Warta Jenaka, 104
Wayang Kulit, 64, 65, 91, 93, 94, 95
Wei Yun, 108, 109
Wen Lang, 110
Wen Renping, 111
Wen Rui'an, 108
Wen Zichuan, 109

Wijaya Mala, 104
Wila', 46
Wildman, Rounsevelle, 120
Wilkinson, R. J., 46
Winstedt, Sir Richard, 22
Wolio, 45
Wong Phui Nam, 119
Woon Swee-tin, Bernard, *see* Wen Renping
Writing systems, 9
Wu Tiancai, 111

X

Xiao Ai, 111
Xiao Ya, 110

Y

Yahp, Beth, 116, 117
Yakan, 42
Yang Jiguang, 111
Yang Lin, 50
Yao Tuo, 109, 111
Yap Ah Loy, 58
Yasmin Yaacob, 125
Yayasan Budaya Melayu Sarawak, 30
Yeoh, Patrick, 124
Yi Jin, 111
Yi Teng, 111
You Cao, 111
You Chuan, 110, 111
Yu Chuan, 108
Yuan Shang Cao, 109
Yue, 51

Z

Za'ba, 23, 25, 105, 106
Zaen Kasturi, 107
Zahari Affandi, 105
Zaihasra, 106
Zainal Abidin Ahmad, *see* Za'ba
Zainun Aruf, 100
Zakaria Ali, 105
Zakaria Ariffin, 123
Zeng Huading, 110
Zhang Fang, 110
Zhang Guixing, 108
Zhao Rong, 108
Zhen Ge, 109
Zheng He, 50
Zheng Yan, 108
Zhong Qi, 111
Zhou Can, 111
Zhou Zimeng, 109, 110
Zi Chun, 110
Zi Xi, 108
Zikir, 78
Zulkarnain Yaakub, 100
Zurinah Hassan, 106

Picture Credits